The Institutional Economics of Water

A Cross-Country Analysis of
Institutions and Performance

R. Maria Saleth

*Senior Institutional Economist, International Water
Management Institute, Colombo, Sri Lanka*

Ariel Dinar

*Lead Economist, Agriculture and Rural Development
Department, The World Bank*

A CO-PUBLICATION WITH THE WORLD BANK

Edward Elgar
Cheltenham, UK • Northampton, MA, USA

Published by
Edward Elgar Publishing Limited
Glensanda House
Montpellier Parade
Cheltenham
Glos GL50 1UA
UK

Edward Elgar Publishing, Inc.
136 West Street
Suite 202
Northampton
Massachusetts 01060
USA

A catalogue record for this book
is available from the British Library

ISBN 0 8213 5656 9

Typeset by Cambrian Typesetters, Frimley, Surrey
Printed and bound in Great Britain by MPG Books Ltd, Bodmin, Cornwall

Contents

Figures

Tables

10.2a Law-related channels: relative share and significance of
impact in all-sample context 273
10.2b Policy-related channels: relative share and significance of
impact in all-sample context 274
10.2c Administration-related channels: relative share and
significance of impact in all-sample context 277
10.3a Law-related channels: relative share and significance of
impact across country groups 279
10.3b Policy-related channels: relative share and significance of
impact across country groups 281
10.3c Administration-related channels: relative share and
significance of impact across country groups 284
10.4a Exogenous variables: relative share and significance of
impact in all-sample context 287
10.4b Exogenous variables: relative share and significance of
impact across country groups 289

Acronyms and Abbreviations

3-SLS	Three-Stage Least Squares
bcum	billion cubic meters
BERI	Business Environment Risk Intelligence
cukm	cubic kilometers
cum	cubic meters
DWAF	Department of Water Affairs and Forestry, South Africa
EC	European Community
EU	European Union
FAO	Food and Agriculture Organization
GDP	Gross Domestic Product
GNP	Gross National Product
GOI	Government of India
IAD	Institutional analysis and development
ICRG	International Country Risk Guide
ICID	International Commission on Irrigation and Drainage
IDA	Institutional decomposition and analysis
IMT	Irrigation management transfer
IWMI	International Water Management Institute
mcum	million cubic meters
mha	million hectares
MEA	Mahaweli Economic Authority, Sri Lanka
MIWR	Ministry of Irrigation and Water Resources, Sudan
MOPT	Ministerio de Obras Publicas y Transportes, Spain
MOWR	Ministry of Water Resources, China and India
NWP	National Water Policy, India
O&M	operation and maintenance
OFWAT	Office of Water Services, United Kingdom
OLS	Ordinary Least Squares
PRC	People's Republic of China
RBO	River basin organization
sqkm	square kimometers
WC	Water Commission, Israel
WUA	Water user association

Acknowledgments

The work leading to this book was supported by funding from the Rural Cluster within the Development Economics Research Group, the Visiting Research Fellows Program and the Agriculture and Rural Development Department of the World Bank as well as the Bank–Netherlands Water Partnership Program, the Norwegian Trust Fund, the Swiss Trust Fund at the World Bank, and the International Water Management Institute, Colombo, Sri Lanka.

The quantitative analysis of the institution–performance interaction reported in this book would not have been possible but for the rich information so willingly provided by 127 international experts on water matters. As a formal acknowledgment of their intellectual contributions, the names of respondents to our questionnaire and others who provided useful material and valuable information are listed in Appendix B. Because of their facilitative role and logistic support during country visits and international surveys, a special note of thanks is also due to the following persons: Miguel Solanes, Sam Johnson, José Trava, Nelson Pereira, Larry Simpson, Alberto Garrido, Mohamed Jellali, Dan Yaron, Yaov Kislev, Saul Arlosoroff, Alan Conley, Gerhard Backeberg, Piet Maritz, Douglas Merrey, Douglas Vermillion, Terrence Abeysekara, Nihal Fernando, Warren Musgrave, John Pigram, Zhang Hai Lun, and Yuri Steklov.

We acknowledge with gratitude the generous invitation of John B. Braden, Elinor Ostrom, and William Easter to present our theoretical framework and methodology in seminars at the University of Illinois, Indiana University, and the University of Minnesota, respectively. We received initial feedback on our work from participants in these seminars, as well as from separate discussions we had with Vincent Ostrom and Vernon Ruttan.

The final manuscript has also benefited from elaborate written comments and suggestions received from several reviewers. In this respect, we are particularly indebted to Vernon Ruttan, Daniel Bromley, William Easter, Roy Gardner, Raymond Suppala, Marie-Leigh Livingston, William Blomquist, Jennifer McKay, Alberto Garrido, Steven Renzetti, Rodrigo Maia, Piet Heyns, Gerhard Beckeberg, Krzysztof Berbeka, J.C. Caldas, Angel Alejandrino, and Peter Mollinga.

The excellent documentation support of Eliza Mcleod of the Sector Library at the World Bank, Washington, DC, and Charlotte Hess of the specialized library on Institutional Economics at the Workshop on Political Theory and

Policy Analysis at Indiana University, Bloomington, is noted with thanks and appreciation.

A special word of gratitude goes to Frank Rijsberman, Director General, International Water Management Institute, Colombo, Sri Lanka for his encouragement and support toward the final stages of the preparation of the manuscript. Similarly, the active support – received in the early stages of the project – from B.D. Dhawan, S.R. Hashim, and Pravin Visaria of the Institute of Economic Growth, Delhi and M. Govinda Rao of the Institute for Social and Economic Change, Bangalore, India, are also gratefully acknowledged.

The excellent secretarial support of Michelle Riguad, Fulvia Toppin, and Shivajirao Padmavathy, efficient programming support of Jaime Yepez, Sridharan, and Krishnachandran, able data-processing assistance of William Fru, and timely communication and logistic support of Santhakumar Sundaram are also appreciated with due credit for their contributions to the study.

Finally, we thank Kathleen A. Lynch for her thorough editorial revision of the entire manuscript.

                                              R. Maria Saleth and **Ariel Dinar**

1. Water challenge: an institutional diagnosis

As the world ushers in the new millennium, water scarcity – in both its quantitative and qualitative manifestations – is emerging as a major development challenge for many countries. In countries racing toward their physical limits to fresh water expansion, the amount of water available is a key concern. In other countries with expanding urban settlements, industrial sectors, and commercialized agriculture, water quality is a major concern. Since pollution-induced deterioration in water quality reduces the utility of the existing water resources, water scarcity is also a growing concern even in countries with no apparent limits for fresh water expansion. Considering the serious economic, ecological, and welfare consequences of floods in many countries, water crisis is also to be viewed in a much broader sense than as a mere scarcity issue.

Although the nature and severity of water problems are different from country to country, one aspect is common to most countries: water scarcity – whether quantitative, qualitative, or both – originates more from inefficient use and poor management than from any real physical limits on supply augmentation. This is the crux of water crisis and such diagnosis raises our hope that the crisis can be averted by improving water use and management. But the task is not easy, as it involves radical changes in the way water resources are developed, allocated, and managed. How to design, initiate, and sustain these changes and tackle the water challenge on a durable basis, within the economic, ecological, and political constraints are at the heart of the ongoing water debate, both nationally and internationally. As a backdrop to subsequent discussion, the water crisis, and its institutional underpinnings must be viewed and understood in all dimensions, especially from a global perspective.

PHYSICAL DIMENSION

Water crisis is usually viewed in terms of an increasing imbalance between water supply and demand. However, it is much more than a simple hydrological or physical phenomenon, as it also stems from pervasive gaps in the economic and institutional dimensions of water resource development, allocation, use, and management.

Water is the most abundant and ubiquitous resource on Earth, but 97.5 percent of the world's water is too salty for human consumption and crop production. Even the rest of the fresh water, an estimated 35 million cubic kilometers (million cukm)/year,[1] cannot be fully accessed; most of it is locked either in the ice cover of Arctic and Antarctic regions or in deep underground aquifers. Thus, the physically accessible fresh water potential of the world is only 90,000 cukm/year. This amount represents just 0.26 percent of global fresh water reserves (Shiklomanov 1993: 13). Close to two-thirds of this potential evaporates back into the atmosphere. Although this portion, known as *green water*, is not accessible for direct human use, it does provide indirect but indispensable ecological benefits by sustaining the life-supporting functions of ecosystems as well as the livelihood needs of people relying on rain-fed agriculture.

Even the rest of the fresh water potential, known as *blue water*, cannot be fully utilized due to economic, technological, and environmental limitations, spatial and temporal mismatch between fresh water availability and demand, and pollution-induced quality deterioration. The spatial distribution is a grave problem as water resources are not available where or when needed. For instance, Brazil, with just a small fraction of global population, has one-fifth of the world's fresh water resources whereas India and China, with more than a third of the world's population, have only one-tenth of global fresh water resources (Shiklomanov 1993: 13). As a result, of the estimated blue water potential of about 40,000 cukm, only about 12,500 cukm can be accessed under present economic and technical conditions [Food and Agriculture Organization (FAO) 1996: 3]. The issue will become even more complicated, as the future utilization of even the accessible blue water is threatened by climatic change-induced variations in the level and spatial pattern of global temperature and precipitation.[2]

Desalinization and water recycling can increase water supply, but these options are costly, relevant in only a few contexts, and offer limited possibilities for augmenting supply. Although desalinization capacity has increased tremendously to reach 18 million cubic meters (million cum)/day at present, it is confined mostly to a handful of countries in the Middle East and a few coastal cities in the United States (Gleick 1998: 30–31). Considering both present capacity and future expansion, the total supply from desalinization is no more than a fraction of total global water demand.[3] The case is similar for water reuse and recycling. Water reuse is not more than 2 percent of total water demand, even in the countries of the Arabian Peninsula where the scarcity of water is most severe (Abdulrazzak 1995: 230). Despite serious ecological and health concerns, the use of treated wastewater for irrigation is substantial and growing in countries such as Israel, Mexico, Chile, and Tunisia.

Improving water use efficiency is a promising avenue for supply augmentation in view of the extensiveness of water losses and resource underutilization. Since this option helps to realize the hidden resource potential within the existing supply limits, it augments supply even in the absence of new water development projects and also preempts the ecological consequences ranging from waterlogging and salinity to aquifer depletion. For instance, a 10 percent improvement in water use efficiency can add 2 million hectare (mha) of additional irrigation in Pakistan and 14 mha of additional irrigation in India (Postel 1993: 60; Saleth 1996: 234). In developing countries where investment constraints and environmental issues limit irrigation expansion, the option of improving irrigation efficiency is very important.[4] The adoption of modern irrigation technologies can improve water use efficiency by up to 95 percent and could lead to water savings of more than 50 percent (Postel 1999: 187). While these technologies have a tremendous water-saving potential, they cover only a limited area and are confined to just a handful of countries.

The total area covered by modern irrigation technologies is estimated to be only about 1.6 mha, a fraction of a percentage of global irrigated area. Five countries account for three-fifths of this area: the United States, Spain, Australia, Israel, and South Africa (Postel 1993: 60–61). The urban sector, too, offers substantial scope for water saving, both by reducing water loss and improving water use efficiency. Water saving through retrofitting of traditional residential water appliances such as toilets can release substantial water for further redistribution. In California, for instance, the retrofitting of toilets alone can lead to a 25 percent saving in indoor water use (Gleick 1998: 22). However, the retrofitting program is costly and requires cooperation from water users. The required investments and public cooperation cannot be obtained without first altering the incentive environment through policy changes.

Despite the stringent limits to supply augmentation, water demand is increasing due to a fast-growing global population and expanding scale of global economic activities. Since 1950, the global population has more than doubled to 6 billion and it is expected to double again, to 12 billion, by 2100.[5] Urbanization, the major consequence of population growth and economic expansion, put serious pressures on both the quantitative and qualitative dimensions of water resources. The urban population, now estimated at 43 percent of global population, is expected to reach 61 percent by 2025 – implying an urban population of about 5 billion (Saleth 2002: xv). The water-related consequences of urbanization will be particularly serious in the already heavily populated developing countries. The growth of urban settlements not only magnifies the task of providing water supply and sanitation services but also increases the health and environmental risks of water pollution from industrial effluent and urban sewage. As many developing countries are concentrating their limited resources on the immediate task of providing water supply, they are unable to invest enough resources either in sanitation programs or in sewage treatment. In Latin America, for example, more than 90 percent of urban waste-water is collected and discharged directly into the water systems (Nash 1993: 32). The situation has not improved much today. In addition to urban sewage, farm chemicals from commercialized agriculture and toxic effluents from energy-intensive industries deplete water quality, aggravating water scarcity.

Apart from the quantitative and qualitative pressures on its physical dimension, water demand is also growing due to the broadening perspective of water and its ecological, ethical, and cultural roles. Water is needed to meet not only human needs but also the needs of the water-based ecosystems that form part of the global life-supporting system. As a result, the minimum instream flow requirement that is now mandatory in many countries also forms an increasing component of water demand. Water also has to be reserved to support indigenous communities and their traditional cultures (Donahue and Johnston 1998). In view of the human-rights implications of meeting basic water needs and the equity aspects of empowering vulnerable groups, including women, water demand now also assumes an ethical and social dimension.

In any case, the demand for water is growing much faster than supply in many countries. The growth in demand is particularly serious in overpopulated but water-scarce regions in developing countries where water is the defining line between poverty and prosperity. With population growth and economic expansion, the scale of global economic activity has also increased several fold. For instance, irrigation, which accounts for more than three-quarters of total water use, expanded from 50 to 250 mha during 1900–2000 and is expected to reach 296 mha by 2020. The expansion in irrigation, drinking, and industrial needs during 1900–2000 resulted in a dramatic increase in global fresh water withdrawals from 500 to about 4000 cukm/year (Gleick 1998: 6–7).[6]

Although current withdrawal represents no more than 5 percent of the physically accessible global fresh water resources, it is close to a third of the planet's economically accessible blue water resources. Postel, Daily, and Ehrlich (1996) predict that global water withdrawal is already close to 54 percent of the accessible blue water and could reach 70 percent by 2025. This prediction is not off the mark. Considering population projections for 2100 and an annual per capita allowance of 200 cum for household needs and 800 cum for irrigation (Falkenmark 1999: 360),[7] the total global human water requirement could increase from 6 bcum at present to 12 bcum by 2100. This means that global water demand, which represents 50 percent of the accessible blue water at present, could be very close to the ultimate water barrier toward the end of the 21st century. But, in a scenario where the withdrawal of 30 to 60 percent of the accessible fresh water resources is considered the practical limit for supply augmentation (Falkenmark and Lindh 1993), it is not farfetched to see many countries reaching their supply limits within the next 20 years.

The telltale symptoms of water scarcity are already evident in 80 countries with 40 percent of the global population. Eighteen of these countries, located mostly in the Middle East, are nearing or exceeding their renewable water supply limit (Falkenmark and Lindh 1993: 80; Gleick 1993: 105–6). Fifty-five countries in Africa and Asia cannot meet the basic water needs of their growing populations. As a result, about 2.2 billion people do not have access to clean water and 2.7 billion people do not have access to sanitation services (Gleick 1998: 40). The increasing water scarcity is also a major threat to irrigated agriculture, especially in developing countries in Africa and Asia with a major share of global population and a predominant dependence on agriculture. Often, the social and economic costs of water scarcity also spill into the social and political arenas, causing severe water conflicts among users, regions, and countries (Gleick 1993; Beaumont 1994; Frederiksen 1998; Postel 1999).[8]

Besides the socioeconomic consequences of its quantitative dimension, water scarcity is also having serious effects on its qualitative dimension. Pollution-induced quality deterioration not only reduces the benefits of available supply but also leads to pernicious environmental and health hazards. As a result of water pollution and poor sanitation services, more than 2 billion people remain exposed to malaria in about 100 countries (Nash 1993: 27). Waterborne diseases kill 5 to 10 million people each year out of the 250 million new cases reported every year (Gleick 1998: 39). At the other side of the spectrum, water-related natural disasters such as floods and famines also take a heavy toll of human life, both directly and indirectly through disease.[9] In addition to the human costs, there are also economic losses from crop and property damage.[10]

ECONOMIC DIMENSION

The long-term ecological consequences of water crisis to global life-supporting systems and the threat to the survival of the human species can be only imagined. However, the immediate economic consequences of water crisis can be easily reckoned given the key role of water in socioeconomic development. Water resources support 40 percent of global food production through irrigation and 20 percent of global fish yield through aquaculture (FAO 1996: 2). Water resources also help in generating 640,000 megawatts of power, constituting 20 percent of the global power supply (Gleick 1998: 70). The direct economic contributions of water resources can be still higher at the regional level. For instance, irrigation contributes to 70 percent of food production in

China and 50 percent of the same in India (FAO 1996: 5). Similarly, the role of hydropower in total power needs is far higher than the world average in many countries. For instance, in 63 countries, hydropower accounts for more than 50 percent of total power production and in 23 of these, it accounts for more than 90 percent of total power supply (Gleick 1998: 71).

The water sector in general and its irrigation segment in particular will soon face much heavier pressure. Expanding population, especially in the developing countries of Asia and Africa, is going to raise the demand for food. Food demand from the developing countries that was at 1,021 million tons in 1993 is expected to jump to 1,634 million tons by 2020, and up to 80 percent of the additional supply will depend critically on irrigation (Rosegrant and Ringler 1999). Similarly, in view of the physical limits, production constraints, technical difficulties, and pollution proneness of fossil energy, the demand for cheaper, technically flexible, and environmentally clean hydropower is also increasing in all countries. This will put additional pressure on the water resources of countries that have the technical potential for hydropower generation and infrastructural capabilities for power trade.[11]

Water resource development has served well its historical function of supporting a world with an increasing population and an expanding scale of economic activities. However, there is some evidence that the positive relationship between water resources and economic development is becoming disturbed, not just in developing countries but in developed countries as well. The negative consequences include ecological and social disturbances in project areas, salinity in irrigated regions, aquifer depletion in arid zones, and pollution-induced water quality and health impairment around urban centers. Such damage raises social costs whereas inefficient use and mismanagement reduce the social benefits possible from additional supply. As a result, the net economic and welfare contributions of water resources decline over time and across countries. Some indirect evidence of this fact is provided by Orloci, Szesztay, and Varkonyi (1985), who evaluate the relationship between per capita Gross Domestic Product and per capita water use based on cross-section data pertaining to 50 countries over three points in time (1965, 1980, and 2000). Despite the conceptual difficulties with the variables and the crude nature of the analysis, the results suggest that the positive association observed between the two variables is getting weaker over time. The weakening trend suggests the simple fact that water use declines with economic development due to a shift from extensive to intensive use patterns facilitated by water scarcity and technology. But, the positive trend still suggests the reality that water remains a major constraint on economic development, especially among countries in the lower income range.

More specific cases provide much stronger evidence for the declining net contributions of water resource development. For instance, in India, with a current irrigated potential close to 90 mha, about a tenth of this potential remains unutilized and close to a sixth of the irrigated area is afflicted with waterlogging and soil salinity (Saleth 1996: 20). While underutilized capacity leads to opportunity costs covering not only the output forgone but also the interest on investment, waterlogging and salinity lead to both a short-term productivity decline and a long-term loss of scarce and productive land resources. The underutilization of water resources developed with costly investment and the production loss from waterlogging and soil salinity are far more serious when considered from a global perspective. For instance, while the total storage capacity of all the world's reservoirs is estimated at about 6,000 cukm, the amount of water actually stored in these reservoirs is far lower than the capacity because of problems such as siltation, catchment deterioration, and flow irregularities (FAO 1996: 8). At the other side of the spectrum, the area affected by irrigation-induced salinity is estimated to be between 20 and 47 mha and yield loss from these areas is estimated to be about 30 percent (Postel 1999: 93; Rosegrant and Ringler 1999: 11).

When the total output is less than its optimum due to the combined effects of capacity underutilization and productivity loss from salinity, the cost of creating additional irrigation potential is also becoming prohibitive in many countries. The capital cost of new irrigation capacity, which is already high in many parts of the world, is increasing faster due to environmental and resettlement costs as well as delay-induced cost escalation. The estimated capital cost of adding a hectare of irrigation varies from between US$1,500 and $4,000 in China and India to between $6,000 and $10,000 in Brazil and Mexico. In parts of Africa, it can be as high as between $10,000 and $20,000[12] (Postel 1993: 57 and 1999: 62). When the output contributions of irrigated area are declining and the environmental and financial costs are increasing, it is no wonder that the net economic and welfare contributions of water development projects decline over time.

Similar examples of water resources' declining economic and welfare contributions can be found in other sectors. In the urban sector, for instance, expanding water supplies can contribute more to costs than to benefits in view of pervasive water loss, lower water rates, and poor cost recovery. Mexico City provides the worst-case example of water losses facing the urban water sector in many developing countries. Water losses in Mexico City were estimated to be high enough to supply the gross water need of a whole city the size of Rome (World Resources Institute 1990).[13] It was ironic that such huge water losses occur in a city that pumps its water from a distance of 200 km and an altitude of 2 km. As in most urban centers in developing countries, cost recovery in Mexico City was only 20 percent. It is, therefore, not surprising that the cost of supporting this city was said to exceed its contributions in terms of goods and services (Falkenmark and Lindh 1993: 86). It is this poor financial and operational performance that has eventually led the Mexican government to privatize the city's water service provision.

The declining trend in the net economic contributions of water resources clearly stems from inefficient use, poor management, declining water productivity, and increasing environmental and financial costs. It is also an outcome of the fact that the initially linear relationship between water resources and economic development now has to incorporate the circularity of multifarious effects that emerge in the interaction among society, water, and the ecosystem (Falkenmark 1999; Varis 1999). In view of the broader perspective of the linkages between water, society, and the environment, the economic dimension of the current water crisis incorporates not only the strict economic aspects but also the economically relevant ecological and social aspects. While the declining net economic contribution of the water sector is understandable in view of the increasing weight given to current and future ecological and social costs, it is difficult to reconcile with the negative financial contributions of the water sector in many countries. The negative financial trend, an obvious outcome of lower water charges and poor cost recovery, jeopardizes the efficient maintenance of water infrastructure as well as the potential for future investments in water development projects. Declining water sector investment and the deteriorating physical health of water infrastructure now cast a shadow on the water sector's existence and sustainability. In view of the close linkages between the financial status, physical health, service quality, and economic performance of the water sector, the overall process of economic development itself depends critically on water sector performance. The key issue in the economic dimension of the water challenge is, therefore, how to improve the financial and economic sustainability of the water sector and thereby enhance and sustain its indispensable contributions to socioeconomic development.

POLICY DIMENSION

The problems facing the water sector show that the era of plenty has ended and the era of scarcity has begun, locally, nationally, and globally. Contrary to the prediction of economic theory that resource use efficiency improves with scarcity, water use is becoming less and less efficient even as water grows more scarce. Why is this? The answer lies in water sector policies, including the approach on which they are based and the framework within which they are formulated and implemented. The basic approach and the institutional framework that dominated the surplus era continue with little change even in the scarcity era. The emphasis on engineering solutions, the treatment of water as a free good, and bureaucratic allocation and management are now inconsistent with the requirements and challenges of the new era. Therefore, how to resolve the conflicts between past policies and the emerging realities is the central issue on the policy dimension of the water challenge.

Water crisis is an outcome of the growing imbalance between water needs (as determined by population growth and economic development) and supply augmentation capabilities (as determined by economic policies, managerial framework, and technological conditions). Policy has a key role both in managing water needs and in enhancing supply augmentation and management capabilities. For instance, policy changes that can capture and reflect the increasing value of water can justify options ranging from desalinization to interregional water transfer either directly or indirectly through the import of water-intensive commodities. However, economic justification for these costly options can occur only when the efficient use of the already available water resources raises the economic and social value of water. A higher value and, hence, price of water, can both justify and pay for the costly supply augmentation options. This argument can be extended to other situations where there is room for fresh water development but involves higher environmental and social costs. In this case, a higher value of water obtained from an efficient use of existing supply can be used to finance ecological restoration and resettlement programs. Through appropriate policies, therefore, supply augmentation can be integrated with demand management so that an efficient allocation and use of the already developed resources can justify and pay for the development of additional supplies. To what extent these policies can succeed in this respect depends on two critical aspects: the economic approach and the allocation framework. It is the absence of policies with an economic approach and the lack of institutions to support an allocation framework that are responsible for the present predicament of the water sector in most countries.

A retrospective review of the approaches and policies followed hitherto shows how inconsistent they are with the emerging resource realities, socioeconomic concerns, and development ethos. While an efficient and durable solution to water scarcity requires an economic approach, decentralized management, market-based allocation, and full-cost pricing, water policies in most countries are characterized by the predominance of an engineering approach, centralized management, bureaucratic allocation, and subsidized provision. Instead of the urgent need for an allocation-oriented paradigm for water resource development and management, the supply-oriented paradigm remains the basis for water resource development and management in many countries.

With hindsight, it is easy to criticize the supply-oriented approach, but it is unfair to underestimate its historical role in supporting a world with a growing population and an expanding scale of economic activity. The massive amount of water resources developed through large schemes did help the emerging countries of Africa and Asia in supporting their expanding agriculture and urban settlements. It also helped to eliminate the food crisis of the 1950s and 1960s and generate environmentally clean energy for supporting industrial development and improving the quality of life. But, the emerging resource realities and development concerns, as well as a century-long accumulation of the negative effects of water development projects and their mismanagement reduce the current relevance of the supply-side approach.

The conceptual basis, assumptions, and policy implications of the supply-oriented paradigm have become not only obsolete but also incompatible with present concerns. With an increasing premium attached to the ecological, social, and cultural aspects of water, the narrow and isolated perspective of water underlying the supply-oriented paradigm is inconsistent with the objectives of sustainable water resource management. In view of the critical linkages that the water sector has with the rest of the economy, viewing water problems as confined strictly to the water sector is no longer appropriate. Similarly, when the scarcity value of water is increasing, it is inappropriate to insulate the water economy from market forces through the politically rooted system of public provision and subsidized water charges. While the water sector is gradually, but steadily, emerging from the grip of political and other myopic considerations, it has not yet reached the stage where economic and sustainability considerations alone can guide decisions about water. Thus, the ability of most countries to face the twin challenge of supply augmentation with the least ecological and social costs, and the development of institutional frameworks for efficient and equitable use of current and future supplies is critically predicated on the speed with which policy reforms are undertaken to create a new governance structure needed for water allocation and management.

Fortunately, the situation surrounding the water crisis is not completely bleak as there are a few positive trends in the policy dimension. Since recognition is growing that the water crisis is mainly an outcome of inappropriate policies and mismanagement, there is now hope that the water problems can be addressed with appropriate national and international policies. There is also a remarkable degree of consensus on the general approach toward water sector reform and its key components. While the approach is rooted in an allocation paradigm that can both ensure efficient management of current resources and justify future addition through water development, the reform agenda includes the key institutional issues related to the legal, policy, and administrative aspects of water resource development and management. Many countries have already undertaken significant reforms in their water sectors and many more are going to undertake such reforms soon (Saleth and Dinar 2000).

INSTITUTIONAL DIMENSION

The crisis in the water sector has also revealed the inherent limitations of today's institutions in dealing effectively with the new set of problems related more to resource allocation and management than to resource development. The multifarious economic and political consequences of water scarcity, including the widespread occurrence of interregional and intersectoral water conflicts, have intensified the need for flexible but effective water allocation and management mechanisms. The traditional perspective of water as a free good is being replaced with a perspective of water as an economic and social good. This means that water pricing, project selection, and other related policies have to be changed to reflect such a new perspective. Allocation and conflict-resolution mechanisms have to be created, strengthened, or updated in both the legal and policy spheres. Water users, who were beneficiaries in the surplus era of water development, have now become 'customers' or 'clients' in the water scarcity era. The water administration and water sector decision processes have to learn to accommodate an increasing role of user organizations, nongovernmental agencies, women, environmental, and other self-help groups as well as to explore the ways in which emerging water and information technologies can be gainfully utilized. Thus, as countries move from a state of plenty to a state of scarcity, water institutions, which define the rules of water development, allocation, and utilization, have to be concurrently reoriented to reflect the realities of changing supply–demand and quantity–quality balance.

The public-good character of water and the scale issues involved in its exploitation necessitated and justified its public ownership and state involvement in its development and distribution. This arrangement worked well in the surplus era. But, as water scarcity becomes economically binding and the magnitude of water-related subsidies, including the administrative overhead costs, becomes fiscally constraining, the social costs of state-dominated institutional arrangements are beginning to surpass the corresponding social benefits. As a result, the current trend is toward an alternative system that can allow private decisionmaking in water resource development, allocation, and management. For the alternative system to function effectively and equitably, legal changes are needed to facilitate a private and transferable water-rights system that ensures full legal, physical, and tenure certainty of water rights (Ciriacy-Wantrup 1956; Milliman 1959; Dales 1968). It also has to address the concerns of the weaker segments of population, which rarely have the economic capacity to benefit from such systems. With such a water-rights system, economic conditions could create the necessary incentives for water exchanges both within and across sectors, and such exchanges, will enhance efficient water use.[14]

While a private water-rights system is crucial to give individuals incentives to use water efficiently, some of the physical features of water also create interdependence and conflicts among water-rights holders. Although such conflicts can be resolved through courts, there are also large incentives for collective action among users to minimize and resolve conflicts outside of courts at lower costs as well as to internalize the long-term effects of their short-term actions (V. Ostrom and E. Ostrom 1972). This means that the private water-rights system has to encompass complementary organizations for collective action and mechanisms to coordinate private institutional arrangements with public or governmental management institutions. Thus, contrary to the general perception, the private water-rights system, collective action institutions, and state management organizations are not alternative institutional options but complementary institutional components of a new governance structure for the water sector. The creation of the kind of alloca- tion-centered institutional mechanisms and governance structures needed to deal with water scarcity on a continuing basis is not an isolated task. It warrants a radical change in the gamut of institutional arrangements govern- ing various facets of the water sector from water resource development through allocation, utilization, and management. The change entails concur- rent reforms in the legal, policy, and administrative spheres of the water sector.

While water-pricing policies and market mechanisms are the key compo- nents of the framework needed to put into effect an allocation-oriented approach to water scarcity problems, they themselves require a set of other supportive arrangements. For instance, the allocative role of water prices requires them to be based on the scarcity value or the opportunity cost of water. Since the administratively determined water prices for various uses are based on average rather than the marginal cost of supply, they reflect neither the supply cost nor the scarcity value (Dinar and Subramanian 1997). To be realistic, the introduction of marginal cost pricing in irrigated agriculture requires volumetric water provision. But, volumetric water provision in turn requires prior institutional and technical changes to support volumetric water allocation. These changes include the introduction of a water-rights system, the development of user associations, and the modification of project design and distribution networks.[15] These institutional and technical changes can influence water prices by providing an implementation framework and by encouraging the emergence of direct allocation mechanisms such as water markets. Besides the legal system of water rights and the physical structure for measuring and conveying water, the efficient operation of water markets depends also on the organizational mechanisms for enforcement and conflict resolution (Easter, Rosegrant, and Dinar 1999).

Institutional reform of the magnitude required at present is a daunting chal- lenge in most countries with outdated and poorly functioning water institutions.

The main issue is whether there are incentives and compulsions powerful enough to induce countries to take on such a large reform task, especially given the political risk and investment needs. One of the key premises in institutional economics literature is that institutional change occurs only when the transaction costs of reform are less than the corresponding opportunity costs of doing nothing.[16] With increasing water scarcity and its economic, ecological, and political costs, the opportunity costs of the prevailing institutional inadequacy within the water sector are great and moving fast to exceed the corresponding transaction costs. While this is a necessary condition for water sector reform, it is not sufficient as long as the political economy constraints remain a powerful obstacle to initiating any substantive institutional reform. Fortunately, in addition to the positive influence of progress in water and information technologies, as well as the pressure from donor agencies and international commitments of countries, a few powerful factors enhance the prospects for water sector reforms in most countries.

Although institutions evolve with changing conditions and social needs, this natural process of institutional evolution is often obstructed by the rent-seeking behavior of politically powerful groups (North 1990a: 7–8). As a result, suboptimal institutions persist by resisting changes. But, with increasing water scarcity and growing macroeconomic problems, these rents are declining, creating conditions where these groups themselves are now open to change.[17] Moreover, the emergence of a middle class – a product of economic development and education – has diluted the political power of the few and improved the political balance necessary for group-neutral reforms. This changed political milieu explains the declining predominance of an engineering approach and the irrigation sector and the increasing importance of economic and environmental concerns and nonirrigation sectors. With the emergence and political influence of pro-reform constituencies, a political urge has now surfaced for institutional reform.

The economic gains likely to be realized from allocation-oriented institutional change are substantial and also increasing with every increase in water scarcity. The magnitude of the net benefits from water institutional change is directly related to the degree of water scarcity, and economic incentives for institutional change increase with every rise in water scarcity. Since water scarcity is induced by factors such as population growth, economic development, and climate change, these factors also have a direct bearing on the extent of net benefits possible from institutional change within the water sector. Increasing water scarcity also magnifies both the real and economic costs of inappropriate water sector policies (e.g., treating water as an 'open access' resource and subsidized water provision), which can be approximated by the gap between the scarcity value of water and the prevailing water charges.

Apart from water scarcity that creates an endogenous pressure for change, the opportunity cost of institutional change within the water sector is also strongly influenced by some factors that originate outside the strict confines of the water sector. These often underestimated factors include macroeconomic adjustment policies as well as sociopolitical liberalization and reconstruction programs (Dinar 2000: 6–10). Macroeconomic reform magnifies the fiscal implications of the opportunity costs of institutional change. In contrast, sociopolitical reform attempts (e.g., in Chile during the 1970s, Spain during the 1980s, China since the 1980s, and South Africa since the 1990s) reduce the transaction costs directly because the institutional changes in the water sector form part of a systemwide reform.[18] The opportunity cost of institutional change is also being magnified by water-related natural disasters such as droughts (e.g., California), floods (e.g., China), and soil salinity (e.g., Australia). In other words, although the original opportunity costs of a crisis-ridden water sector remain a potent force for change, they also get additional support as well as a context to gain the much needed political economy thrust to prompt and sustain the process of institutional change.

WHY THIS STUDY?

Institutional reforms within the water sector, though urgent, need not be undertaken simultaneously. They can be spaced within a well-planned timeframe. For instance, the cost of transacting institutional reform in a given political economy context can be minimized, and the usual inertia associated with the stupendous nature of the reform task can be overcome through a strategy of gradual but sequential reform. Since such a strategy continuously builds on the synergy generated by selected reforms in key institutional components, subsequent reforms become easier to transact both politically and institutionally. Similarly, with an increasing integration of the world economic system under the ongoing process of globalization, countries have begun to realize that learning from each other's experience is an important means of improving their mutual performance in many spheres, including water management. In this context, cross-country flows of knowledge and experience in the realm of water sector reforms are valuable for the demonstration effect they create and the key inputs and insights they provide for designing and implementing institutional strategies.

While cross-country experience can minimize the costs and risks involved in experimenting with institutions, insights into the components, priority setting, and sequencing of institutional reforms can be useful for identifying technically feasible and politically acceptable reform strategy format and design. Thus, well-conceived policy research could itself be a powerful instrument for promoting institutional changes within the water sector, but present literature leaves a major gap in this important area of institutional research. This study aims to fill this serious gap with an attempt to review and document recent institutional changes in the global water sector in a comparative context and quantitatively evaluate the process of interaction between institutions and performance in the water sector from a cross-country perspective.

Country-specific studies dealing with either water institutions or water sector performance in isolation are common, whereas studies evaluating them with a cross-country perspective are rare or dated. Although country-specific approaches are useful, the 'best practice' cases identified through a cross-country exercise are particularly relevant for revealing motivations for institutional change. Documentation and analytical evaluation of cross-country experience in the context of the water sector and its institutional arrangements are valuable on at least two counts. The knowledge base created from cross-country experience allows countries to learn and adapt from mutual experience with minimal transaction costs and uncertainty. It also enables international funding agencies to develop and perfect their national and global institutional initiatives to improve water sector performance.

The identification of a strategy for water institutional reform with minimum transaction costs and maximum political acceptability requires a sharpened understanding of the analytical and operational linkages among various components of water institutions as well as the ultimate impact of such linkages on the overall water sector performance. Current knowledge allows the nature and direction of this causative change to be traced, but not the quantification of its true transaction and opportunity costs. Existing methodologies are also unable to allow a rigorous evaluation of the two components of institution–performance interaction; that is, institutional interlinkages and institution–performance linkages. From the standpoint of both institutional theory and water sector policy, it is important to evaluate the nature and strength of linkages both among institutions and between institutions and performance. Such an evaluation, if performed within an analytical framework permitting qualitative and quantitative considerations, can provide immense policy insights into the relative significance of various institutional components in terms of the nature and magnitude of their institutional interlinkages and performance effects. This sort of functional analysis of institutional components evaluated within a quantitative framework and carried out within an appropriate empirical context can provide critical inputs for the policy task of designing effective water institutions and identifying politically the most acceptable sequence of institutional reforms in different contexts.

The literature also presents a similar gap on the nature and mechanics of institution–performance interaction, especially in the water sector context. The theoretical literature elaborating the additional gains possible from institutional changes – in the general and in the water sector contexts – is vast and growing.

The literature in a general institutional context covers the seminal works of Olson (1965), Bromley (1989a), E. Ostrom (1990), and North (1990a). The same in the water institution context includes the important works of Fox (1976), Frederiksen (1992), Le Moigne, *et al.* (1994), Picciotto (1995), Saleth (1996), Hearne and Easter (1997), Saleth and Dinar (1999a, 1999b, and 2000), and Challen (2000). With the exception of Saleth and Dinar (1999b), the literature on the subject – both theoretical and empirical – provides little guidance, as its focus is either too narrow to consider water institutions as a whole or too descriptive and anecdotal to provide any quantitative evaluation.[19]

The limitation of the literature is understandable for two reasons. First, most studies have either ignored or underestimated the strategic roles of the critical linkages evident among institutional components (e.g., between property-rights system and conflict-resolution capabilities or between water technology and information application, and enforcement and monitoring capabilities of water administrations). Second, the inherent difficulties in quantifying institutional issues have discouraged attempts at quantitative evaluation of institutional linkages and their performance impacts. Besides, the quantitative evaluation of institutional issues presents immense empirical difficulties, not only because of their nonquantitative nature but also because of the unavailability of the right kind of data. While the analytical challenges and empirical difficulties are too real to discount, the strategic value of a quantitative institutional inquiry within the water sector provides the urge to venture into this uncharted course of policy research. The present study attempts to make a modest beginning in this critical, but least explored area of institutional research by considering the context of water sector.

APPROACH, SCOPE, AND OBJECTIVES

Before specifying the objectives and approach, let us specify the scope and focus. Since water institutions fall into a domain intersected by economics, law, and public policy and are also strongly influenced by factors such as resource endowment, demography, and science and technology, the basic approach here is inherently interdisciplinary in orientation and analytical in character. The term 'water sector' encompasses all its subsectors; 'institutional change' covers changes in water law, water policy, and water administration. The water sector and water institutions are approached from a national perspective in an attempt to capture their essential and policy-relevant characteristics and features. While such a macro perspective involves a sacrifice of micro details, it is taken deliberately to sharpen the focus on the main thrust of this study: institutional interlinkages and their performance impacts.

Since the process of institution–performance interaction within the water sector is influenced by factors including historical forces, political arrangements, demographic conditions, resource endowment, and economic development, the critical roles of these exogenous factors are also to be included within our evaluation framework. The role of these factors will be evaluated based on a cross-country comparative review of major water sector challenges and recent institutional responses. The cross-country review of the water sector and water institutions goes far beyond simple documentation and comparative analysis in the sample countries as it is organized within a stage-based perception of institutional change and performed within an institutional transaction cost framework. Although both the nature and direction of the institutional changes observed among countries vary by country-specific economic, political, and resource realities, some trends and patterns are clearly identifiable. To unravel these trends and patterns of change at the international level, this study attempts to address the following questions: What are the nature and direction of these changes? Which are the key factors that motivate these institutional changes? How adequate are these changes for addressing both existing and emerging water sector challenges? Can cross-country experience be used to derive a workable agenda for institutional changes, especially among countries at the threshold of water sector reform? The answers to these and related questions can help in understanding the water sector challenges and in delineating the contours of ongoing institutional responses at the global level.

In the context of the quantitative evaluation of the institutional interlinkages and institution–performance linkages within the water sector, the approach underlying the analytical framework and evaluation methodology can be briefly explained in terms of the following four interrelated steps. First, the concepts of water sector, water institution, and water sector performance are defined to set the broad contour of analysis. Second, both the major components of water institution and water sector performance are conceptually decomposed to define the analytical framework that captures major institutional interlinkages and institution–performance linkages. Third, given the nonquantitative character of most institutional components, a set of variables amenable to either objective observation or judgmental evaluation is identified for characterizing the functional linkages among institutional components and between institutional components and water sector performance. Finally, the characterized functional relationships are empirically evaluated using data collected through a cross-country survey of water sector experts to quantitatively appraise the nature and strength of the institutional interlinkages and institution–performance linkages.

The value and credibility of the cross-country approach as a tool of analysis are critically predicated on the choice of sample countries selected for evaluation. The sample has to be large enough to capture variations in socioe-conomic conditions, political settings, and water sector realities but small enough to permit a rapid appraisal of major water sector challenges and key institutional responses. After careful screening, a sample of 43 regions – 39 countries and four US states – is selected for the cross-country comparison. Since the sample covers different continents, historical backgrounds, political systems, development stages, demographic trends, water law traditions, and, more importantly, levels of water scarcity, it can represent well the reality of global water sector in all its relevant dimensions. The representative charac-ter of the sample is further enhanced by its coverage of the full spectrum of recent institutional changes and water sector reforms in terms of their inclu-siveness and effectiveness. Although the comparison is confined almost exclusively to the 43 sample countries or regions, experience from other countries and regions will be brought in to reinforce some points in a few relevant contexts.

The database for the quantitative evaluation of the linkages between water institutions and water sector performance has been developed from both factual and perceptional information obtained by administering a predesigned questionnaire (Appendix A) to 127 water experts from the sample countries and regions. These experts, with considerable international experience, have different disciplinary backgrounds and represent both governmental and nongovernmental perspectives. As such, the sample can be expected to repre-sent various viewpoints on the nature and strength of the linkages between water institutions and water sector. Apart from the perception-based survey information, anecdotal evidence and available secondary data are also used to evaluate some aspects of institution–performance linkages within the water sector.

Having delineated the scope and described the approach and empirical context of our study, let us now state its objectives. As is clear from the ratio-nale and context of our study outlined above, the overall objectives of this inquiry are twofold. The first is to document and evaluate water sector features, institutional arrangements, and recent institutional initiatives of sample countries within a comparative context. The second is to analytically demonstrate and empirically evaluate the process of institution–performance interaction using observed, anecdotal, and perception-based information from an international survey of water experts designed and conducted specifically for this study. The specific objectives are to:

• Attempt a detailed and critical review of the theoretical and empirical literature dealing with the institution–performance interface both in general and in water sector contexts so as to provide background, context, and methodological foundation.

- Delineate an analytical framework capable of capturing the operational linkages within and between different water institutional components as well as between water institutions and water sector performance.
- Develop an evaluation methodology to translate various layers of institutional interlinkages and institution–performance linkages into a set of models defined by interrelated equations.
- Describe and justify the empirical context used for the evaluation of the models of institution–performance interaction within the water sector.
- Undertake a cross-country review of water sector reforms within a stage-based conception of institutional change and institutional transaction cost framework so as to provide anecdotal evidence for institutional and performance linkages, and set the context for their quantitative evaluation.
- Attempt a quantitative evaluation of the models of institution–performance interaction to identify the relative role, significance, and robustness of institutional aspects in terms of their institutional and performance linkages as well as to derive empirical insights on reform design principles such as institutional priority setting, sequencing, and packaging as well as reform timing, scale, and dose.
- Conclude by identifying key implications for both institution theory and water sector policy.

The chapter scheme of this book is organized, more or less, in terms of the above stated objectives, but the next section provides more details on its outline and structure.

STRUCTURE OF THE BOOK

From here on, the book is organized into 10 chapters. Chapter 2 provides the background and motivation for subsequent chapters, with a brief but comprehensive review of the theoretical literature on institutional economics. The review focuses on the nature and definitions of institutions, their key features and their analytical and methodological implications, the relationship between institutions and economic performance, theories of institutional change, and the forces initiating and sustaining the process of institutional change. Against an overview of the approaches and methodologies used for institutional analysis, including the institutional transaction cost approach, Chapter 3 presents a critical review of the theoretical and empirical literatures that attempt to evaluate institutions and their performance, both in general and in water sector contexts. The review is intended to justify our study by identifying some serious gaps in the literature and to provide contrast to our approach and methodology by highlighting the points of their departure from traditions.

Having delineated the scope and focus of our attempt, Chapter 4 develops the main components that together constitute the theoretical and methodological foundation of our study. These are the institutional ecology principle, ex-ante approach, subjective theory of institutional change, and the institutional decomposition and analysis framework. Decomposing water institution and water sector performance into their constituent components and defining variables to capture the status of these components, Chapter 5 analytically depicts and mathematically models some of the main layers of institutional and performance linkages evident in the process of institution–performance interaction under alternative assumptions. Since the process of institution–performance interaction within the water sector evolves within the general institutional environment as defined broadly by the socioeconomic, political, legal, and resource-related factors, a separate model is developed to empirically evaluate the relative effects of some of these exogenous factors.

Chapter 6 describes and justifies the empirical context based on the perceptional data on all institutional and performance variables collected from an international panel of 127 water experts from 43 countries and regions. Besides providing key water sector features and sociopolitico-economic profiles of sample countries, it also gives the descriptive statistics for both perceptional data from expert surveys and observed data from secondary sources. Chapter 7 attempts a cross-country review of water sector and institutional reforms within the stage-based conception of institutional change and explains institutional change in terms of an institutional transaction cost approach. It also provides some anecdotal evidence and practical instances for a few of the layers of institutional and performance linkages. Based on this review, policy-relevant best practices observed in the sample countries are identified, and certain common trends and patterns evident both in water problems and institutional arrangements are delineated.

Chapters 8, 9, and 10 present and evaluate the empirical results derived from the regression-based estimation of the models of institution–performance interaction in different estimation contexts. Comparing the single-equation model representing conventional conception and a system model representing a realistic conception of the process of institution–performance interaction, Chapter 8 provides econometric evidence both for the existence and performance implications of institutional linkages as well as for the relative role and significance of institutional aspects. Chapter 9 evaluates the robustness and sensitivity of results by estimating the model in various contexts defined by three sample sizes, two expert groups (engineers and social scientists), and two country groups (reform countries and others). Empirically evaluating the relation between performance variables and exogenous variables representing socioeconomic, political, and demographic factors, it also provides insights on the relative role of exogenous factors and on the interface between subjective perception and objective reality.

Chapter 10 takes the analysis to its next logical and, in terms of policy, more insightful stage. Considering the estimated coefficients of various equations within the system model as a quantitative representation of prevailing international consensus on various key aspects of institutions and their performance, this chapter traces the multifarious routes through which the effects of a marginal change in an institutional variable are transmitted to reflect ultimately on sectoral performance. Based on the relative size and significance of the institutional variables involved in various impact-transmission channels, this chapter sheds light on institutional design and implementation issues. Finally, Chapter 11 concludes by identifying the major implications of this study for institutional theory and water sector policy.

NOTES

1. One cukm is equal to one billion cubic meters (bcum).
2. Spatial variations in global precipitation and temperature are expected to cause considerable shifts in regional agricultural patterns and accentuate the already serious spatial mismatch between water supply and demand. Warming in the winter is predicted to be greater in the northern latitudes than toward the equator. Precipitation is expected to fall consistently throughout the year in high latitudes and in the tropics but may increase by as much as 10 to 20 percent in certain zones, such as 35 to 50°N (Gleick 1993: 107).
3. However, in the context of the seven countries on the Arabian Peninsula, the supply from desalinization is substantial, about a tenth of their current total water demand (Abdulrazzak 1995: 232).
4. For instance, the additional irrigation development possible in the developing countries during 1995–2020 is predicted to be only 37 mha, implying an annual growth rate of just 0.7 percent as compared to the rate of 1.7 percent actually observed during 1982–93 (Rosegrant and Ringler 1999: 12).
5. With the recent slowdown in population growth rate, other more optimistic estimates place the global population at about 8 billion by 2100.
6. There are, in fact, many estimates available on total global water withdrawal by 2000. These estimates vary from 3,940 to 6,826 cukm/year, depending upon the expert and the year of estimation (Gleick 1998: Table 1.1: 14).
7. Per capita demand could be still higher in areas with poor rainfall as the irrigation allowance of 800 cum/person/year assumes that only 50 percent of all irrigation needed for food production comes from manmade irrigation while the rest comes from soil moisture from precipitation (Falkenmark 1999: 360). Besides, in view of the heavy evaporation demand and percolation losses, the amount of water (in the form of soil moisture) needed to produce the annual per capita diet may be as high as 2,000 cum. This is particularly apt to apply in countries such as India and China, both of which have a major share of global irrigated area and population (FAO 1996: 5).
8. Some of these conflicts have the potential to become full fledged water wars as a large part of the surface flow in several countries originates from outside their borders. In 19 countries, the proportion of surface water originating beyond their borders ranges from 21 percent (Israel) to about 97 percent (Turkmenistan and Egypt). Moreover, the share of global population that will face the predicament of water conflict in these hotspots is projected to increase from 44 to 75 percent by 2025 (Postel 1999: 138–40).

9. Of the many recent examples of the human costs of such disasters, the most serious ones include the death of between 0.9 million and 1.2 million people in 1887 and between 1.0 million and 3.7 million people in 1931 (Wijkman and Timberlake 1984; McDonald and Kay 1988).

10. For instance, the annual economic loss due to floods in China alone is estimated to be as high as $5 billion (Qishun and Xiao 1995).

11. There is considerable scope for regional power trade. For a case study of the economic and technical potential for such trade in Europe, see von der Fehr and Sandsbraten (1997).

12. Currency is expressed in US dollars here and elsewhere in this book unless noted otherwise.

13. Another case with equally serious water losses is the Indian city of Bangalore. Like Mexico City, the water supplied in Bangalore is moved from a distance, 100 km, and is lifted, almost 1 km up. The current water loss in the city is reckoned at 305 million liters/day (81 million cum/year). This wasted amount of water would more than eliminate the city's current demand gap (Saleth and Sastry 2004).

14. In many cases, in addition to the quantity specification, water quality needs also to be specified as part of the water rights so as to avoid quality-related externalities (Howe, Schurmeier, and Shaw 1986).

15. Although the introduction of volumetric water supply does not require the water-rights system, the volumetric water distribution policy will be more effective in achieving its efficiency and equity objectives with the water-rights system than otherwise.

16. In the particular context of water institutions, transaction costs cover both the real and monetary costs of instituting the regulatory, monitoring, and enforcement mechanisms needed for water resource development, allocation, and management. Similarly, the opportunity costs cover both the real and the economic value of opportunities forgone (i.e., the net social loss in preserving the status quo).

17. For instance, the institution of subsidized and bureaucratic provision of water protected so long by politically powerful farm groups is coming under tremendous pressure for change because the financial and performance crisis engendered by this arrangement now threatens the very benefits that these groups used to receive.

18. This means that institutional change brings significant scale economies. Institutional initiatives within the water sector, if well designed and timed, can be used to exploit such scale economies and minimize overall transaction costs.

19. Saleth and Dinar (1999b) is the only study that attempts a quantitative evaluation of the institution–performance interaction in the context of the water sector, but a number of other studies evaluate the interaction in other contexts. They are reviewed and contrasted with the present approach in Chapter 3 of this volume.

2. Understanding institutions: nature, performance, and change

The institutional underpinnings of development, in both the general and water sector contexts, are increasingly recognized because the policy prescriptions based on the neoclassical approach and on public choice theory have proved equally ineffective in many contexts. In the context of natural resource management, with all its many forms of externalities, neither the price mechanism nor the creation of property rights can provide a durable solution. Therefore, policy prescriptions, which have moved from 'getting the prices right' to 'getting the property rights right,' now center on 'getting institutions right' (Williamson 1994: 3).

For a better appreciation of this policy shift and as background for our subsequent analysis, we begin with a short but critical review of the theoretical literature on institutional economics. The review focuses on the nature and definitions of institutions, their key features and their analytical and methodological implications, the relation between institutions and economic performance, theories of institutional change, and the forces initiating and sustaining the process of institutional change in a generic context.

INSTITUTIONS: NATURE AND DEFINITION

Institutions are a pervasive phenomenon with diverse origins as they affect various dimensions of human relationships and interactions. Consequently, they have diverse definitions and interpretations, reflecting different disciplinary perspectives and theoretical traditions. But, beneath this diversity lies an undercurrent of convergence on the generic meaning and purpose of institutions. This section will show this convergence by sifting through various interpretations and definitions of institutions presented in the literature.

Institutions, Knowledge, and Information

Simon observes that 'it is because individual human beings are limited in knowledge, foresight, skill, and time that organizations are useful instruments for the achievement of human purposes' (1957: 199). In other words, human beings substitute institutional forms for knowledge and skill in an effort to enlarge their capacities and offset their limitations. Since institutions are codified knowledge, they evolve from the wisdom derived from natural principles found in nature and distilled out of the accumulated collective knowledge of human beings. Thus, there is a two-way relationship between knowledge and institutions, and, in this sense, knowledge and institutions are viewed as substitutes. In view of this substitutability, Coase (1960) states that institutions are not needed in a world of perfect knowledge and full information. But, as economies develop and become more diverse and complex, uncertainty also increases, requiring an increasing reliance on institutions to minimize behavioral uncertainty by providing predictive information. Institutions are, therefore, a substitute for accurate information because they provide a basis for making reasonably sound decisions by ensuring the behavior of others (North 1990a: 6, 27).

Institutions, Choice, and Behavior

Institutions are also viewed as instruments for interpreting and transforming information into knowledge. For instance, Hodgson (1998: 171) considers institutions as essential for providing a cognitive framework to interpret sense data, habits, and routines and transform and signal them as economically and socially useful knowledge. Attention is also directed on the way knowledge and information embodied in institutions are used to enable individual and collective decisions and to coordinate societal interactions. Since institutions define what individuals can and cannot do in a given context, they in effect delineate the action sets for both individual and collective decisionmaking (Commons 1968; Bromley 1989a and 1989b). Thus, institutions constitute a society's rules of the game, as they are the humanly devised constraints for coordinating human interaction (North 1990a: 3). As they define and delimit the set of choices, institutions determine the incentive structure for human exchanges and reduce uncertainty by providing structure to everyday life (North 1990a: 3–4).

Institutions not only constrain choices but also open up opportunities (Bromley 1989b; Achesen 1994b). Institutions set parameters for the system and state variables, 'constrain' the menus of actions available to actors, shape the vision of the world, and define the identity of the actors themselves (Granovetter 1985; March and Olsen 1989; Coriat and Dosi 1998). Commons (1968) provides a comprehensive definition of institutions by viewing them as the 'working rules of going concerns.' Together, these rules indicate what 'individuals *must* or *must not* do (compulsion or duty), what they *may* do without interference from other individuals (permission or liberty), what they *can* do with the aid of collective power (capacity or right), and what they *cannot* expect the collective power to do on their behalf (incapacity or exposure)' (Commons 1968: 6).

From another perspective, Schmid (1972: 893) considers institutions as 'sets of ordered relationships among people, which define their rights, exposure to the rights of others, privileges, and responsibilities.' Since institutions define the choice sets of individuals and groups and define relationships among individuals and groups, they are at the core of choice and behavior (Bromley 1989b: 740). Institutions – viewed either as 'working rules' or as the 'set of ordered relationships' – together determine the economic conditions or the action situations (Bromley 1989b: 740; E. Ostrom 1990: 52–3). Since institutions are fundamentally linked to knowledge and information, they play a powerful role in delimiting action sets, delineating action situations, and determining the incentive environment and behavioral conditions for the players.

Institutional Environment and Institutional Structure

Although institutions work as a system, they can be analytically grouped into two distinct segments to enhance our understanding of their functions. These segments are based on the distinction between institutions and organizations (North 1990a: 4–5) or between the institutional environment and institutional arrangements (Davis and North 1970: 131; North and Thomas 1973: 5–6). *Institutional environment* is defined by a set of fundamental political, social, and legal rules that establish the basis for production, exchange, and distribution. *Institutional arrangements* provide a structure within which members of a society – individually or collectively – cooperate or compete. The institutional environment covers the rules of the game whereas institutional arrangements include the governance structure and its evolution within and interaction with the institutional environment.

Governance structure incorporates the economic and political organizations that form part of the institutional arrangement (Williamson 1994: 2). The specific focus on organizations or institutional arrangements is to highlight their role as 'agents of institutional change' (North 1990a: 5). While the rules determine the outcome, the players or actors – as individuals and as organizations – can also change the rules depending on their relative share of the outcome or their political bargaining power. As such, institutional arrangements function as mechanisms to effect changes in the institutional environment.

The line demarcating institutional environment and institutional arrangement (or governance structure) is not fixed but varies with the focus and level of analysis. As a result, some segments of the institutional arrangement can become part of the institutional environment and vice versa. For instance, when considering water institutional arrangements, the overall economic, political, and resource-related institutions become part of the institutional environment. Similarly, when the focus is on the institutional arrangements of a particular region or subsector, the institutional arrangements at the national and sectoral levels become part of the institutional environment. In any case, institutions, whether they are part of the institutional environment or institutional arrangements, can be considered a constellation of rules linked and structured in such a way as to achieve a 'human purpose' or to address a 'going concern.'

FEATURES OF INSTITUTIONS

To understand the linkages between institutions and economic performance, some key features of institutions must be understood. Institutions operate at different levels and contexts. There are formal institutions and informal institutions; macro-level institutions and micro-level institutions; procedural institutions and behavioral institutions. Institutions are also classified as ceremonial and instrumental institutions (Bush 1987). Schotter (1981: 3–4) identifies two distinctive interpretations of institutions: collectivist and organic. Collectivist interpretation corresponds to what Hurwicz (1972 and 1998) calls a 'designer' perspective, and the organic perspective is similar to the 'endogenous or induced' institutional innovation perspective (Ruttan 1999: 1). While the immediate purposes and spheres of influence of these institutions vary, they are interrelated and usually have the common objective of providing information and reducing uncertainty in human–human and human–resource relationships in different social, economic, and political contexts.

Institutions as Subjective Constructs

Though hard to accept, the reality is that institutions are subjective constructs. The old institutional economics tradition recognizes the subjective nature of institutions by characterizing them as 'belief system' and 'habits.' Veblen (1919: 239) considers institutions 'settled habits of thought common to the generality of men.' Similarly, Commons (1934: 69) considers behavioral habit and institutions as mutually self-reinforcing. Although the new institutional economics does not include habit in the definition of institutions, North (1990a) places a strong emphasis on the 'mental construct' or the 'subjective model' of individuals as a major factor affecting institutional change. Institutions are not considered objective phenomena, but subjective mental constructs or 'artifacts' that think and act through the medium of human beings (V. Ostrom 1980; Douglas 1986; North 1990a; Stein 1997; E. Ostrom 1999).

Because institutions are the mental construct of human beings, 'we cannot feel, touch, or even measure institutions' (North 1990a: 107).

Since institutions shape the world vision and identity of actors (Granovetter 1985; March and Olsen 1989; Coriat and Dosi 1998), they have a subjective influence beyond their objective impact. While institutions shape people's cognition, views, vision, and action, they are also influenced by the same factors (Johnson and Nielsen 1998: xiv–xvii).[1] Precisely for this reason, Hodgson (1998: 181) views institutions as 'both "subjective ideas" in the heads of the agents and "objective" structures faced by them.' The agents and structures, though distinct, are connected in a circle of mutual interaction and interdependence (Bhaskar 1979; Hodgson 1998: 181). Although institutions are formalized in tangible formats as constitutions, laws, or codes of conduct, their ultimate impact depends on the extent to which they permeate the thinking and actions of individuals. The subjective nature of institutions does not preclude their objective manifestations (e.g., constitution or traffic signal), their susceptibility to objective influence (e.g., economic crisis and war), or the objective nature of their ultimate impact. Thus, institutions are subjective in terms of their origins and operations, but objective in terms of their manifestations and impacts.

Path Dependence

The evolution of institutions and their performance implications are affected strongly by their path-dependent nature. *Path dependency* means that history does matter: the direction and scope of institutional change cannot be divorced from its early course or past history.[2] Because of their path-dependent characteristics, institutions are the 'carriers of history,' reproducing themselves well beyond the time of their usefulness (David 1994; Coriat and Dosi 1998: 7). The idea of institutional change as a process of 'cumulative causation' (Veblen 1919: 70–77) suggests not only path dependence but also the linkages among institutions in a temporal sense. Institutional linkages – over time and at a specific time – receive special attention in institutional economics (North 1990a: 22). Since informal institutions play an important role in the incremental way in which institutions evolve, they remain a major source of path dependence (North 1990a: 44). Informal institutions change more slowly than formal institutions. As a result, there is always tension between altered formal rules and persisting informal rules (North 1990a: 45). In addition to informal institutions, there are such self-reinforcing mechanisms as network externalities, learning effects, and the historically derived subjective modeling of issues. Since all these mechanisms reinforce the current course of the development path, reversing the course of that path becomes extremely difficult or costly (North 1990a: 99).

Stability and Durability

The features of institutions that are important from the standpoint of institutional change are their relative durability, self-reinforcing nature, and persistence (Hodgson 1998; Keohane 1988). While the notion of structure-induced equilibrium tries to capture the durability feature of institutions (Shepsle and Weingast 1981; Levi 1990: 404), North (1990a: 94–100) explains this durability in terms of path dependence and self-reinforcing mechanisms such as network externalities and learning. The relative durability aspects of institutions make institutional change gradual and incremental in nature (North 1990a: 89). Even when conquest or revolution suddenly changes formal institutions, the informal rules derived from the formal rules continue to have their hold, providing institutional continuity and stability (North 1990a: 83–91). Institutional stability is a necessary condition for enabling complex transactions over time and space. This is accomplished partly by the anchoring role of the slowly changing informal rules and partly by the complexity of formal rules wherein rules are nested in a hierarchy, each level more costly to change than the previous one (North 1997: 6).[3]

Hierarchic Nature and Nestedness

Institutions are not a single entity but comprise a number of fundamentally linked and carefully structured components. Since these components assume the form of either a single rule or a subset of sequentially nested rules, institutions can be viewed as a constellation of hierarchically nested rules. Institutions, whether as part of institutional environment or institutional arrangements, are mutually nested and structurally embedded within each other (North 1990a: 83; E. Ostrom 1999: 38). For instance, by distinguishing three levels of rules, that is, constitutional-choice rules, collective-choice rules, and operational-choice rules, Kiser and E. Ostrom (1982) show how they cumulatively affect actions and outcomes. These rules are nested and sequentially linked within a hierarchical system such that the collective-choice rules are derived from constitutional-choice rules and the operational-choice rules are, in turn, derived from the collective-choice rules (E. Ostrom 1990: 52–3). There are also linkages among the rules within each set of rules as they are 'organized in multiple layers of nested enterprises' (E. Ostrom 1990: 101). The constitutional-choice rules for a micro setting also nest and link with the constitutional- and collective-choice rules of larger jurisdictions (E. Ostrom 1990: 50). Besides their hierarchical linkages, institutional arrangements exhibit spatial nestedness. Boyer and Hollingsworth (1997a: 469–77) illustrate this with their analysis of the structural and spatial features of markets, hierarchies, and alliances.

Embeddedness and Complementarity

Although the factors governing institutions can range from pure market selection or transaction cost criteria to cultural, social, and political requirements, institutions themselves are embedded with and complementary to each other (North 1990a: 22). Thus, formal institutions are embedded within informal institutions and the former cannot be effective without the latter. For instance, modern capitalistic institutions are embedded within a system of trust, reciprocity, tacit or shared knowledge, and risk-sharing arrangements (Boyer and Hollingsworth 1997a: 445–7). Market institutions, in particular, are embedded within social and political institutions at both national and regional levels (Lazonick 1991). This embedded character ensures the prerequisites for the operation of market institutions. Institutional embeddedness also has contextual and spatial dimensions. In view of these dimensions, markets and their institutional substitutes such as hierarchies, networks, and alliances are constantly influenced by socioeconomic transformation, technical change, and changing status of regions and nation-states (Boyer and Hollingsworth 1997b: 54).

IMPLICATIONS OF INSTITUTIONAL FEATURES

The institutional features discussed above are germane to our study in view of their theoretical significance and analytical and methodological implications. While some of the implications are already recognized in the literature, others are still to be further explored or better understood. Because of their direct relevance to the approach and methodology of our study, these implications need to be identified and elaborated at the outset.

Subjective Approach to Institutional Analysis

The subjective nature of institutions presents a major challenge for their evaluation with existing approaches and methods, particularly because extensive, detailed information is needed on multiple institutions of which the agents are only a part (Coriat and Dosi 1998: 7). But, at the same time, the subjective perspective of institutions also opens up new approaches for evaluating institutional change and its performance impact.

As we know, the empirical difficulties of dealing with the internal and subjective aspects such as 'utility' and 'welfare' – the two central concepts that drive modern economics – are overcome by considering their external reflections expressed in demand–supply relations and observed in income–consumption patterns. Even when demand–supply relations or income–benefit levels cannot be observed (e.g., missing markets for several environmental amenities), techniques such as contingent valuation are widely accepted to elicit information on their implicit forms. Similarly, the delphi approach is used to evaluate uncertain and futuristic events (e.g., the impact of genetically modified organisms and climatic change) with information gained from subject specialists. The expert system approach (Hayes-Roth, Waterman, and Lenat 1983; Hoffman 1987) is used to evaluate issues by combining observed data with information embodied in and specific to experts. Participatory appraisal techniques, the approach widely used to evaluate many micro-level issues, also rely on largely subjective information from participants. The reliance on subjective and qualitative considerations is also common in many organizational and managerial environments, especially for evaluating employee, project, and program performance.

An approach similar to those discussed above is equally legitimate and relevant for dealing with the problems associated with the subjective nature of institutions. This is particularly so when information problems can be overcome by tapping the hitherto underexplored information sources related to the subjective dimensions of institutions. For instance, a carefully designed and conducted survey of key players in a given context can be used to unearth their implicit preference over existing institutions, their demand for institutional change, or their aspirations for creating new institutions. The information obtained in the process can be viewed as the participants' 'revealed preferences' on the institutional configurations and components. If this approach is feasible and acceptable, a conceptual and methodological basis can be laid for anticipating the nature and direction of institutional changes – one that allows a considerable lead-time for preparation and adjustment.

Another methodological implication of the subjective perspective of institutions is also little recognized in the literature. The subjective perspective can provide a framework for an integral treatment of subjective factors, including ideology, bias, and ignorance, as well as their objective counterparts such as relative change in prices, technological developments, and political conditions. As this framework relies on subjective perception as a mechanism for integrating both subjective and objective factors, it has the potential to complement both transaction cost analysis and the political economy approach. Besides, the subjective framework can also formally capture the influence of aspirations, expectations, and anticipations. As such, the subjective framework can enable us to explicitly incorporate an ex-ante approach in institutional analysis. Much more importantly, the subjective approach shifts the attention from the influence wielded by organizatioins to the role played by individuals in the process of institutional change. Despite its theoretical consistency and practical significance, the subjective approach has not yet been tested in the literature as a framework for institutional analysis.

Institutional Decomposition

The path dependency of institutions allows a more reliable prediction of the path of institutional change. Although the short-run path is difficult to predict, the long-run path as well as the overall direction and thrust of institutional change are more predictable (North 1990a: 104). While path dependency implies institutional stability and durability, these institutional features require close attention, considering their implications for institutional change. The stability and durability features do not mean institutions are stagnant or changeless. It means only that the changes are so slow and marginal as to escape notice. They also mean that institutional stability at the macro level coexists with their variety and diversity at the micro level (Hodgson 1998: 171). As a result, distinct forms of institutional structures and their key components are easier to identify, especially in the case of formal institutions at the macro level. The decomposition of institutions and the identification of their institutional forms, including their common principles and typologies, are very valuable for understanding how various institutional components are related to each other (Boyer and Hollingsworth 1997b: 51).[4]

Institutional Performance and Transaction Costs

The linked and nested nature of institutions, on the other hand, has a strategic role to play in the cost and effectiveness of institutional change. In view of this feature, institutional change is not a one-step result, but a process involving gradual, sequential, and incremental transformation. The cost of changing an institutional rule varies across its components, levels of analysis, political regimes, and time periods (E. Ostrom 1990: 140–41). Since each institutional change becomes the foundation for subsequent and higher level institutional changes, the cost of each subsequent institutional change can decline, suggesting the presence of substantial scale economies in institutional change (North 1990a: 95). Knowledge of the cost implications of institutional linkages and their practical advantages for institutional sequencing and priority setting is valuable, especially for specifically planned institutional reform programs.[5] This knowledge is equally valuable even in the case of naturally evolving or self-organizing institutions. This knowledge can facilitate both the creation of the second- and third-order institutions and the promotion of autonomous and voluntary changes in the first-order institutions themselves (E. Ostrom 1990: 141).

The hierarchical feature of institutions has a considerable significance both for deepening institutional change and for enhancing institutional performance. 'Institutional thickening' in terms of increasing interlinkages and complementarity among institutions determines their ultimate performance efficacy. As institutions get more functionally interlinked, individual implications for their overall performance become inseparable. Not only does the performance of lower level rules hinge on the performance of their higher level counterparts but their synergy and scale economy effects also ensure that the aggregate performance implications of a set of hierarchically nested rules are much more than the sum of their individual performances.[6] Apart from the scale economy effects on the performance side, the nested nature of institutions and their linkages can also be exploited to minimize the total transaction cost of institutional change through a careful strategy of institutional sequencing and packaging.

Pluralistic Approach to Institutional Analysis

The nested and embedded character of institutions has four key implications for the nature and sources of institutional change. First, there are many sources – both economic and noneconomic – for institutional change since many institutions are linked with each other and embedded within an environment characterized by the interaction of economic, social, and political factors. Second, partly because of this diversity of sources and partly because of the network externalities and lock-in effects, change in one institutional component is difficult without concurrent changes in other institutional components and in the institutional environment itself. Third, embeddedness leads to culturally distinct institutional configurations that require normative, cultural, and political explanations of institutional arrangements (Schmitter 1997: 312).[7] And, finally, the internal embeddedness and complementarity of institutions suggest that it is impractical to consider a particular institutional form to be superior or universally valid.

While markets are often projected as the ideal and universally valid institutional arrangement, they cannot perform efficiently unless embedded in a nexus of obligational rules and public interventions. Similarly, the state cannot be effective without reliance on the market and delegation of some of its functions to private groups. Since society needs a variety of institutions to govern different spheres of human interactions at various levels, institutional mechanisms (e.g., markets, hierarchies, associations, and the state) cannot be considered alternatives. Just as an excess of markets leads to instability (Polanyi 1957) so, too, does an excess of state. This means that the pervasive and unrealistic dichotomy between state and market has to be discarded and a broader array of institutional arrangements has to be considered. What is needed, therefore, is an ideal combination of institutional mechanisms that support and complement each other to improve their mutual and collective efficiency (Boyer and Hollingsworth 1997b: 51–3). From a methodological perspective, this points to the need for an ideologically neutral and pluralistic approach to institutional analysis.

INSTITUTIONS AND PERFORMANCE

The intricate linkages between institutions, agents of change, and economic performance can be depicted using a stylized schema involving: (a) institutional environment, (b) institutional arrangements or governance structure (the combination of economic and political organizations), and (c) individual decisionmakers. These linkages, as depicted in Figure 2.1, integrate and summarize the main arguments of Williamson (1993: Figure 1) and Eggertsson (1996a: Figure 3). Figure 2.1 can be used to show how institutional change originates from the dynamics of interactions among the three constituents. This dynamic includes both the key role played by the 'agents of change' and the interaction of subjective factors (i.e., endogenous preferences and behavioral attributes) with the objective environment. Before interpreting the import

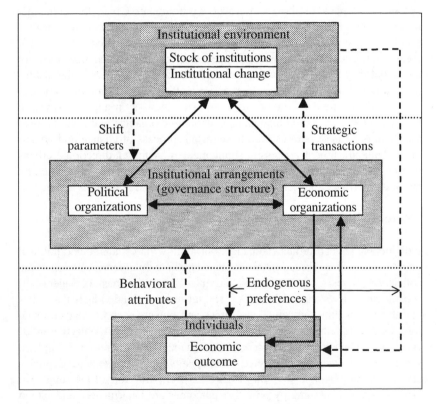

Source: Modified from Williamson (1993) and Eggertsson (1996a).

Figure 2.1   Institutional environment and governance structure.

of Figure 2.1, the embeddedness of the depicted system of institution–performance interaction within the physical, social, cultural, and economic systems has to be recognized.

Agents of Change

Though a part of the institutional arrangements or governance structure, the economic and political organizations (including government and bureaucracy) play a different role in the process of institutional change. The economic organizations that determine the economic outcome for their constituents can influence the institutional environment only through political organizations. Similarly, exogenous changes such as technology, trade, and investment affect institutional changes through their effects on economic outcomes which, in turn, prompt economic organizations to induce political organizations to make necessary changes in the institutional environment. Given the economic impact of political institutions and the political impact of economic institutions, these two sets of organizations are also intimately linked. The fact that these organizations are considered agents of institutional change does not mean that they themselves will not change. Since they are part of the institutional environment, they both affect and are affected by institutional change. In view of the circular flow of interaction (the two-way triangular arrows in Figure 2.1) among institutional change, economic organizations, and political organizations, these entities are in a constant process of change and adjustment. This adjustment process is supplemented by the unidirectional effects between institutional environment and institutional structures (as denoted by the broken arrows representing shift parameters and strategic transactions).

Subjective Influence

Individuals can also influence change, but mainly via economic and political organizations. Since these organizations are nothing but a representation of the collective interests of their individual members, they must consider their constituents' views and preferences.[8] The influences of individuals that originate from economic outcomes are direct and objective; those that originate from behavioral attributes, implicit and subjective. The direct, objective influences are channeled via the economic organizations whereas the implicit, subjective influences are channeled via the institutional arrangements or governance structure taken as a whole (Figure 2.1). The true role of the subjective aspects and their shaping by objective outcomes are inadequately understood and treated in the literature. This is why endogenous preferences are considered to operate only with the one-way flow of effects to individuals from institutions (both institutional environment and institutional arrangements). However, when preferences can be defined over the entire choice space covering not only commodities and services but also the institutional forms, endogenous preferences should be able to influence institutional choice and, hence, institutional arrangements. In the same way, the effects of behavioral attributes, currently considered to flow from individuals to institutional arrangements, need also to flow in the reverse direction because institutions are known to produce new behavioral attributes.

Institutional Change and Economic Performance

Institutions influence economic performance through their effects on the cost of exchange (transaction costs) and production (transformation costs) (North 1990a: 5–6). Since efficiently functioning institutions minimize uncertainty, they facilitate exchange directly by providing information and indirectly by reducing transaction costs. The economic benefits conferred by institutional change should, logically, ensure efficient institutional evolution. Alchian (1950) argues that competition weeds out inefficient institutions and ensures the survival of efficient ones. North and Thomas (1973) argue that changes in relative prices provide incentive for the creation of efficient institutions. However, North (1981) abandons the view that institutions evolve into efficient forms and refines the explanation for the persistence of inefficient institutions. The explanation starts with the distinction between institutions and organizations and shows how the interaction between them shapes the direction of institutional change. Although this explanation seems to hinge on rent-seeking behavior (strategic transactions in Figure 2.1), it goes much deeper. It incorporates the role of the lock-in effects and the attendant network externalities emerging from the symbiotic relationship between institutions and organizations in reinforcing the ongoing path and resisting any shift to a new path of institutional change (North 1990a: 7–8).

Since the changes in formal institutions reflect the power as well as the constraints of rulemakers, the role of changing power relationships as a source of institutional change cannot be ignored (Eggertsson 1996a: 14–17). While the prevailing system of property rights describes the distribution of private power, the power of the state emerges from its capacity to change or alter the distribution of property rights or economic opportunities and advantages. The politically dominant groups can wield these powers to enhance their economic control. As long as the institutional changes are brought about by politically dominant interest groups for favoring their own interests, such changes need not necessarily minimize transaction costs and enhance social welfare. Nevertheless, the mere role of power and bargaining need not imply that such institutional changes always have to be Pareto inferior. Other powerful mechanisms can moderate or neutralize the predatory behavior of power groups and government by bringing some consistency between the individual rationality of people controlling power and the collective rationality of society.

Institutional thickening is generally considered to improve institutional effectiveness and hence, overall economic performance, but Olson (1982) argues that a proliferation of institutions can be a source or an indicator of economic decline. The reasoning is based on the politically divisive role of 'distributional coalitions' that dominate the organization 'space' of the society and the attendant slowdown in the adoption of new technologies and the emergent constraints on efficient resource reallocation. But, North (1983: 163–4) contests this view. To him, the negative political and economic roles of interest groups are exaggerated and there is a corresponding underestimation of the normalizing roles of political and economic institutions such as the constitution and collective efforts to avert socially harmful economic decline. Apart from factors such as altruism and ideology, some mechanisms such as the constitution, congress or parliament, multiparty system, and bureaucracy broaden policymakers' time horizon and reduce the extreme role of power and self-interest in institutional change.[9] In any case, due to the emergence of political and technical constraints from path dependency, institutions may not evolve automatically into their efficient forms. Due to the persistence of inefficient institutions or the emergence of second- or third-best institutional arrangements, institutional changes do not always lower transaction costs or improve social welfare.

THEORIES OF INSTITUTIONAL CHANGE

The stage is now set for a look at some of the main theories explaining institutional change, each focused on the role of one or more factors. The old institutional economics places considerable importance on cultural context (Rutherford 1995: 443) and the way ethnic, cultural, and religious beliefs influence exchange and contracts (Landa 1994; Greif, Milgrom, and Weingast 1994). North (1990a), in an attempt to synthesize the old and new institutional economics, incorporates some of the central ideas of the old institutional economics such as the role of ideology, mental models and belief systems, and cultural influences in shaping the learning process. These ideas help to explain anomalies left unexplained by a simple extension of the neoclassical approach to institutional issues (e.g., the existence of inefficient institutions and the role of noneconomic factors in institutional change).[10]

The two main theoretical traditions within institutional economics converge on the set of factors underlining institutional change, but significant differences remain in terms of the proximate factors considered to lead or initiate the change. Broadly speaking, there are three distinct theories of institutions: theories of the evolutionary emergence of social conventions, market-based theories of exchange and selection through competition, and a bargaining theory explaining institutions in terms of asymmetries of power (Knight 1995). Commons (1934) views institutional evolution in terms of political and judicial processes of decisionmaking and the activities of private collective organizations, where economic efficiency may be important but not necessarily the sole or dominant factor. The earlier works of North (North and Thomas 1970 and 1973) treat institutional change as endogenous to the economic system. In view of the critical role of exogenous factors, Field (1981) critically contests such a partial perspective. But subsequent works of North (1990a) recognize the scope for exogenous sources of institutional change, including ideology, conquest, and war. New insights on the role of exogenous factors can be obtained by treating institutional change as a 'shift in the demand for institutional innovation' as induced by the interactive effects of resource endowments, cultural conditions, and technological developments (Ruttan 1978, 1988 and 1999; Ruttan and Hayami 1984).

The emergence and change of different sets of institutions require different kinds of theoretical explanations. Theories of planned or intentional design generally adopt a contractarian approach, describing institutional change as a product of free and voluntary exchange in the political market (Buchanan and Tullock 1962). In contrast, market-based theories of institutions (e.g., public choice theory) predict that institutional changes occur whenever their benefits exceed costs. These theories are consistent with the new institutional economics perspective of institutional change, but with three amendments. The first is to avoid the confusion of equating property rights with institutional arrangements as property rights are but one of many components of institutional arrangements. The second is to recognize and capture the political economy aspects of institutional change by incorporating the institutional implications of the distribution of both benefits and costs of institutional change across various groups. Since these distributional effects are an outcome of the initial system of property rights, the initial resource endowment and the attendant bargaining strengths of individuals and groups determine the nature of subsequent institutional evolution.[11] Finally, the effects of exogenous and nonmarket forces (e.g., natural disasters, war, revolution, and ideologies) on the relative bargaining strength of these groups have to be accounted for.

The rational choice approach (Rawls 1971; Harsanyi 1977) models the choice of institutional arrangements within a decision situation involving extreme uncertainty or a 'veil of ignorance.' In other words, individuals and groups choose the primordial institutional configurations such that they are not worse off regardless of the change in the state of nature. This model can provide a reasonable explanation for the choice of only the primordial institutional configurations. But, it does not explain well subsequent changes in institutional

structure because maintaining the 'veil of ignorance' argument is not reasonable in these cases. The other rational choice theorists (Twight 1992), therefore, consider institutional choice in a situation where institutional
arrangements already exist and individuals or groups invest in institutional
maintenance or modifications to change the distribution of payoffs, economic
opportunities, or economic advantage. The emergence of hierarchies as an
alternative to market can be understood well from this perspective. Boyer and
Hollingsworth (1997a: 442–3) describe the theory of voluntary and rational
self-building of institutions where organizational innovations derive from the
rational calculus of individuals and firms comparing alternative solutions.

Some noteworthy attempts to synthesize competitive selection with intentional efforts to create institutions through market exchange have their own
value as independent explanations for different kinds of institutions (Coase
1960; Williamson 1975 and 1985; North 1990a). Theories of intentional
design have been invoked primarily to describe the creation of political institutions based either on the transaction cost approach or on purely intentional
efforts. Implied in the explicit emphasis on the distributional consequences of
institutions is the role of political bargaining as a mechanism of institutional
change (Knight and Sened 1995b: 4–5). Riker (1995), in his study of the framing of the US Constitution as a case of the more general phenomenon of intentional institution creation, identifies two important factors: the importance of
predecessor institutions and internal consistency within institutions. Internal
consistency means that various provisions of constitutions are all tuned to
achieve the overall objective in an ordered way.

Institutions created purely on intentional efforts include bureaucratic organizations and constitutions as well as property rights. In these cases, the explanations for creating and changing institutions are based on the relative
bargaining power of relevant social actors (Knight and Sened 1995b: 5). The
papers included in the Knight and Sened book provide a detailed commentary
on both the evolution of informal institutions and on the intentional design of
formal institutions. Levi (1990: 407) views formal institutions as an outcome of
social bargaining and institutional change is 'most likely when there is an
increase in the bargaining powers of individuals seeking change and a decrease
in the blocking power of individuals whose interests are served by the current
institutional arrangements.' This bargaining-based logic of institutional change
clearly applies only to formal institutions. From an anthropological perspective,
Douglas (1986) argues that most informal institutions and their formal counterparts have evolved from natural principles and hence are a social reflection
of arrangements found in nature. This consistency is one reason as to why informal institutions are more durable than formal institutions.

Not all writers supporting evolutionary theory subscribe to the view that the
process will automatically lead to socially efficient institutions. For instance,

Posner (1980), Schotter (1981), Coleman (1990), and Williamson (1975 and 1985) expect that socially efficient institutions of different forms will evolve. Coase (1960), North (1981 and 1990a), Barzel (1989), and Libecap (1989) believe that the evolutionary process can yield socially inefficient institutions as well (Knight and Sened 1995a: 2–3). Demsetz (1967) argues that institutions emerge when benefits outweigh costs. But, this does not mean that the emergent institution will always be efficient, as the distribution of benefits and costs across economic groups is not taken into account. According to North (1990a: 9 and 73), institutions tend to be inefficient because they are devised by people with the bargaining power to create new rules. As a result, institutions are always a mixed pack, some inducing efficiency, others constraining efficiency.

The efficiency motive is endogenous to the model of institutional change whereas the case of income redistribution is exogenous. The emergence of additional gains from changes in relative prices and technology and the inability of existing institutions to capture such gains are the primary reasons for institutional innovation. The essential requirement for initiating institutional change in such conditions is that the discounted expected gains should exceed the expected costs of undertaking the change (North and Thomas 1970: 3). A study by Libecap (1978) uses the institutional transaction cost approach to explain institutional changes in the context of mineral resources in the US West. The empirical analysis leads to the conclusion that, as long as there are private gains to be realized and they are higher than the additional cost of institutional change, there will be demand for refining the precision of legal rights (Libecap 1978: 341). In the context of water resources, the switch from the riparian to the prior appropriation doctrine can also be explained in terms of the additional net gains of the institutional change under conditions of increasing water scarcity and their impact on private investment in irrigation technologies (Bromley 1989b: 738–9).

Theories of competitive selection through market processes are useful to explain some institutions, but they cannot be generalized. The selection of institutional arrangements through market mechanisms can be myopic and inefficient (Polanyi 1957) and may lead to dead ends (Hayek 1976). By incorporating an explicit role for transaction costs into welfare diagrammatic analysis, Griffin (1991: 607) concludes that zero transaction costs need not ensure an efficient economic outcome when relevant institutions or their major components are imperfect (e.g., property-rights system). It is impossible to invoke economic efficiency in a Pareto sense as a norm to guide institutional choice because the selection is only from a subset of the actually available institutions and also because of our limited ability to characterize and consider many other alternatives (Griffin 1991: 614). Williamson (1999) also recognizes this in terms of his 'remediableness criterion', according to which an inferior governance mode is chosen for lack of any feasible alternative mode of governance. For institutional economists with a strong belief in the evolutionary nature of institutions, efficiency can never be invoked because institutions, being in a constant process of evolution, never reach the equilibrium that would allow the derivation of their efficiency properties.

Institutional maintenance and stability can be explained in terms of their capacity to produce either collective benefits for all social groups or distributional advantage for the powerful. But, the explanation cannot be complete without explicit recognition of the connection of institutions with power structure as well as knowledge and learning. The power connection necessitates a political economy consideration; the knowledge and learning connection requires a subjective consideration. For a better understanding of the process of institutional change from this particular perspective, North (1994) suggests close examination of the role of four factors: ideology (culture), historical specificity (path dependency), power (political economy), and, most of all, the learning process (subjective processing of knowledge and information). Of particular relevance from the perspective of our study is the importance of learning, especially its effects on the subjective processing of knowledge and information as well as on the mental construct of the world. Learning has wider ramifications as it underlines the role of knowledge, interaction, and information exchange. Thus, research on and documentation of the internal dynamics of institutions as well as international experience on the institutional reform process could add much to the learning of policymakers, executives, and ultimately, the users.

Despite the importance of economic factors, the actual direction of institutional change is essentially an outcome of the prevailing power balance among interest groups. But, there are limits on the extent to which changes in power balance can alter the course of institutional change. For instance, institutional path dependency leaves only a few alternative routes open for change. As a result, normal changes in the power structure affect institutions only within a range. Furthermore, interests are not fixed, but change in response not only to changes in economic conditions but also to the features of the reform program itself (Haggard and Webb 1994b: 5). Therefore, working with a pro-reform coalition, the reform program can be designed to minimize political opposition and counter special interest groups. In this sense, reform program design also indirectly involves coalition building. The importance of interest groups should not dwarf either the independent role of government and commitments of political leaders or the power and 'politics' of ideas (White 1990: 11).

The inevitability of subjective and incomplete processing of information allows ideology, bias, and ignorance to play a major role in human choices. This is an additional source of inefficient institutions. According to North (1990a: 26), 'institutions alter the price paid for one's convictions and hence, play a critical role in the extent to which nonwealth-maximizing motivations influence choices.' A parallel argument can show how resource degradation, fiscal crisis, and natural calamities resulting from inefficient institutions enhance conviction for radical reform. In these circumstances, partisan politics and interest group considerations weaken. While politically dominant groups may favor the status quo, crisis weakens their bargaining power and strengthens new ideas and policies, in the process removing most of the previously insurmountable obstacles (White 1990: 16).

MOTIVATION FOR AND SOURCES OF INSTITUTIONAL CHANGE

When discussing theories of institutional change, we did touch on motivating factors and sources of institutional change. These aspects deserve special attention, as none of the theories satisfactorily explains change in different institutions and contexts. The conventional view holds that institutional change occurs either to enhance efficiency or to improve equity (North and Thomas 1970 and 1973; Binswanger and Ruttan 1978; North 1981; Ruttan and Hayami 1984). However, Bromley (1989b) argues that institutional change is also motivated by two other considerations: the reallocation of economic opportunity and the redistribution of economic advantage. Although these considerations appear to be related to equity, they have a broader meaning than and different origin from the conventional equity argument, as they are not related to the redistribution of income stream or motivated by changes in relative prices and technology. Their real origin is the changes in the collective attitude about the society's full consumption set and social welfare function (Bromley 1989b: 745–7).[12] The fact that some institutional changes motivated by these considerations (e.g., import restrictions) do not achieve social efficiency (Bromley 1989b: 756) is an additional reason why institutional changes may not always be efficient. This apparent reason is linked closely to the logic based on interest groups (or organizations) and the subjective model of individuals (or social attitudes) that led North (1990a: 7) to accept the persistence of inefficient institutions.

Technological developments are another major source of institutional change. Institutional change is an outcome of a growing 'tension between an existing structure of property rights and the production potential of the economy' (North 1981: 62). That is, the tension between the 'structural production frontier', as determined by the prevailing property-rights systems, and the 'technical production frontier', as determined by resource endowment and technology (Eggertsson 1990: 319).[13] Eggertsson (1990: 319) notes that 'for each structure of property rights, there is a *structural production frontier*, which is reached by selecting, from a set of feasible organizations, those that minimize costs and maximize output.' Given the prevalent state of technology and other exogenous factors, the set of feasible forms of organizations is defined by the property-rights structures, which, in turn, depend on the political structure. According to Eggertsson (1990: 319), some political systems provide incentives to place the economy close to its technical production frontier while others do not.

Institutional change can also be viewed from a supply–demand perspective (Feeny 1993; Ruttan 1999). This perspective delineates the demand side from the supply side of institutional change and then focuses on the role of both the proximate and fundamental factors operating on both sides (Alston 1996: 26–7). The demand for institutional change originates from the latent gains emerging from disequilibria induced by changing resource endowments, product prices, and technical change (North and Thomas 1971 and 1973; North 1990a; Ruttan 1999). Demand for institutional services should increase substantially to overcome the transaction costs involved both in negotiating and in implementing changes in institutional arrangements (Williamson 1985: 15–42). The supply side of institutional change is a less studied aspect in institutional economics. Institutional supply assumes importance for various reasons. Although institutions evolve naturally through time and respond to market forces, purposive changes are also necessary to expedite the process and shape the direction of institutional change. It is here that the supply side of institutions assumes significance.[14]

From the perspective of institutional supply, the state plays a major role as a source of institutional change. In fact, the new institutional economics assigns a key role to the state in creating and enforcing stable systems of property rights. These institutional functions enable the state to reduce the transaction cost per unit of exchange (North 1986: 236). This scale economy effect makes the state a more efficient mechanism than other governance arrangements for lowering the overall transaction costs of both market and nonmarket institutions (Eggertsson 1996a: 9).[15] In addition to these maintenance roles, the state also has a more active role as the supplier of institutional change (Alston 1996: 27).[16] The state (as well as international donors and funding agencies) can also promote other suppliers of institutional change, such as research and information systems, by supporting the identification, evaluation, and dissemination of institutional best practice and success stories from around the world. Moreover, given the coercive and persuasive powers of modern states, they can also play mediating and facilitative roles, particularly in avoiding dead ends and in defending societal values (North 1981 and 1990a).[17]

Institutional change is an incremental process in which short-run profitable activities cumulatively create the long-term path of institutional change (North 1990b: 397). The change in relative prices has been a dominant source of institutional change throughout history (North and Thomas 1973). Changes in relative prices are only the proximate factor as they just capture and reflect the effects of changes in fundamental factors such as technology and resource endowments (Ruttan 1999). The scope for reducing the cost of economic and social transactions also remains as the major source of institutional inventions and change. Other major sources of institutional change include power (Marglin 1991) and ideas or ideologies (North 1990a and 1990b; White 1990). Likewise, the existence of dense networks of social relations (e.g., family, religion, and culture) and other noneconomic institutions can also be used to build useful economic institutions (Polanyi 1957; Granovetter 1985). Since traditional norms and values provide the framework within which economic institutions are embedded, social and cultural aspects play a strong role in institutional evolution and change, mainly through their role in reducing the cost of transactions.

Other forces, including donor agencies and multilateral and bilateral economic and political agreements, also affect the supply and demand sides of institutional changes (White 1990: 3; Haggard and Webb 1994b: 25–9).[18] Similarly, the widespread and dominant trend toward political liberalization and democratization in recent decades (Huntington 1991) has enhanced prospects for institutional changes (Haggard and Webb 1994b: 1–2). Depending on the level of analysis, these and related factors can be viewed as either exogenous or endogenous to institutions. For instance, in the case of the layer schema depicted in Figure 2.1, the main sources of institutional change are individual preferences, strategic motives (e.g., rent seeking), and institutional environment. While the first two are obviously endogenous, the last factor can be treated as either exogenous or endogenous to the analysis. Since the institutional environment is defined broadly to include a set of 'fundamental political, social, and legal ground rules that govern the economic and political activity' (Davis and North 1970: 133), it is considered endogenous in Figure 2.1. But, the political and social factors have to be treated as exogenous, in view of the powerful role that war, revolution, ideology, and the social impact of natural calamities play in institutional change.

Changes in institutional structure are affected by the exogenous influence of factors constituting the institutional environment as well as by the endogenous influence of features internal to the institutional structure. To capture this important idea, Shepsle (1979: 135) puts forward a model of structure-induced equilibrium. This model argues that the attributes of the institutional structure themselves induce institutional equilibrium, unlike other equilibrium models of institutional change where equilibrium is driven by individual preferences and the physical aspects of the game. This argument provides an additional dimension to the path-dependency notion of North (1990a) by underlining the roles that the inherent features of institutional structure play in the process of institutional change.

To understand and evaluate these roles more clearly, we need first to understand the institutional structure, especially by decomposing its constituent parts and analyzing their features, including their complementarities and interlinkages. In this sense, the notion of structure-induced equilibrium has a special meaning and relevance for the analytical basis of our institutional analysis.

NOTES

1. In the latter sense, subjective perception of reality or the actors' mental construct of the world becomes a key factor affecting the nature and direction of institutional change (North 1990a: 17).
2. Path dependence implies limited scope for sudden and radical changes. Although most institutional change is gradual and continuous, discontinuous institutional changes through conquest or revolution are also possible. However, institutional change through conquest and revolution affects only the formal rules. The informal rules derived from the previous formal rules change far more slowly than their formal counterparts and linger on with little change (North 1990a: 6).
3. Here, two points must be recognized. First, the stability and durability features, as discussed here, are free from efficiency considerations. Second, these features do not preclude the malleability or adaptive flexibility of institutions, which are the key to initiating and sustaining the process of development (Adelman, *et al.* 1992: 106).
4. Although the approach toward the decomposition of institutions and the identification of their typologies remains the same, the criteria and relevant particulars vary by the kinds of institutional arrangements being considered.
5. In this respect, we share the main message of a carefully conducted study of the reform process and policy implementation (White 1990) that the way in which the reform program is structured and packaged has much to contribute to its successful implementation.
6. Although there was a large initial setup cost in creating de-novo institutions such as the US Constitution of 1787, the 'interdependent web of an institutional matrix produces massive increasing returns' and could also minimize the negative performance implications of inefficient institutional components (North 1990a: 95 and 100).
7. Although transaction cost analysis minimizes the roles of these noneconomic considerations, they are inevitable in view of distinct variations even in the same institutions across cultural contexts. Hall (1986) and Wilks and Wright (1987) are examples of comparative studies that consider nationally distinct capitalist institutions and doctrines.
8. While organizations are the agents of change, they are not the origin of change. Since the demand for change originates from individual agents as a response to economic outcomes and endogenous preferences, organizations channel only the collectively expressed need for change.
9. This is especially true in a democratic system. For instance, political parties in a democracy may require the incumbent to protect the interests of their successors. Similarly, factors such as the creation of the rule of law, empowerment of technocrats, and international influence dilute or neutralize excessive and exploitative forms of political power (Bates 1996: 22–3).
10. As a result, the distinction between the 'old' and 'new' institutional economics is declining as the new institutional economics incorporates some of the most important aspects of the old institutional economics, such as culture, habit, and ideology (Groenewegen, Kerstholt, and Nagelkerke 1995; Rutherford 1995; Hodgson 1998). As a result, institutional economics is departing from neoclassical economics, although transaction cost economics, one of the major branches of institutional economics, retains the analytical rigor of neoclassical economics.
11. The pattern of distribution of institutional impact also determines both the occurrence and effects of institutional change. For instance, when the externalities are so widely distributed

across a vast number of unorganized individuals, the transaction cost may be too high to be Pareto relevant to support a market-driven institutional change (Livingston 1987: 285).

12. Instances of institutional changes, as induced by these considerations, range from mine safety and antipoverty laws to environmental acts and trade regulations (Bromley 1989b).

13. For a theoretical illustration of this point with recent South African experience, see Dollery (1995).

14. The desirability of developing and supplying institutions that strengthen voluntary exchanges and interactions must be recognized. But, supplying institutions determined only by the market process itself is not necessarily desirable. Since imaginative collective forms of coordination mechanisms are necessary, nonmarket-based and purposive institutional changes are also needed (Boyer and Hollingsworth 1997a: 477).

15. This cannot be an argument for unrestrained state power, as it can also create social costs when excessive interventions provide disincentives for decentralized decisionmaking. One way to minimize such social costs is to contain state power by strengthening the rule of law (North and Weingast 1989; North 1990a and 1993; Weingast 1993).

16. For instance, economic development in Western Europe is historically connected with the state's role in establishing and enforcing property rights, weights, measures, legal institutions, banking institutions, and capital markets (North 1990a: 52–3 and 64).

17. The rule of law can both contain and strengthen the powers of the state, especially when political deadlocks and intergovernmental disputes render the state powerless. For instance, in India, but for the increasing influence of the judicial system, the union government could not have enacted some recent environmental regulations or resolved some serious interstate water disputes.

18. The importance of multilateral economic agreements, especially trade agreements, for institutional changes at the national level can be judged from the increase in the number of trade blocs from about 30 in 1994 to about 50 by 1999 (Li 1999: 1).

3. Existing literature: approaches, attempts, and limitations

To explain institutions, performance, and change in different cultural, social, economic, and political contexts, a variety of theories are used. Paralleling the diversity in theories, a variety of approaches are also used to develop the methodologies needed to evaluate institutions in theoretical and empirical settings. The relevance of these approaches and methodologies varies with the nature of the institutions, the level, scope, and focus of the analysis, and the evaluation context.

To identify the institutional approach or approaches suitable for our purpose, a basic understanding of these approaches is essential. We attempt here an analytical overview of these approaches, including the institutional transaction cost approach. Against this overview, we also attempt a methodological review of the analytical and empirical literature dealing with institutions and their performance both in general and in water sector contexts. The review is intended to justify our study by identifying some serious gaps in the literature and to provide contrast to our approach and methodology by highlighting their points of departure from existing wisdom and tradition.

INSTITUTIONAL APPROACHES: A STYLIZED COMPARISON

Considering the subject matter and objectives of our study, its reliance on an institutional approach is natural and straightforward, but the approach itself has many strands and variants. A comparative overview of these variants can bring out their strengths and weaknesses. In terms of overall approach, the theoretical traditions in institutional economics can be grouped into five analytical categories (Landry 1996: 9). Table 3.1 shows how the approaches in each category differ in terms of generic scope, assumptions, unit of analysis, focus, explanations, and limitations.[1] Of particular relevance for our study are the differences between these approaches in terms of their assumptions about institutional interdependence, level of analysis, unit of institutional evaluation,

Table 3.1 *Stylized comparison of institutional approaches*

Aspects of comparison	Approaches				
	Old institutionalism	Neo-institutionalism	Meso-corporatism, policy community, networks	Game theory	Transaction cost theory, agency theory, theory of contract
1. Generic scope	Macro-analysis of complete institutions	Macro-analysis of incomplete institutions	Variations on micro-analysis of incomplete institution	Micro-analysis of complete institutions	Mico-analysis of incomplete institutions
2. Assumptions					
• Interdependence	No	No	Yes	Yes	Yes
• Information	Complete	Incomplete	Incomplete	Complete	Incomplete
• Rationality	Comprehensive	Bounded	Bounded	Comprehensive	Bounded
3. Unit of analysis	Institutional structures	Institutional structures	Meso-institutional structures	Institutional structures	Institutional transactions
4. Causal explanations	Institutional structures determine individual behaviour	Incomplete institutions create incentives for opportunistic behaviour	Actions of individuals are rendered compatible through efficient and equitable use of incomplete institutions	Rational individuals select equilibrium solutions	Incomplete institutions create incentive for opportunism which induces individuals to invest in institutions that minimize cognitive competence and opportunism
5. Focus	On formulation of classifications of institutional structures	On opportunities and constraints built into institutional structures	On opportunities and constraints built into meso-institutional structures	On the degree of stability of equilibrium solutions	On technical coordination, warranty, monitoring, and costs of incentives
6. Limitations	• High level of aggregation • Ad-hoc description • Individuals do not calculate	• High level of aggregation • Ad-hoc explanations	• Average level of aggregation • Ad-hoc explanations	• Institutions are highly abstract • Institutions are exogenous • Institutions are minimal	• Difficult to derive equilibrium solutions

Source: Adapted from Landry (1996).

47

and the degree of institutional disaggregation. Although these approaches have differences, they are not alternatives but complements for a comprehensive understanding of institutions and their performance implications at various analytical levels and in different evaluation contexts.

Our macro focus on formal institutional structures precludes the game theoretic approach. Similarly, since our interest is not on evaluating the macro institutional formations but on the performance implications of the internal features and linkages within an institutional structure, the approaches classified under the category of meso-corporatism, hierarchies, and networks are also not directly relevant for our purpose. The same applies to public choice theory, which falls naturally under the fifth category of approaches in Table 3.1. Public choice theory makes institutions endogenous to its framework of analysis and also highlights issues such as rent seeking and transaction costs that are outside the scope of the neoclassical approach, but it does not allow a comparison of alternative institutional configurations or explain institutional change that occurs through political means (Livingston 1987: 282–3). Although the role of government is recognized by public choice theory, the state's role is limited to defining and protecting property rights. Since a precise definition of rights by the state does not guarantee how the rights should be structured (Randall 1974), the issue of evaluating alternative institutional configurations remains outside the purview of analysis within public choice theory.

Neither agency theory nor the theory of contract are much help, as our focus is not on the role of organizations or on the issues of enforcement and monitoring. We are looking directly at the critical role of individuals (stakeholders, policymakers, opinionmakers) in the process of institutional change. Specifically, we are looking into change and convergence in the subjective construct of individuals as to the nature and performance of institutions and inquiring how such convergence can serve as a basis for gauging consensus on the extent and direction of present and future institutional change. As noted, organizations function as a conduit for reflecting and consolidating the views of their constituent members. While agency and organizational theories can provide the framework for treating the role of individuals indirectly via organizations, there are no corresponding theories to account directly for the role individuals play in the process of institutional change. As a result, the issue presents considerable analytical and methodological challenges. We believe that these challenges can be overcome easily if we can create a methodological framework that combines the elements of the old and new institutional economic theories, especially within the institutional transaction cost framework.

Since we want to study a completely specified institutional structure from a macro perspective with a focus on structural features, we come closer to the old institutional economics. But, recognizing the limitations on the information and rationality dimensions takes us closer to new institutional economics. On the issue of institutional linkages, the central issue from the perspective of our study, we depart from both old and new institutional traditions and get closer to the other three categories of approaches as they all assume institutional interdependence. We do, however, believe that the issue of institutional linkages can be handled within both the old and new institutional economics framework. A generic evaluation framework can be developed by combining aspects of old and new institutional economics traditions as well as the transaction cost approach, but it presents major conceptual and analytical challenges.

Treating old and new institutional economics within the same analytical framework is not easy because of serious epistemological and methodological differences between these two traditions. Old institutional economics is more comprehensive and realistic, but it lacks rigorous analytical methods. In contrast, the new institutional economics approach could retain the analytical rigor and precision due to its complementary relationship with the neoclassical approach.[2] But, at the same time, the new institutional economics approach has retained its originality by distancing itself from both old institutional economics and neoclassical economics. For instance, unlike its counterparts, it explicitly recognizes the facts of bounded rationality and incomplete information. At the same time, it recognizes the role of market forces while also allowing for an explicit consideration of the role of economic and political organizations as well as other noneconomic factors such as culture and ideology and changing social goals (Bromley 1985; North 1990a). This approach therefore allows the evaluation of both the positive and normative aspects of institutions (Tool 1977).

The preference for new institutional economics as a general framework for our analysis is clear, but a few issues have to be settled first. The application of an institutional approach can be taken either 'as an exercise in (general) theory or as an exercise in governance mechanisms. [The former attempts] a general conceptual framework that provides an overview of the entire transition process, viewing it through a wide-angled lens' (Williamson 1994: 5). The latter, in contrast, attempts an 'exhaustive conceptual classification of the decisions that have to be made, the players that have to make them, the institutional structures within which decisionmaking will take place, and a set of performance criteria against which the process can be evaluated' (Rausser and Simon 1992: 270). These two exercises represent, in a way, the differential perspectives of old and new institutional economics. In other words, when the institutional approach is treated as an exercise in general theory, it approximates the evolutionary perspective of institutions underlying the old institutional economics. In contrast, when it is treated as an exercise in governance, it resembles the equilibrium perspective of institutions underlying the new institutional economics.

The evolutionary vs. equilibrium perspective of institutions is not just a reflection of the old vs. new institutional economics divide. It has deeper implications, especially for the conceptualization and evaluation of institutional change. The central question in the old institutional economics was not about the influence of institutions on economic behavior but about understanding of the process of institutional change itself. Veblen (1899) viewed this process essentially in evolutionary terms whereas Commons (1934) viewed it as a manmade process characterized by collective rule making, purposive selection, and constructivism.[3] Although events such as constitutional change, war, or revolutions can lead to dramatic and discontinuous changes, especially in formal and macro institutions, institutional changes are intrinsically a slow and continuous process. Davis and North (1970: 9), therefore, view institutional changes as a cumulation of an incremental or evolutionary process such as the gradual modification of contractual relations or shifts in the boundaries between market and nonmarket activities.

Although there is consensus on the evolutionary nature of institutional changes, there is a fundamental disagreement as to whether the change process will arrive at an equilibrium. Many institutional economists, especially those having some affinity with the neoclassical tradition, believe in the relevance of the equilibrium notion to institutional change. But others with the old institutional traditions believe that the notion of equilibrium is inconsistent with a phenomenon that is constantly evolving. Since institutions always respond to new changes, they are *always in the process of becoming* and *never reach equilibrium*. When the system is always evolving (i.e., in disequilibrium), the normative considerations underlying the concept of efficiency become meaningless and, hence, a criterion is lacking for evaluating institutional change (Bromley 2002, personal communication). Although institutions evolve constantly, when the evolution is so slow and marginal as to be almost stable, periodic but brief equilibrium is conceivable in the sense of a motionless state. But, since such a transient state provides no guarantee for the convergence of true social costs and benefits, it cannot be a basis for any efficiency analysis. The evolutionary–equilibrium debate does not constrain our methodology, however, because we want to evaluate institutions and their performance in a relative context through the subjective construct and instrumental valuation of individuals.

INSTITUTIONAL TRANSACTION COST APPROACH

Among the approaches listed in Table 3.1, the transaction cost approach deserves closer attention in view of its relevance both for explaining the extent and direction of institutional reforms observed across countries and for evaluating the transaction cost implications of institutional linkages within macro institutional structures. The transaction cost approach that originated with Coase (1937) and was developed further by Williamson (1975, 1985) was first applied to explain the evolution of market and nonmarket organizations within an institutional environment. Although transaction cost theory is considered to have micro focus in a generic sense, one of its variants, the institutional transaction cost approach, as developed by North and Thomas (1971) and North (1988, 1990a, 1990c), can be generalized to deal with macro-level institutional change. This generalization requires two major amendments to the original version. The first amendment is to enable the transaction cost approach to account also for the impact of noneconomic factors, especially the political economy aspects, on institutional transactions. The second amendment is to enable the approach to account for the transaction cost implications of internal and structural features of institutions such as institutional linkages. Let us now see what these amendments mean for the generalization of the transaction cost approach.

The incorporation of political economy considerations, though involves some loss of rigor and precision, can generalize the transaction cost framework far beyond its original scope and application context. For instance, organization theory within transaction cost economics focuses mainly on changes in contractual relations within an institutional arrangement (more specifically, within an organization).[4] Even though transaction cost economics is interdisciplinary in nature, focusing on economics, law, and organization, it cannot explain changes in either institutional arrangements or institutional environment.[5] To explain these changes, transaction cost economics has to also look into the political economy aspects of institutional change. In new institutional economics, in contrast, the political economy aspect is central to explaining how the governance structure and other extraneous factors shape the institutional environment (North 1990a).[6]

Since the transaction cost approach deals with the relationship between transaction costs and institutional evolution within a given institutional environment, it encounters problems in capturing the transaction costs pertaining to the creation of new institutional arrangements as well as modifications in existing institutional environments. In the context of such institutional transactions, a complicated and hierarchically inter-related choice must be made between institutional alternatives, institutional configurations, and methods of implementing them. In view of this limitation, the institutional transaction cost approach may miss or undervalue interdependencies among a series of contracts (Williamson 1985: 393). This incompleteness of the approach is especially serious, as it cannot capture the transaction cost implications of linkages and synergies evident within the institutional structure. While institutional linkages can be demonstrated analytically as well as with historical case studies, their implications for institutional transaction costs are hard to quantify. Observational evidence, experimental approaches, and survey methods can, however, provide some initial breakthrough in this respect and could also provide some indicative and qualitative information on the transaction cost implications of institutional design principles.

Let us now see how the concept of transaction costs has to be modified to account for the factors affecting both general and institutional transactions. Transaction costs are opportunity costs, just like any other cost in economic theory. There are both fixed and variable transaction costs.[7] *Transaction cost* refers to the effort, time, and expense involved in obtaining the information necessary to negotiate, make, and enforce an exchange (Williamson 1985: 2). The exchange can include the enactment of laws, declaration of policies, and the creation of and changes in organizations. All the relevant transaction costs cannot be fully accounted for in narrow economic terms because institutional transactions, like other transactions, are embedded within a society's normative and cultural systems (Commons 1934; Granovetter 1985). As a result, transaction costs are also influenced by behavioral factors such as reputation and credible commitments (Williamson 1994) as well as social capital such as moral standards, shared norms, and trust (Coleman 1987, 1990; Yaffey 1998).

In a general sense, transaction costs are sensitive to a number of factors. North (1997: 2–3) identifies four variables: the cost of measuring the valuable attributes of a commodity or service, the size of the market, the need for monitoring and enforcement, and ideological attitudes.[8] North's emphasis on the ideological variable (1990a, 1997) assumes both theoretical and practical significance. More pertinent here is the direct relationship between the level of transaction costs as determined by the first three variables and the importance of the ideological variable (North 1997: 3). Thus, ideology counts the most when measurement and enforcement costs are high, and vice versa.[9] Since ideology is related to the subjective models that individuals use to explain and evaluate the events around them, it involves noneconomic aspects and motives. As a result, the incorporation of ideology makes the transaction cost approach more realistic and enables it to explain institutional choices not only from an economic perspective but also from a social and political perspective. Since the cost of transacting in political markets is high even in the most perfect political markets (North 1990: Ch. 12), the political actors have substantial freedom as they are not constrained by their political constituents (Bates 1989; North 1990a). In these circumstances, issues such as leadership and its commitment to reform as well as pressure from international actors become far more important than otherwise.

Three factors, besides those discussed above, can have profound effects on transaction costs. They are opportunism, frequency of exchange, and asset specificity. The last factor raises the transaction cost because the exchange in question depends on a specific person, specific location, or specific physical assets. In this condition, bargaining ability becomes low and the potential for opportunism tends to be high (Acheson 1994b: 11). Many sociologists and anthropologists (e.g., Granovetter 1985; Douglas 1986) find, however, that the emphasis on opportunism misses the neutralizing role of social and cultural factors within which economic relationships are embedded. For instance, the rules or institutions that make the activities of others predictable can reduce opportunism and, hence, the transaction costs. Since the frequency of exchange and repeated interaction can enhance behavioral predictability and reduce the scope for opportunism, they also have a significant transaction cost minimization role.

Another set of factors that influence transaction costs both directly and indirectly relates to the effects of the changing physical and sociopolitical environment. In a particular physical and sociopolitical environment, each distinct institutional structure is associated with a specific level of transaction costs (Eggertsson 1990). But, when the physical and sociopolitical environment undergoes changes, the level of transaction costs varies, leading to the emergence of a new institutional structure that corresponds to the changed transaction costs. The state also has a double-edged role with respect to institutional transaction costs. The state is in a position to provide institutional services (e.g., creation and protection of property rights) at lower costs than private or volunteer groups (North and Thomas 1973: 8). But, the fiscal needs of the state as well as its susceptibility to interest-group politics can also lead to higher transaction costs and inefficient institutions (North and Thomas 1973; North 1981, 1990a, 1990b; Olson 1982; Eggertsson 1990).

The more relevant issue for the purpose of our study is the transaction cost implications of the internal features of institutions themselves. The cost of an institutional transaction or reform program can be reduced by factors such as increasing returns or scale economies in institutional change (North 1990a: 95). But, these factors are predicated on the existence of linkages and synergies among institutional aspects. Thus, besides the scale-related factors, there are also structure-related factors with significant implications not only for the economic and political costs of institutional transactions but also for overall institutional performance. These structural factors relate to institutional design principles covering issues such as institutional prioritization, packaging, sequencing, scaling and timing. To evaluate the political economy and transaction cost implications of these factors, we need a clear understanding of the internal structure and composition of the prevailing institutions, including their relationships to proposed institutions and existing socioeconomic, political, and physical conditions. That is, a greater knowledge of the institutions' specific features can itself play an important role in reducing institutional transaction costs in various contexts.

Such knowledge can be gained from a finer decomposition of institutional structure, identification of key institutional components or aspects, and an evaluation of their structural and functional linkages. From this exercise, the institutional components and aspects can be categorized in terms of their relative performance implications, political feasibility, and upstream and downstream linkages with their counterparts. Such an analysis can, in turn, enable us to identify various schemes of institutional priority setting, sequencing, and packaging, and select those with lowest transaction costs and highest political acceptance. Since the choice here is not institutional components and aspects but their configurations, the transaction costs include the effects of scale economies, structural features, path dependency properties and political economy aspects. As will be seen from our literature review below, these aspects, though they received attention in the literature, have not been systematically treated, especially within an empirical context.

THE LITERATURE: A REVIEW OF ISSUES AND APPROACHES

In the previous chapter, we carefully reviewed the theories of institutional change and, earlier in this chapter, we evaluated the approaches used for evaluating institutions. The review in this section focuses on the analytical and empirical literatures that attempt to evaluate institutions and their performance both in general and in water institution contexts. No single attempt at a comprehensive review of institutional economics can be adequate given the vast amount of literature on the subject with its varying strands of perspectives, levels of analysis, disciplinary orientations, and methodological bases. For our present purpose, the focus is narrowed by limiting the review to the issues addressed and approaches used in studies dealing with macro institutional aspects. Even here, the attempt can be unwieldy in view of the growth in the volume and diversity of theoretical and empirical studies on macro institutional aspects since the works of Coase (1937), Williamson (1975, 1993), North (1981, 1990a), and Bromley (1989a). The task is all the more formidable as we cannot completely avoid the studies dealing with micro institutional aspects as the approach and methodology underlying some of them can also be relevant for our purpose.

Grouping the literature in terms of analytical level of analysis is a useful strategy for producing a manageable yet comprehensive review. In this respect, the approach suggested by Alston (1996: 26) and Eggertsson (1996a: 10–11) is of direct value. Eggertsson (1996a), in particular, suggests that current research in the economics of institutions can be organized into three analytical levels.[10] The first and second levels deal, respectively, with the linkages between institutions and economic performance and with the influence of institutional environment on the structure of economic organizations and contractual arrangements. Analysis at the third level covers a panorama of miscellaneous issues that attempt to explain various elements of the institutional framework and the structure of property rights.[11] Although the analytical levels identified are only a few of many possible constellations, they are extremely useful as a framework for organizing our review of existing literature – both theoretical and empirical – on institutions in general and water institutions in particular. This review will revolve mainly around the studies falling under the first two analytical levels that, broadly, correspond to the two distinct segments of the institution–performance interaction depicted in Figure 2.1.

Theoretical Literature

Although we concentrate on the analytical and empirical literatures, a brief look at the highlights of the generic literature on the theoretical aspects of institutions and performance will help to ensure the completeness of our review. The theoretical literature in the first two analytical categories assigns different roles to different segments of institutions (Eggertsson 1996a: 10). The literature at the first analytical level deals with the effects of institutions on economic performance and treats as exogenous both the institutional environment and institutional arrangements (the governance structure or the organizations and other contractual arrangements). The literature in the second analytical level deals with the effects of institutional environment on the evolution and structure of organizations and contractual arrangements, but institutional structure becomes endogenous while institutional environment remains exogenous. Thus, there is a fundamental difference in the theoretical and methodological basis of studies falling under the two analytical categories.

The general literature at the first analytical level, inquiring into the interface between institutions and economic performance, is substantial. Among the most noteworthy are the works of North (1981, 1990a) and Bromley (1989a). Also included in this category is a substantial part of the works in the law and economic literature that explores the economic consequences of legal arrangements (e.g., Posner 1986 and Cooter and Ullen 1988). The studies at the second level deal with the way the institutional environment defines and limits the sets of practical economic organizations available to a society. Examples of such studies include the seminal works of Coase (1937) and Cheung (1968) as well as the pioneering works of Williamson (1975, 1985, 1993). Unlike these studies that focus on industrial organizations and rely on a transaction cost perspective, North (1981, 1990a),[12] Douglas (1986), Greif (1989), E. Ostrom (1990), and Landa (1994) generalize the relation between institutions and organizations to a noncapitalistic environment and incorporate noneconomic factors such as ethnicity, culture, religion, and ideology. As to the basic methodologies employed at both analytical levels, the general theoretical literature relies mostly on teleological analysis, case studies, or analytical and theoretical treatments.

Empirical Literature: General Institutional Context

Concurrent with the consolidation of the main theoretical foundations of institutional economics, tremendous growth has occurred in the empirical literature on issues related to institutional structures, institutional change, and economic performance. Let us attempt here a review of a subset of studies in the institutional economics literature that try to evaluate empirically the issue of institution–performance interaction both in general and in water sector contexts. The focus of this review is mainly on three aspects: the dimensions of the institution–performance interaction being evaluated, the nature of the variables being developed to capture institutional aspects, and the analytical framework and methodological evaluation being used. Although our attention is mainly on empirical studies on macro institutional aspects, a few analytical and descriptive works and micro attempts are also included in view of their potential significance for our approach and methodology.

Most of the research on institutions is either too descriptive or too abstract to be of much use for policy (Alston 1996: 25). But, there are studies with a fair degree of analytical and quantitative reliance. Some of the most important are reported and reviewed in edited volumes such as Alston, Eggertsson, and North (1996a) and Clague (1997a). The central question addressed by the papers in Cook and Levi (1990) is related to factors behind the secular changes in institutions. The debate here centers on biological evolution, social evolution, contracting and recontracting, leadership (or ideas and ideologies), or their combination. The volume by Acheson (1994a) includes a number of empirical analyses of both macro and micro institutions, especially from an anthropological perspective. The coverage of the study ranges from the institutions generated by military governments to the institutional shift from collective farms to family farms in China. From a methodological perspective, the works reported in these volumes and others reviewed here are based either on detailed case studies or regression-based, cross-country analysis. Since institutional change is a multidimensional and multilevel phenomenon, empirical studies, even those with a relatively sophisticated methodology, cannot be expected to capture the process in all its complexity and detail. Limiting the scope, detail, or the context of analysis forces considerable degree of simplification (Alston, Eggertsson, and North 1996b: 3).

A vast body of literature relies on quantitative approaches to varying degrees. Although Williamson (1985: 21–2) considers transaction costs basically unmeasurable, there are some noteworthy and successful attempts at the empirical measurement of transaction costs, especially within an economywide context (Wallis and North 1986, 1988; Porat and Rubin 1977). Wallis and North (1986, 1988) rely on a temporal or teleological analysis to study the size, structure, and implications of the 'transaction sector' (the institutional structures that facilitate, enforce, and maintain economic exchanges within a market setting) in the United States between 1870 and 1970. As per the estimates of Wallis and North (1986), the transaction sector accounted for 47 to 55 percent of US Gross National Product in 1970. Porat and Rubin (1977: 8), who estimate the US transaction sector from the perspective of information, give a figure of 46 percent of US GNP in 1967.[13]

Cross-country comparative studies carried out within the quantitative framework by Adelman and Morris (1967) and Morris and Adelman (1988) provide some interesting generalization about institutions and performance. Although institutions are found to be more important than resources, technology, and capital, they are only the necessary, but not the sufficient conditions for stimulating economic growth. Adelman and Morris (1974) and Adelman and Lohmoller (1994) combine both temporal and cross-section analysis to study the impact of political structures and economic institutions on economic growth in the context of 23 countries between 1850 and 1914. The study by Adelman and Lohmoller (1994) is particularly important in view of its implications for the methodological basis of the present study. It evaluates the institution–performance interaction within a quantitative framework using a latent variable regression model where many latent or unobservable institutional variables are captured by their relationship with manifest or observable variables. Notably, most of the latent variables (e.g., the character of national political leadership, amenability of land institutions to improvements, and the spread of technology in different sectors) have also been formulated as categorical variables. These categorical variables are also ordered based either on actual evidence or on a priori reasoning (Adelman and Lohmoller 1994: 351–4).

A combination of temporal and cross-sectional analysis has also been used to study both general and specific aspects of institution–performance interaction. For instance, the study by Remmer (1998) uses this hybrid approach to evaluate the relationship between democracy and international cooperation in the Mercosur region (comprising Argentina, Brazil, Paraguay, and Uruguay) in 1947–85. While the actually observed economic and international treaty data are combined to quantitatively evaluate the democracy–cooperation linkages within a logistic regression framework, the main dichotomous variable (democracy) has been created using secondary information from comparative research on Latin American democracy. There are also theoretical and analytical studies addressing particular aspects of the institution–performance interaction such as

the relationship between organizational performance and economic development status (e.g., Clague 1994) and the role of the state in building new institutions and managing conflicts during the structural change process (Chang
1994). Although these issues can be addressed quantitatively, since both studies use only a small cross-section of countries, they evaluate these issues only
theoretically within an analytical framework.[14]

Another interesting set of studies shows how data problems inherent in an
empirical evaluation of institution–performance interaction can be overcome
by combining subjective information with objective data, particularly in
cross-sectional contexts. Knack and Keefer (1986), for instance, in their
logistic regression-based cross-country study of institutions and economic
performance, combine observable variables such as investment, Gross
Domestic Product, and prices with subjectively evaluated institutional variables such as quality of bureaucracy, corruption level, expropriation risk, and
infrastructural quality. They obtain these institutional variables – evaluated
within a 0–10 or 0–4 scale – from the data compiled by private professional
bodies providing international investment risk services such as the
International Country Risk Guide (ICRG) and Business Environment Risk
Intelligence (BERI).[15] These investment service firms, in turn, develop data
on institutional indicators based on opinion surveys of international executives.[16] Similarly, Gray and Kaufmann (1998) evaluate the linkage between
corruption and development in a cross-country context utilizing the executive
perception-based institutional information compiled by the World Economic
Forum (1997).

Cukierman, Webb, and Neyapti (1998) study the nature of the relationship
between the degree of independence of central banks and the level of inflation within a regression framework. This study provides an interesting case
not only for combining temporal and cross-sectional analysis but also for
obtaining institutional information from a cross-section of policy experts
through a custom-made questionnaire. While their dependent variable, inflation, is observable and objective, their independent variable, the independence of central banks, is reflected by a set of coded and appropriately
weighted legal aspects pertaining to the functioning of these banks and their
top executives. The survey of experts in 23 of the 72 sample countries has
been used to obtain both parallel information and perceptional weights on all
relevant institutional variables. Brinkerhoff (1994) evaluates the effects of
institutional design features on project performance by considering a random
sample of 80 World Bank-funded projects implemented in different countries
during 1983–90. The scope of this study is confined to a cross-section of
projects and its evaluation technique is limited to a statistical analysis of tabulated data. Nevertheless, it is noteworthy for its detailed analytical decomposition of institutional design features and for its use of a rating scheme for the

numerical conversion of some of the institutional aspects on a scale of –3 to +3.[17]

Using simple statistical analysis within a cross-country context, Clague (1997a) evaluates how measures of property rights and contract enforcement explain differences in income, growth rates, and investment. The institutional variables for the regression analysis are developed from the cross-country ratings obtained and reported by private investment and risk-rating services such as the ICRG and BERI. The same set of institutional variables, including variables capturing political aspects such as regime type and duration, have also been used by Clague (1997b) to evaluate the impact of political regimes on economic growth, again within a cross-country context. Based on his evaluation of how different features of democracy affect economic policy, Haggard (1997) finds that well-organized interest groups that facilitate the compromise needed for effective policy reforms can play a much more positive role in promoting economic growth than envisaged by Olson (1982).

The study by Li (1999) is noteworthy for its innovative approach to developing institutional variables from secondary data. The basic objective of this study is to evaluate the causal link between institutional arrangements and the trade performance of trade blocs. Central to the analysis is the 'institutional variations index' that captures the inter-bloc variations in the features of both institutional environments and institutional arrangements. The index is constructed by summing the respective values obtained by seven dummy (0–1) variables representing trade-related institutional aspects such as tariff elimination, nontariff elimination, free trade in service, free movement of labor, free movement of capital, specific timetable for liberalization, and dispute settlement procedures.

Based on quantitative and qualitative data for 1,088 households from India and Sri Lanka, Isham and Kahkonen (1999) evaluate how institutional aspects such as service rules and practices, social capital, and governmental and nongovernmental organizations affect the impact and performance of rural water supply projects. A noteworthy aspect of this paper is the use of a 'social capital index' developed from the number of community groups to which a household belongs, with the 'group characteristics' being defined in terms of caste, religion, occupation, decision process, and performance rating (Isham and Kahkonen 1999: 23). The use of proxies for evaluating institutional performance is a common practice in many empirical studies in institutional economics. The choice of the proxy variables depends upon the particular purpose. For instance, Ostrom, Parks, and Whitaker (1978) use variables such as the number of streetlights and trashcans as proxies for evaluating the effectiveness of the neighborhood police system.

Relative costs can be a criterion for comparing alternative institutional arrangements. For instance, Demsetz (1964) and Hurwicz (1972) suggest relative costs as a criterion for comparing the efficiency of market (private) and nonmarket (public) provision of services. But, in contexts involving sovereign transactions (e.g., defense, foreign affairs, and judiciary) as well as in cases where no better alternative is available, nonmarket institutions such as public bureaucracies are the most suitable mode of governance (Williamson 1999).[18] Utilizing the transaction cost economics framework, Williamson (1999) makes a qualitative comparison of four main alternative governance structures (markets, hybrids, hierarchies, and public bureaucracies). He also makes a similar comparison of three alternative organizational forms of public bureaucracies (privatization, regulated privatization, and public agency). In both cases, the qualitative comparison is based on the relative performance of the alternatives in terms of key institutional attributes such as incentive intensity, administrative control, adaptation (autonomous and cooperative), and the relevance of contract law (Williamson 1999: 314, 336).

Based on a detailed case study of a Philippine village, Ruttan (1999) evaluates the interrelated effects of resource endowments and technical changes on the demand for institutional changes in the sphere of land tenure and labor relations. In contrast to micro or partial studies of institutional change, other studies take a macro or general equilibrium view by explaining institutional change in terms of its complex relations with a diverse set of economic, political, and organizational factors. Examples of macro studies include North and Weingast (1989, 1996) on the political foundation of secure markets in 17th century England and Alston and Ferrie (1996) on the linkages among production methods, technological change, labor contract, and political system in the southern United States. The set of case studies reported in Haggard and Webb (1994b) evaluate how the process of political liberalization and democratization initiated and sustained economic reform, including institutional change, in eight countries. The main emphasis of these studies was on the differential sequencing of economic and political reforms and on the roles played in the reform process by political parties, the electoral system, and bureaucratic organizations (Haggard and Webb 1994a: 3–5). These studies also provide evidence for the influence on the reform process wielded by political variables (e.g., number of political parties and election cycle) and economic variables (e.g., level of fiscal deficit and inflation).

Besides the quantitative and quasi-quantitative attempts discussed above, other studies evaluate institutions essentially from an analytical and descriptive perspective. The work of E. Ostrom provides an interesting instance in this respect. Based on a critical review of several informal and formal irrigation and water institutions around the world, Ostrom (1990:

Chs 3, 6) identifies some key principles underlying their success and failure. She also evaluates their performance in terms of eight design principles related to the nature of rules, mechanisms for monitoring, sanctions, and conflict resolution, and institutional nestedness (E. Ostrom 1990: 180). As we will see later, the analytical frameworks of this and related works provide valuable insights for developing an approach for decomposing institutions into their main components and subcomponents or aspects. For now, let us turn to a review of the empirical literature dealing specifically with water institutions.

Empirical Literature: Water Institutional Context

Both the general and specific aspects of the institution–performance interaction within the water sector are well recognized in the literature (Hartman and Seastone 1970; Dinar and Latey 1991; Frederiksen 1992; Guggenheim 1992; Le Moigne, et al. 1992, 1994; Gazmuri and Rosegrant 1994; Hearne and Easter 1997; Howitt 1998). These studies try to evaluate the interaction within a theoretical, anecdotal, or case study framework. While their scope, purpose, and methodology vary, the common element binding them together is their focus on the performance implications of one or more aspects of water allocation and management institutions. Let us now briefly review these and other studies dealing with different aspects of the relationship between water institutions and sector performance.

To begin with, the description-based analysis of V. Ostrom and E. Ostrom (1972) of the Southern California water economy is an interesting original analysis of the way water institutions (water law and water-related organizations) evolve with the changing water resource realities of the region. Besides focusing on the way the macro water institutions are crafted within the physical and economic environment of the region, the authors also explore the role of private incentives for collective action. The idea of coevolution is taken further both on the theoretical and empirical fronts. For instance, Rausser and Zusman (1991) provide a theoretical model that considers the political, economic, and physical aspects of the water systems as parts of a coevolutionary process. Although this study does not deal with either institution or its performance directly, it suggests a way of endogenizing the context of institution–performance interaction within the evaluation process itself. Similarly, utilizing the case of the Platte River in the US Midwest, Yang (1997) describes the way water institution, resource system, and competing economic and social interests interact and coevolve through time.

Wade (1982) compares the yield and employment performances of irrigation water control institutions (the water distribution system and procedure) in southern India and in South Korea within an essentially descriptive and nonquantitative framework. South Korea's better performance is explained in terms of a better water supply, small, decentralized, and demand-controlled system, and good management structure. Lo and Tang (1994) utilize, again, a descriptive case study framework to explain the differential performance of institutional arrangements (governance and management structures) in controlling water pollution from different sources (industrial and domestic) by considering the case of Guangzhou Municipality in China. The main result is that, since no one set of institutional arrangements can solve all types of collective problems, only by designing institutions to be compatible with the type of problems they confront can a better institutional performance be ensured. Another interesting study deserving attention here is Oswald (1992), evaluating a tank irrigation system in south India based on an expert system that combines secondary data with primary information developed by experts. Among the studies that have been reviewed so far, this study assumes particular significance in view of its attempt to rely on expert knowledge as an information source.

Although most of the studies reviewed so far are descriptive, analytical, or theoretical in orientation, a few studies attempt a quantitative or numerical analysis of different dimensions of the process of institution–performance interaction within the water sector. Their general approach centers either on game theory or on optimization-based simulation models. Utilizing a simulation of a multilateral bargaining model of a water allocation problem under different property-rights regimes, information conditions, and water supply levels, Saleth, Braden, and Eheart (1991) and Saleth and Braden (1995) identify price and quantity-based exchange rules capable of minimizing inefficiency due to strategic behavior. Both studies focus on the evaluation of alternative rules in terms of their impact on the efficiency properties of the water market from a micro perspective. In contrast, other studies attempt an evaluation of water institutional aspects from a regional perspective. For instance, Dinar and Latey (1991) use the results from a large-scale simulation of the irrigation and drainage issues in the San Joaquin Valley, California to evaluate how water markets can improve water use efficiency and reduce the negative economic and environmental consequences of drainage-induced waterlogging and soil salinity problems.

Practically no study either posits or evaluates the issue of institution–performance interaction within the water sector taken as a whole. However, a few studies attempt to estimate or elaborate the overall benefits possible from institutional changes within the water sector. Literature tackling the issue of institutional change from a larger water sector perspective covers the important works of E. Ostrom (1990), Frederiksen (1992), Le Moigne, et al. (1994), and Picciotto (1995). Apart from this theoretical literature on the rationale for and gains from water institutional change, there are a few studies that try to quantify the magnitude of potential gain from changes either in particular segments of water institutions or in water institutions taken as a whole. Studies that evaluate the potential gains from institutional changes in the context of water markets, interregional transfers, and water quality management include the works of Vaux and Howitt (1984), Dinar and Latey (1991), Howitt (1994), Hearne and Easter (1997), and Zilberman, et al. (1998). Studies that provide some rough numerical estimates of the opportunity cost (the potential social gain) or transaction costs of change in water institutions as a whole include the works of Colby (1990), Gazmuri and Rosegrant (1994), Saleth (1996), Archibald and Renwick (1998), and McCann and Easter (1999).

Gazmuri and Rosegrant (1994) and Saleth (1996) estimate the opportunity cost of sectorwide institutional reforms by calculating first the actual or potential efficiency-induced additional irrigated area and then the cost of creating that area through new water development projects. The estimated opportunity costs vary from $400 million for Chile (Gazmuri and Rosegrant 1994: 24) to $14 billion for India (Saleth 1996: 274). Similar, but simulation-based, estimates for the San Joaquin Valley place the opportunity costs at $223 million (Archibald and Renwick 1998). These opportunity cost estimates are related to institutional transaction costs because they provide an upper bound for the latter. As distinct from the approach of trying to estimate transaction costs indirectly via the opportunity costs of institutional change, others attempt to directly estimate the transaction costs of institutional reform (Colby 1990; McCann and Easter 1999).

The present approaches toward estimating both the opportunity and transaction costs of institutional change in the water sector remain admittedly partial, for they do not adequately account either for the segment-specific institutional needs of different water subsectors or for the component-specific cost variations across various components of water institutions (water law, water policy, and water organization). Variations in opportunity and transaction costs across water subsectors and water institution components make institutional changes easier in some contexts but more difficult in others.[19] Since institutional change is a continuum, the easier reforms initiated in the early stages brighten the prospects of further and higher level institutional changes. This means that there is an intricate and functional linkage between the transaction costs of subsequent reforms and the opportunity costs of earlier reforms. Although these linkages appear to be highly abstract and theoretical, their practical influence within the political economy of the reform process should neither be ignored nor underestimated. In the same way, the transaction cost implications of changes both within and outside the water sector have not been understood well, especially their implications for institutional design and implementation principles. However, in view of the critical need for political economy thrust to prompt and sustain the process of institutional change, the opportunity or transaction costs are only necessary but not sufficient for inducing institutional reforms both in general and in water sector contexts.

DARK AND GRAY SPOTS IN CURRENT LITERATURE

Despite a vast and growing literature in the theoretical and empirical dimensions of institutional economics, dark and gray spots still persist in our knowledge. North (1986, 1995) identifies some of these weak spots as the 'frontier area for research' in institutional economics, and others are implied in his seminal work (North 1990a). In fact, these dark and gray spots in institutional economics in general and water institutional economics in particular provide the rationale, justification, and motivation for our study. Although we touched on some of these weak spots in the course of our literature review, let us now explicitly identify them and their implications for institutional economics theory and methodology.

Failure to Reckon the Role of Perception

The main function of institutions is to provide information and reduce uncertainty in human interaction, but information alone cannot solve every problem because individuals differ in their interpretation of the same information. In this sense, institutional economics overestimates the importance of the role of information. Differential interpretation of the same information stems from differences in individual perception or, more accurately, in individual mental models. Factors such as religion, culture, ideology, education, experience, bias, and ignorance color individual perceptions. Thus, the perception of information rather than information itself becomes important for institutional performance and change. Recognizing this fact, North (1990a, 1993, 1995) and Eggertsson (1996a), among others, emphasize the 'mental model' as the software that people use for processing information. The mental model approach, which requires an extension of cognitive sciences to institutional economics, is an important frontier of research in institutional economics (North 1995: 25; Eggertsson 1996a: 20). Unfortunately, either due to an aversion to subjective aspects or due to the formidable challenges posed by the issue, the true role of subjective perceptions, including how they are shaped by subjective aspects and objective outcomes, is inadequately understood and treated in current literature.

Underestimation of the Role of Individuals

With the failure to evaluate the influence of subjective and perceptional aspects, the basic role played by individuals in the institutional change process has not been reckoned adequately within the institutional economics literature. Instead, economic, political, and social organizations are considered as the agents of institutional change. Individuals influence institutional change essentially through these organizations. But, as argued in Chapter 2 in the context of Figure 2.1, since the organizations are nothing but a representation of the collective interests of their individual members, they have to consider their constitutents' views, preferences, and interests. While organizations can be the agents of change, they are not the originators of change because the real demand for change originates from individual agents both as a direct, objective response to economic outcomes and as an implicit, subjective response to endogenous preferences. A careful reading of the literature can also reveal that the focus on organizations was essentially to bypass the analytical and methodological difficulties involved in tackling directly the role that individual actors play in the process of institutional change. As a result, the critical roles that stakeholders and opinionmakers as well as their perceptional convergence and consensus formation play in the process of institutional change could not be systematically treated in existing literature.

Absence of an Ex-Ante Approach

Since institutions and their performance are evaluated mostly in ex-post rather than in ex-ante contexts, the results often lack relevance for designing long-term and anticipatory strategies for institutional reform, both at micro and macro levels. Although ex-post and historical analysis of institutional change provides considerable insights into the factors affecting the process of change, it is of little help in evaluating the future course of institutional change and its performance implications. As a long-term process with a long gestation period before impact, institutional change has to be evaluated from an ex-ante angle. In such evaluation, subjective factors such as ideology, bias, and ignorance are as important as objective factors such as expected economic gains, changing resource realities, and political and technological developments. We believe that an ex-ante approach can be operationalized through the perception-based subjective approach where economic and noneconomic factors can be treated within the same analytical framework. In other words, perception can be used as a mechanism to capture the effects of both subjective and objective factors. In this sense, we can analytically address another frontier area identified by North (1995: 25): how institutions and the mental construct of the players interact during the process of institutional change.

Inadequate Treatment of Institutional Linkages

The interest in the structure of institutions and linkages among them is as old as institutional economics itself. In fact, Veblen's analytical scheme (1914) is one of 'cumulative causation' in which each stage in institutional evolution is shaped by what happened before. North (1990a) elaborates the same fact more formally in terms of his concepts of path dependency and increasing returns on institutional change. Although these concepts are considered to capture the main implications of temporal linkages among institutions, they also capture the effects of structural linkages where institutions of different kinds hang together, more or less, as coherent systems characterized by interactions of various institutions (Johnson and Nielsen 1998: xiii). Unfortunately, since the present literature is content with a mere recognition and analytical treatment of these institutional linkages, the real significance of the innate structural features of institutions for institutional design and performance has not received much analytical or empirical attention. As a result, the issue of how initial institutions constrain upstream and downstream institutional choices remains a frontier area for research in institutional economics (North 1995: 25).

Need for Institutional Decomposition

Despite a fast growth in the institutional economics literature, we still hear complaints about the absence of a comprehensive taxonomy of institutions and institutional change and the imprecise and tentative nature of the description and comparison between institutional settings (Johnson and Nielsen 1998: xiii). Institutional decomposition attempts can contribute toward such a comprehensive taxonomic exercise, but they are more relevant for enhancing our understanding of the structural composition and inner dynamics of institutions. When a well-delineated institutional structure is analytically decomposed, various layers of institutional linkages can be traced, mapped, and evaluated for their institutional and performance implications. This sort of analysis is valuable for developing reform programs based on institutional design and implementation principles such as institutional priority setting, sequencing, and packaging and reform timing, scale and speed. However, the strategic role that institutional decomposition can play in providing an analytical framework for institutional analysis has not received the appropriate attention in either the analytical or the empirical literature on institutional economics. Although there are noteworthy exceptions in this regard,[20] further research could advance our understanding of the analytical and policy value of institutional decomposition exercises.

Research-Based Knowledge for Institutional Change

The supply side of institutional change is one of the most ignored dimensions in institutional economics. Supply-side factors include the existing stock of knowledge, the costs of institutional design, incentives for political entrepreneurs to innovate, and the expected benefits for elite decisionmakers (Feeny 1993). The supply of institutional innovation is also strongly influenced by the cost of achieving social consensus, which, in turn, depends on power structure, cultural tradition, ideologies, resource endowment, and knowledge about institutions themselves (Ruttan 1999: 9). Research-based knowledge can contribute to institutional change in terms of learning externalities and consensus formation. It can both enhance the institutional options available to society and improve the effectiveness of institutions.[21] In this respect, the cross-country flow of information on institutional best practice has a powerful role. Since institutional performance can be improved by the way institutional options are designed, structured, timed, sequenced, and packaged (Haggard and Webb 1994a; Saleth and Dinar 1999b), research-based knowledge on institutional design principles assumes additional strategic significance. To better exploit these strategic aspects, we need a more detailed knowledge of the internal aspects of institutional structure than what is available now.

NOTES

1. Despite their fundamental differences, these approaches share one feature: they all attempt to overcome the major limitations of the neoclassical approach, especially its inability to explicity incorporate the institutional aspects within its analytical framework.
2. This is despite the significant amendments that new institutional economics has made in some of the basic premises of neoclassical economics, especially in terms of the 'bounded rationality' postulate and the explicit recognition of noneconomic factors. Still, the new institutional economics is seen as a generalization of neoclassical economics in many respects. For instance, the neoclassical view of firms as production units has evolved to see them as governance structures, and the emphasis on technology and production costs has shifted to economic contracting and transaction costs (Williamson 1994: 1).
3. For a critical review of the old institutional economics and its linkages with the new institutional economics, see Groenewegen, Kerstholt, and Nagelkerke (1995).
4. This fact underlies the assertion of transaction cost economics that each generic mode of governance is supported by a distinctive form of contract law (Williamson 1994: 16).
5. For a set of papers discussing such reservations about the conventional transaction cost approach, see Groenewegen (1996).

6. Extraneous factors include not only the role of war, revolution, natural calamities, and bilateral and multilateral agreements (contracts) but also the changes in the physical and social attributes of the economy within which the institutional environment evolves and governance structures operate.
7. See Dahlman (1979) for various definitions of transaction costs.
8. In the case of an institutional transaction, the costs are influenced by institutional attributes such as their structure, linkages, and embedded characters as well as the size of the political market as characterized by the size and power of groups demanding institutional change.
9. The importance of ideology also increases with a declining cost of conviction (ideas, dogmas, and prejudice). See North (1990a: 40; 1997: 5) for the elaboration of this point and Nelson and Silberberg (1987) for empirical evidence.
10. Moving down these three levels, the relevance of the neoclassical approach declines, but the need for new methods and transdisciplinary approaches increases. Even at the first analytical level, the neoclassical approach has to be extended to cover transaction cost and property-rights approaches. Otherwise, neither the variety of institutional arrangements nor their economic consequences can be understood and evaluated properly (Eggertsson 1996a: 10).
11. These elements often transcend the boundaries of economics to enter into the domain of politics, sociology, anthropology, law, and history because the institutional framework consists of both formal and informal rules including the mechanisms for their monitoring and enforcement. For a survey of these issues, see Eggertsson (1990: Chs 8–10).
12. Although North's studies fall properly into the first analytical level dealing with the linkages between institutions and economic performance, they also have implications for the second-level analysis.
13. According to Eggertsson (1990: 15), the transaction costs 'are in one way or another associated with the cost of acquiring information about exchange.' Thus, the transaction costs are identical with the information costs in all contexts where an exchange is involved.
14. This is not, however, meant to undermine the importance of these and other similar studies but to illustrate how the subject of inquiry, evaluation context, data problems, and evaluation techniques are interrelated. This is particularly true of institution–performance interaction because of the innate difficulty in quantifying an essentially qualitative and subjective phenomenon.
15. The ICRG has published its ratings since 1982 with monthly updates; the BERI has published its scores since 1972 with quarterly updates.
16. For instance, the 1997 Global Competitiveness Report of the World Economic Forum compiled and processed the responses from 3,000 firms in 59 countries.
17. The rating scheme involves subjective considerations in the sense of 'learned judgment.' A few instances of the rated variables are the level of government, stakeholder, and public support; economic, policy, and social contexts; and environmental stability.
18. Williamson (1999: 316) uses the absence of such superior and feasible alternatives as the basis for his 'remediableness criterion.' To him, the mere survival of some governance modes within a comparative institutional competition can be taken as a 'rough-and-ready test' for the remediableness criterion in practice. However, the survival of certain extant modes, for example, the QWERTY typewriter keyboard (David 1985), is also due to the path-dependency problem reflected in the exorbitant cost of switching to more efficient alternative ways of organizing the keyboard. In the presence of these costs, therefore, comparing the existing institutions with their new alternatives is not reasonable (Williamson 1999: 316).
19. For example, it is easier to formulate and declare a water policy than to design and promulgate a water law. Similarly, it is much easier to promulgate both water policy and water law than to create new or to reform existing administrative structures needed to effectively translate and apply the legal provisions at the field level.
20. For instance, E. Ostrom, Gardner, and Walker (1994) and E. Ostrom (1999) attempt a rule-based decomposition of micro-level institutions by identifying their nested structure or configural relationships. Saleth and Dinar (1999b), on the other hand, rely on a

component-based decomposition of macro-level water institutions for an analytical and quantitative evaluation of institutional interlinkages and their performance implications.

21. North (1990a: 137) underlines the option-enhancing role of research by stating that 'the existence of relatively productive institutions somewhere in the world and low-cost information about the resultant performance characteristics of those institutions can provide a powerful incentive for change in poorly performing economies.'

4. Evaluating institutional linkages: toward an alternative methodology

The identification of the theoretical and methodological gaps present in current institutional research, though very important, is much less challenging than the task of addressing these gaps, especially within an empirical context. Difficult though it is, however, the task is not insurmountable. Our ability to face the challenge lies in developing an alternative methodology for systematic evaluation of institutional linkages and their strategic implications through the subjective and ex-ante perception of stakeholders and decisionmakers. In this chapter, we develop such an alternative methodology using a few theoretical and analytical components as its basic building blocks. These components include the contextual delineation, ecosystem perspective and ex-ante approach, subjective theory of institutional change, pluralistic approach and methodological complementarity, and institutional decomposition and analysis (IDA) framework. Although the rationale and basis of the subjective approach and IDA framework form part of the methodological description in this chapter, their analytical representation and empirical translation will receive a more focused treatment in the next two chapters.

Before describing the components of the methodological framework, two key aspects should be recognized so as to know how our methodology departs from others in the literature. First, it allows an explicit and multipronged evaluation of the role that factors, both exogenous and endogenous to institutional structure, play in the process of institutional performance and change. In the application of our methodology, the exogenous factors are evaluated both heuristically, using observed cross-country evidence within an institutional transaction cost framework, and quantitatively, using secondary data within a cross-country regression context. Endogenous institutional features or institutional linkages are evaluated both analytically, using an institutional decomposition procedure, and quantitatively, using subjective and ex-ante information from a cross-section of stakeholders. Second, our methodology is rooted in a new theory that views perceptional changes – affected by both subjective and objective factors – as the core of institutional change. Justifying the subjective approach, this theory focuses on individuals as the source of change and the instrumental approach as the basis of evaluation. With these aspects in mind, let us look at the key components that together constitute the methodological framework for our analytical model of institution–performance interaction and empirical analysis of institutional linkages and their performance implications.

CONTEXT, LEVEL, AND FOCUS OF ANALYSIS

The first step in developing our methodological framework involves the delineation of its analytical contour and application context as these aspects determine both the specifics and details of the required methodology. Although we develop here a subjective theory of institutional change, our interest is not in its empirical evaluation but in its utility in providing a theoretical basis for the subjective approach underlying our methodology. While we do deal with observed institutional changes across countries, the purpose is essentially to see how they relate to political economy aspects and institutional transaction cost considerations. Our main concern here is not in evaluating institutional change per se but in understanding how the design and transaction implications of institutional linkages and exogenous factors can be exploited to foster institutional change and its performance impact. Even while considering institutional change, we focus not on radical and discontinuous changes that are brought from above but on gradual changes that emerge from below as a natural response to changing conditions. As such, the evaluation of the grassroot forces for institutional change such as perceptional convergence and consensus formation among stakeholders and/or decisionmakers remains central in our scheme. However, the deliberate changes brought about by economic and political organizations in their own organizational structures or elsewhere in the institutional system undertaken for their own gains are beyond the scope and purview of our study.[1]

For more specific aspects of the application context, we need to wait until Chapter 6, as these aspects will be understood better as we complete the description of the methodology attempted in this chapter and the analytical framework presented in the next one. Here, it is enough to say that we intend to develop the methodology in the particular context of water institutions. Although water institutions can be evaluated with a focus on their informal and micro segments, the methodology being developed here focuses only on the formal and macro segments of water institutions.[2] The methodological focus on these segments of water institutions is justifiable in view of the particular requirements of our twin objectives of having a cross-country evaluation of institutional changes and quantitative analysis of institution–performance linkages. There are also equally valid theoretical justifications for our focus on formal and macro institutions. Let us now discuss these justifications.

Focus on Formal Institutions

Informal institutions are not purposively designed but evolve through sponta-
neous interaction, whereas formal institutions can be purposively designed
(Commons 1968; North 1990a). The difference between formal and informal
institutions is one of degree, not of kind, and in many cases some informal
institutions gradually become part of their formal counterparts and some
formal institutions take informal forms. Informal institutions are also considered extensions and local-level translations of formal institutions. In reality,
however, formal institutions are also derived from and dependent on informal
institutions, especially for their stability and strength. This is because informal
institutions remain the foundation on which the formal institutions operate.
Thus, any effort to design efficient formal institutions has to consider the way
new formal institutions interact with prevailing informal institutions
(Eggertsson 1996a: 22). Therefore, the formal–informal categorization of
institutions is based more on analytical grounds than on any functional
reasons.

Although the formal and informal institutions are closely related and
linked, analytical considerations warrant their differential treatment because
of the fundamental differences in their sources and rates of change (North
1990b: 386) as well as their amenability for inclusion in formal analysis. For
instance, changes in formal institutions can be evaluated within either a
simple or an extended transaction cost framework. But, changes in informal
institutions cannot be explained purely from an economic perspective
(Eggertsson 1996a: 6–7). Formal institutions can be changed through deliberate reform programs, but their informal counterparts cannot be changed.
Similarly, unlike the formal institutions created and maintained usually by the
state or through a political process, informal institutions such as norms,
customs, and conventions evolve essentially through a sociocultural process.
Informal institutions, unlike their formal counterparts, involve self-enforcing
arrangements, especially those operating close to the point where actual decisions are made. As a result, they function with low or no social costs.
However, since informal institutions change very slowly (North 1990a: 45),
they can be taken for granted in studies dealing with marginal changes in
formal institutions (Eggertsson 1996a: 13). This is particularly true when the
main focus is on the macro aspects of the structure and change in formal institutions, as is the case with our study.

Focus on Macro Institutions

As stated already, the focus on macro institutions is a direct outcome of our
main objective: the evaluation of institutional linkages and their performance

implications. Institutions are often examined from a macro perspective to identify their patterns and regularities as well as to find the extent of imitation, inertia, lock-in, and 'cumulative causation' (Hodgson 1993: Ch. 9; 1998: 171). While micro institutional analysis considers stylized institutions as exogenous factors at a highly abstract level, macro institutional analysis tackles institutions at a high level of aggregation while focusing on the production of ad hoc descriptions and taxonomies. Understandably, these descriptions and taxonomies are easier at the macro level in view of the relative stability and durability of macro institutions. As a result, macro institutions are more amenable to institutional decomposition, which is indispensable for developing the analytical framework needed to map, characterize, and evaluate various layers of institutional and performance linkages.

The macro–micro dichotomy also has a bearing on the choice of approach and, hence, on the ethical basis of institutional analysis. For instance, Williamson (1994) considers that the normative approach works well at the macro level of institutional environment, but that the positive approach works better at the micro level of institutional arrangements or governance structures. While this can be true, the association between the level of institutional analysis and the relative relevance of these approaches can be understood better when we recognize the relative and contextual nature of both the macro–micro distinction and the institutional environment–institutional arrangement categorization.[3] Since our interest is mainly in the macro features of institutional arrangements in appropriately defined regional contexts, our approach is essentially positive in nature. However, taking a positive approach does not mean that the evaluation has to be completely free of normative elements. In many real world situations, even when evaluating an aspect for what it is, there is always some consideration of what it ought to be or is expected to be. This fact is particularly relevant for institutions, especially when there is no objective basis for their evaluation either due to information problems or due to the slow or delayed process of their impact. This is an important caveat to the positive approach implied by the predominant macro-analytical orientation of our study.

ECOSYSTEM PERSPECTIVE AND EX-ANTE APPROACH

Two key aspects underpin the analytical and theoretical basis of our methodological framework: the ecosystem perspective and the ex-ante approach. The ecosystem perspective allows us to view the institutional structure as an ecosystem that evolves within an environment defined by social, cultural, political, economic, and resource conditions to produce performance outcomes. The ex-ante approach enables us to integrate anticipatory and futuristic aspects into the process of subjective evaluation of objective factors. In view of their analytical and methodological significance, the logic and role of these two aspects require a close examination.

Institutional Ecology Principle

We are now in a position to formally consider what implications the institutional features discussed in Chapter 2 have for our methodological framework. As we can see, the features that characterize institutions – interlinkages, malleability or adoptive flexibility, and hierarchical and embedded nature – are similar in principle to those that characterize an ecosystem. This commonality allows us to propose what we call the *institutional ecology principle*. By extending the concept of 'ecosystem' to institutional systems, this principle enables us to present most of the institutional features as a single idea. It considers institutional structures at various levels as an interconnected ecosystem that evolves and coevolves with the institutional environment as characterized by cultural, socioeconomic, political, environmental, and resource-related factors.[4]

The institutional ecology principle and its underlying ecosystem perspective may seem trivial and superficial, but its roles in our scheme are crucial. From a pedagogical perspective, this principle enables us to conceptualize clearly the idea of interlinkages among institutions and the interaction between institutions and their environment. Such a conceptual clarity can dispel the confusion over institutions prevalent at popular and political levels. From a theoretical perspective, the institutional ecology principle can also resolve the conflict between the evolutionary and equilibrium approaches. Just like a natural ecosystem, even though institutions evince constant changes, they can be in periodic but brief equilibrium specifically because their changes are so slow and marginal over a long time span. Thus, as part of the same process, evolution and equilibrium do not exclude each other.[5]

From an analytical perspective, the institutional ecology principle also provides the conceptual basis for institutional decomposition and linkage-mapping exercises. This fact enables us to evaluate both forward and backward linkages and synergetic and discordant effects among institutional aspects as well as the nested and embedded nature of institutions within the physical, social, economic, and political systems. The institutional ecology principle also enables us to treat both institutional segments – that is, institutional environment and institutional structure – together as a system and separate this system from its physical, socioeconomic, and political settings. This separation allows a different perspective from the one that is widely held in the institutional economics literature (Figure 2.1).

Ex-Ante Approach

As seen in the previous chapter, most studies attempt institutional evaluation in ex-post rather than in ex-ante contexts. Ex-post and historical analysis can provide valuable insights on the likely course of institutional change and the factors influencing that course. But such an analysis can capture neither the influence of evolving conditions and conceivable future events nor the effects of institutional changes with a long gestation period. As a consequence, the results often lack relevance for designing adaptive, anticipatory, and long-term strategies for institutional reform both at the micro and macro levels. This is a serious limitation, as it can distort both theory and policy. It is often considered an outcome of the information gap because the observed and secondary information, representing past situations, cannot incorporate the present and future situations. But, valuable information about the present and future situations is both available and used regularly by society for evaluating many aspects, including institutions and their performance. Information on present and future situations is embodied in the minds of individuals. That information is being constantly processed and updated through the individuals' subjective evaluation of objective factors evolving around them.

The information obtained from an individual may contain bias, but the same information obtained from the perceptional convergence of a cross-section of individuals having stakes and influence can provide a more balanced picture of the situation. Since this is valuable and legitimate information, the main issue here is how to tap and treat it within a formal process of institutional evaluation. Unfortunately, no methodology in the institutional economics literature enables us to both tap the embodied knowledge and use this information for institutional evaluation, even though such information is often used in other contexts such as contingent valuation, the delphi procedure, expert system, and participatory appraisal. What we have here is a gap in methodology rather than in information. In our effort to address this methodology gap, the ex-ante approach is used as an important tool. Specifically, this approach is used as a mechanism for endogenizing an anticipatory dimension to the subjective process of evaluation by individuals so that the factors that are highly relevant to institutional change and performance, such as learned judgments, aspirations, and expectations of stakeholders, can be formally incorporated and evaluated. In this way, the ex-ante approach forms an important component of our methodological and empirical framework.

SUBJECTIVE THEORY OF INSTITUTIONAL CHANGE

To provide a theoretical foundation for our methodological framework, we develop an alternative theory of institutional change that explicitly recognizes individuals as the source of change by tracing the linkages between their subjective perceptions and institutional change. Such an alternative theory of institutional change, where the main motive force is the changes in the subjective perception of individuals, is not radical, as it is a refinement and restatement of ideas present in the literature. In fact, the critical role that subjective factors play in the process of institutional change is underlined by institutional economists of all schools and traditions (Veblen 1919; Commons 1934; Bhaskar 1979; Douglas 1986; North 1990a, 1997; Hodgson 1998). But, no systematic theory explains the roles of these subjective factors in the process of institutional change, and no approach exists for their analytical incorporation within an evaluation framework amenable to empirical analysis. For a better articulation of our alternative theory of institutional change, the meaning and role of subjective perception as found in the literature must be understood.

Subjective Perception and Institutional Change

The subjective perception idea is closely linked to the subjective nature of institutions. However, our emphasis here is more on the mechanisms with which it affects the process of institutional evaluation and change. As noted already, North (1990a: 17) represents subjective perception in terms of his ideas of 'mental construct' and 'subjective model.' Understandably, these ideas are closely related to the notion of 'prevailing habits of thought' (Veblen 1919: 239) as well as the idea of 'habitual assumptions' (Commons 1934: 69). Notably, Commons (1934: 654) links ideology, habitual assumptions, and knowledge within a single process as he views ideological evolution as a process of modifications in 'habitual assumptions' brought about by experimental problem solving by individuals, organizations, courts, and governments. However, it is North (1990a) who explicitly recognizes the important role that the 'mental construct' or the 'subjective model' of individuals plays in the process of institutional change. According to him, subjective perception has a powerful role in institutional choice and change, especially when formal institutions make it possible for individuals to express preferences at little cost to themselves.[6]

Bromley (1989b) assigns an important role to 'collective attitude' as a source of institutional change. Attitudinal change acquires power to induce institutional changes because most people, including those at the interface between public perception and political decisionmaking, concur with the need for change. In other words, most individuals' 'mental constructs' of the institutional reality converge on the issue of initiating change. In this sense, there is a clear conceptual link between the role of 'collective attitude' and the role of the 'subjective model' or the 'mental construct' of individuals underlined by North (1990a). From another perspective, perceptional convergence also implies the articulation or solidification of the demand for institutional change. More relevant from the viewpoint of institutional change is the fact that the presence of such perceptional convergence and the emergence of demand for institutional change provide political entrepreneurs with incentives to lobby or take initiatives for institutional change.[7]

Conditions for Perceptional Convergence

The basic issue is whether perceptional convergence can occur in the face of factors creating divergence, such as ideology, bias, and information gaps, including sheer ignorance. The rationality postulate assumes that the actors possess cognitive capacity to see the true models of the world about which they make choices or, at least, they receive enough information to correct their initial models. Unfortunately, when the information being received is incomplete or subject to multiple interpretations, the subjective models of individuals are bound to diverge (North 1990a: 17). But, other factors tend to minimize perceptional divergence. These factors include both the cultural influences and persuasive powers of the state or other moral authorities that reduce transaction costs and motivate people for collective action (Bates 1994). The prospects for perceptional convergence are also enhanced by the powerful effects of information flow and mutual learning. Although the subjective perceptions of actors are culturally derived, they undergo continuous modifications through experience, interaction, information, and learning. The lower the cost of information and learning, the faster will be the alterations in subjective perceptions (North 1990a: 138).[8]

Since the subjective perception of the actors is also not independent of objective influences, perceptional convergence is also induced by objective factors such as price, technology, and resource endowments. In fact, the perceptional influences of subjective and objective factors are often too mingled to enable a clear distinction and separation. Therefore, it is not clear how conventional transaction cost theory can account for the direct effects of subjective factors or the extent to which they capture the effects of objective factors. Subjective factors are also affected by institutions themselves through what can be called the 'legitimacy effect' or the tendency to 'go with the majority.' As institutions reinforce their own moral legitimacy, whatever endures is often seen – rightly or wrongly – as morally just (Hodgson 1998: 179). Thus, the institutions operating in most countries or contexts gain legitimacy as do those repeatedly pronounced as 'the best type' in various national and international forums. These considerations, including the role of international and interpersonal interaction and knowledge flow, play an important role in creating convergence in individuals' subjective perceptions. Because of such perceptional convergence, we often observe a certain amount of regularity and pattern in the evaluation of institutions by individuals with diverse backgrounds.

The general tendency for convergence in institutional choice and valuation does not, however, negate the potential for divergence. Such divergence emerges from practical experience with poorly performing 'best' institutions (due to contextual and implementation snags) and from the ideological moorings of individuals. Knight and Sened (1995b) allude to the slippage in socially shared knowledge about the rules as one of the explanations for the violation of even self-enforcing institutions. Such slippage comes from 'lack of knowledge of these rules on the parts of members of the community, or from the differences in [the interpretations of] the substantive content of the rules' (Knight and Sened 1995b: 11).[9]

Finally, it is important to understand the nature of the relationship between convergence in social expectations and convergence in the choice of institutions and their configurations. While Knight and Sened (1995b: 12–13) recognize the major role that convergence in social expectations plays in the process of institutional change, they consider that the former does not guarantee institutional convergence because of path-dependency constraints. We contest this view, as it considers social expectations to be independent of prevailing institutions. When subjective perception or social expectation is influenced by institutions, it will only be over the alternative paths permitted by the current state of institutions. As a result, perceptional convergence can indeed lead to convergence in institutional choice as well.

Process of Institutional Change: A Stage-Based Perspective

The central role that the subjective perception of individuals plays in the process of institutional change can be understood better by viewing the change process within a stage-based perspective. In this perspective, the following four stages are crucial: mind change – the changing perception of stakeholders and decisionmakers both at the micro and macro levels; political articulation and programmatic translation of perceptional change; practical implementation of a reform program – beginning with symbolic and procedural changes and continuing with real and substantive changes; and ultimate impact of institutional changes. These stages progress, not as a linear process, but as a circular process, subject to constant subjective and objective feedbacks and adaptations. As a result, the circular process is influenced both by subjective factors (e.g., ideology, bias, and ignorance) and by objective factors (e.g., relative prices, technological change, and other economic and physical factors). The process is also affected by the significant intervening roles of other factors operating both at the macro and individual levels. These factors include political lobbying and bargaining, information flow and learning

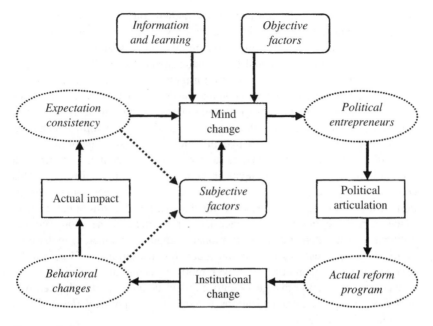

Source: Authors.

Figure 4.1   Subjective theory of institutional change.

externalities, and behavioral changes and performance expectations. More importantly, the circular process of change is not free from the influence of existing institutions, due partly to their technical features such as path dependency and partly to their effects on the worldview of main actors. Our conceptualization of the stage-based process of institutional change can be depicted in a stylized form (Figure 4.1).

Despite a fair amount of simplification, Figure 4.1 highlights the central role that changes in perception play in initiating institutional change as well as in evaluating its behavioral and performance impacts. Of the four stages in the process of institutional change, the first stage, involving mind change, assumes a critical significance. The mind change of individuals signifies a change in their mental construct of the world, and it gathers power when a critical mass of perceptional convergence builds up about the need for, and the extent and direction of institutional change. In addition to the subjective and objective factors noted above, mind change is also affected by the behavioral and performance impacts of existing institutions and by the nature and direction of the ongoing process of institutional change itself. In this respect, the total benefit and its individual shares expected from institutional changes can also play a powerful role in influencing the mental construct of desirable insti-tutions. As long as the expectation of a majority of individuals is not fulfilled by the ongoing institutional changes, the circular process shown in Figure 4.1 will continue to create new and additional demand for institutional reform. While underlining the positive role of information and learning on the process of mind change, we also need to recognize the deleterious effects of the purpo-sive and biased campaign by powerful interest groups to alter or distort general perception and, hence, the demand for institutional reform and change.

As a consequence of mind change, the thinking and language of those who can influence institutional change undergo gradual change, creating an economic and political environment propitious for institutional reform. This characterizes the interface between the first and second stages, where percep-tion strongly converges on the need for and nature of institutional change. Since such perceptional convergence also crystallizes in the economic and political spheres, demand for institutional change is articulated, motivating political entrepreneurs to initiate and lobby for institutional reforms on the desired lines. As economic incentives motivate economic organizations to convert perceptional convergence into political demand, political incentives also motivate political organizations to convert this political demand into concrete policy actions.

Although economic and political organizations can agree on the need for change, they usually disagree on the details of change because they cater to different social and economic groups, each with divergent perspectives on and expectations about institutional change. Therefore, the reform program that emerges at the end of the political process is an outcome of the relative bargaining strengths of political parties and other interest groups. Their rela-tive strengths change not only with changing resource realities and the national and international economic environment but also during the process of adjustment within the reform program itself. The reform package is subject not only to the political bargaining process but also to the technical constraints that delimit feasible paths of change (path dependency). Thus, the final reform program reflects political compromises and technical adjustments.[10]

This process leaves considerable scope for slippage between reform imple-mentation and actual change in existing institutions, especially in a democra-tic system. In many contexts, most of the initial changes following a reform program are ceremonial and procedural in nature (e.g., policy declaration, legislation enactment, and renaming or merging of organizations). These cere-monial changes and the false impression that the substantive changes will eventually follow may even keep the demand for reform dormant for some time. This is likely to happen when the institutional changes contemplated by the original reform program run counter to the interests of the economically and politically powerful groups. Therefore, perceptional convergence and political consensus for the reform program have to be powerful and enduring to take the reform process to its next stage where substantive changes in institutions will be implemented. In some cases, the procedural changes can also facilitate realignment of political groups and creation of a pro-reform atmosphere. In a strongly pro-reform climate with pressing economic compulsions and increasing political commitment to reform, institutional change gradually moves from the stage of procedural changes to the stage of substantive changes (e.g., legal reform, policy changes, and organizational restructuring). If the predominant thinking is against any reform, a business-as-usual trend continues without any institutional changes – either procedural or substantive.

Instrumental Approach and Adaptive Evaluation

Even when substantive changes take place in institutions, their impact on economic performance has a long gestation period. The direct outcome of institutional change is a process of cumulative behavioral changes, and the ultimate outcome depends on the extent to which these behavioral changes improve actual production and exchange.[11] The material outcome of the process is, therefore, not immediate, and measurable benefits often become manifest only long after the program period. In the interim, the performance impacts of institutional change can be measured in other ways, such as by the extent to which policy decisions in the new setting conform to the policy intent (Tool 1977; Bromley 1985).

The 'instrumental value' approach to institutional performance, though considered as the 'ultimate problem-solving criterion,' is not free from difficulties and problems in practical situations (Livingston 1987: 287). Without knowing the outcome of the implementation process, there is no objective means for evaluating consistency between decisions and goals or for ensuring that consistency leads to the realization of goals.[12] Thus, the application of an instrumental value approach for institutional evaluation necessarily involves subjective judgments (Livingston 1993: 816). With the inevitability of subjective aspects, the instruments or reference points used in instrumental valuation can vary across individuals and could also include noneconomic considerations.

Another major problem in evaluating institutional change through an instrumental approach is the substantial difference between intended outcome and actual outcome due to the limited capabilities of individuals and the complexity of the problem (North 1997: 8). One important way in which individuals overcome these human limitations is through a constant process of adaptation of their subjective evaluation of both the action (institutional change) and outcome (performance impact) with information available at each point in time.[13] In this way, performance can be evaluated to adjust the decisions without having to wait a long time to observe the actual outcome.

Subjective evaluation is inevitable even during the third and fourth stages, where the actual institutional reforms, behavioral changes, and performance impacts occur. Subjective feedback occurs not only at the end of the third stage, in which the institutional changes are initiated, but also during the fourth stage, in which the economic impacts of these changes begin to take shape. While perceived behavioral changes can be used to evaluate the effectiveness of institutional changes, the perceived gap between expected performance and actual performance could be used to evaluate the magnitude of the impact of institutional changes. These subjective evaluations, feeding constantly into the mind change process together with the objective factors and learning experience, become internalized within the circular process of institutional change.

Methodological Implications

The subjective theory, though deceptively simple and descriptive, brings together and synthesizes several theoretical traditions within institutional economics. As described above, although the theory underlines the central role of individuals as agents of change, it recognizes the role of economic and political organizations as well as the political economy process through which the reform program is designed and implemented. While the focus on individuals gives an impression that our theory is rooted in methodological individualism, the recognition of the role of economic and political organizations allows it to account for the influence of broader social and group interests. Besides, the subjective theory uses individuals and their perceptions not as an end in themselves but only as a means for endogenizing the participatory process through which perceptional convergence and consensus formation emerge among key players, including stakeholders and decisionmakers. Moreover, the role of interest groups and political entities is also implicit during the course of perceptional change and during the process of political bargaining from which the final reform program emerges. As outlined above, the subjective theory looks far beyond the role of individuals and their subjective perceptions.

The role of information and learning is incorporated explicitly, while the role of economic and political transaction costs is incorporated implicitly. To the extent that perception change is influenced by the expected benefits and costs (including their individual shares) of existing and alternative institutions, the role of transaction costs – both economic and noneconomic – is implicit in the subjective theory of institutional change. By extension of the same logic, the role played by political transaction costs during and after the second stage of political articulation and reform formulation has also been incorporated into the process of institutional change. Transaction costs – both economic and political – remain a key force both in the cognitive and observed phases of the process of institutional change. Similarly, the role of political economy aspects such as political entrepreneurs, interest group politics, and political bargaining is also explicitly incorporated within the subjective theory. Since we consider that the subjective process of evaluation is based on the instrumental valuation of the players, the theory is free from the normative aspects associated with conventional efficiency analysis.

Subjective perception is important throughout the process of institutional change, but its role in the first stage, involving mind change, is critical. It is in the first stage that the effects of individual-specific subjective aspects, objective conditions, information flow and learning process, and subjective or instrumental feedback of both institutional change processes and performance impact usually converge and are captured.[14] That is precisely why we consider a careful evaluation of the first stage of institutional change to be very instructive for understanding such important issues as the following. How is interaction between institution and performance perceived? What are the causal linkages implied in the perception of such interaction? What are the preferred types of institutional configuration? These issues can provide key insights into the prevailing perceptions, evolving expectations, and emerging consensus on institutional linkages, performance, and change. Attention to the insightful first stage and the pervasive role of subjective perception has been missing from the literature. In this study, these two aspects are, in fact, the centerpiece of the evaluation methodology and its empirical application.

COMPLEMENTARY METHODOLOGIES

Since institutions are entities that emerge, evolve, and operate in the intersection of economic, legal, organizational, political, social, and physical spheres, no single model or theory can suffice for their evaluation. What is needed is a framework for organizing various theories to gain both diagnostic and prescriptive insights into the subject of inquiry (E. Ostrom, Gardner, and Walker 1994: 23–5).[15] As these theories can be from various disciplines, the framework has to be multidisciplinary in orientation. Although various theories and their underlying approaches are relevant for institutional analysis, they need not be equally relevant to evaluate institutions varying by type (formal and informal or market or nonmarket), level (macro and micro), or context (exogenous and endogenous). With these facts in mind, let us now specify the theories, approaches, and methodologies used in our study to evaluate institutions at different levels and contexts.

Empirical works attempt to evaluate institutions and their performance using one or all of the following three methods: case studies, comparative methods examining several cases together, and econometric analysis of cross-country data (Alesina 1994: 55; Alston 1996: 29–30). Here, we use all three methods in a complementary way. Case studies, especially the analysis of successful and unsuccessful episodes of policy reform, are a standard approach in the study of political economy of policy reform (Nelson 1990; Bates and Krueger 1993; Haggard and Webb 1994a; Dinar 2000). Success stories and anecdotal cases are especially useful for illustrating the general principles operating at the interface between institutional change and performance impact.[16]

In the context of our study, the cross-country comparative analysis of recent institutional changes is used to evaluate water institutional changes heuristically within the framework of institutional transaction costs. However, we also rely on econometric analysis of cross-country data to evaluate both the role of exogenous factors and the performance implications of institutional linkages. In other words, the observed or secondary data on social, political, and economic variables and perceptional data on performance are used to evaluate the relative role of exogenous factors in explaining institutional and water sector performance. But, perception-based subjective and ex-ante information from a cross-section of stakeholders is used to evaluate the performance implications of endogenous or structural features of institutions.

The pluralistic methodologies needed for a multilevel evaluation of institution–performance interaction require diverse theories to underpin our analysis and explanation. The subjective theory outlined above can help us meet this theoretical requirement as it incorporates several theoretical traditions within a simple but unified framework. But, its significance lies mainly in justifying our reliance on subjective perception both as a methodological basis and as an information source for an empirical evaluation of the process of institution–performance interaction. Therefore, we need other theories to support other aspects of our methodological framework. In this respect, we require essentially the theories of political economy of reforms (Nelson 1990; Bates and Krueger 1993; Haggard and Webb 1994a; Dinar 2000) and mainstream institutional economics, especially institutional transaction cost economics (Williamson 1975, 1985; Bromley 1989a; North 1990a). These theories, related to different phases of our subjective theory, can supplement our theoretical approach.

The institutional transaction cost approach and political economy perspective are used for explaining the nature, extent, and direction of the ongoing process of institutional changes in the global water sector. The institutional transaction cost approach is applied not in terms of calculating the transaction costs and social benefits of institutional change, but in terms of a simple heuristic calculus. The occurrence of institutional change in one or more countries is taken as observational evidence that its transaction costs exceed its corresponding opportunity costs (or potential benefits). The same is also considered as evidence for the fact that the change is also consistent with the political economy of interest group bargaining. However, more explicit political economy considerations – ranging from macroeconomic crisis and natural calamities to international influence from donor agencies and international agreements – are also incorporated into the evaluation process and analysis. While the institutional economics approach remains pervasive throughout our analysis, it is especially so in the evaluation of institutional linkages and their implications for the institutional design and implementation principles such as institutional sequencing, priority setting, and packaging as well as reform scale and timing.

The institutional ecology principle clarifies the perspective with which we approach structural and functional relationships among institutional components. If we can identify a modeling framework that can enable us to characterize and decompose institutional structure and its environment, these relationships can indeed be traced, mapped, and translated into forms that can be both analytically visualized and empirically evaluated. For this purpose, the 'pattern model,' used to describe the analytical linkages among various elements evident within a general pattern together with their logical connections (Fusfeld 1980: 33), is highly relevant.

Given the multicausal nature of the relationships of such a pattern model, it is always 'open,' as it cannot include all relevant variables and relationships (Wilber and Harrison 1978; Caldwell 1982). Ruttan (1999) has, in fact, used such a pattern model to show multicausal relationships among resource endowments, cultural endowments, technology, and institutions. In a broader sense, the framework conception of E. Ostrom (1990) resembles the pattern model insofar as both encompass a set of logically linked relationships based on various theories and warrant a multidisciplinary approach. The 'pattern model' or the 'framework' conception can be specialized to characterize water institutions, decompose their constituent components and aspects, and map and evaluate various layers of linkages evident in the process of institution–performance interaction within the water sector.

INSTITUTIONAL DECOMPOSITION: RATIONALE AND BASIS

The final component of our methodology involves the identification of a framework for institutional decomposition that is most suitable for the particular analytical and methodological requirements of our study. As is clear from the institutional ecology principle, institutions operate as a system characterized by intricate and multiple layers of relationships. As a result, it is difficult to isolate and evaluate the effects of individual institutional components from those of other interlinked and nested components. One analytical approach to solve this difficulty is to decompose an institution first into its major components and subcomponents, and then trace the linkages and map the relationships among them. This is the rationale for developing the institutional decomposition and analysis framework as an operational basis for our evaluation methodology. Since space here is insufficient to detail how the IDA framework is used for decomposing water institutions and how the decomposition exercise is used for characterizing their functional linkages, these operational aspects are reserved for an exclusive treatment in the ensuing chapter. Here, our attention is confined in providing the rationale and justification for institutional decomposition in general and for our IDA framework in particular, essentially through a review of previous attempts in existing literature.

Decomposition Attempts in Literature

Institutional decomposition is nothing new; it has received considerable attention in both the analytical and empirical literature on institutional economics. Institutions are decomposed in varying levels of abstraction and detail, depending upon the way the institutions are conceived and the level at which they are evaluated. As a result, decomposition attempts in the literature are either too broad and macro in nature or too narrow and micro in focus. Since these decomposition attempts are made for reasons ranging from pedagogic exposition to practical application, a brief review will help us in laying a solid analytical and theoretical foundation for the IDA framework that we attempt to develop for the specific purpose of our study.

Institutions are usually treated as a single entity but, in reality, they are made up of analytically and functionally distinguishable components or elements. That is why North (1997) considers the idea of the 'composition of institutions' very important and many studies have indeed attempted to decompose institutions in varying contexts and details. For instance, Adelman and Head (1983) decompose institutions by placing them in one of three categories: social mores and norms, laws and regulations, and contractual arrangements.[17] Feeny (1993) and Clague (1997b) identify three categories of institutions: constitutional order, institutional arrangements, and cultural endowments. The cultural endowment forms part of social capital (Coleman 1987, 1990). Since constitutional order and cultural endowments change slowly (except in extreme cases of revolution or disasters), the focus of much of the literature on institutional innovation and change is on the institutional arrangements (Clague 1997b: 18). Coriat and Dosi (1998: 6) distinguish three components of institutions: formal organizations (e.g., firms, other social and economic organizations, and state); shared pattern of behavior (e.g., routines, social conventions, and ethical codes), and norms and constraints (e.g., moral prescriptions and formal laws).

There are also more systematic approaches to institutional decomposition. For instance, institutions can be decomposed in broader terms based on the distinction between institutional environment or institutional framework and institutional structure or governance structure (Bromley 1989a; North 1990a; Williamson 1994). Even with such a broad decomposition of institutions into institutional environment and institutional arrangements, Williamson (1975, 1985) provides new insights into the economic and institutional implications of the interaction between the two segments utilizing the transaction cost approach originally articulated by Coase (1937).[18] This illustrates the utility of institutional decomposition for theoretical and practical analysis.

The two segments of the institutional sphere (institutional environment and institutional arrangements) can be further decomposed from various perspectives and in different formats. For instance, the institutional environment can be further decomposed into broad categories such as formal rules (constitution and other laws, contracts, and declared policies), informal rules (shared values, social conventions, and social capital such as norms, trust, and moral codes of conduct), and enforcement mechanisms. Each of these categories can be decomposed into still finer categories depending upon the analytical requirements. For instance, the property-rights system, one of the many important components of the legal system, can be classified into some of the feasible forms or types that can range from open access system to private property-rights system (Hanna, Folke, and Maler 1996: 4–5; Bromley 1989a: 204–6). In a similar vein, institutional arrangements are classified into economic and political organizations, which themselves can be classified, in turn, into alternative modes of governance.

The governance modes include the state, markets, contracts, hierarchies, and hybrids, which form the basis for identifying broad typologies or taxonomic categories of institutional arrangements (Landry 1996; Boyer and Hollingsworth 1997a; Williamson 1999). Besides these modes of governance, broad structural features are also used to categorize and decompose institutions. For instance, Williamson (1985: 73–8) classifies governance structures into market governance, bilateral governance, trilateral governance, and unified governance. The institutional forms including the state, market, and hierarchies, though interrelated, differ in terms of their basic features and performance implications. For instance, markets take different forms, ranging from perfect competition to monopoly, and a similar feature is also shared by other institutional counterparts such as hierarchies, contracts, and networks (Williamson 1975: 151–4). Broader typologies of institutional arrangements are also identified by classifying them in terms of the way they relate the pursuit of individual self-interest with the principle of coordination (Boyer and Hollingsworth 1997b: 51). For instance, Hage and Alter (1997: 100, 116) use the modes of coordination and the number of organizations as two criteria for identifying the typologies evident in interorganizational relationships and for characterizing their symbiotic and competitive linkages.

In view of the structural linkages among institutional forms, the relevant issue in most contexts is not the choice of one or the other form but the choice of their effective configurations.[19] In this respect, the decomposition attempts by Boyer (1987) and Coriat and Dosi (1998) deserve special attention, partly because of their interest in alternative configurations of governance modes and partly because of their focus on institutional configurations on a spatial scale. Boyer (1987: 127) identifies different 'regimes of regulation'[20] that capture the specific characteristics in the 'mechanisms and principles of adjustment associated with the configurations of wage relations, competition, state interventions, and hierarchization of the international economy.' Coriat and Dosi (1998: 10) attempt a similar kind of taxonomic decomposition of 'regimes of accumulation' in terms of distinct sets of institutional arrangements.

The major factor that determines the criteria for institutional decomposition is the conception and features of institutions themselves. Institutions are conceived predominantly as rules (Buchanan and Tullock 1962; Shepsle 1979; E. Ostrom 1990), norms emerging from social conventions (Schotter 1981; Axelrod 1984; Coleman 1990), property rights (e.g., Bromley 1989a), and contracts (Williamson 1990). North (1990a) conceives institutions as comprising of formal rules, informal rules (norms), and economic and political organizations. Although Williamson (1975, 1985) shares a similar conception, he separates the organizations from the rule configurations to show how organizations evolve within these rules. Although he considers the way the organizations change these rules, this aspect receives more intensive treatment from North (1990a) with his decomposition of institutions into institutional environment (rules) and institutional arrangements (organizations).

North (1997: 4) decomposes formal institutions into their major components such as 'political and judicial rules, economic rules, and contracts' and the political rules are, in turn, further decomposed into 'the hierarchy of polity, its basic decision structure and the explicit characteristics of agenda control.' The important point to note here is that the administrative structure dealing with the decision process is included as part of the formal rules. Since the laws and constitution are not self-enforcing, organizational mechanisms are needed for their enforcement. Such mechanisms, if effective, correct some of the defects associated with the legal system.[21] All the institutional components and the organizations can also be reduced to a system of interrelated sets of rules. For instance, E. Ostrom and her coworkers (E. Ostrom 1986, 1990, 1999; E. Ostrom, Gardner, and Walker 1994) characterize institutions in terms of seven sets of rules: position rules, boundary rules, scope rules, authority rules, aggregation rules, information rules, and payoff rules. Although this rules-based conception of the institution is developed in the particular context of local institutions for common pool resources, it can very well be generalized to characterize even macro-level institutions.

Institutions are also viewed purely as a system of property rights. For instance, by taking a very broad view of property rights, Bromley (1989a: 133) classifies rights into *institutional rights*, concerned with 'negotiations and bargains over the structure of choice sets' and *commodity rights*, concerned with 'market transactions from within choice sets.' This is the basis for his distinction between 'institutional transactions' and 'commodity transactions.' From a contractarian perspective, since institutions are generated through a 'nexus of contracts' (Williamson 1990), they can also be decomposed in terms of a set of linked and embedded contracts. For instance, by highlighting the differences between contracts and structures (set of contracts), Landry (1996) shows how formal rules can be added to enhance the rational choice of individuals.[22] White (1990: 109) provides another instance of decomposition when he makes a detailed mapping of various aspects of the policy arena in a generic context. This work is instructive in that it shows how the understanding of a complex situation can be deepened with an unbundling or unpacking procedure.

Institutional Decomposition and Analysis Framework

Now, we must advance the analytical focus to the still more interesting but less studied aspects of tracing and evaluating the performance implications of institutional linkages. From a general perspective, institutional decomposition can proceed either from an abstract schema of institutions or from a typology of institutions (Levi 1990: 405). These strategies are not alternatives but complementary in the sense that the institutions can be decomposed first into components and different typologies can then be identified for each institutional component. Although broader decomposition can be useful, further and finer decomposition is needed to facilitate a deeper understanding of the inner dynamics of the process of institution–performance interaction. For a detailed but manageable analysis, however, the decomposition exercise must be performed in a more specific institutional context (e.g., water institutions, trade institutions, and environmental institutions) and focused on the main components of the institutional environment and institutional structures. This is exactly what we attempt in developing our institutional decomposition and analysis, or IDA, framework.

The rudiments of our IDA framework have emerged from our earlier work (Saleth and Dinar 1999b), but further refinements are largely inspired by the institutional analysis and development (IAD) framework of E. Ostrom and her coworkers (E. Ostrom 1986, 1990, 1999; E. Ostrom, Gardner, and Walker 1994). The analytical basis of the IAD framework is the characterization of institutions in terms of three hierarchically related categories of rules: constitutional choice rules, collective choice rules, and operational rules. This framework is note-worthy for three very important reasons. First, as the rules are separated from their physical, social, and economic environment, the latter aspects form part of the 'institutional environment.' Second, since the focus is on micro-level institutions, the rules cover the elements of both institutional environment (laws and policies) and institutional arrangement (organizations). And, third, although the three categories of rules involve an implicit decomposition of a generic institution, the framework itself is developed mainly to characterize and classify local institutions operating in various settings.

As we will see, our IDA framework for institutional decomposition shares several features with the IAD framework. For instance, our IDA framework also distinguishes water institutions from their physical, social, political, and economic settings. This institutional setting includes general institutions deal-ing with other spheres of the economy, ranging from constitution and macro-economic policies to social and political institutions. Despite the fact that our framework is based on a component and aspect-based decomposition of insti-tutions, insofar as these aspects and components can be interpreted as rules or their configurations, our decomposition exercise is similar in spirit to the rules-based decomposition followed in the IAD framework. In an important sense, the three sets of rules underlying the IAD framework can be approxi-mated by the three main institutional components underlying our IDA frame-work: laws (legal rules), policies (policy guidelines), and organizations (organizational or administrative rules).[23]

Since the decomposition exercise in the two frameworks covers both segments of institutions (institutional environment and institutional arrange-ments depicted in the layer schema of Figure 2.1), the institutional environ-ment in both contexts covers only the general socioeconomic, political, and physical aspects. The close resemblance between the two frameworks cannot, however, undermine some fundamental differences between them, especially at their application or evaluation stage. For instance, the IAD framework has been developed essentially for a comparative evaluation of local institutions with information on their features and performance as observed in various contexts and settings. The researcher does the evaluation in the IAD frame-work based on observed (ex post) information on relevant institutional features.

Admittedly, our IDA framework can also be used for a comparative evalu-ation of micro institutions in different countries or regions based on observed information on their features. But, we have developed this framework essen-tially as a tool for eliciting the subjective and ex-ante evaluation of macro institutions by stakeholders facing different objective realities and subjective attributes. Thus, the institutional evaluation becomes a participatory process involving stakeholders and decisionmakers, and not an exercise performed by the researcher. In a more important departure, however, our IDA framework also allows us to map and evaluate layers of linkages evident in the process of institution–performance interaction, especially through empirically testable models of relationships. These models also include the relationships that capture the effects of exogenous factors on the interaction process. With these as background, let us now move to the specification of our IDA framework as an analytical translation of our methodology.

NOTES

1. Such changes include the structural and spatial evolutions of firms into networks and alliances. It is these changes that Williamson (1975, 1985) evaluates within his transaction cost framework. Although deliberate changes can include constitutional amendments, the creation of bureaucratic organizations, and trade and political agreements, they need eventual public support for their stability.
2. The contextual nature of its development does not mean that the methodology cannot be generalized to other resource contexts or applied to micro contexts. Although informal institutions may not be amenable for treatment within our methodology, its general principles can indeed be applied at the micro level and in the context of other natural resources with suitable adjustments, especially in its analytical representation involving institutional decomposition.
3. For instance, when evaluating sectoral or regional institutions to be part of the institutional environment, national institutions become macro. Similarly, while evaluating transnational institutions (e.g., river basin institutions), national, regional, and sectoral institutions become part of the institutional environment. In view of the changing boundaries between institutional segments, a rigid correspondence cannot be maintained between them and the nature of the approach to be used.
4. Do institutions have life like an ecosystem? The stability, durability, and path-dependency features of institutions do ensure their endurance far beyond the lifetime of their creators. Even institutions no longer used for the purposes for which they were originally designed are often revived later for use in different contexts. For instance, the Torrens property title registration system that dramatically simplified and improved land dealings around the world is based on a 19th-century system used for ship registration in Germany. Similarly, the organizational concept that has revolutionized modern commerce, the limited liability share company, evolved from the British Companies Act of 1862 (Young and McColl 2002).
5. The relative relevance of the two approaches depends on the length of the timeframe being considered for institutional analysis. Thus, when institutions are evaluated from a historical or teleological perspective, the changes that become prominent require an evolutionary approach. But, when the timeframe is short and the evolutionary changes are so slow as to be almost stable, then an equilibrium approach is indicated.
6. North (1990a: 43) cites voting and lifetime tenure for judges as instances of formal institutions that lower the cost of acting on one's own conviction.
7. The issue of whether such initiatives – considered as public goods – will be taken up by political entrepreneurs depends not on any ex-post benefit–cost analysis but on their *ex-ante perception* of a tangible political benefit to themselves or to their political parties (Knight and Sened 1995a: 12).
8. Perceptional convergence, in turn, has critical effects both on the overall cost and the ultimate gains from institutional transactions. The magnitude of this effect, however, depends on the extent to which changes in subjective perceptions lead to actual changes in attitudes and behaviors.
9. From the perspective of our methodology, this means that due to the divergence in the subjective models of individuals, the approach of relying on subjective perception as an

empirical basis for institutional evaluation need not lead to self-fulfilling prophecies or ignore genuine differences in perceptions or expectations of stakeholders.

10. The technical adjustments required to account for path dependency constraints need not occur only at the reform design stage. They can occur even during the stages of mind change and its political articulation as processes at these stages are also influenced by existing institutions. Thus, for instance, when the institutions are characteristic of a democratic system, there cannot be any perceptional convergence or political lobbying for dictatorial institutions.

11. An instance from the water sector can clarify this point. In a water resource *development* project, the measure of outcome is the size of the resource created and its use in meeting irrigation and other water needs. In a program to reform water *institutions*, the outcome is a process of change. The ultimate effect of an institutional reform program depends on the ability of the process to sustain itself and produce the ultimate effects of improving economic performance through better resource allocation, use, and management.

12. For instance, although water rights can be legally obtained for instream and environmental purposes in Colorado, in reality there are few instream water rights because the issuing power for such water rights is with the Colorado Water Conservation Board with a traditional orientation toward irrigation and municipal water supply. Under this condition, the acquisition of rights by private environmental groups rather than by a public agency may serve well the policy intent (Livingston 1987: 293).

13. The process of 'mental accounting' in which people organize the outcomes of transactions and evaluate them relative to a 'reference point' (Kahneman and Tversky 1984: 341) can be identified as the mechanism individuals use to adjust their subjective evaluation. The reference point can be either their instrumental values or the outcomes at status quo position, or both.

14. In the context of policy reforms initiated by donor and lending agencies such as the World Bank, White (1990: 10–12) considers perception and understanding of the reform package by the country officials as the most important prerequisite for its effective implementation. This observation is equally valid in the context of institutional change as it indicates the potential for the subsequent stage of procedural and substantive changes in the institutional structure.

15. The rationale for a framework for accommodating such multiple methodologies or approaches can be explained by distinguishing between models, theories, and frameworks. *Models* capture the elements of a particular situation. *Theories* are concerned with the features of a class of models. *Frameworks* help to organize various theories. For details, see E. Ostrom, Gardner, and Walker (1994: 23–5).

16. This approach can also enable us to show how subjective perceptions of institutional features and their performance impact are consistent with the observational evidence as depicted by these success stories and anecdotal episodes.

17. The first two categories define the 'rules of the game' within which the third category emerges and operates. Confusion of the second category with the third leads to the error of equating property rights with institutions as found in both neoclassical economics and public choice theory.

18. In his analysis of governance structures, Williamson (1975, 1985) considers the institutional environment or institutional framework as given (North 1990b: 392). While Williamson (1993, 1994) recognizes the important interaction between the governance structure and the institutional framework, his main concern remains the explanation of alternative modes of governance structures within a given institutional framework.

19. This is due to the fact that the overall performance can be improved by exploiting the competitive and cooperative relationships that exist between the polycentric governance structures consisting of, for instance, federal, state, and local governments as well as nongovernmental enterprises (V. Ostrom, Tiebout, and Warren 1961: 831).

20. The term 'regulation' here does not mean the legal regulatory apparatus but is used to capture the notion of system theory that different parts of the process, under certain conditions, reciprocally adjust yielding certain orderly dynamics (Coriat and Dosi 1998: 9).

21. But, when these mechanisms are themselves defective, they can also turn an otherwise effective legal system into an ineffective one (Williamson 1994: 18–19). In fact, this is an instance of the performance significance of the linkages among institutional components.

22. These rules pertain to coordination, warranty (or assurance), monitoring, sharing of benefits, and the duration of the contracts. Different combinations of the variants of these rules produce different structures of contract (Landry 1996: 26).
23. Laws are nothing but the outcome of constitutional choice, just as policies are the result of collective choice. Operational rules come into play when laws and policies are applied through the administrative mechanisms involved in implementation, monitoring, and enforcement. Laws and policies are also related insofar as policies are the political translation of laws, and policies of fundamental importance often become formalized as laws.

5. Analytical framework and empirical models

This chapter outlines the institutional decomposition and analysis (IDA) framework and identifies a set of empirically testable models that capture the major facets of the process of institution–performance interaction within the water sector. The specification of the analytical and empirical components of the IDA framework underlying our evaluation methodology can be done in four steps. First, the concepts of *water sector*, *water institution*, and *water sector performance*, as used in this study, are defined to set the broad contours of analysis. Second, *water institution* and *water sector performance* are conceptually decomposed to identify some of their major components and subcomponents (or aspects). Third, using this decomposition exercise and the institutional ecology principle, the analytical linkages among water institutional aspects are demonstrated, and the influences of exogenous factors affecting the process of institution–performance interaction within the water sector are illustrated. Finally, by defining variables to represent different institutional, performance, and exogenous aspects, the major layers of institution–performance interaction and their impact-transmission channels are translated into a set of empirically testable models. These models are used to evaluate the effects of factors both endogenous and exogenous to the process of interaction between water institution and water sector performance.

CONCEPTUAL BASIS

Let us begin by specifying the way in which the water sector, the water institution, and their performance are conceived and approached in our study. The specification of the conceptual basis of these three key entities is essential to delineate the scope and context of our analytical framework and its empirical translation.

Water Sector

For the purposes of this study, *water sector* covers surface, subsurface, and reclaimed or recycled sources. Similarly, the coverage includes all water uses

– both consumptive and nonconsumptive – and all major water issues ranging from quantity–quality conflicts to drought–flood syndromes. However, since the water sector is viewed from an overall macro perspective of a country or region within a country, attention is more on the overall sectoral trends and features rather than on specific details and particulars. Although the macro perspective of the water sector involves a sacrifice of micro details, such a perspective is taken deliberately to sharpen the focus on the main thrust of our study: the evaluation of the process of institution–performance interaction within the water sector. The macro focus offers the additional advantage of enabling us to consider the intervening effects that some of the factors exogenous to both the water sector and the water institution have on the interaction process.

Water Institution

As in the case of the water sector, *water institution* is also approached from a macro perspective of a country or region and covers particularly the formal dimensions. Consistent with the literature, institutions are conceived in a much broader sense than mere organizations. In this broader sense, institutions are considered to cover the legal framework, policy regime, and administrative or organizational arrangements.[1] In a similar sense, the water institution can be conceptualized as an entity defined interactively by three main components: water law, water policy, and water administration. Thus, for the purposes our study, we define *water institution* as an integrated system covering both its institutional environment and institutional arrangements. This is in contrast to the approach discussed in Figure 2.1 where they are distinguished as separate segments.

The analytical separation of institutional arrangements from their institutional environment is relevant for studying issues such as the influence of one segment on another (e.g., Williamson 1975, 1985). However, it may not be relevant for cases such as the water institution where the study of the evolution of water organizations within water law and policy regimes is less meaningful from the standpoint of water sector performance. Since water organizations are the executive and implementation arms created for the translation and enforcement of the legal and policy provisions, neither they nor the laws and policies can exist independently of each other. It is true that the water administration itself – dominated by public sector bureaucracies in most contexts – becomes another player with a vested interest in enhancing and protecting its power and influence. However, the vested interests are related mainly to budgetary claim and interbureaucracy competition for power rather than to water allocation and use. From the perspective of water sector performance, therefore, water administration should be treated as part of the rules of the game rather than as part of the players.

In the scheme of our study, the integrated conception of water institution is essential to meet two analytical requirements. The first is to allow a different approach to institutional decomposition, and the second is to distinguish the water institution from its general environment. Our approach for the decomposition of *water institution* involves an analytical distinction among the three institutional components: water law, water policy, and water administration. The water institutional system, as defined by these three institutional components, has to be separated from its general environment to understand how the system and its performance are influenced by a variety of factors exogenous to the strict confines of the water sector. These exogenous factors include the nonwater-related legal, policy, and administrative aspects (e.g., constitution, land and environment laws, and farm and fiscal policies) as well as the noninstitutional aspects (e.g., resource endowments, historical precedents, political arrangements, demographic conditions, and development status).

An important distinction of water institution is that, unlike the general social and economic institutions, informal and local-level rules and conventions change faster than formal and macro-level rules that are beset by political economy and bureaucratic constraints.[2] Although this feature of the water institution provides one important exception to the observation of North (1990a: 45) that informal institutions change slowly, it still does not contradict his main point that formal and macro-level institutions are more susceptible to purposive modification than informal institutions. Furthermore, from the perspective of theoretical and empirical evaluation, formal institutions, unlike their informal counterparts, are also more amenable to treatment with transaction cost and political economy-based analysis.

ANALYTICAL DECOMPOSITION

Since an institution is an amalgamation of nested and embedded rules, it can be decomposed entirely in terms of rules or their configurations. But, for the purpose of our study, this approach is less relevant, as it cannot capture some of the important aspects that are crucial for institutional linkages and their performance impact. Although rule-based decomposition can capture the properties of individual rules, it cannot capture certain macro features shared by two or more rules (e.g., integration or consistency among legal rules or linkages between law and policy dimensions). Similarly, the rule-based decomposition also faces a problem in capturing the performance implication of the linkages among rules. In view of these limitations, we follow a different approach that decomposes water institution in terms of its major *institutional components* and *institutional aspects*.[3] These components and aspects capture not only the rules or their configurations but also their common features and performance implications. In this sense, our approach is thus more general than the rule-based approach to institutional decomposition.

Decomposing Water Institution

Using the decomposition approach, the analytical decomposition of *water institution* is performed at two levels. At the first level, the water institution is decomposed in terms of its three broad institutional components (water law, water policy, and water administration or organization). At the second level, each of these institutional components is decomposed further to identify its constituent institutional aspects. While it is easy to identify all the institutional aspects involved in each of these three components of the water institution, it is difficult to consider all of them within a single and tractable framework. For a focused and manageable evaluation, therefore, it is necessary to concentrate on some of the major institutional aspects noted frequently – both in the literature and in policy debate – as key factors for institutional and sectoral performance. The institutional aspects that are finally selected under each of the three institutional components of the water institution are given below.

The *water law* component of the water institution includes the following law-related institutional aspects:

(a) Legal treatment of water and related resources
(b) Format of water rights
(c) Provisions for conflict resolution
(d) Provisions for accountability
(e) Scope for private sector participation
(f) Centralization tendency
(g) Degree of legal integration within water law.

Similarly, the *water policy* component of the water institution includes the following policy-related institutional aspects:

(a) Project-selection criteria
(b) Pricing and cost recovery
(c) Interregional and/or sectoral water transfer
(d) Private sector participation
(e) User participation
(f) Linkages with other economic policies
(g) Law–policy linkages.

Likewise, the *water administration* component of the water institution includes the following administration-related institutional aspects:

(a) Spatial organization
(b) Organizational features
(c) Functional capacity
(d) Pricing and finance
(e) Regulatory and accountability mechanisms
(f) Information, research, and technological capabilities.

As can be seen, the institutional aspects selected here for evaluation capture some of the policy issues that dominate current debate on water sector reform. These issues are: integrated water resources management, conflict resolution, accountability, financial viability, decentralization, and capacity building within water sector. All these issues also have a strong bearing on the overall performance of both water institution and water sector. The coverage of institutional aspects can, therefore, be considered adequate for capturing the major thrust and features of water institution and for evaluating most of the currently relevant policy issues concerning water institution and water sector performance. From a more general perspective, with a finer decomposition of water institution in terms of key aspects and the identification of the alternative forms that each of these institutional aspects can take, various macro-level institutional configurations and institution–performance typologies can be identified. These configurations and typologies are based on various combinations of the forms taken by different institutional and performance aspects.[4]

Decomposing Institutional Performance

Besides the institutional aspects, we also need to decompose performance to identify a set of *performance aspects* to capture the overall effectiveness or performance not only of each of the three institutional components but also of the water institution taken as a whole. They are:

(a) Overall effectiveness of water law
(b) Overall effectiveness of water policy
(c) Overall effectiveness of water administration
(d) Overall effectiveness of the water institution.

The overall effectiveness of each of the three institutional components depends not only on the effectiveness of constituent institutional aspects but also on the strength of their linkages with other institutional components and their constituent aspects. Similarly, the overall effectiveness of the water institution depends both on the individual and interactive effects of its three institutional components. In this way, the overall performance of the water institution is linked ultimately to both the individual and joint effects of the institutional aspects underlying all three institutional components. In addition to the direct impacts of institutional components and their underlying institutional aspects, the performance of water institution is also influenced by the exogenous effects emanating from the general socioeconomic, political, and resource-related environment within which it is embedded.

The overall performance of the water institution is more difficult to conceive and measure than that of its components, but it can be captured indirectly in terms of its progressiveness. Broadly speaking, the progressive nature of the water institution can be evaluated in terms of four interrelated factors: adaptive capacity, scope for innovation, openness to change, and ability to tackle emerging problems. While adaptive capacity is indicative of the flexibility of the water institution to change in time and space, scope for innovation allows it to acquire a new and more appropriate institutional structure with constant updating. Similarly, openness to change suggests the absence of institutional rigidity. All these factors are fundamentally interrelated in the sense that the openness of the water institution to change is a basic condition for ensuring its adaptive capacity and innovation potential, and all three factors are indispensable for ensuring a progressive and performance-oriented water institution.

Decomposing Water Sector Performance

Rigorous performance criteria have been developed and applied at the project level in the irrigation subsector (Sampath 1990; Bos 1997; Burt and Styles 1997; Renault 1998), but not for evaluating the overall performance of the entire water sector. Efforts to develop objective and internationally comparable economic and equity criteria are severely constrained both by the data and methodological problems involved in capturing the economic or scarcity value of water and by the subjective issues inevitable in evaluating equity performance. While there are indicators for the physical gap (demand vs. supply) and financial gap (water charges vs. supply cost), their aggregate and sector-specific nature and data problems limit their ability to serve as objective criteria for the overall water sector performance.

Even with well-developed objective performance criteria, water sector performance cannot be evaluated in all its dimensions due to the presence of crucial subjective but pertinent aspects of performance such as the smoothness of water transfers and the adaptive ability of the water institution. Although the number of water conflicts can be used as a proxy for the smoothness of water transfers, how the relative seriousness of such conflicts can be factored into the evaluation is not clear. The situation is similar in the application of science and technology, because the number of scientific and technical instruments does not necessarily reflect the effectiveness with which they are used. Even where objective criteria are available or theoretically possible, subjective aspects (in the sense of learned judgments of stakeholders and water experts) will still be needed to substitute for or supplement with available knowledge.

Since water sector performance is viewed here as a concept with physical, financial, economic, and equity dimensions, decomposing it in terms of these four performance dimensions or components is logical. The *physical performance* of the water sector is evaluated in terms of the following aspects:

(a)   Demand–supply gap
(b)   Physical health of water infrastructure
(c)   Conflict-resolution efficiency (low cost and less time)
(d)   Smoothness of water transfers across sectors, regions, and users.

The *financial performance* of the water sector is evaluated in terms of the following aspects:

(a)   Investment gap (actual vs. required)
(b)   Financial gap (expenditure vs. cost recovery).

The *economic efficiency* of the water sector is evaluated in terms of the following aspects:

(a)   Pricing gap (water prices vs. supply cost)
(b)   Incentive gap (actual water prices vs. scarcity value of water).

And, finally, the *equity performance* of the water sector is evaluated in terms of the following aspects:

(a)   Equity between regions
(b)   Equity between sectors
(c)   Equity between groups.

Parallel to the interdimensional synergy evident among institutional components and aspects, there are also strong linkages among the physical, financial, economic, and equity dimensions of sectoral performance. For instance, pricing and cost-recovery aspects influence the physical health of water infrastructure because of their implications for funding maintenance and system improvement activities on a regular basis. Similarly, enhanced service quality, as induced by a healthy water infrastructure, is likely to facilitate cost recovery. Likewise, efficient conflict-resolution mechanisms can ease the process of intersectoral and interregional water transfers, contributing thereby to a more efficient and equitable allocation of water resources. Besides their financial implications, efficient water prices can also contribute to water use efficiency and conflict resolution. It is in view of its ability to capture such linkages that the IDA framework assumes importance as a methodological tool for systematic evaluation of the institution–performance interaction within the water sector.

WATER INSTITUTION AND SECTOR PERFORMANCE: LINKAGES AND INFLUENCE

With the analytical decomposition of the water institution and sector performance and the distinction of the process of their interaction from the general environment within which they are embedded, we can demonstrate the performance implications of both the linkages within a water institution and the influences of exogenous factors. For this purpose, it is useful to distinguish various layers of linkages evident within the process of institution–performance interaction within the water sector. The endogenous linkages within water institution (*institutional linkages*) can be distinguished from those between water institution and sector performance (*institution–performance linkages*). The institutional linkages can also be distinguished further as *intra-institutional linkages*, the linkages among institutional aspects within a given institutional component, and *interinstitutional linkages*, the linkages among institutional aspects across institutional components. Finally, there is also the influence of exogenous factors, especially on the performance of both the water institution and the water sector. These linkages within and among the water institution, water sector, and exogenous factors are considered as the dimensions or layers of the process of institution–performance interaction.

Institutional Linkages

The overall performance of the water institution and its ultimate impact on water sector performance depend not only on the capabilities of its individual components and aspects but also on the degree of integration among them. We will begin with the institutional linkages because they are the underlying causes of institution–performance linkages. Within institutional linkages, let us first consider their interinstitutional dimensions. Although water law and water policy are related, it is difficult to establish whether water law precedes or succeeds water policy, as history provides evidence for both cases. But, in any case, neither law nor policy alone can be effective in view of their mutual feedbacks and adjustments over time. Under ideal conditions, water law empowers water policy and water policy, in turn, provides a political economy translation for water law. Together, they define the framework and determine the capacity of the water administration that implements the legal and policy provisions at field level. Intuitively speaking, water laws and water policies form the software component of the water institution and water administrations or organizations, its hardware component.

The extent of integration within the water institution can be formalized in terms of the strength of institutional linkages. An illustrative set of these institutional linkages and their intra- and interinstitutional dimensions is depicted in Figure 5.1. To begin with, the legal aspects dealing with the way water sources as well as water, land, and environmental resources are treated influence such water policy aspects as priority setting for water sources and project-selection criteria. For instance, a water law that does not differentiate water by its source but recognizes the ecological linkages between water and other resources is more likely to encourage a water policy that assigns a higher priority to environmental imperatives and hydrological interconnectivity in project selection. Such a law–policy linkage also creates a favorable institutional environment

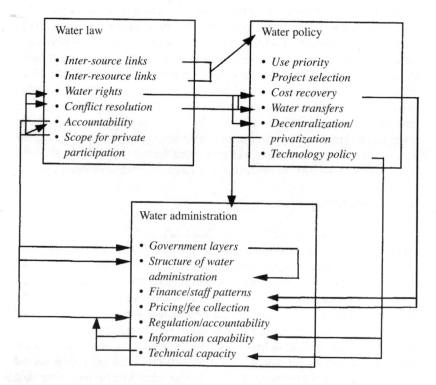

Figure 5.1   Institutional linkages within a water institution.

for promoting an integrated approach to water resources management. This particular linkage also indicates the way in which water law and water policy are influenced by the laws and policies related to other resources such as land and environment.

The most important legal aspect, one with multiple linkages to other legal, policy, and administrative aspects, is related to water use rights. It reinforces the linkages between the two legal aspects: conflict resolution and accountability. It also influences water policy through its linkages – both implicit and explicit – with policy aspects such as water pricing, cost recovery, management decentralization, and private sector participation. The three legal aspects – water rights, conflict resolution, and accountability – also have strong linkages with water administration insofar as they require special administrative mechanisms and technical/functional capabilities. Similarly, different policy aspects also strongly influence water administration. The most important of these are the aspects pertaining to user participation, management decentralization, and private sector participation. These policy aspects can strengthen water administration by tapping private skills and funds while contributing to the process of decentralization and debureaucratization. Policy aspects related to the application of water, information, and management technologies contribute to infrastructural development, skill formation, and capacity building.

Institution–Performance Linkages and Exogenous Influence

The strength of institution–performance linkages depends directly on the operational and functional effectiveness of various layers of linkages evident within the water institution. Since the interaction between water institution and water sector occurs within an environment characterized by many factors outside of their strict realms, institution–performance linkages are also subject to exogenous and contextual influences. The roles that these exogenous factors play in the institution–performance interaction within water sector are illustrated in Figure 5.2.

Figure 5.2 has two analytical parts. In the first part, depicting the institution–performance interaction, the two-way arrow links water institution and water sector performance. While institutions influence water sector performance through the economic medium, both the nature of the water sector and the efficiency of its performance can influence the water institution through the hydrogeological and political media. This two-way linkage has a few important implications. First, it indicates the obvious role that economic factors play in initiating institutional changes in the water sector. Second, it shows how hydrogeological factors can explain institutional variations across countries and regions. Since the water institution is shaped by the nature of the

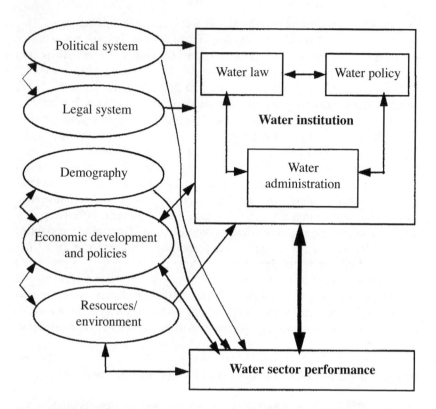

Figure 5.2   Exogenous influence on institution–performance interaction.

water sector, they are not entirely independent of the basic characteristics of the water sector itself. Thus, water institutions in areas with abundant water can differ from those in areas with acute scarcity. And, third, the two-way linkage also indicates the way crisis in the water sector can build political pressure for institutional change. The crisis-induced institutional responses observed in many countries around the world (Saleth and Dinar 1999a and 2000) provide ample evidence for this phenomenon.

The political impact of the hydrological phenomenon of water crisis also has an underlying economic urge for change. With a crisis-ridden water sector, the marginal benefits of institutional change in terms of improved performance become very high relative to both the real and monetary costs of transacting the institutional change. Although the incremental net benefits from institutional change can decline as the water institution matures, they are high in the initial stages of institutional evolution. This can be so purely from an economic perspective. But, the calculus can change once the political economy aspects are taken into account because the evaluation of the benefits and costs of institutional change is often blurred by political considerations. Since political expediency involves myopic considerations, the transaction costs – both real and monetary – are overestimated while the benefit streams, which continue over a longer time span and spill over far beyond the water sector, are underestimated. When water crisis assumes serious proportions (e.g., worst drought), causing popular concern, the economic calculus attains the much-needed political legitimacy. In this sense, the logic for initiating institutional and sectoral reforms is consistent with both welfare theoretic and political economy arguments.

The context within which the institution–performance interaction occurs is as important as the mechanics of the interaction because of its conditioning effect on the two-way linkages between water institution and water sector performance. In reality, the general context, or the environment, is defined by an interplay of innumerable factors that are strictly exogenous to water sector. For analytical convenience and simplicity, Figure 5.2 focuses only on the most important factors, such as the political system, legal framework, economic development, demographic condition, and resource endowment. Although these factors are themselves interrelated, for expositional purposes, we highlight only the nature of their influence on the process of the institution–performance interaction. While the political system and legal framework affect mainly the structure of the water institution, the other factors influence and are also being influenced by water sector performance. Since these factors represent the exogenous constraints and opportunities facing the water sector, they play a major role in shaping both the nature and character of the institution–performance interaction within the water sector.

Although institutional differences provide the major explanation for variations in water sector performance, the general context of the institution–performance interaction is still important for providing residual and complementary explanations.[5] In many instances, the context can even better explain why similarly placed water institutions (or their components) lead to a differential water sector performance. Performance variations in turnover policy across countries (Johnson 1997; Vermillion 1997) and basin-level organizations (Kliot, Shmueli, and Shamir 1997) are cases in point. These instances show that political and legal commitments to declared policies, though necessary, are not sufficient in the face of administrative inadequacy and other bottlenecks, including the structural basis of the political system (e.g., federal vs. unitary form or presidential vs. parliamentary form).

Economic factors, including macroeconomic reforms and trade policy changes, also play a strong role in providing impetus for institutional changes within the water sector. The success of the turnover program in Mexico, the extensive water sector reform initiated in China, and the growing policy attention to water sector reform in India can all be traced to macroeconomic reforms of the late 1980s (Saleth and Dinar 1999a and 2000). The role of environmental factors including drought and floods is similar, as illustrated by the cases of California and China, respectively. These instances of the powerful role played by exogenous factors in institution–performance interaction within the water sector underline the need to incorporate within the evaluation framework the synergy and the discord emanating from both within and outside the water sector.[6]

IDENTIFICATION AND DEFINITION OF VARIABLES

The decomposition framework provides a basis for developing a methodology for a quantitative evaluation of the institutional linkages depicted in Figure 5.1 and the institution–performance linkages described in Figure 5.2. To translate the analytical framework into an empirically applicable form, let us identify and define the variables that can capture various layers of institutional linkages and institution–performance linkages within the water sector. In this respect, we identify two sets of variables. The first set tries to capture features that are endogenous to the water institution and the water sector. The selection of these variables is guided not only by their ability to reflect the status of institutional and performance aspects but also by their amenability to numerical translation within an empirical setting. Some of these variables are quantitative or quantifiable by proxies, whereas others are inherently qualitative and, therefore, relative, involving subjective or judgmental considerations. The second set of variables aims to capture some of the exogenous factors, such as economic development, demographic change, educational status, extent of water scarcity, and the resource and environmental situations, that affect the institution–performance interaction within the water sector. The selection of these exogenous variables is based on their relative importance and the possibility of developing comparable data.

Definition of Institutional and Performance Variables

The definition of both the institutional and performance variables flows directly from the analytical decomposition of *water institution* and *water sector performance*. Each decomposed institutional and performance aspect is captured by one or more variables depending upon the desired level of detail. To facilitate interpretation of these variables, their nature and format must be described, as well as the range of values they can take. The selected set of institutional and performance variables are defined below.

Water law variables

LTRWSA = Legal treatment of water sources, a dummy variable with a value of 1 if all sources are treated alike, but 0 otherwise

LPRSRF = Format of surface water rights having a value range of 0–7 with 0 for no rights; 1 for unclear, unauthorized, or scattered rights; 2 for common or state property; 3 for multiple rights; 4 for a riparian system; 5 for an appropriative system; 6 for a correlative (proportional sharing) system; and 7 for a license or permit system

LCRMEE = Effectiveness of conflict-resolution mechanisms[7] captured in terms of judgmental perception and expressed on a 0–10 scale

LACPRE = Overall effectiveness of accountability provisions[8] evaluated in terms of judgmental perception and expressed on a 0–10 scale

LINTRE = Overall ability of water law to provide a legal framework for an integrated treatment of water from various sources evaluated in terms of judgmental perception and expressed on a 0–10 scale

LOECEN = Extent of a centralization tendency within water law evaluated in terms of judgmental perception and expressed on a 0–10 scale

LOEPRV = Legal scope for private sector participation in the water sector evaluated in terms of judgmental perception and expressed on a 0–10 scale

LOEFWL = Overall effectiveness of water law[9] evaluated in terms of judgmental perception and expressed on a 0–10 scale.

Water policy variables

PPSCRI = Project-selection criteria having a value range of 0–6 with 0 for no response, 1 for political dictates, 2 for equity factors, 3 for ecological factors, 4 for benefit–cost ratio, 5 for internal rate of return, and 6 for multiple criteria

PCOREC = Cost-recovery status with 0 for nonresponse, 1 for full subsidy, 2 for partial recovery, and 3 for full cost recovery

PIRSWE = Effectiveness of interregional and intersectoral water transfers evaluated in terms of judgmental perception and expressed on a 0–10 scale

PGPIPP   = Impact of private sector promotion policy evaluated in terms of judgmental perception and expressed on a 0–10 scale

PGPIUP   = Impact of the policy for promoting users' participation evaluated in terms of judgmental perception and expressed on a 0–10 scale

POPAWE   = Extent of the influence of other policies[10] on water policy evaluated in terms of judgmental perception and expressed on a 0–10 scale

POELWL   = Extent of the linkages between water law and water policy evaluated in terms of judgmental perception and expressed on a 0–10 scale

POEFWP   = Overall effectiveness of water policy[11] evaluated in terms of judgmental perception and expressed on a 0–10 scale.

Water administration variables

AORGBA   = Spatial organization of water administration taking a value of 0 for nonresponse; 1 if organized in terms of administrative divisions; 2 for the hybrid basis, that is, in terms of both geographic divisions and hydrogeological regions; 3 for broad hydrogeological regions; and 4 for river basins

ABALFS   = Balance in functional specialization, a dummy with a value of 1 if balanced and 0 otherwise

AIBDWP   = Existence of an independent body for water pricing, a dummy with a value of 1 for existence and 0 otherwise

ASBUDC   = Seriousness of budget constraint facing the water administration evaluated in terms of judgmental perception and expressed on a 0–10 scale

AACCME   = Effectiveness of the accountability arrangements[12] evaluated in terms of judgmental perception and expressed on a 0–10 scale

AARINF   = Adequacy and relevance of the information base evaluated in terms of judgmental perception and expressed on a 0–10 scale

AEXTST   = Extent of science and technology application[13] in water administration evaluated in terms of judgmental perception and expressed on a 0–10 scale

AOEFWA = Overall operational ability of the water administration evaluated in terms of judgmental perception and expressed on a 0–10 scale.

Performance variables

WSPPHY = Physical performance[14] of the water sector evaluated in terms of judgmental perception and expressed on a 0–10 scale

WSPFIN = Financial performance[15] of the water sector evaluated in terms of judgmental perception and expressed on a 0–10 scale

WSPECO = Economic performance of the water sector evaluated in terms of judgmental perception and expressed on a 0–10 scale

WSPEQU = Equity performance of the water sector evaluated in terms of judgmental perception and expressed on a 0–10 scale

WSPOEV = Overall performance of the water sector obtained by averaging *WSPPHY*, *WSPFIN*, *WSPECO*, and *WSPEQU*

WIPOEV = Progressiveness or overall adaptive capacity of the water institution taken as a whole evaluated in terms of judgmental perception and expressed on a 0–10 scale.

Although the variables, as defined above, are self-explanatory, a few words should be said about some of their general characteristics. The institutional and performance variables can be grouped into two broad categories: factual and perceptional variables. The factual variables can be observed, but the perceptional variables, involving judgmental considerations, cannot be observed. Even though the factual variables are observable, problems such as uncertainty and incomplete information can lead to multiple answers. For instance, the legal format of water rights is subject to multiple interpretations notwithstanding a complete legal clarity in water law. In contrast, institutional and performance variables specifically require judgmental considerations to obtain numerical information on them. Some examples are the variables intended to capture the overall performance of water institution and the same of its components.

Some institutional aspects can be captured through observable and quantifiable variables. For instance, the effectiveness of the conflict-resolution aspect of water law can be expressed in terms of the number of unresolved water conflicts. Similarly, the size of water administration can be expressed in terms of staff strength and the effectiveness of cost-recovery policy can be captured by the gap between water rates and supply costs. But, apart from the usual information problems, the need to incorporate factors such as expectational aspects, futuristic considerations, qualitative dimensions, and regional variations increases the relevance and value of subjective and judgmental information. For the same reason, value judgments are also unavoidable even in the case of water sector performance where objective and observable measures can be developed. Despite their objective basis, these measures can only be relative and contextual in terms of time and space as they are defined with past data and in specific contexts.

The variables can also be grouped into three categories based on the value they take: dummy (0 or 1) variables, categorical variables taking integer values within a given range, and scale variables taking a value in the 0–10 range. The first two groups of variables are essentially factual and are involved only in the case of water institution whereas the variables in the third group are basically perceptional or judgmental in nature and are involved in all cases where performance evaluation is needed. The dummy variable indicates the existence or otherwise of a given institutional aspect whereas the categorical variable tries to place a given institutional aspect into a fixed number of feasible categories. Thus, the categorical variables can be used to capture the institutional features observed or perceived in various contexts. In contrast, the scale variables are used to capture the institutional and performance aspects as evaluated in terms of the subjective and the instrumental valuation of objective information against expectations and aspirations.

In the case of categorical variables, the categories are identified either in terms of their actual occurrence or in terms of theoretical possibilities. For instance, the categories identified for water rights are based on an extension and adaptation of the classification of property rights made by Bromley (1989a) and Eggertsson (1996b) to the particular context of water resources. In the context of all categorical variables, the numerical value for each category is assigned consciously to obtain an ascending order in terms of their relative performance and significance. While some value judgments are involved in the ordering of categories, the process does utilize the available empirical evidence and acceptable theoretical justification. For instance, in the case of water-rights format, the appropriative-rights system is assigned a higher value than the riparian- and common-property systems because of its superior allocation efficiency (Hartman and Seastone 1970; Burness and Quirk 1980; Saleth, Braden, and Eheart 1991). Although the literature considers the correlative-rights system inferior to the appropriative-rights system, we assign a higher value in view of its better equity performance.

The ordering of categories in cases such as project-selection criteria and cost recovery is based purely on economic reasoning. In the case of project-selection criteria, as long as all the costs and benefits are reckoned and internalized, there is a theoretical correspondence between benefit–cost ratio and internal rate of return. Still, these criteria differ considerably in terms of the way they are perceived. While the benefit–cost ratio is considered socially oriented and soft, the internal rate of return is considered business oriented and stringent. We have therefore assigned a higher value to the internal rate-of-return criterion. The bounded nature of the scale variables within the 0–10 range also has important implications. Since 0 means the worst situation and 10 means an ideal situation, the intermediate values on the scale can be interpreted as the extent to which the actual situation deviates from either the worst or the ideal situation. In this sense, the scale variables add a relativity dimension to evaluation of various institutional and performance aspects. Finally, we have assigned a few variables a zero value for nonresponse. Although this is an outcome of a respondent's ignorance or lack of clarity, we treat it as a reflection of the inability of the institution rather than as a limitation of the individual.

Definition of Exogenous Variables

Let us also identify and define a few additional variables to capture factors that are exogenous to both the water institution and water sector performance but have significant effects on both of them. The exogenous factors are many, diverse, and contextual. For analytical convenience, they can be broadly grouped under the following general categories: economic development, social equity, demographic changes, cultural factors, and physical status of resources (water, land, and environment). From the perspective of a particular sector such as the water sector, the exogenous factors also include the institutional conditions facing the economy as a whole (e.g., legal systems and regulatory arrangements) as they affect sectoral performance indirectly through their effects on sectoral institutions. To capture the effects of some of the most important exogenous factors, we define the following set of variables.

GNPPPC = Purchasing power parity-based GNP per capita in US dollars

POPDEN = Population density in people per km^2

DCUPOP = Decadal change in urban population as a percentage

FWATWC = Freshwater withdrawal per capita per year in cum

PWATAG = Agricultural share in total water withdrawal as a percentage

ALANDC = Arable land per capita in hectares (ha)

FPIIND   = Food production index

EXPEDU = Public expenditure on education as a percentage of GNP

GININD   = Gini index

NCNATW = Share of natural capital in total wealth as a percentage

ENVRRI   = Environmental Regulatory Regime Index in score

ININCR   = Institutional Investors' Credit Rating index.

Before proceeding further, four points on the listed set of exogenous variables need clarification. First, these variables are defined essentially at the national or regional level for a given time period. Second, while the first nine variables are too obvious to need any clarification, a few words are in order to explain the last three. The variable *NCNATW*, representing the share of natural capital in national wealth, is based on the total value of six natural capital assets: timber, nontimber, cropland, subsoil resources, protected areas, and pastureland.[16] The variable *ENVRRI* is defined as a composite index of seventeen variables pertaining to the stringency of regulations, the structure, information, and enforcement aspects of regulatory institutions, level of energy subsidies, and membership in international environmental organizations.[17] The variable *ININCR* is an index of credit rating by institutional investors and hence captures a country's overall creditworthiness.[18] Third, although many variables can capture the exogenous factors in the economic, social, demographic, physical, and institutional realms, we have identified these twelve variables mainly in view of their close relationship with water institution and water sector performance. The other obvious reason for their choice relates to the availability of comparable data. And, finally, but more importantly, although both *FWATWC* and *PWATAG* are directly related, and hence, endogenous to water sector, we consider them to be exogenous because they capture the pressures placed on water resources by economic development, demographic growth, and agricultural expansion.

While *GNPPPC* captures economic growth as adjusted to regional differences in population and purchasing power, *POPDEN* and *DCUPOP* represent two of the key demographic aspects. *POPDEN* captures the interface between demography and geography, and *DCUPOP* takes stock of the impact of population growth on urbanization. *FWATWC*, selected to provide a general measure of water scarcity, also captures the effects of development and demographic pressures on water resources, whereas *PWATAG* captures the extent to which the water sector is oriented toward agriculture. Although *ALANDC*, which captures demographic pressure on cultivated land, can also serve to indicate the overall scope for equity in access to arable land, *GININD* is also selected to have an explicit focus on overall equity in terms of income distribution. *FPIIND* can take stock of the production and food security implications of the water sector in particular and the agricultural sector in general, whereas *EXPEDU* can capture not only the importance assigned to social sector investment in general but also the role of education in particular. The variable *NCNATW*, which represents the value of natural resources relative to human and produced assets, can also provide some indication of the ecological status. The variable *ENVRRI*, which captures the effectiveness of the environmental regulatory regime, can also provide an indirect measure of the effectiveness of the overall legal and regulatory apparatus. Finally, the variable *ININCR* is selected to capture the external perception of the overall fiscal and economic health of the economy.

With the identification and definition of the set of exogenous variables, at this stage, the following three aspects should be noted for distinguishing them from the institutional and performance variables defined in the previous section. First, in contrast to the institutional and performance variables that can vary across individuals both within and across countries, regions, and periods, the exogenous variables vary across countries, regions, and periods but remain the same for any country or region at a given point in time. Second, in contrast to the subjective nature of the institutional and performance variables, most of the exogenous variables listed above are observable, and data on all of them are easily obtainable from secondary sources.[19] Finally, while the exogenous variables capture the objective status of a given magnitude as observed in the past, the institutional and performance variables as defined here can incorporate past and future trends observed or perceived not just in a given dimension but also in all related dimensions. Thus, the evaluation of how the values of the subjectively derived variables, representing the endogenous institutional and performance features, are influenced by objective conditions, as represented by the endogenous variables, constitutes an important challenge for our modeling exercise and empirical analysis.

EMPIRICAL MODELS OF INSTITUTION–PERFORMANCE INTERACTION

With the definition of the institutional, performance, and exogenous variables, various facets of the institution–performance interaction evident in Figures 5.1 and 5.2 can now be translated into a set of functional models that can be empirically estimated within a regression framework. A closer look at these figures reveals two distinct sets of relationships to be formalized for a quantitative evaluation of the institution–performance interaction. The first set of relationships characterizes the institutional linkages and institution–performance linkages. The second set of relationships characterizes the effects that the exogenous factors have on the overall process of institution–performance interaction. We therefore need two sets of empirical models. The first set will formalize both the institutional linkages and institution–performance linkages by relating institutional and performance variables with those representing various institutional components and aspects. The second set of models will capture the exogenous influence on institution–performance interaction by relating the exogenous variables to the institutional and performance variables.

Models of Institutional and Performance Linkages

Given the selected set of institutional and performance variables and the illustrative set of linkages evident in Figure 5.1, it is straightforward to specify the models that characterize some of the layers that are most important for policy formulation. To provide contrast, we specify two versions of the models – one representing the popular conception of institution–performance interaction that does not recognize institutional linkages and the other, a more realistic conception, that explicitly recognizes the performance implications of institutional linkages.

Model A, capturing the conventional conception of the relationship between water institution and water sector performance, can be represented in the following equation.

$$
\begin{aligned}
WSPOEV = f_1[&LTRWSA, LPRSRF, LCRMEE, LACPRE, \\
&LINTRE, LOECEN, LOEPRV, PPSCRI, \\
&PCOREC, PIRSWE, PGPIPP, PGPIUP, \\
&POPAWE, POELWL, AORGBA, ABALFS, \\
&AIBDWP, ASBUDC, AACCME, AARINF, \\
&AEXTST]
\end{aligned}
\tag{A1}
$$

Equation [A1] shows water sector performance as a simple and direct function of 21 variables representing various legal, policy, and administrative aspects. This model is obviously unrealistic, as it fails to account for the performance implications of the interrelationships among these institutional variables. We still specify and include it for evaluation to provide a contrast to the more realistic Model B, which explicitly recognizes the performance effects of institutional linkages and synergy.

To allow a clear specification of model B, we need first to trace the major institutional linkages and their performance implications so that we can identify the layers of linkages and the channels of their impact transmission. Given Figures 5.1 and 5.2 and the defined set of institutional and performance variables, these layers of linkages and channels of impact transmission can be traced and formally represented as shown in Figure 5.3. To see how these layers and channels are characterized in Figure 5.3, we note first that, of the 26 variables shown in this figure, five are performance variables – four related to water institution and its three components and one related to water sector. The rest are all institutional variables representing 21 institutional aspects. Only 16 of these 21 institutional variables are truly independent and are, therefore, distinguished by placing them within ovals. The impact of these independent variables on institutional performance is channeled both directly (as indicated by the double-line arrows) and indirectly (as indicated by the single-line arrows).

The five institutional variables, placed in rectangles, are dependent as they are affected by different subsets of the 16 independent institutional variables. The institutional variables – both independent and dependent – affect the three variables representing the performance of the three water institution components (placed in rounded rectangles). These three variables affect the variable representing the overall performance of the water institution (placed in a hexagon), which, in turn, affects the ultimate dependent variable in the system, water sector performance (placed within a cross). In addition to their indirect effects on water sector performance via institutional performance, some of the institutional variables also have direct effects on water sector performance (indicated by dotted lines). These variables include both the independent ones (*POPAWE, AARINF*, and *AEXTST*) and the dependent ones (*PCOREC* and *ASBUDC*). Note that their indirect effects are in terms of their institutional influence, whereas their direct effects are in terms of their role as proxies for economywide policy, fiscal, information, and technology trends.[20] Thus, we can see that the effects of the variables representing both the institutional and performance aspects are transmitted through various layers and multiple channels. Once these layers of linkages and channels of impact transmission have been identified, the task of representing them as a set of interdependent equations is straightforward. Together, these equations specify our Model B.

$$LCRMEE = g_1(LPRSRF, PGPIUP, POPAWE, ABALFS, \\ AARINF, AEXTST) \qquad [B1]$$

$$PIRSWE = g_2(LPRSRF, LCRMEE, PGPIUP, AEXTST) \qquad [B2]$$

$$PCOREC = g_3(LPRSRF, PGPIUP, POPAWE, AIBDWP) \qquad [B3]$$

$$ASBUDC = g_4(AIBDWP, PCOREC, PGPIPP, PGPIUP) \qquad [B4]$$

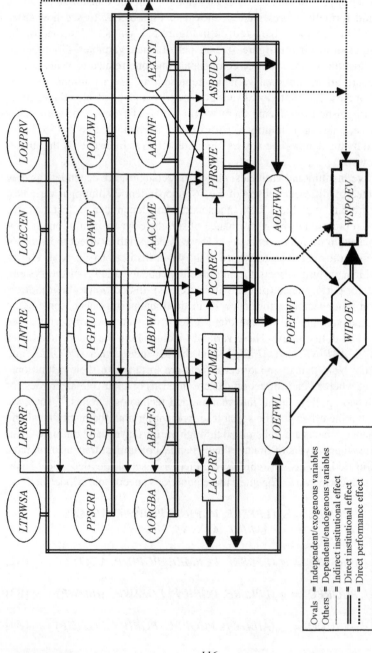

Ovals = Independent/exogenous variables
Others = Dependent/endogenous variables
——— = Indirect institutional effect
═══ = Direct institutional effect
▬▬▬ = Direct performance effect

Figure 5.3 Institution–performance interaction: layers of linkages and channels of impact transmission.

$$LACPRE = g_5(LPRSRF, LOEPRV, PCOREC, POELWL, \\ AACCME) \qquad [B5]$$

$$LOEFWL = g_6(LTRWSA, LPRSRF, LCRMEE, LACPRE, \\ LINTRE, LOECEN, LOEPRV) \qquad [B6]$$

$$POEFWP = g_7(PPSCRI, PCOREC, PIRSWE, PGPIPP, \\ PGPIUP, POPAWE, POELWL) \qquad [B7]$$

$$AOEFWA = g_8(AORGBA, ABALFS, AIBDWP, ASBUDC, \\ AACCME, AARINF, AEXTST) \qquad [B8]$$

$$WIPOEV = g_9(LOEFWL, POEFWP, AOEFWA) \qquad [B9]$$

$$WSPOEV = g_{10}(WIPOEV, POPAWE, ASBUDC, PCOREC, \\ AARINF, AEXTST) \qquad [B10]$$

Of these equations, the first five capture the interinstitutional linkages evident across institutional aspects under the three institutional components. Hence, they are very important for capturing the performance effects of inter-dimensional synergy within water institution. Since these equations describe the way some of the institutional aspects are influenced by other institutional aspects both within and across institutional components, they capture the institutional linkages that transcend individual institutional components. Equation [B1], for instance, considers the legal variable capturing the effectiveness of conflict-resolution mechanisms as a function of one legal variable (surface-water-rights format),[21] two policy variables (effectiveness of user participation policy and influence of other policies on water policy), and three administrative variables (balanced functional specialization, information adequacy, and science and technology application). Similarly, equation [B2] shows the policy variable representing the effectiveness of intersectoral and regional water transfers as a function of two legal variables (water rights format and effectiveness of conflict-resolution mechanisms), one policy variable (effectiveness of user participation policy), and one administrative variable (extent of science and technology application).

Equation [B3] considers the policy aspect of cost-recovery status as a function of one legal variable (water-rights format), two policy variables (effectiveness of user participation policy and influence of other policies on water policy), and one administrative variable (existence of independent water-pricing body). Equation [B4] postulates the administrative variable capturing the seriousness of budget constraint as a function of one administrative variable (existence of an independent water-pricing body) and three policy variables (cost-recovery status, effectiveness of privatization policy, and effectiveness of user participation policy). Equation [B5], on the other hand, views the legal variable capturing the effectiveness of accountability provisions as dependent on two legal variables (water-rights format and privatization provisions), two policy variables (cost-recovery status and overall law–policy linkage), and one administrative variable (effectiveness of administrative accountability). In addition to their role in capturing the interdimensional institutional synergy, these five equations are also crucial in view of their structural linkages with the rest of the equations.

With the description of the first five equations that formalize the interinstitutional linkages transcending individual institutional components, let us now describe the three equations that capture the intra-institutional linkages evident within each of the three institutional components. Equation [B6] postulates the overall performance of water law as a function of seven water law-related institutional aspects. These institutional aspects are: the legal treatment of water sources, the format of water rights, the effectiveness of a conflict-resolution mechanisms, the effectiveness of accountability provisions, the level of internal consistency within water law, the degree of centralization tendency within water law, and the legal scope for private sector participation. Similarly, equation [B7] considers the overall performance of water policy as a function of seven water policy–related institutional aspects. These institutional aspects are: the project-selection criteria, the cost-recovery status, the effectiveness of interregional and intersectoral water transfer policy, the effectiveness of government policy toward private sector involvement and the same toward user participation, the effects of other policies on water policy, and the extent of linkage between water law and water policy.

Likewise, equation [B8] specifies the overall performance of water administration as a function of seven administration-related institutional aspects. These institutional aspects are: the organizational basis of water administration, extent of balance in functional specialization, existence of an independent body for water pricing, severity of budget constraint, effectiveness of administrative accountability, adequacy and relevance of information, and the extent of science and technology application within water administration. While equations [B6], [B7], and [B8] are designed to capture the functional linkages within each of the three water institution components, equation [B9] shows how the overall performance of the water institution is linked with the effectiveness of its three institutional components. Finally, equation [B10] postulates the performance of the water sector as a function of water institution performance and five institutional variables taken as proxies, respectively, for policy bias against the water sector (*POPAWE*), cost-recovery commitment (*PCOREC*), overall fiscal health (*ASBUDC*), information level (*AARINF*), and technology application (*AEXTST*) in the country.

Together, these 10 equations – with different levels of detail and disaggregation – can help in evaluating some of the most important and policy-relevant layers in the institution–performance interaction. While equations [B1] to [B5] formalize the interinstitutional linkages, equations [B6] to [B8] represent the intra-institutional linkages. The last two equations represent the institution–performance linkages within water institution and between water institution and water sector, respectively. As we observe these equations, it is evident that they are nested with sequential relationships among them. Among the first five equations, the dependent variable in equation [B1] enters as an independent variable in equation [B2] and that in [B3] enters as an independent variable both in equations [B4] and [B5]. While all the dependent variables in the first five equations also enter as independent variables in equations [B6], [B7], and [B8], those in the next three equations enter as independent variables in equation [B9]. The dependent variable of equation [B9] as well as those in equations [B3] and [B4] becomes the independent variable in equation [B10]. Thus, it is equation [B10] that captures the ultimate effects of various sequential relationships among all the other equations within the system. It is this sequential property of the equations in Model B that enables us to systematically evaluate various layers of linkages and channels of impact transmission evident in institution–performance interaction within water sector.

The sequential feature of the equation system has major implications both for the choice of econometric technique and for the method of analysis. From an econometric perspective, since equations [B1] to [B10] form an integrated system in view of their sequential relationships, they should be estimated within the framework of a simultaneous equation system. Such an empirical approach will allow us to econometrically account for both the direct and indirect effects that the institutional aspects have on water sector performance. When these equations are estimated within an appropriate empirical context, the sign and size of their coefficients could provide valuable insights on the relative role played by various institutional aspects in determining the performance of both water institution and water sector. Given the sequential nature of the equation system and the estimated coefficients, the complete chains of effects (or channels of impact transmission) can be traced between a marginal change in any institutional variable and its ultimate impact on water institutional and sectoral performance. As we will see, this exercise is valuable for identifying various configurations of institutional sequencing and packaging.

Models of Exogenous Variables

The models of exogenous variables are specified to capture the exogenous influence emanating from the general environment within which both the water institution and the water sector are embedded. Since we do not have any objectively

observed measures for institutional and sectoral performance, the models specified below relate the actually observed exogenous variables to the subjectively
derived variables capturing the performance of a water institution, its three institutional components, and the water sector. In this respect, these models differ
from both Models A and B, which are based exclusively on subjectively derived
institutional and performance variables. Recognizing this important difference,
let us specify the set of equations representing Model C as follows.

$$LOEFWL = h_1(GNPPPC, POPDEN, DCUPOP, FWATWC,$$
$$PWATAG, ALANDC, FPIIND, EXPEDU,$$
$$GININD, NCNATW, ENVRRI, ININCR) \qquad [C1]$$

$$POEFWP = h_2(GNPPPC, POPDEN, DCUPOP, FWATWC,$$
$$PWATAG, ALANDC, FPIIND, EXPEDU,$$
$$GININD, NCNATW, ENVRRI, ININCR) \qquad [C2]$$

$$AOEFWA = h_3(GNPPPC, POPDEN, DCUPOP, FWATWC,$$
$$PWATAG, ALANDC, FPIIND, EXPEDU,$$
$$GININD, NCNATW, ENVRRI, ININCR) \qquad [C3]$$

$$WIPOEV = h_4(GNPPPC, POPDEN, DCUPOP, FWATWC,$$
$$PWATAG, ALANDC, FPIIND, EXPEDU,$$
$$GININD, NCNATW, ENVRRI, ININCR) \qquad [C4]$$

$$WSPPHY = h_5(GNPPPC, POPDEN, DCUPOP, FWATWC,$$
$$PWATAG, ALANDC, FPIIND, EXPEDU,$$
$$GININD, NCNATW, ENVRRI, ININCR) \qquad [C5]$$

$$WSPFIN = h_6(GNPPPC, POPDEN, DCUPOP, FWATWC,$$
$$PWATAG, ALANDC, FPIIND, EXPEDU,$$
$$GININD, NCNATW, ENVRRI, ININCR) \qquad [C6]$$

$$WSPECO = h_7(GNPPPC, POPDEN, DCUPOP, FWATWC,$$
$$PWATAG, ALANDC, FPIIND, EXPEDU,$$
$$GININD, NCNATW, ENVRRI, ININCR) \qquad [C7]$$

$$WSPEQU = h_8(GNPPPC, POPDEN, DCUPOP, FWATWC,$$
$$PWATAG, ALANDC, FPIIND, EXPEDU,$$
$$GININD, NCNATW, ENVRRI, ININCR) \qquad [C8]$$

$$WSPOEV = h_9(GNPPPC, POPDEN, DCUPOP, FWATWC,$$
$$PWATAG, ALANDC, FPIIND, EXPEDU,$$
$$GININD, NCNATW, ENVRRI, ININCR) \qquad [C9]$$

The independent variables in all nine equations are the 12 exogenous variables whereas the dependent variables are the subjectively derived performance levels of the water institution and its three components (equations [C1] to [C4]) as well as the water sector and its four performance components (equations [C5] to [C9]). While equations [C1] to [C4] capture the effects of the exogenous variables on the performance of the water institution and its three components, equations [C5] to [C9] capture the same for water sector performance and its four components. As these exogenous variables capture the economic, social, demographic, resource, and institutional context within which the institution–performance interaction occurs, equations [C1] to [C9] could help in understanding the relative level and direction of the influence of these contextual factors on institutional and sectoral performance. Since these equations relate only the subjective performance variables with the exogenous variables, they evaluate the effects of exogenous factors on institutional and sectoral performance not directly but indirectly in terms of their effects on the subjective process that generates these performance variables. The evaluation of these equations is still valuable, partly to validate the consistency of subjective evaluation with the objective state of the general conditions surrounding water institution and water sector and partly to understand the relative role of exogenous factors in performance evaluation.

NOTES

1. In this study, the terms *administration* and *organization* are used interchangeably because we conceive administration as covering all relevant organizational modes – both public and private – involved in a given context.
2. Instances supporting this fact include the emergence of local-level water-sharing arrangements among users, including informal water markets in many parts of the world lacking formal water laws and policies (Easter, Rosegrant, and Dinar 1998). Similarly, the innumerable instances of collective action in the context of water resources and other common pool resources also indicate that informal and local rules change faster than formal and macro-level rules (E. Ostrom 1990).
3. Note the specific sense in which the terms *institutional components* and *institutional aspects* are used in our study. While the former is used to denote a broader decomposition of institution, the latter is used to denote a further decomposition of the three water institution components.
4. For instance, an institutional profile including a private water-rights system, full cost pricing, and decentralized water administration characterizes one institutional typology whereas the same with undefined water rights, subsidized pricing, and centralized water administration defines another institutional typology. Similarly, many more institutional configurations and typologies can be identified by considering various combinations of the institutional aspects and their forms.
5. Regarding the important role played by the social and political contexts in determining the effectiveness of institutions in general, North (1990a: 101) provides an interesting instance. That is, the adoption of the US constitution by many Latin American countries and western property-rights laws by many developing countries have not been successful because 'the enforcement mechanism, the norms of behavior, and the subjective model or models of the

actors are not the same.' This means that institutional similarity does not necessarily assure performance consistency across contexts.

6. One way of conceptualizing and analytically tracking the influence of these exogenous factors is to consider their effects on the social benefits and transaction costs of institutional change. While political and legal factors have a dominant role in determining transaction costs, others have a larger role in defining the social benefits of institutional changes within the water sector.

7. The conflict-resolution mechanisms considered for evaluation include: bureaucratic systems, national water councils and the like, tribunals, water court systems, judicial–legislative mechanisms, river boards, basin-level organizations and the like, water user associations, and multiple arrangements.

8. The accountability provisions considered for evaluation include those related to officials (e.g., indemnity clause, penalty provisions, and administrative actions) and those related to users (e.g., injunctions, sanctions, and tortious liabilities).

9. The key issues considered in the evaluation of the effectiveness of water law include: its current and future relevance, synergy with other laws, capacity for conflict resolution and accountability, and ability to adjust with environmental issues and emerging technologies.

10. These policies include agricultural policies, energy–power policies, fiscal policies, economic policies, credit and investment policies, environmental policies, trade policies, and foreign policy.

11. The overall effectiveness of water policy is obtained by averaging the judgmental values reported for the effectiveness of policies with respect to project selection, cost recovery, water pricing, regulatory and incentive aspects, water education and extension, and application of water, information, and management technologies. To get the score for the composite variable, the simple addition of scores reported for various variables represented by the composite variable is a normal practice in the quantitative literature within institutional economics (e.g., Clague 1997b: 72; Isham and Kahkonen 1999: 23; Li 1999: 6–7).

12. The accountability arrangements considered here include the following categories present both within and outside a formal water administration: administrative oversight, financial auditing (public accounts committees), work auditing, grievance cells, monitoring procedures for sectoral and regional water allocation, interministerial committees, statutory bodies, local administrations, user groups, and nongovernmental organizations.

13. The extent of science and technology application is evaluated by considering the use of computers, remote sensing and satellite tools, research and experimental information, modern accounting and auditing techniques, management information systems, geographic information systems, wireless communications, water-measuring technologies, and computerized dynamic control of canal and water delivery networks.

14. The physical performance of the water sector is evaluated by considering the following aspects: ability to bridge the overall demand–supply gap, physical health of water infrastructure, conflict-resolution efficiency (low cost and less time), and smoothness of water transfers across sectors, regions, and users.

15. While financial performance is evaluated in terms of overall cost recovery and investment adequacy, economic performance is evaluated with due consideration to both the gap between water charges and supply cost and the gap between water charges and the economic or scarcity value of water.

16. For the calculation procedures and data sources for this variable, see Kunte, et al. (1998: 4–10).

17. All the variables except the last one on membership are based on judgmental information from a panel of 4,022 executives from 50 countries collected by the World Economic Forum and reported regularly in its *Global Competitiveness Report*. For further details on the construction of and data sources for *ENVRRI*, see Esty and Porter (2000: 74).

18. For details on this index, as reported in *World Development Report: 2000*, see World Bank (2000a).

19. The subjective nature of the institutional and performance variables does not, however, mean that they are temporally unstable. This is partly because institutional change is a slow and gradual process and partly because the subjective process of evaluation can summarize

the temporal change in institutional and performance aspects as observed in the recent past and also as expected in the foreseeable future.

20. In this respect, *POPAWE*, representing the effect of other policies on water policy, is considered a proxy for the overall policy bias against the water sector whereas *AARINF* and *AEXTST*, representing information adequacy and science and technology application, respectively, are taken as indicators for the overall information and technology status. Similarly, *PCOREC* and *ASBUDC*, representing cost-recovery status and seriousness of budget constraint, respectively, are considered proxies for general cost-recovery commitment and fiscal health of the state.

21. The format of surface water rights is used here as well as in equations [B2], [B4], [B5], and [B6] as a proxy for the general format of water rights.

6. Empirical context: description and justification

Despite their macro focus and partial coverage of institutional and exogenous aspects, the models presented in the previous chapter are able to capture some of the most important layers of linkages inherent in the process of institution–performance interaction within the water sector. When these models are empirically estimated, some of the critical linkages that we have shown analytically can be evaluated quantitatively as well. Such a quantitative analysis can provide a basis for formal statistical analysis of the relative role, direction, and significance of the influences that various institutional aspects and exogenous factors have on the performance of both water institution and water sector. However, the validity and credibility of such a statistical analysis are predicated on the relevance and suitability of the empirical context, and its underlying sample selection procedure and data generation process. The main purpose of this chapter is, therefore, to describe and justify the empirical context selected for a quantitative analysis of institutions and performance.

STAKEHOLDERS' PERCEPTION AS AN EMPIRICAL BASIS

All the three models described in the previous chapter can be quantitatively addressed by using either time-series data for a country or region or cross-section data for a set of countries or regions, or by combining both the time-series and cross-section data within a panel framework. Unfortunately, obtaining enough actually observed and internationally comparable time-series or cross-section data for an empirical estimation of our models, though not impossible, is extremely costly in terms of both time and resources. Even if such data are available, there is still a problem, as they represent the past, static situation and cannot, therefore, capture the ex-ante dimensions representing ongoing and future changes as well as stakeholders' aspirations and expectations. Since observed data can allow only ex-post rather than an ex-ante analysis, they have an obvious limitation, especially for designing anticipatory and long-term strategies for institutional reform.

Overcoming Data Limitations

To overcome the problems of the nonavailability and limitations of observed data, this study relies on stakeholders' perception as an information basis for the empirical analysis of the models of institution–performance interaction. As seen in Chapter 3, the empirical reliance on perception-based data is nothing new in the institutional economics literature. There is a long tradition of using such data for institutional analysis (Knack and Keefer 1986; Cukierman, Webb, and Neyapti 1998; Gray and Kaufmann 1998; Barrett and Graddy 2000; Chong and Calderon 2000). As we have recognized, perception-based information sources are also used regularly both in economics and in other social science disciplines. Carefully conducted perception surveys can unearth the untapped but highly relevant information used regularly by individuals and society to make many important social, economic, and political decisions. Such information embodied in individuals is particularly valuable for institutional analysis primarily because of the role of subjective aspects and the long gestation period involved in the process of institutional change and its performance impact. Our reliance on perception-based information is, therefore, not just for substituting or complementing observed data, but equally for a number of other legitimate theoretical and practical reasons. Let us explain some of these reasons that legitimize the reliance on perception-based information for institutional analysis.

Theoretical and Methodological Legitimacy

As noted in Chapter 2, a critical mass of literature underlines the subjective dimensions in institutions (e.g., Bhaskar 1979; Douglas 1986; North 1990a; E. Ostrom 1990, 1999; Stein 1997; Vira 1997). Since this literature views institutions as a human mental construct that thinks and acts through the medium of individuals, it shifts the focus from organizations to individuals as the main source of institutional change. This point is articulated effectively by North (1990a: 5) when he notes: 'Institutions are a creation of human beings. They evolve and are altered by human beings; hence our theory must begin with the individual.' As we have argued in Chapter 4, subjective perception can be considered as a major analytical tool for incorporating explicitly the central role that individuals play in the process of institutional change. Since the subjective perception of individuals includes the effects of both objective and subjective factors, it can also be used as a methodological tool to bring together and evaluate the role of many methodologically and conceptually different factors within a common evaluation framework. Moreover, subjective perception allows us not only to give an ex-ante dimension to institutional evaluation, but also to incorporate the important role of knowledge and learning into the process of institutional change. As pointed out by Kaufmann, Kraay, and Mastruzzi (2003), perceptional evaluation is also apt to capture the de facto features of institutions as opposed to their de jure counterparts.

The main rationale for our reliance on subjective perception as an empirical basis, therefore, comes directly from our approach and evaluation methodology, both rooted in the subjective theory of institutional change as outlined in Chapter 4. Of the four stages of institutional change – mind change, political crystallization of reform, actual institutional change, and performance impact (Figure 4.1) – the first stage is critical. In contrast to the present literature that focuses mainly on the last three stages, our study concentrates on the first stage so as to highlight and elaborate the central role that the mind change of stakeholders and decisionmakers plays in the whole process of institution–performance interaction. At this stage, the subjective and objective factors, knowledge and learning, and the interactive feedback from the actual and expected outcomes of previous, ongoing, and future institutional changes all tend to converge. Since the interactive effects of all these factors are captured by subjective perception, the latter remain a critical interface between present realities and future changes.

When the subjective perception of individuals, as observed at the first stage of institutional change, is evaluated, we can gain valuable insights on the way stakeholders perceive the process of institution–performance interaction. Since subjective perception captures the subjective aspects, objective factors, learning effects, and the feedback from past, ongoing, and expected changes in the water institution and the water sector, it can be used to evaluate institutional change either before, after, or during the actual change.[1] As the subjective perception of stakeholders plays a major role in determining the reform direction, actual implementation, and final impact, a careful evaluation of the first stage, capturing the process of mind change, could also provide key insights into the other three stages of institutional change.

Convergence and Comparability

Our evaluation of the subjective perception of stakeholders in the first stage can also indicate the extent of perceptional convergence on the need for and nature of institutional change. Since perceptional convergence can identify the institutional configuration preferred by most stakeholders, it can also be interpreted as a revelation or representation of an implicit demand for institutional configurations. It is this institutional demand, as revealed by perceptional convergence on a given institutional configuration, that prompts political entrepreneurs to lobby for change in their quest for political returns. When demand for institutional change is very strong, the effects of perceptional convergence can also both flow into the second stage of reform design and the third stage of reform implementation. In view of its possible effects during the second and third stages, strong institutional demand, as created by perceptional convergence, can also speed up and enhance the impact of institutional change.

Considering the significant roles that perception and its convergence play in the process of institutional change, it is necessary to ensure their freedom from the diversionary effects of value judgment. As we know, the subjective nature of institutions itself makes value judgments unavoidable even in their evaluation (Bhaskar 1979: 773), but the question is 'can perception converge in the presence of the individual-specific properties of value judgments?' The answer to this question is important for ensuring the comparability of subjective evaluation across stakeholders. As we will see later in this chapter, such comparability is essential to justify the treatment of subjectively derived information within a statistical context.

Although the phenomenon of value judgment is determined by individual-specific subjective aspects, it is not free from objective influence. More specifically, when the effects of the objective factors predominate over those of the subjective factors, both the subjective perception and its convergence tendency will be little affected by the effects of value judgments.[2] We can also see many real world situations wherein individual views or value judgments are often relegated to the background so as to consider larger community or social interests. Instances of these conditions include extreme events such as economic crisis, war, floods, and droughts. Under these conditions, we usually observe a general convergence or shared perception among people having fundamental socioeconomic and political differences. The contributory fact to such convergence here is the common threat or the same predicament facing most or all members of the society.

Even in normal situations where subjective aspects can add power to the divisive role of value judgments, perceptional convergence between individuals is possible. The mechanism that can lead to convergence in this case is the instrumental valuation that individuals rely on for evaluating phenomena such as institutions where the generally acceptable objective criteria are neither available nor applicable. In these conditions, individuals use some reference points as instruments for evaluating the extent to which an aspect deviates from or approaches an ideal situation or agreed standard. These reference points can be either subjectively derived ideals (expectations or aspirations) or objectively available standards (declared policy intentions and best-practice cases). The subjectively derived reference points are often inspired by some objective phenomena (e.g., best or worst practices), historical experience, or theoretical results. As far as these factors are common to most individuals, the subjectively derived reference points of most individuals are likely to be close, if not identical. This possibility is underlined further by the role of interaction, learning, and experience, which create common and generally acceptable standards for evaluating various aspects including institutions. Even when the reference points of individuals are dissimilar, there can still be convergence in a relative sense.[3]

Practical Advantages

The approach of using stakeholders' perception as an empirical basis has a number of other advantages. First, it allows us a considerable freedom in the choice of institutional and performance variables and enables us to derive all the relevant information within the same analytical context. Second, it enables us to tap the accumulated wisdom, expectations, and futuristic considerations that are neither captured by observed data nor used normally in institutional evaluation. Third, perception not only synthesizes different types of information (objective data, subjective observation, and expected trends) but also internalizes some complicated and difficult-to-measure concepts (e.g., performance, efficiency, and equity). Finally, given its empirical reliance on a cross-section of countries and experts, it can capture the effects of variations both in the exogenous factors (e.g., political system, demographic conditions, economic development, and resource endowment) and in the individual-specific subjective factors (e.g., disciplinary background, experience, and ideological orientation).

SUBJECTIVE INFORMATION: RATIONALE AND CAVEATS

While subjective perception can be a legitimate and rich source of information, much depends on the way such information as embodied in individuals is tapped and interpreted. The usual instrument for capturing such implicit information involves reliance on a 'perception' survey of a carefully selected group of stakeholders, experts, and decisionmakers. Since the survey approach enables us to capture the diversity of perspectives and identify areas of agreement, it remains an important diagnostic tool (White 1990: 89–90). Relying on this empirical approach, we try to obtain information on all relevant institutional and performance variables by administering a structured questionnaire to a carefully-selected sample of key water sector experts from a group of representative countries.

Information even on the variables capturing institutional and sectoral performance is also obtained within the judgmental or subjective framework for two reasons. First, observed data, though available on some aspects of water sector performance, are neither adequate to cover all performance aspects nor capable of capturing the ongoing as well as prospective performance changes. As a result, information on all performance variables is also obtained within the framework of subjective evaluation. And, second, in addition to its role in solving the data problems, this approach provides a consistent data set where each set of institutional observations has its own set of corresponding performance observations. This allows us to relate the subjectively derived information on institutional aspects to the same on performance aspects across individuals. Since the information derived from the subjective perception and judgmental values of the respondents is central to our evaluation of institutional linkages and their performance implications, the ramifications of three key aspects must be recognized: bounded rationality, asset specificity, and information impactedness. While the implications of these conditions for contracts and organizational arrangements have been treated elaborately by Williamson (1975, 1985), our concern about these conditions here is related to their implications for the appropriateness of the survey technique as well as for the quality of subjective information.

The asset-specificity condition is related to the 'idiosyncratic employment' concept of Marshall (1948: 626) and the 'personal knowledge' idea of Polanyi (1962: 52–3). It refers to the special knowledge possessed by individuals in particular and the economically useful special attributes possessed by economic assets in general (Williamson 1985: 52–4). Although this knowledge and these attributes are valuable, they may remain unrecognized, unrewarded, and underutilized. Many situations pose difficulties in transferring and displaying such knowledge or attributes because of the 'information impactedness condition.' *Information impactedness* refers to the condition where the 'true underlying circumstances relevant to a transaction, or related set of transactions, are known to one or more parties but cannot be costlessly discerned by or displayed for others' (Williamson 1975: 31). It is a derivative condition arising from a combination of uncertainty, opportunism, and bounded rationality. *Bounded rationality* refers to human behavior that is '*intentionally* rational but only *limitedly* so' (Simon 1961: xxiv). This condition explicitly recognizes the cognitive and computational limitations of the human mind, especially relative to the size and complexity of the problem at hand (Simon 1957: 198). As these limitations differ across individuals, there are bounded rationality differentials across individuals (Williamson 1975: 47).

Reflecting the three concepts in the context of our survey approach, we find that the survey instrument can indeed enable us to capture the special knowledge possessed by key water experts through their practical experience and accumulated wisdom derived from their proximity to various layers of decisionmaking. But, we need to recognize that our survey approach is not free from the cognitive and communication limitations imposed by the information impactedness and bounded rationality conditions. One way to minimize the impact of these conditions on the evaluation process is to design the survey instrument in such a way as to ensure a more efficient and less biased knowledge capture. The finer decomposition of institution and performance attempted within our institutional decomposition and analysis framework enables the questionnaire to present the institutional alternatives and typologies in a simple and disaggregated manner.[4] This allows the respondents to focus their attention on each of the institutional and performance aspects and summon their knowledge and perception on that aspect so as to provide us with a more accurate response to the best of their intentions and judgments.

SAMPLE SELECTION AND DESCRIPTION

The key challenge for the evaluation of the mind change lies less with the method than with the empirical approach, especially the identification of an appropriate evaluation context and the selection of a suitable focus group. With a detailed, yet manageable, analytical framework based on institutional decomposition as described in Chapter 5 and the legitimacy of using perceptional information, we can use a perception survey to capture the required information from a focus group selected from a representative set of countries. While the choice of country can be made in such a way as to capture economic, social, physical, and historical diversity, the choice of focus group is somewhat tricky. This is because of the requirement that the focus group should *simultaneously* have all four of the following characteristics. First, the group under consideration should be directly related to the water sector, particularly with a major stake in its performance. Second, it should have a strong influence on the overall decisionmaking process affecting the water sector. Third, it should have some basic understanding of the technical aspects of water institutional arrangements and their performance implications. And, finally, it should have sufficient international exposure to enable a relative perspective of institutional arrangements and water sector performance.

Identifying a focus group that satisfies all four of these selection criteria simultaneously is not easy. In the water sector context, the three groups that satisfy one or more of the selection criteria are water users, political decisionmakers, and water experts. While water users have a larger and more direct stake in water institutions and their performance implications, their lack of technical knowledge on the structural features of water institutions and their limited international exposure exclude them from being an effective focus group for our survey. Despite their influential status and considerable international exposure, the political decisionmakers are also in the same predicament as they lack both technical knowledge and the time necessary to provide the required level of institutional and performance details. In terms of the selection criteria, therefore, it is neither advisable to include the micro-level water users nor feasible to select macro-level political decisionmakers.

Unlike the water users and political decisionmakers, a cross-section of carefully selected water experts – both subject specialists and sector executives – satisfying most of the criteria can be considered as a more viable group to represent and capture the prevailing mindset toward water institutions and their performance implications. They have a stake in sector performance, hold the required technical knowledge, and possess considerable international exposure. Although they are generally considered less influential than the political decisionmakers, they do have considerable impact on the decision-making process, both directly through their technical and policy advice to political actors and indirectly through their research and advocacy roles. In most contexts, in view of their influence on opinion and policymaking circles, they can also be considered as a pivotal group representing the critical interface between grass-roots users and macro planners.

Sample Countries

The value and credibility of the subjective information needed for an evaluation of the models of institution–performance interaction depend also on the composition and randomness of sample countries. Tables 6.1a and 6.1b show the sample countries together with some key information on their political arrangements, demographic conditions, water resource potential and sectoral features, and socioeconomic status. Due to variations in their legal traditions, institutional arrangements, and water sector status, four states in the United States (California, Colorado, Illinois, and Texas) are considered as separate regions for survey purposes. Together, these 43 countries and regions provide the empirical context for subjective evaluation of the process of institution–performance interaction within the global water sector. To gather some first-hand information on institutional arrangements, sector performance, and recent reforms, a representative subset of these 39 sample countries was visited in October–December 1997.[5]

As we can see from Table 6.1, the sample countries and regions jointly account for 52 percent of global land area, 68 percent of global population, 63 percent of global renewable water resources, and four-fifths of global freshwater withdrawal and irrigated area. Although data on people living below poverty line are not available for a number of countries, the data available indicate that the sample covers at least 60 percent of the global population suffering from poverty. From a continental perspective, the sample covers 6 African countries, 19 Asian countries, 8 European countries, and 10 countries

Table 6.1a Socioeconomic profile and water sector features of sample countries[a]

Sl. no.	Sample countries[b]	Political regime[c]	Population (million)	Area (million km²)	Annual rainfall (cm)	Renewable water resources (bcum)	Annual water withdrawal			Hydropower as percentage of total power
							Total (bcum)	Percentage of total resources	Percentage used for irrigation	
		(1997)	(1999)	(1999)	(2000)		(Various years)			(1998)
1	Argentina	1	37	2.78	5.0–500.0	1031.01	28.6	2.8	75.0	90.00
2	Australia	2	19	7.74	12.7–127.0	356.67	15.1	4.2	33.0	68.00
3	Bangladesh	1	128	0.14	101.6–203.2	1233.41	14.6	1.2	86.0	0.00
4	Bolivia	1	8	1.10	25.4–177.8	309.00	1.4	0.5	48.0	0.00
5	Brazil	3	168	8.55	60.0–360.0	7133.11	54.9	0.8	61.0	6.00
6	Cambodia	4	12	0.18	38.1–76.2	496.88	0.5	0.1	94.0	98.50
7	Canada	5	31	9.97	38.1–203.2	2856.40	45.1	1.6	9.0	62.40
8	Chile	1	15	0.76	5.0–125.0	480.11	21.4	4.5	84.0	18.00
9	China	6	1250	9.60	12.7–76.2	2856.25	525.5	18.4	77.0	17.40
10	Egypt	1	62	1.00	5.0–20.0	58.84	55.1	93.6	86.0	55.00
11	France	1	59	0.55	63.0–140.0	191.51	40.6	21.2	12.0	12.80
12	Germany	3	82	0.36	50.0–250.0	177.86	46.3	26.0	0.0	97.00
13	India	3	998	3.29	13.0–1100.0	1943.11	500.0	25.7	92.0	13.70
14	Indonesia	1	207	1.91	100.0–500.0	2613.38	74.3	2.8	93.0	12.90
15	Israel	1	6	0.02	2.5–35.5	1.10	1.7	154.0	64.0	18.60
16	Italy	1	58	0.30	76.2–127.0	168.72	57.5	34.1	45.0	2.00
17	Japan	7	127	0.38	76.2–203.2	432.05	91.4	21.2	64.0	1.00
18	Lao PDR	6	5	0.24	110.0–370.0	283.19	1.0	0.4	82.0	74.00
19	Mexico	8	97	1.96	15.0–170.0	463.56	77.8	16.8	78.0	19.30
20	Morocco	7	28	0.45	12.7–76.2	30.24	11.1	36.7	92.0	92.20

21	Myanmar	9	45	0.68	76.2–127.0	1058.18	4.0	0.4	90.0	90.10
22	Namibia	1	2	0.82	5.0–70.0	54.75	0.3	0.5	68.0	0.00
23	Nepal	10	23	0.15	100.0–400.0	211.58	29.0	13.7	99.0	0.20
24	Netherlands	3	16	0.04	62.5–92.5	92.75	7.8	8.4	34.0	0.09
25	New Zealand	10	4	0.27	60.0–150.0	344.21	2.0	0.6	44.0	25.00
26	Pakistan	1	135	0.80	30.5–162.5	261.63	155.6	59.5	97.0	77.60
27	Philippines	1	77	0.30	236.0	338.26	55.4	16.4	88.0	1.00
28	Poland	10	39	0.32	60.0–100.0	63.53	12.1	19.0	11.0	2.56
29	Portugal	1	10	0.09	50.0–100.0	72.23	7.3	10.1	48.0	20.00
30	South Africa	1	42	1.22	5.1–134.6	50.74	13.3	26.2	72.0	3.00
31	South Korea	1	47	0.10	130.0	70.55	23.7	33.6	63.0	20.00
32	Spain	11	39	0.51	15.2–139.7	111.03	35.5	32.0	62.0	94.00
33	Sri Lanka	1	19	0.07	30.4–233.7	44.25	9.8	22.1	96.0	71.00
34	Sudan	9	29	2.38	70.0–100.0	31.15	30.0	96.3	99.0	81.00
35	Thailand	4	62	0.51	127.0–230.0	415.28	33.1	8.0	91.0	12.00
36	Tunisia	1	9	0.16	10.0–25.0	3.95	2.8	70.9	86.0	41.00
37	United Kingdom	4	59	0.25	50.0–400.0	146.85	9.3	6.3	3.0	9.90
38	United States	3	273	9.36	17.8–213.4	2502.86	447.7	17.9	27.0	88.00
39	Vietnam	6	78	0.33	111.8–223.5	908.47	54.3	6.0	86.0	82.00

Notes:

[a]Some reviewers, especially from Poland and South Africa, have indicated that the values for some of the variables listed here are not in agreement with those noted in the statistical sources of their countries. However, we continue to use the data available in the sources cited for the sake of cross-country consistency.

[b]Data for Taiwan are not available.

[c]Republic = 1; Federal Parliamentary State = 2; Federal Republic = 3; Multiparty Liberal Democracy under Constitutional Monarchy = 4; Confederation with Parliamentary Democracy = 5; Communist State = 6; Constitutional Monarchy = 7; Federal Republic operating under a centralized Government = 8; Military Regime = 9; Parliamentary Democracy = 10; Parliamentary Monarchy = 11.

Sources: World Bank (1997, 2000a), Gleick (1998), Seckler, et al. (1998), and World Resources Institute (1999).

133

Table 6.1b Socioeconomic profile and water sector features of sample countries[a]

Sl. no.	Sample countries[b]	Net irrigated area		Annual water demand (bcum)	Groundwater resources			GNP (PPP) per capita ('000 $)	Urban population (%)	People below poverty line (%)[c]
		Total (mha)	As percentage of arable land		Annual recharge (bcum)	Extraction				
						Total (bcum)	As percentage of recharge			
		(1994–97)		(1998)	(1975–95)			(1999)	(1999)	(1999)
1	Argentina	1.58	6.30	10.5	128	4.7	3.7	11.32	90.0	25.5
2	Australia	2.40	5.10	3.5	–	2.5	–	22.45	85.0	–
3	Bangladesh	3.67	43.40	6.9	34	3.4	10	1.48	24.0	42.7
4	Bolivia	0.09	4.10	0.5	130	–	–	2.19	62.0	65.0
5	Brazil	2.31	4.80	8.5	1874	–	–	6.32	81.0	17.4
6	Cambodia	0.27	7.10	0.2	30	–	–	1.29	16.0	39.0
7	Canada	0.73	1.60	1.4	369.6	1.1	0.3	23.73	77.0	–
8	Chile	2.16	54.30	6.3	140	–	–	8.37	85.0	21.6
9	China	34.69	37.70	181.2	870	74.6	8.6	3.29	32.0	6.0
10	Egypt	2.87	99.80	26.2	1.3	3.4	261.5	3.30	45.0	22.9
11	France	1.56	8.50	3.3	100	6.2	6.2	21.90	75.0	–
12	Germany	0.46	3.90	0.9	45.7	7.7	16.9	22.40	87.0	–
13	India	53.82	32.40	192.4	350	150	42.9	2.15	28.0	40.9
14	Indonesia	2.65	15.50	4.6	226	–	–	2.44	40.0	11.3
15	Israel	0.16	45.50	0.7	1.1	1.2	109.1	15.94	91.0	–
16	Italy	2.07	24.90	14.3	30	12	40	20.75	67.0	–
17	Japan	2.51	62.80	1.6	185	12.9	7	24.04	79.0	–

18	Lao PDR	0.16	18.60	0.2	50	–	–	1.73	23.0	46.1
19	Mexico	5.28	22.80	27.6	139	23.5	16.9	7.72	74.0	10.1
20	Morocco	1.13	13.10	4.7	7.5	3	40	3.19	55.0	13.1
21	Myanmar	1.47	15.40	1.5	156	–	–	0.70	27.0	–
22	Namibia	0.01	0.90	0	2.1	–	–	5.37	30.0	–
23	Nepal	1.03	38.20	1.6	–	–	–	1.22	12.0	42.0
24	Netherlands	0.54	61.00	1	4.5	1.1	25.3	23.05	89.0	–
25	New Zealand	0.13	8.70	0.5	198	–	–	16.57	86.0	–
26	Pakistan	16.94	80.80	72.6	55	45	81.8	1.76	36.0	34.0
27	Philippines	0.90	16.30	4.5	180	4	2.2	3.82	58.0	40.6
28	Poland	0.10	0.70	0.2	36	2.4	6.7	7.89	65.0	23.8
29	Portugal	0.49	21.80	1.5	5.1	3.1	60.1	15.15	63.0	–
30	South Africa	1.16	7.90	6.8	4.8	1.8	37.3	8.32	52.0	–
31	South Korea	1.12	60.60	2	–	1.2	–	14.64	81.0	–
32	Spain	2.83	18.10	10.9	20.7	5.5	26.6	16.73	77.0	–
33	Sri Lanka	0.28	30.70	3	17	–	–	3.06	23.0	40.6
34	Sudan	1.95	15.09	9.8	7	0.3	4	0.24	23.0	–
35	Thailand	4.08	23.90	9.5	43	0.7	1.6	5.60	21.0	18.0
36	Tunisia	0.22	7.60	1.4	1.2	1.2	101.7	5.48	65.0	19.9
37	United Kingdom	0.10	1.70	0.2	9.8	2.7	27.6	20.88	89.0	–
38	United States	22.29	12.00	105.9	1514	110	7.3	30.60	77.0	77.0
39	Vietnam	1.71	31.00	6.9	84	–	–	1.76	20.0	50.9

Notes:
a Note a to Table 6.1a also applies here.
b Data for Taiwan are not available.
c – means data not available and in the particular case of people below poverty line, it also means the percentage is smaller than 5 percent.

Sources: World Bank (1997, 2000a), Gleick (1998), Seckler, et al. (1998), and World Resources Institute (1999).

and regions from the Western Hemisphere. The sample is dominated by Asian countries because the mismatch between water demand and supply is more acute on this continent and hence, the need for institutional reform more urgent. From a climatic perspective, the sample covers countries and regions in tropical, subtropical, and temperate zones with differential rainfall patterns, water resource potential, and water demand conditions.

The sample also captures well the variations in water challenges facing different countries. For instance, Israel, Sudan, and Tunisia represent the problems of absolute water scarcity whereas Bangladesh, China, Cambodia, and Japan represent the problems of floods, drainage, and water quality. While California, Australia, and India represent the problems of sporadic drought, most of the European countries represent the problems of poor water quality and its health and environmental consequences. From the perspective of development status, the sample covers 27 developing countries and 16 developed countries and regions. Equally important is the political diversity represented by the sample. Coverage includes dictatorships (e.g., Myanmar), kingdoms (e.g., Morocco), communist arrangements (e.g., China), and democratic systems – both parliamentary and presidential (as represented by many other countries). The structure of government also varies from unitary to federal. These variations in political arrangements and government structures as well as in legal traditions are important in view of their obvious effects on the legal, policy, and administrative aspects governing the water sector.

Since the sample covers different continents, historical backgrounds, political systems, development stages, demographic trends, water law traditions, and, more importantly, levels of water scarcity, it can represent well the reality of the global water sector in all its relevant physical, economic, and institutional dimensions. The representative character of the sample is further enhanced by its coverage of the full spectrum of recently observed institutional changes in the global water sector in terms of their extent, depth, and effectiveness (Saleth and Dinar 1999a, 2000). Of the 43 countries and regions, 15 have undertaken a series of recent initiatives to reform their water institution in particular and water sector in general.[6] Thus, from any perspective, the sample provides a rich contextual background for obtaining the information on the subjective perception of institution–performance interaction within the water sector.

Sample of Experts and Survey Process

Just as the sample countries were chosen to ensure diversity of situation and context, so were the sample water experts selected to represent various regions, disciplinary backgrounds, professional specializations, experience levels, and organizational affiliations. Special attention was also given to ensuring that the water experts have the necessary knowledge and international exposure. In this sense, the initial list of water experts forming the prospective sample for the perception survey is certainly purposive. Considering this list of experts as a preliminary sample, an extensive but pretested questionnaire (Appendix A) was either personally handed over or mailed to participants with a detailed explanation of the objective and scope of the exercise.[7] The final sample includes only the experts who responded with a completed questionnaire, providing all the required information. In this sense, the actual sample that constitutes the information basis of our study is *almost* random, though more by chance than by design.[8] The alphabetical list of respondents who constituted our final sample of experts, as well as other experts who supported us with logistics, information, and materials is given in Appendix B.

The survey was conducted in three phases between October 1997 and May 2000. In the first phase, October 1997–March 1998, a total of 98 key water sector experts from 12 countries were identified and contacted. These countries were: Australia, Brazil, Chile, China, India, Israel, Mexico, Morocco, South Africa, Spain, Sri Lanka, and the United States (Illinois, California, Colorado, and Texas). Of the 98 experts contacted in the first stage of the survey, only 48 responded with a completed questionnaire and only 43 of these turned out to be complete, with comparable information on all the variables. Large gaps or partial responses precluded the use of the rest.[9] In the second phase of the survey, conducted in April 1998–November 1999, another 164 water experts in 27 additional countries were approached with questionnaires. They included some of the experts contacted in seven of the countries covered in the first phase. But of the 164 water experts contacted during this phase, only 73 responded with full information.

In the third phase of the survey, covering December 1999–May 2000, 16 water experts were approached from some of the same countries covered in the second phase as well as from four additional countries (France, Germany, Italy, and Poland). Of these, 11 responded with a completed questionnaire. All in all, the final sample consists of 127 water experts from 43 countries and regions, implying a response rate of about 46 percent. The information derived from the responses of these 127 experts forms the database for the quantitative evaluation of institution and performance. The distribution of these experts by country and survey phase is shown in Table 6.2. As can be seen, we have a single response from 13 countries and regions, but multiple responses from 30 other countries and regions. Thus, the number of responses from the sample countries varies from one to nine.

The continental pattern of country coverage and survey response can be seen in Figure 6.1. Asia, which accounts for 44 percent in both country coverage and survey response, dominates other regions. As noted, since this region

Table 6.2   Distribution of sample experts, by country and survey round

Countries	Code		Recent reform[a]	Questionnaires obtained (1997–2000)			
	Number	Letter		Survey 1	Survey 2	Survey 3	Total
Argentina	1	AR	No	–	1	–	1
Australia	2	AU	Yes	3	3	–	6
Bangladesh	3	BD	No	–	4	–	4
Bolivia	4	BO	No	–	1	–	1
Brazil	5	BR	Yes	4	2	–	6
California	6	CA	Yes	–	3	–	3
Canada	7	CD	No	–	4	–	4
Chile	8	CL	Yes	5	1	–	6
Cambodia	9	CM	No	–	1	–	1
China	10	CN	Yes	3	2	–	5
Colorado	11	CO	Yes	2	–	–	2
England	12	ED	Yes	–	1	1	2
Egypt	13	EG	No	–	2	–	2
France	14	FR	Yes	–	–	1	1
Germany	15	GM	No	–	–	2	2
Indonesia	16	IA	No	–	4	–	4
Illinois	17	IL	No	1	–	–	1
India	18	IN	Yes	5	4	–	9
Israel	19	IS	Yes	4	–	–	4
Italy	20	IT	No	–	–	3	3
Japan	21	JP	No	–	4	–	4
South Korea	22	KR	No	–	1	–	1
Laos PDR	23	LP	No	–	1	–	1
Morocco	24	MO	Yes	–	6	–	6
Mexico	25	MX	Yes	6	–	–	6
Myanmar	26	MY	No	–	1	–	1
Namibia	27	NB	No	–	1	–	1
Netherlands	28	ND	No	–	2	–	2
Nepal	29	NP	No	–	2	–	2
New Zealand	30	NZ	No	–	1	–	1
Philippines	31	PH	No	–	3	–	3
Pakistan	32	PK	No	–	3	–	3
Poland	33	PO	No	–	–	3	3
Portugal	34	PT	No	–	1	1	2
South Africa	35	SA	Yes	2	4	–	6
Sudan	36	SD	No	–	2	–	2
Sri Lanka	37	SL	Yes	3	–	–	3
Spain	38	SP	Yes	5	1	–	6
Thailand	39	TL	No	–	1	–	1
Tunisia	40	TU	No	–	2	–	2
Taiwan	41	TW	No	–	1	–	1
Texas	42	TX	No	–	1	–	1
Vietnam	43	VN	No	–	2	–	2
Total			15	43	73	11	127

Note: [a]The recent reform status of the countries is based not only on literature review but also on the authors' subjective considerations as to the extent and depth of the recently observed reform initiatives.

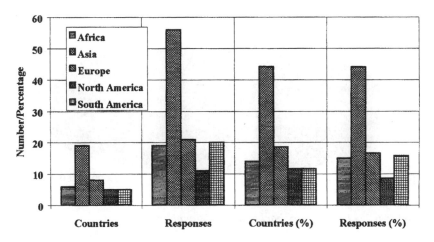

Figure 6.1   Continental breakdown of sample countries and sample experts.

accounts for the largest share of global population, poverty, and irrigated agriculture, it has to be well represented in the sample. While both the Western Hemisphere and Europe are represented relatively well, Africa comes last with a share of around 15 percent in both country coverage and survey response.[10] Except for this fact, the sample in both terms of its country coverage and survey response is, more or less, consistent with the continental pattern of demographic, resource, and institutional potential.

Figure 6.2 depicts the disciplinary background of the 127 experts included in our final sample. The majority of the respondents are engineers (48 percent) and economists (32 percent). The rest of the respondents are either lawyers or represent other social science disciplines such as management and sociology. This pattern is somewhat consistent with the disciplinary composition common to the water sector of most countries. We recognize that this strict disciplinary characterization of experts does not fully reflect their vast transdisciplinary knowledge gained from experience or learned through interaction. The fact that they were able to provide complete answers to all the legal, policy, administrative, and performance issues covered in our exhaustive questionnaire is in itself an ample testimony to their wide knowledge base, extending far beyond their strict disciplinary background.

Another relevant aspect related to the sample composition is that the sample also covers experts from both the government and nongovernmental sectors. While experts within government are officials at the highest echelon of water administration in their respective countries, other nongovernment experts include retired officials, academics, and international consultants. As

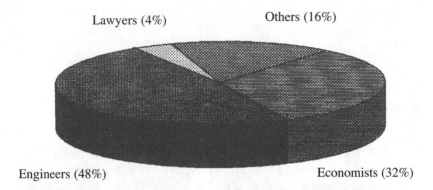

Lawyers (4%)   Others (16%)

Engineers (48%)   Economists (32%)

Figure 6.2   Disciplinary background of sample experts.

noted, since international exposure was one of the major criteria for their selection, the experts included in the sample have considerable knowledge about the water sector and its institutional arrangements in other countries. As we have argued, international exposure and learning possibilities are necessary conditions for the similarity or closeness of reference points across the respondents. This fact ensures the scope for comparability and convergence in perceptional evaluation. Overall, we can consider that the sample displays a wider diversity not only in terms of the background and experience of experts but also in terms of the development status, political arrangements, and resource endowments of their countries. It can, therefore, provide a broader spectrum of both country-specific and cross-country perspectives on the subjective perception of various linkages evident both within and between the water institution and water sector performance, and on the way such perception is influenced by objective and exogenous factors.

PERCEPTIONAL INFORMATION: EMPIRICAL VALIDITY AND INTERPRETATION

As shown, to evaluate mind change that forms the logical first stage of institutional change, we require specifically subjective and perceptional information. Similarly, it is also clear that the use of executive perception as an empirical basis for institutional analysis has empirical precedence, theoretical justification, and practical advantages. While perception-based subjective information has methodological legitimacy, pertinent questions remain, especially those related to the nature of such information, its interpretation, and its amenability to a formal statistical analysis. Since the validity of the results and the credibility of their policy implications are predicated ultimately on the quality of the information and the appropriateness of the method used for its analysis, some of these questions have to be answered at this stage. These answers will be valuable both to facilitate and to clarify the interpretation of the results presented in subsequent chapters.

Is the Perception-Based Information Comparable?

We have established the comparability properties of perceptional evaluation in the context of our discussion on instrumental evaluation and perceptional convergence. However, we need to consider a few additional aspects related to the comparability of perceptional information. The comparability of information is a precondition for its use in a regression context. The question about comparability arises both from the perceptional basis of the information and from the structure of the sample with different countries and different experts from the same country. Since water institutions and water sector issues differ both within and across countries, the responses of the experts are considered to reflect their subjective evaluation of different and apparently distinct institutional arrangements and performance conditions, especially using different reference points. While this suggests a problem for comparing perception-based information across individuals, we will argue to the contrary by showing that neither institutional diversity nor the reference point differences can be a constraint for comparison. The key to the argument lies in the conceptual basis assumed for the process of subjective evaluation.

Conceptually speaking, each country's water institution can be considered as a set containing all its legal, policy, and administrative features. For convenience, we can visualize this institutional set of each country as a circle. Although water institutions differ across countries, they share many common features. To reflect this fact, we consider an intersecting set of circles, each representing water institutions in different countries. The water institutional arrangements at the global level can then be represented by a larger circle that contains all these intersecting circles and includes country-specific and common institutional aspects.[11] This is depicted in Figure 6.3 where, for expositional convenience, we have considered the institutional arrangement in only three countries evaluated by six experts, with two of them evaluating the situation in each of the three countries.

In Figure 6.3, the segments denoted by A, B, and C represent country-specific institutional features; those denoted by D, E, and F represent the institutional features common to two countries. Segment G represents the institutional features common across all three countries. When these common institutional features are evaluated by experts even with a moderate level of cross-country knowledge on key institutional aspects, it is reasonable to expect

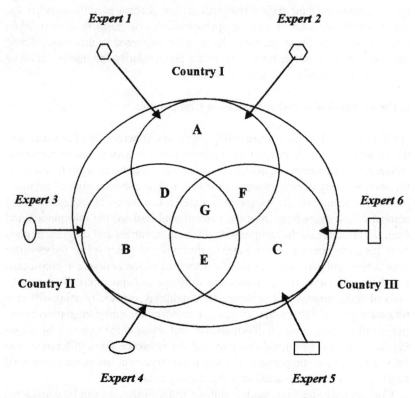

Figure 6.3   Logic for cross-country comparison of perceptual evaluation.

that they evaluate their country-specific situation with reference to a best or worst situation found elsewhere in the world or derived from theory. In this sense, the reference points being used by the experts for their evaluation are also likely to be similar, if not the same. This is exactly the case in the context of subjective evaluation being considered in our study. As we can see from the institutional and performance aspects identified and defined in Chapter 5, although their typologies and performance levels can vary across countries, these aspects as such are common across countries. Similarly, since the sample experts were purposively selected with consideration of their subject expertise and international exposure, they also have enough technical and cross-country knowledge on major institutional and sectoral features. Based on this reasoning, we consider the independent observations of the sample experts on various institutional and performance aspects to be comparable and hence, amenable to statistical treatment.[12]

Does Micro Institutional Diversity Inhibit the Evaluation?

This study evaluates how institutional variations affect the performance of the water institution and the water sector, but such an evaluation is essentially in terms of variations observed in major institutional typologies rather than in micro-level details. While country-specific and micro-level institutional details are definitely an important concern for studies dealing with institutional diversity at regional and local levels, they are not pertinent for the main purpose of this study. This can be illustrated by considering the legal format of water rights. While the format of water rights displays wider variations across countries, regions, and water sources, a generic set of key typologies of water-rights formats can still be identified and used for cross-country comparison. An illustrative set of such typologies of water-rights formats are the common-property rights, riparian rights, appropriative rights, correlative rights, and water permits.[13] Since this study requires only the evaluation of the relative effects of these broad categories rather than their micro-level variants, the evaluation is not constrained by institutional diversity at micro-level.

How to Interpret Variations in Experts' Responses?

When water institutions are effective in the sense that they are powerful enough to pervade the minds of decisionmakers and thereby influence their water allocation and use decisions, variations in the responses of experts are likely to be smaller. Otherwise, variations in the responses will be larger due to ambiguity where subjective factors, including ideology, can contribute to differential interpretations. If the subjective factors are powerful enough to disorient perception, it means that water institutions have failed in their basic role of providing a transparent framework for human–water interaction. Intuitively speaking, the magnitude of these variations can be considered a measure of institutional ineffectiveness. For instance, variations in factual information (e.g., the format of water rights or conflict-resolution mechanisms) among experts from the same country represent the degree of ignorance or uncertainty, which can be considered more as a measure of institutional ineffectiveness than a limitation of sample experts.

Similarly, since variations in the judgmental information of experts from the same country will be greater when institutions are ineffective and subjective factors such as bias and expectations are dominant, the magnitude of such variations can also be considered as a measure of institutional ineffectiveness. While intercountry variations in both kinds of information can be considered as an indication of cross-country variations in performance of both water institutions and the water sector, their intracountry variations can be interpreted as an indicator of uncertainty about the features of water institutions and their performance impacts. Since the main function of institutions is to reduce uncertainty and increase transparency, the extent of uncertainty or ambiguity evaluated in this manner can also provide comparative insights on the relative efficacy and performance of water institutions in different contexts. Irrespective of whether such ambiguities are inherent in institutions or are created deliberately by vested interests, they remain as an example of the failure of the institutionalizing function of institutions.

Can Perception-Based Data Be Used in a Regression Context?

The comparability of information, though necessary, is not sufficient to justify its use within a regression framework. The sufficient condition for the use of perception-based information in a regression context comes from the following observation that forms the very foundation of our evaluation methodology outlined above. Experts often say that the water sector performance of a given country or region is low because of poor institutional arrangements. This is not a casual statement, but is based on a mental process of evaluation that compresses both observed data and subjective information on water institution and water sector performance. If we can magnify the mental process of evaluation and derive the information used to reach the conclusion, a similar evaluation can be performed outside of that mental process. This is precisely what our evaluation methodology is trying to do. Since the regression exercise mimics the process of evaluation that occurs in the minds of experts and relies on the revelation of the same set of information used in such a process, the use of the perception-based information within a regression framework is intuitively consistent and justified.

Do the Regression Results Reflect Only the Expected Linkages?

The responses of experts are an outcome originating both from their observations of reality and from their expectations of a desirable situation. Hence, the regression results cannot be considered to reflect only the expected linkages. As long as the responses are truthful, the results can reflect the perception of actual linkages. Since the sample covers internationally known experts with a considerable stake on their reputation when revealing their knowledge and judgment, it is unreasonable either to question the integrity and objectivity of their responses or to consider the evaluation a hypothetical exercise for making self-fulfilling prophecies. Even when the regression results reflect only the expected linkages, they are still valid for evaluating the relative performance impact of institutional aspects. In this sense, the regression results can be considered as a means for finding an international consensus on the relative role and significance of various institutional aspects. As noted, such a consensus can be interpreted as an implicit demand for institutional configurations.

Can the Presence of an Institutional Aspect Ensure Better Performance?

Some of the equations in the model of institution–performance interaction postulate that the presence of an institutional aspect can improve performance on the reasoning that the performance of both the water institution and the water sector is likely to be better with than without their presence. This does not mean any mixing up of the 'cause' and 'effect.' Since there are sequential linkages and synergy among institutional components, institutional components that are considered to induce changes in the institutional and water sector spheres are themselves an outcome of prior changes in other institutional components. Considering a water-rights system as an example, the presence of such a system implies also the presence of some of the legal, policy, and administrative arrangements that are necessary to support its operation. While a water-rights system is a means for improving sector performance, it is also an end from the standpoint of institution building. Similarly, financial self-sufficiency or cost recovery, which is an end from the financial angle, is also a means for improving the physical health and operational efficiency of water projects. Thus, the cause–effect categorization is path dependent in the sense that a 'cause' can be an 'effect' and vice versa depending upon the objective of the evaluation and the route through which such evaluation proceeds.

DATABASE

The database for the study includes both the survey data obtained through our questionnaire from 127 sample experts as well as secondary data pertaining to sample countries. Given the three sets of models specified and described in Chapter 5, it goes without saying that the survey data provide the basis for estimating Models A and B whereas both the survey and secondary data provide the basis for estimating Model C. Since Models A and B are based exclusively on survey information, they are estimated with a sample consisting of the 127 experts' individual responses.

In contrast, Model C, with a hybrid information base, is estimated with a sample consisting of 39 countries. This is because comparable secondary information on all the exogenous variables that form the independent variables of this model can be obtained mostly at the national level. In view of this fact and the attendant need to ensure cross-sectional consistency, all the performance variables that form the dependent variables in all nine equations of

Model C are obtained by taking the average of individual responses from each of these 39 countries. In the case of the four US states (California, Colorado, Illinois, and Texas), considered as separate regions for survey purposes, the performance variables of the states were also averaged to represent the overall performance at the national level. With these facts in mind, let us have a brief look at both the survey and secondary database.

Survey Data

Given the elaborate and detailed nature of the questionnaire and the meticulous nature of the information provided by the respondents, our survey enables us to generate at least 75 variables. This list comprises 17 legal variables, 25 policy variables, 27 administrative variables, five water sector performance variables, and a water institution performance variable.[14] Of these 75 variables, we have selected only 26 to build Models A and B as specified in Chapter 5. These variables include 21 institutional variables (seven each of the legal, policy, and administrative variables), four institutional performance variables, and a water sector performance variable. As can be seen from the model specification, the selected institutional variables represent some of the most important institutional aspects receiving attention worldwide in the ongoing policy debate. The coverage of institutional aspects includes, among others, water rights, conflict resolution, accountability, privatization, user participation, decentralization, project selection and cost recovery, water transfers, organizational basis, pricing body, balance in functional specialization, information adequacy, and science and technology application. The descriptive statistics for the 26 institutional and performance variables included in Models A and B are given in Table 6.3.

Secondary Data

The objective of collecting secondary data is to develop variables to capture the role of physical, demographic, socioeconomic, and institutional factors that are exogenous to both the water institution and the water sector, but are having a strong influence on their performance. While these exogenous factors are many, attention is focused on the following crucial aspects. They are development status, demographic condition, resource scarcity, sectoral orientation of water economy, food production, social sector investment, distributional equity, ecological status, overall institutional effectiveness, and external perception of the creditworthiness of the country. To represent these aspects related to the overall environment within which institution–performance interaction occurs, a set of 12 variables is selected.

Table 6.3 Descriptive statistics for perception-based institutional and performance variables

Sl. no.	Variables			Mean values	Standard deviation	Range	
	Names	Acronyms	Types			Min.	Max.
Legal variables							
1	Treatment of surface and subsurfaces water	*LTRWSA*	Dummy	0.331	0.472	0.00	1.00
2	Format of surface water rights	*LPRSRE*	Category	2.606	1.470	0.00	7.00
3	Effectivesness of conflict-resolution provisions	*LCRMEE*	Scale	5.235	2.566	0.00	10.00
4	Effectiveness of accountability provisions	*LACPRE*	Scale	4.427	2.684	0.00	10.00
5	Degree of integration within water law	*LINTRE*	Scale	3.622	3.326	0.00	10.00
6	Tendency for centralization in water law	*LOECEN*	Scale	5.063	2.878	0.00	10.00
7	Scope for privatization in water law	*LOEPRV*	Scale	4.662	2.601	0.00	10.00
8	Overall effectiveness of water law	*LOEFWL*	Scale	5.361	2.059	0.00	10.00
Policy variables							
9	Project-selection criteria	*PPSCRI*	Category	3.530	1.561	0.00	6.00
10	Level of cost recovery	*PCOREC*	Category	2.230	0.712	0.00	4.00
11	Effectivness of water transfer policy	*PIRSWE*	Scale	3.277	2.384	0.00	8.75
12	Impact of private sector promotion policy	*PGPIPP*	Scale	4.284	3.105	0.00	10.00
13	Impact of user participation policy	*PGPIUP*	Scale	3.654	2.844	0.00	10.00
14	Impact of other policies on water policy	*POPAWE*	Scale	5.622	1.715	0.00	7.00
15	Overall linkage between law and policy	*POELWL*	Scale	5.660	2.429	0.00	10.00
16	Overall effectiveness of water policy	*POEFWP*	Scale	4.615	2.003	0.00	8.67

Table 6.3 continued

Sl. no.	Variables		Types	Mean values	Standard deviation	Range	
	Names	Acronyms				Min.	Max.
Administrative or organizational variables							
17	Organizational basis of water administration	*AORGBA*	Category	2.504	1.463	0.00	5.00
18	Balance in functional specialization	*ABALFS*	Dummy	0.472	0.501	0.00	1.00
19	Existence of independent water-pricing body	*AIBDWP*	Dummy	0.252	0.436	0.00	1.00
20	Seriousness of budget constraint	*ASBUDC*	Scale	3.381	3.289	0.00	10.00
21	Effectiveness of administrative accountability	*AACCME*	Scale	4.364	2.518	0.00	10.00
22	Adequacy of information	*AARINF*	Scale	6.217	2.190	0.00	10.00
23	Extent of science and technology application	*AEXTST*	Scale	4.463	1.989	0.00	10.00
24	Overall effectiveness of water administration	*AOEFWA*	Scale	4.828	2.050	0.00	9.00
Performance variables							
25	Overall evaluation of water institution performance	*WIPOEV*	Scale	5.499	2.033	0.00	10.00
26	Overall evaluation of water sector performance	*WSPOEV*	Scale	5.165	1.583	0.00	8.67

These 12 variables form the independent variables in all 9 equations of Model C as specified in Chapter 5. Since obtaining information on these variables at the national level is more meaningful and also easier, they are collected for the 39 countries covered in our country–regional sample.

Table 6.4 shows the descriptive statistics for the 12 exogenous variables obtained from secondary sources as well as the nine institutional and water sector performance variables obtained from our perception survey. As noted, the nine performance variables for each country are obtained by averaging the corresponding responses from all the experts from that country. That was done for all countries except the 13 for which there is only one response. The secondary information for most of the exogenous variables comes from the World Bank (1997, 2000a). The information on the share of natural capital in national wealth and the Environmental Regulatory Regime Index comes from Kunte, et al. (1998) and Esty and Porter (2000).

While the objective and rationale for the selection of the set of exogenous variables are obvious, we find two difficulties in getting comparable information for all 39 countries in the sample. First is the difficulty in getting data on all variables for the time period coinciding with that of the survey information. As a result, the time period of the data differs across variables as shown in Table 6.4. Although this problem is difficult to overcome, we tried to collect data for periods as close to the survey period as possible subject to data constraint. The second difficulty is related to the nonavailability of data on a few variables for one or more countries. In the case of these variables and countries, we used the corresponding data from similarly placed other countries as surrogate information following the approach used by Kunte, et al. (1998). The variables and the countries for which the surrogate data are used are listed in Table 6.5. As can be seen from this table, the surrogate information is used more heavily in the case of the two variables representing, respectively, the share of natural capital in national wealth and the Environmental Regulatory Regime Index as this information is not available for many countries in our sample.

In any case, these two problems related to the secondary data on the exogenous variables are not expected to affect the results of Model C in any serious manner for the following reasons. First, these exogenous variables are used essentially as indicators of the overall environment within which the process of institution–performance interaction occurs in the water sector of different countries. As a result, the differential time period of the variables is not going to have any serious effect. Second, since the surrogate approach is used mostly in the case of variables that take into account some of the qualitative and relative magnitudes, we expect that this approach will have little effect on the overall results. Tables 6.3 and 6.4 are instructive not only to give a flavor of the kind of survey and secondary information underlying the estimation

Table 6.4 Descriptive statistics for perceptional and observed variables used in hybrid models

Sl. no.	Variables				Mean values	Standard deviation	Range	
	Names	Units	Periods	Acronyms			Min.	Max.
Perception-based performance variables								
1	Overall effectiveness of water law	Scale	1998–00	*LOEFWL*	5.42	1.62	1.55	10.00
2	Overall effectiveness of water policy	Scale	1998–00	*POEFWP*	4.30	1.73	0.00	7.12
3	Overall effectiveness of water administration	Scale	1998–00	*AOEFWA*	4.84	1.72	0.00	8.75
4	Overall evaluation of water institution performance	Scale	1998–00	*WIPOEV*	5.43	1.73	0.00	8.50
5	Overall evaluation of physical performance	Scale	1998–00	*WSPPHY*	5.32	1.57	0.00	8.30
6	Overall evaluation of financial performance	Scale	1998–00	*WSPFIN*	5.17	1.80	0.00	8.25
7	Overall evaluation of economic performance	Scale	1998–00	*WSPECO*	4.41	1.93	0.00	8.75
8	Overall evaluation of equity performance	Scale	1998–00	*WSPEQU*	5.53	1.90	0.00	9.33
9	Overall evaluation of water sector performance	Scale	1998–00	*WSPOEV*	5.11	1.58	0.00	8.66

Observation-based exogenous variables

		(units)	Year	Abbrev.				
10	GNP(PPP)/capita	($)	1999	GNPPPC	9.97	8.80	0.24	30.60
11	Population density	(People/km²)	1999	POPDEN	154.95	186.49	2.00	981.00
12	Decadal change in urban population	(%)	1980–90	DCUPOP	7.15	7.48	–1.00	34.00
13	Freshwater withdrawal/year/capita	M³	1980–98	FWATWC	614.34	400.50	41.67	1639.90
14	Agricultural share in total water withdrawal	(%)	1987–98	PWATAG	65.10	29.87	0.00	99.00
15	Arable land/capita	(ha)	1995–97	ALANDC	0.33	0.48	0.03	2.75
16	Food Production Index (1989–91 = 100)	(Index)	1996–98	FPIIND	117.92	14.93	88.20	153.5
17	Public expenditure on education	(% of GNP)	1997	EXPEDU	4.73	1.95	1.20	9.10
18	Gini Index	(Index)	1985–97	GININD	37.64	8.20	24.90	60.00
19	Share of natural capital in total wealth	(%)	1990–94	NCNATW	8.08	6.30	1.00	22.00
20	Environmental Regulatory Regime Index	Score	1990–95	ENVRRI	–0.06	0.81	–1.52	2.71
21	Institutional Investor Credit Rating	(Index)	2000	ININCR	55.99	24.36	16.90	92.90

Table 6.5   Details on the use of surrogate data

SI. No.	Variables	Countries	Surrogates
1	*GININD*	Sudan	Tunisia
2	*EXPEDU*	Sudan	Tunisia
3	*ALANDC*	Sudan	Tunisia
4	*FPIIND*	Sudan	Tunisia
5	*ININCR*	Sudan	Tunisia
		Cambodia	Vietnam
		Laos PDR	Vietnam
6	*NCNATW*	Sudan	Tunisia
		Cambodia	Vietnam
		Laos PDR	Vietnam
		Poland	Netherlands
		Bolivia	Chile
		Israel	Jordan
		Myanmar	Thailand
7	*ENVRRI*	Sudan	Zimbabwe
		Tunisia	Zimbabwe
		Morocco	Zimbabwe
		Namibia	Zimbabwe
		Bangladesh	India
		Pakistan	India
		Sri Lanka	India
		Nepal	India
		Myanmar	Thailand

process but also as a necessary background for the interpretation of estimation results of the various models to be presented in Chapter 8 and 9.

NOTES

1. The fact that the subjective perception and mind change of stakeholders are considered as the motive force initiating institutional change does not mean that subjective perception can be used as a tool only in contexts where institutional changes have already occurred. Since the circular nature of the four stages of institutional change (Figure 4.1) ensures that subjective perception also captures the feedback effects from the fourth stage, it can equally be used as a basis for evaluating past, ongoing, and expected changes in institutions.
2. For instance, when water sector performance is good (poor) with objective results such as better (worse) cost recovery and higher (lower) agricultural production, the perception of sectoral performance by individuals will converge as the influence of objective factors predominates over that of the subjective aspects and value judgments.

3. For instance, suppose that person A considers that the performance of one institutional aspect deviates by 30 percent and another institutional aspect deviates by 20 percent from the ideal whereas the comparable figures for person B are 40 percent and 70 percent. In this case, we can see a relative convergence in the evaluation of the first institutional aspect as compared with its counterpart. If more and more people have evaluations closer to that of person B, there is a trend toward convergence around the valuation of person B. Such convergence also means that the ideals or the reference points of most individuals also remain identical or closer to that of person B. In this sense, it is relative rather than absolute comparability that is necessary to ensure convergence.

4. Bounded rationality is manifested not just in terms of cognitive and computational limitations but also in terms of communication limitation (Williamson 1975: 255). The limitations imposed by both bounded rationality and information impactedness can be minimized through the use of simplified language and commonly used idioms.

5. The countries visited were: Australia, Brazil, Chile, China, India, Israel, Mexico, Morocco, South Africa, Spain, Sri Lanka, and the United States.

6. Chapter 7 gives a comparative account of the water sector and recent water institutional changes observed across the sample countries.

7. Since they were not aware of the models of institution–performance interaction that we were going to use, the experts, while answering the questionnaire, did not have any idea that their responses to different questions would be linked in a particular way. This ensured unbiased and independent responses to different institutional and performance aspects included in the questionnaire.

8. This random element engendered into the sampling process has considerable value in minimizing possible bias in the process of institutional and performance evaluation.

9. The 43 questionnaires received in the first phase of the survey represented only 10 of the 12 countries as the experts contacted in Morocco and the four US states (California, Illinois, Colorado, and Texas) did not respond in time. As a result, their responses were subsequently included with the questionnaires received in the second phase of the survey.

10. We did try to cover more countries in Africa, especially Ghana, Kenya, Nigeria, Tanzania, and Zimbabwe, but the questionnaires sent to these countries were not returned. Despite a lower coverage of countries in terms of numbers, the survey did cover other important countries of the continent such as Egypt, Morocco, Namibia, Sudan, Tunisia, and South Africa.

11. A similar analogy can be extended to conceptualize the water sector at the global level.

12. Even if the ideal situation is not exactly the same, the independently reported judgmental values can still be comparable – within and across countries – in the same sense as consumption expenditure or poverty level are compared across individuals and countries with different utility for money and living-standard norms. Again, from another perspective, the values are conceptually not much different from those obtained from willingness-to-pay or contingent valuation surveys among individuals with different socioeconomic backgrounds and other subjective characteristics.

13. Various combinations of two or more of these water-rights formats can also be taken as an institutional typology.

14. The full data set containing the 127 observations on these 75 variables can be obtained from the authors upon request with an understanding that the information will be used for academic, policy, and noncommercial purposes.

7. Institutional changes in the water sector: a cross-country review

Institutional arrangements governing the water sector have been undergoing remarkable changes worldwide. Although the extent and depth of these changes vary by country-specific economic, political, and resource realities, they evince noteworthy commonalities. What are the nature and direction of these institutional changes? What prompts and sustains such changes? How pronounced are the common trends and patterns? Are there 'best practice' cases? How relevant are they for universal application? This chapter is intended to provide some answers to these and related questions based on a review of institutional changes in our sample countries. Given the scope of our study and purpose of this chapter, the cross-country review reported here is brief, focusing on key features and thrusts of reforms observed up to the survey period.

Though neither complete nor comprehensive, this review is significant on four counts. First, since it highlights the relative influence of exogenous factors (e.g., socioeconomic, demographic, political, and resource-related aspects), the review provides cross-country anecdotal evidence for the effects of the overall institutional environment both on institution–performance interaction (Figure 5.2) and on the perception of sectoral performance (Model C). Second, since the review is performed within an analytical framework rooted in institutional transaction cost theory, the occurrence and depth of reforms across countries can be understood and explained as a direct outcome of a transaction cost–opportunity cost calculus. Third, despite its brevity, the review can place sample countries in the four stages of our perception-based conception of institutional change. And, finally, the review provides a physical and political economy context for the quantitative analysis of institution–performance interaction within water sector presented in the ensuing chapters.

WATER INSTITUTIONAL CHANGE: AN ANALYTICAL FRAMEWORK

Cross-country review can be illuminating when performed within an analytical framework based on institutional transaction cost theory. The institutional transaction cost approach, as developed by North (1990a), is more general than the original transaction cost approach, as it can also incorporate the real costs associated with many noneconomic and nonmarket aspects. Thus, this approach can capture the individual and interactive effects of both economic and noneconomic factors within a common analytical framework. In the water sector context, the factors affecting water institutions are many, with diverse origins and varying impacts. For analytical convenience, they can be grouped into endogenous factors internal to the water sector and exogenous factors outside the confines of both the water institution and the water sector.[1] Since the exogenous and endogenous factors are interrelated and their relative impacts differ by context, it is difficult either to isolate their individual roles or to generalize the direction of their effects. However, their effects can be tracked within the institutional transaction cost framework by conceptualizing them as part of either the transaction costs or the opportunity costs of institutional change. For water institutions, the transaction costs cover both the real and monetary costs of instituting regulatory, monitoring, and enforcement mechanisms related to water development, allocation, and management. Similarly, the opportunity costs cover both the real and economic values of opportunities forgone or the net social costs of maintaining the status quo. Since the transaction cost theory asserts that institutional change occurs when the opportunity costs exceed the transaction costs to trigger a political thrust for reform, it is consistent both with the welfare-theoretic logic and the political economy argument.

Although the opportunity and transaction costs are difficult to quantify exactly, they can be identified and approximated. Unfortunately, the prevailing approaches for the estimation of the opportunity and transaction costs of institutional change are static and partial, as they account neither for the dynamics of institutional interlinkages nor for the impact of exogenous factors. Since institutional interlinkages and exogenous factors often exert a powerful influence on the nature, direction, and speed of institutional change, their exclusion leads to an underestimation of the true potential for institutional change in a given context. Institutional change is not a one-time event but rather a continuum that moves in line with changing resource realities, socioeconomic needs, and political power structure. As reforms initiated in the early stages brighten the prospects for downstream reforms, intricate and functional linkages develop between the transaction costs of subsequent reforms and the opportunity costs of earlier reforms.[2] Similarly, since institutional changes within the water sector derive considerable synergy from exogenous factors reflecting changes elsewhere in the economy, the transaction costs of water sector reforms can also decline due to scale economies in institutional change.[3]

The opportunity and transaction costs of institutional changes are not static but change continuously due to the effects of institutional interlinkages as well as the impacts of endogenous and exogenous factors. For instance, when water scarcity becomes acute due to economic development and population growth, the real and the economic costs of inappropriate water institutions rise, creating both an economic and a political urge for change. Similarly, economic reforms magnify the fiscal implications whereas natural calamities such as droughts and floods aggravate the political implications of the opportunity costs of inappropriate institutions. Political reforms involving nationwide institutional changes, on the other hand, reduce the transaction costs of water sector reforms directly because the institutional changes within the water sector form only a small part of the overall reform process. Likewise, technical progress (e.g., satellite and information technologies and computer-based water control structures) can also reduce the transaction costs of institutional changes. As the exogenous factors magnify the opportunity costs of water crisis and reduce the transaction costs of water sector reforms, they often provide a powerful economic and political thrust for institutional change within the water sector.

The analytical framework based on transaction cost theory captures not only the role of factors both within and outside the water sector but also the strategic significance of certain dynamic aspects of institutional change such as institutional interlinkages and scale economies. Although the set of factors affecting institutional change varies little across countries, their relative significance in the opportunity and transaction costs calculus vary by country-specific contexts. The contextual nature of these variations explains why countries differ in the extent and depth of water institutional reform. As the transaction cost theory provides a unified framework to track and account for the effects of myriad factors affecting institutional change, it can be used as a theoretical basis for explaining both country-specific and cross-country variations in the nature and the direction of water institutional changes.

WATER INSTITUTIONAL CHANGES: A CROSS-COUNTRY REVIEW

Before attempting a review of institutional changes across sample countries, the following aspects must be recognized. First, we need to keep in mind (a) the institutional transaction cost framework discussed above; (b) the subjective theory of institutional change with its stage-based conception of the change process (Chapter 4), and (c) the socioeconomic profile and water sector features of sample countries (Table 6.1). Since these aspects provide the framework and context, they can enhance our understanding of the 'why' and 'how' of the observed institutional changes. Second, from an analytical perspective, the review can be organized on a country-by-country basis or by classifying the sample countries in terms of their reform status, resource situation, development status, or geographic location. However, we chose to organize the review in terms of eight geographic regions: North America, Latin America, Europe, Africa, Middle East, South Asia, Southeast Asia, and Oceania. This is to reflect regional variations in development status, water resource realities, and reform initiatives. And, finally, the review has a varied focus and coverage of country-specific situations, partly because countries with recent reforms need more attention and partly because we lack comparable information. Let us now present a quick review of water institutional changes.

North America Region

Water quality and environment are the major concerns in *Canada*'s water sector and the focus of recent legal and policy initiatives there (Canadian National Committee on Irrigation and Drainage 2000; International Commission on Irrigation and Drainage 2000b). The Federal Water Act and Federal Water Policy, formulated in the mid-1980s, provide a national framework for protecting water quality and enabling sustainable water management. While the federal–provincial body, the Canadian Council of Ministers of the Environment, has a policy and oversight role at the national level, regional interests and locational aspects have led to noteworthy changes in provincial water laws and policies. For instance, the Federal Irrigation Act has undergone changes in Ontario and Quebec. Ontario is preparing the Water Resources and the Environmental Protection Act, as well as the Pesticides Act, to address its water quality and environmental problems. Similarly, Quebec is preparing a new Water Management Policy with an integrated approach to water resources management. Since Canada shares several transboundary rivers and water bodies with the United States, water management in Canada has an international dimension. The water implication of climatic change is a major long-term issue for the Canadian water sector.

Latin America Region

Prompted by the macroeconomic crisis of the late 1980s, *Mexico* has initiated unprecedented reforms in the water sector beginning with its irrigation sector in 1988. This reform involved a transfer of 2.9 mha – representing 87 percent of the area under major and medium irrigation and 46 percent of the entire irrigated area – to 386 water user associations (WUAs). On the legal front, the National Water Law and the Federal Law of Regulations in Water Matters were enacted in 1992 and 1994, respectively. On the policy front, the accent is on decentralization and privatization, including water transfers via a rights market (Hearne, 1998). While water supply functions are being moved to provinces and municipalities, financially self-dependent utilities and private companies are being created in urban areas (Hazin 1998). With the successful experience of the Llerma Basin Council (1989), the basin approach has been extended to the Rio Bravo (1994) and the Valley of Mexico (1996) Basins. To encourage private irrigation investment, the New Agrarian Act has relaxed the ceiling for irrigated land from 20 ha to 100 ha. The legal and policy changes coupled with the irrigation management transfer (IMT) have also led to other changes in water administration. The Commisión Nacional del Agua, the key organ of water administration, has been moved from the Ministry of Agriculture to the Secretariat of Environment, Natural Resources, and Fishing.

Chile has well-developed institutional arrangements favorable to market-based water allocation, decentralized management, and private sector partici-pation. Under the 1981 Water Code and the 1988 Constitution, water use rights are treated as private property, independent of land, that can be traded, used as collateral, and classified as assets for tax purposes (Gazmuri and Rosegrant 1994). Responsibilities have also been better demarcated within Chilean water administration. The state grants quantified water rights to users, and active water markets reallocate such rights within and across sectors. Water user associations (WUAs) distribute water, collect fees, and maintain the system. WUAs and courts resolve conflicts (Gazmuri and Rosegrant 1994; Hearne and Easter 1995, 1997). In the urban sector, corporatization and privatization of state-owned water supply agencies and the consequent entry of private water companies have improved the coverage and quality of water and sanitation services (Gazmuri and Rosegrant 1994: 25). To avoid speculation and discour-age large-scale water-rights transfer from agriculture to the power and urban sectors, legislation has been proposed to allow forfeiture of water rights after five years of nonuse and to create sector-specific water rights. The Environmental Law of 1994 mandates water supply agencies to treat waste-water and stipulates minimum instream flow for ecological purposes.

The Constitution of 1988 marks the beginning of water sector reforms in *Brazil*. By distinguishing 'federal waters' from 'state waters,' the Constitution makes both federal and state governments responsible for water management. The National Water Resource Policy Law, delayed since 1991 due to federal–state disagreements, was passed in 1997. Eight major states have also passed their own water laws. While law precludes ownership rights, it does allow private use rights. On the water administration front, the long predomi-nance of the power sector in national water policy ended in 1995 with the transfer of water from the Ministry of Mining and Energy to the newly created Ministry of Environment, Water Resources, and Legal Amazon. Despite the attempt to consolidate water issues within a single administrative apparatus, many water-related functions (e.g., irrigation, extension, urban water supply, and water quality) remain administratively dispersed. There are also trends toward administrative decentralization and privatization of urban systems. The creation of the National Water Resource Management System and the establishment of national-, basin-, and state-level water councils are expected to improve coordination.

Water sector reforms in *Argentina* are less extensive than in Mexico, Chile, and Brazil, but there were some significant institutional initiatives (Artana, Navajas, and Orbiztondo 1999; World Bank 2000b). Argentina has made several significant reforms and is planning more changes. While water scarcity, salinity, and drainage problems, water quality and pollution issues, and floods create constant pressure for reform, the immediate impetus came from financial and performance crises in the irrigation and water supply systems and the severe fiscal problems facing both national and provincial governments. The reforms focused on decentralization and privatization. Most irrigation districts under federal administration were transferred to the provinces with plans for the eventual transfer of management to WUAs. A hundred major dams with a total capacity of 160 bcum are being operated by the private sector. The Buenos Aires concession of 1993 and similar arrangements in Corrientes province are the chief examples of privatization of the water supply and sanitation systems. Currently, efforts are afoot to create a common regulatory framework for all provinces, prepare a national water master plan, and modernize the water sector in general and irrigation sector in particular.

European Region

The major features of the water sector and its management systems in the *United Kingdom*[4] are urban orientation, quality-induced scarcity, and centralized regulation with decentralized service provision by private companies [Department of Environment, Transport and the Regions 1998a, 1998b; Rees and Zabel 1998a, 1998b; Office of Water Services (OFWAT) 1999a, 1999b]. Water is a shared resource with private use rights and public management rights. The United Kingdom has no exclusive water law; the legal principles for water management are derived from common law and case law. Apart from water rights, some of the long-standing UK institutions include regional water authorities, private involvement, and a system for charging for water use and pollution. Privatization of water services started in the late 1970s, gained momentum in 1985, and was completed in 1989. The Regional Water Authorities have become Water and Sewerage Companies, regulated by OFWAT and by the Drinking Water Inspectorate. The Department of Environment is responsible for water planning; the National River authority, for planning coordination. Although the planning and implementation processes are participatory, there are also several avenues for dispute resolution. Water policies in the United Kingdom, as in other members of the European Union (EU), are affected by European Community (EC) water framework directives. The separation of regulatory functions from operational functions and public–private partnership have contributed to effective management and improved services, although rigid price regulations and mixed payment systems have some negative effects on efficiency and equity.

The water sector and its institutional arrangements in *France* have undergone significant changes in recent years (Agence Loire-Bretange 1998; Barraque, Berland, and Cambon 1998: 85–182; Barraque, Berland, and Floret-Miguet 1998; Betlem 1998a, 1998b; Rees and Zabel 1998a, 1998b; Rees, Zabel, and Buckland 1998; Santos and Rodrigues 1998). These changes have created and strengthened a basin-based and participatory framework for water management in France. In 1964, basin-based institutional arrangements were created with six basin agencies and 25 departments. The water law of 1992 has further sharpened their managerial, regulatory, and monitoring functions. Since the basin agencies lack enforcement power, the 'river contract', an institution based on voluntary collective action, and Police de l'Eau, an institution responsible for monitoring water withdrawal and discharge, have evolved to strengthen monitoring and enforcement. Since basin committees are more heavily represented, state power in these committees has declined from one-half to one-fifth of the seats. A reform prepared in 1998 has intended to improve the financial means for water law enforcement, for example by charging for agricultural pollution and flood-risk aggravation. Latest policy trends include the introduction of catchment planning agencies at basin and subbasin levels, partial transversalization of water services in large cities, and the creation of municipality-owned water companies in other urban areas. The EC has also substantially influenced water sector reforms in France. Since 1989, legal changes have been introduced to comply with EC directives on water subsidies, water quality, and environment.

The water sector in *Spain* is spatially organized into 14 river basin organizations (RBOs) known as Confederaciones Hidrograficas. These RBOs, though operating under the Ministerio de Obras Publicas y Transportes (MOPT), are the real executive arm of water administration responsible for water development, bulk allocation, pricing, monitoring, and enforcement. Operating below the RBOs are the municipalities and irrigation communities that distribute water, collect charges, and resolve conflicts locally. The 1985 water law allows users to obtain use- and source-specific water and discharge permits from the RBOs. As mandated by this law, a comprehensive National Water Plan and Basin Water Plans were prepared in 1993 (MOPT 1993). Since Spain is an EU member, its water policies – especially those related to water subsidies and water quality – are strongly influenced by EC agricultural and environmental policies. As per the EC water framework directives, Spain prepared, in 1994–95, a plan for time-bound improvement in water quality. In addition to meeting the subsidy and water quality targets, the EC also requires Spain to reduce its irrigated area by 10 percent.[5] Recent initiatives include proposals to introduce transferable use rights, grant financial autonomy to RBOs, construct new projects only with users' prior agreement to pay the full costs, and encourage private participation in construction, distribution, sewage treatment, and pollution control.

Portugal's major water problems are regional water disparities, heavy evapotranspiration (50 percent of available water), and substantial trans-boundary flow (a third originating from Spain). Responding to these and other problems, Portuguese water institutions are changing significantly (Correia, et al. 1998; Maia 2000). By law, surface water is largely public, and groundwater is private but subject to public regulation. Legal changes in 1990 reoriented the legal framework from agency- and sector-specific regulations to an integrated approach to water management. In 1993, significant changes were initiated in both policy principles and administrative structure. The policy principles are: (a) to prepare water plans at the national, basin, and subbasin levels; (b) to implement them through the national and basin-level water councils; (c) to license water use rights; and (d) to introduce the polluter-and-user-pays principle in all sectors by 2004. The Ministry of Environment was restructured to create the Secretariat for Natural Resources with a national mandate and five regional directorates with basin-level mandates for water management. Created by dismantling previous basin structures, the new river basin management structures need time to develop and mature. Since the 1993–94 legislation, privatization of urban water supply has been initiated in five metro regions, including Lisbon, and the corporatization initiative has created 12 state-owned water companies in other urban centers. While environmental auditing and inspection and public–private partnership are the main vehicles used to comply with EC water framework directives, relatively old water treatment technologies continue to limit progress.

Apart from the internal pressure from water quality and scarcity problems, the water sector in *Germany* is also affected by the political aspect of German reunification and the international aspects of EC directives related to water sector and water-sharing agreements. Although the legislative framework for water management in Germany is recent, the regulatory regime is more matured with a reliance on permitting and licensing procedures as well as on economic instruments (Kraemer and Jager 1998; Rees and Zabel 1998b; Rees, Zabel, and Buckland 1998). The principle that water should be managed as part of the environment is maintained in both law and policy. Germany's three-tiered political arrangement is reflected in its water administration. Since reunification, East Germany's centralized administrative structure has been being gradually reformed. The multiple organizational arrangements at the

federal, provincial, and local levels create coordination and enforcement difficulties. Although a centrally coordinated research and education system is
absent, there are successful private sector initiatives in this important area. The
German water institution has several strong points: separation of managerial
and operational functions and integration of direct regulation with economic
incentives. Its main weaknesses are lack of coordination and insufficient articulation of water quality and environment in water policy.

The evolution of water management institutions in the *Netherlands* is
dictated not only by factors such as economic development and population
expansion but also by two geographical features (Perdock 1998). With a
significant area (30 percent) and population (60 percent) below mean sea
level, the Netherlands faces the problems of both water scarcity and water
excess. Since nearly three-quarters of water inflow originates outside the
border, two-thirds of inflow from the Rhine alone, the international dimension
is inescapable. Both these features also create water quality and drainage-
related problems. The most important legislation is the Organic Law, which
consists of constitutional rules for various organizations involved in water
management, such as the state, provinces, municipalities, and water boards.
Besides this law, there are the State Act (1971), stipulating the water tasks of
the state, and the Water Boards Act (1992), specifying the operational rules for
water boards. In terms of the legal framework, water management is mainly
the task of public administration, with the state, province, and local and
regional bodies sharing management responsibilities. However, the planning
and management process is highly participatory and transparent. The water-
rights system is well established, allowing users to acquire water rights by
property transfer, acquisition, inheritance, or reallocation subject to public
regulatory rights. Despite its institutional maturity and resilience, the Dutch
water sector still faces major challenges in managing floods, controlling
nonpoint pollution, ensuring the financial viability of water boards, and meeting the EC water directives. Many provinces have adopted the National Water
Policy, but it is not yet fully operational.

Irregular water distribution, weak water retention (only 5 percent of annual
precipitation), pollution and nitrate contamination, and extreme dependence
on the Wisa and Odra River Basins (sources of 80 percent of available water)
are the major features of the water sector in *Poland*. The legal system is weak
and water management issues are approached from an environmental perspective (Berbeka 2000; Lorek 2000; Polish National Committee on Irrigation and
Drainage 2000). Thus, the Ministry of Environment, the chief body responsible for water management at the national level, has a broad mandate, including environmental protection, and pollution prevention and monitoring. The
national policies are being implemented by corresponding agencies at the
provincial and local levels. Each province (*voivodship*) has a Department for

Environmental Protection with both management and regulatory functions, including issuing permits and setting discharge standards. The main responsibilities of *gminas*, the local governments in Poland, include water supply and wastewater treatment. Agencies outside the Ministry of Environment (e.g., the state- and provincial-level Inspectorate for Environmental Protection and the National Fund for Environmental Protection and Water Management) also play important roles in areas such as enforcement, data gathering, and financial support.

Pressed by increasing water scarcity and the EC water framework directives on water and the environment, the water sector and its institutions in *Italy* are witnessing noteworthy changes (Massarutto 1999; Italian National Committee on Irrigation and Drainage 2000; United Nations 2000). Although Italian legal and institutional water policy frameworks have undergone major reforms to conform to EC directives, implementation and enforcement still lag. Only with the Law 36/1994 was the government able to establish that all water uses need licenses. However, licensing is difficult to implement and enforce, as it is implemented by the peripheral administration of the Ministry of Public Works through its regional organs. Besides, regional autonomy and diverse management structures (e.g., an almost exclusive reliance on public irrigation in the south but heavy involvement of private water users in the north) also create their own constraints. Water issues concerning more than two regions are dealt with by the relevant basin authorities with the involvement of some state ministries. Despite significant progress in the last 20 years, many areas still need urgent reform. These include the framing of a comprehensive water policy applicable across uses and regions, enhancing the coverage and effectiveness of economic instruments, and strengthening administrative coordination among public agencies at various levels.

Africa Region

The radical changes witnessed in the water sector of *South Africa* are part of the ongoing process of post-Apartheid economic and political reconstruction. The water law enacted in 1998 defines a modern legal system conducive to management decentralization, market-based water allocation, full cost recovery, and integrated water resource management (Department of Water Affairs and Forestry (DWAF) 1999). By law, private and tradable use rights can be obtained from the DWAF. Natural Resources Courts are created to resolve water conflicts. The White Paper on National Water Policy (DWAF 1997) gives top priority to capacity building, information needs, and human resource development. Water charges – applicable only in the public irrigation system – will be extended to all irrigation systems. Similarly, the WUAs – currently operating mostly in sugarcane zones – are to be extended to other areas. On the administration front, the creation of a National Public Water Utility has been proposed to finance, develop, and operate all water infrastructure (DWAF 1997: 29). Basin entities – known as Catchment Management Agencies – are being created to involve farmers, irrigation boards, and municipalities as stakeholders. The relative success of water boards – the regional public utilities for bulk water supply – is paving the way for the creation of new regional water organizations (e.g., the Lesotho Highlands Water Project and Komati Basin Water Authority).

Despite a centralized political structure, water administration in *Morocco* evinces remarkable decentralization tendencies. The water law of 1995 has led to significant changes in the spheres of water policy and water administration. It makes the Supreme Water Council (involving all major water sector stakeholders) the key organ for national water policy and the RBOs – each covering one or more Regional Authorities for Agricultural Development – the regional nodes of water administration. The national and basin water plans mandated under the law are to provide the technical framework for formulating national and regional water management strategies. By advocating the user-pay principle and full cost recovery, the law requires water abstraction and pollution taxes. Recent ministerial reorganization has brought together agriculture, water, and environment under the Ministry of Agriculture, Equipment, and Environment. The ongoing programs for canal lining, pressurized supply of canal water, and installation of sprinkler and drip systems are intended to enhance water use efficiency in irrigation. Urban water conservation achievements in Rabat, through demand-side management, and in Casablanca, through a privatized water supply system, suggest new avenues for reforming the urban water sector.

The water sector in *Sudan* is characterized by acute regional variations (drought in the north but floods in the south), heavy dependence on shared Nile water (79 percent), meager share of groundwater (16 percent), high evapotranspiration, and extreme irrigation orientation (91 percent). Water issues top the policy agenda, but actual reforms are inversely proportionate to intentions and requirements (Adam 1997; Economic Intelligence Unit 2000c; World Bank 2000c; Government of Sudan 2001). The legal framework of the water sector has seen a major change since the enactment of the Water Resources Act in 1995, which updated and consolidated all previous water-related acts. The Ministry of Irrigation and Water Resources (MIWR) handles nearly all water resources under the overall policy guidance and coordination of the National Council for Water Resources. The National Water Corporation is responsible for drinking water supply. The Irrigation Water Corporation – established under the MIWR in 1995 – is responsible for managing the irrigation sector, but the Gezira irrigation scheme, accounting for 35 percent of Nile supply, is under the Sudan Gezira Board. On the policy front, pricing mechanisms remain weak, and pricing reform, including a 15 percent to 20 percent increase in water rates, is being resisted. Policies are also needed to create additional supplies (by increasing storage in the Roseires dam and by managing the wetlands[6] in the Nile Basin) and to improve allocation of the existing supply. Current dialogue is dominated by issues such as the National Water Policy and the reorientation of water administration to improve coordination, transparency, and capacity building.

The water sector in *Namibia* is marked by water scarcity due to poor rain and regular droughts, predominance of domestic and livestock needs (50 percent), dispersed population settlement, and the international nature of all rivers. These features affect the water institutional structure and its direction of change (Heyns 1997, 1999; Economic Intelligence Unit 2000b). The legal framework of the water sector is based on the largely outdated Water Act of 1954. The Department of Water Affairs within the Ministry of Agriculture, Water, and Rural Development is the main nodal agency for water management. Among the last decade's changes on the policy and administrative fronts, a 1993 policy for the water supply and sanitation sector calls for cost sharing and community management. While water tariffs are fixed to cover mainly the operation and maintenance (O&M) costs, they increased by 17 percent to 30 percent a year between 1993 and 1998. The Water Supply and Sanitation Coordination Committees were established to ensure functional and operational integration. The Namibia Water Corporation Limited (NamWater) – a state-owned autonomous body – was established in 1998 to manage bulk water supply and create and maintain water infrastructure. The comprehensive sector review, conducted in 1996 with World Bank assistance, calls for major reforms in the spheres of capacity building, economic incentives, and law and regulation. Regional cooperation is another critical area needing attention to meet Namibia's growing water needs.[7]

The water sector in *Egypt* has a strong orientation toward irrigation and relies almost exclusively on Nile water that is shared with other Nile riparians – Sudan and Ethiopia – under an international agreement. Thus, water institutional arrangements in Egypt revolve mainly around the Nile system and its agriculture (World Bank 1994, 2000c; Amer 2000; Saghir, Schiffler, and Woldu 2000). The Nile-based canal system is operated by the Irrigation Department within the Ministry of Public Works and Water Resources, the chief body for water management under Law No. 48 of 1982 and Law No. 12 of 1984. The National Water Research Center supports the ministry in its policy and management tasks. The Egyptian water sector is also influenced by other agencies (e.g., Environmental Affairs Agency) and ministries (e.g., Health, Housing, Public Utilities and New Communities, and Agriculture and Land Reclamation). Besides external pressures from population growth and economic development, the Egyptian water sector, with its small resource base, also faces mounting pressures from salinity, lower water productivity, and poor financial and system performance. As a result, water policies are slowly moving away from reliance on the Nile system to focus on groundwater development, water harvesting from flash floods, and desalinization. In addition, some success has been achieved in water conservation and drainage water reuse.

The water sector in *Tunisia* is noted for its meager resource base due to low rainfall, vulnerability to droughts, and susceptibility of aquifers to seawater intrusion. Other features include the predominance of irrigation (79 percent), high user involvement, and increasing reliance on water reuse (World Bank 1993; Zekri 1997; Saghir, Schiffler, and Woldu 2000). Laws 58-63, 60-6, 63-18, and 71-9 are the early legislative attempts for government management and users' cost-sharing obligations. Besides the refinements in the overall legal framework, the 1975 Water Code also transformed the concept of 'water rights' from ownership rights to use rights. In 1989, the Tunisian parliament approved Law 89-44 to allow the creation of an independent public institution with financial autonomy to be responsible for managing and maintaining irrigation infrastructure. While the government finances most water and irrigation development schemes, a tradition of user involvement in operation, maintenance, and management functions dates to the Law of 1933, passed by the French colonial administration. Of the 2,450 WUAs operating in Tunisia, 800 are in irrigation schemes, 1,500 are in water supply schemes, and 150 are in irrigation-cum-water supply schemes. Efforts are being made to reduce state involvement, improve finance and administration, strengthen private sector involvement, and implement demand-management strategies.

Middle East Region

The 1959 water law remains the foundation for water policy and water administration in *Israel*. The Water Commission (WC), previously under the Ministry of Agriculture but now under the Ministry of Infrastructure, is the implementing organ of water law. At the operational level, the WC relies on Mekorot,[8] a state-owned water company handling 70 percent of Israel's water supply. The WC receives technical support from Tahal.[9] Despite the political overtones, economic factors have a decisive impact on water use through metered allocation and volumetric pricing. While politics favors water allocation toward domestic sectors, urban water prices cover the full supply cost. Although irrigation water is subsidized, the subsidy has declined from 75 percent to 50 percent since the introduction of progressive block-rate pricing in 1987 to penalize large freshwater consumers (Yaron 1997).[10] In its 1997 report, the Public Commission on the Water Sector proposed several changes to improve the institutional basis of Israel's water sector (Arlosoroff 1997).

The heart of the reform proposal involves a market-based approach and privatization within a strong framework of public regulation. A legislative proposal, still before the Israeli parliament, aims to enhance the private sector's role in urban water distribution, O&M, and sewage treatment.

South Asia Region

After the 1987 constitutional amendment in *Sri Lanka*, water sector responsibilities were divided between the union and provincial governments. Sri Lanka, like India, has neither an exclusive water law nor a declared water policy, but some 50 acts influence the water sector to varying degrees. A draft Water Resources Bill, under discussion since the early 1980s, has all the ingredients for a modern water law, including water permit systems, full cost pricing, an interministerial coordination mechanism, and water courts for conflict resolution (World Bank 1992: 168). Although 40-odd government agencies influence the water sector, only a few form the core of national water administration (Nanni 1996). A new institutional structure, as conceived in the Action Plan for Comprehensive Water Resources Management (Water Resources Secretariat 1997: 3), though delayed since 1998, is being put into place. Besides these macro changes, Sri Lanka has been following an integrated management transfer program since 1989. Under this progam, 757 WUAs have been registered with an operating area of 85,700 ha (Mahaweli Economic Authority (MEA) 1997).[11] Although Sri Lanka has a lengthy experience with basin organizations, the dissolution of basin organizations such as Gal Oya and the conversion of the Mahaweli Development Authority into a ministry are viewed as a reversal of its declared policy of decentralization. However, as a part of its policy of promoting privatization, in 1997 the government piloted a water company with shares owned by farmers in the Ridi Bendi Ela area.

India has no exclusive water law but many water-related and irrigation laws, most of them passed during colonial times. The drought of 1987 and the macroeconomic crisis of the late 1980s led to some important changes in water policy. While the drought led to the National Water Policy (NWP) of 1987,[12] the economic crisis of the 1980s forced many states to raise internal resources by improving cost recovery and external resources by mobilizing private funds.[13] The 1992 Committee on Pricing of Irrigation Water advocates water rate increases and group-based volumetric water distribution (Government of India (GOI) 1992). The 1992 Model Groundwater Bill, though not adopted by any state so far, advocates well permits, water metering, and withdrawal limits. A high-level national committee has advocated the promotion of private investments in the water sector (GOI 1995). A few states are already trying to obtain private funds directly, by inviting bids for project construction, and indirectly by issuing water bonds to tap the funds from the public for irrigation development (Saleth 1999). Water sector reforms are substantial in a few states (e.g., Andhra Pradesh, Madhya Pradesh, and Tamil Nadu) that have undertaken irrigation management transfer (IMT) and reorganized their water administration. Changes are visible in the policy and administrative spheres, but India still requires a radical restructuring of its water institutions based on the reform blueprint (World Bank 1998) developed jointly by the government and the World Bank.

The water sector of *Nepal* – the landlocked kingdom in the Himalayas – is noteworthy for its poverty reduction role, high share of public expenditure (37 percent), scarcity–floods syndrome, gross underutilization of hydropower potential (1 percent), and transboundary resource base. Some striking changes have recently occurred in the Nepalese water sector and its management institutions (Nepalese Delegation 1996; Economic and Social Commission for Asia and the Pacific 1997; World Bank 1997; Regmi, Sharma, and Vaidya 1998; Upadhyay and Regmi 1999; Sharma 2000). The legal framework of the water sector is defined by four acts: the Water Resources Act (1992), Electricity Act (1992), Nepal Water Supply Corporation Act (1989), and Environmental Protection Act (1996). The Water Resources Act makes water a state resource and licenses it for private use. The agencies directly responsible for the water sector are two departments (hydrology and meteorology, and irrigation) in the Ministry of Water Resources and one department (water supply and sewerage) in the Ministry of Housing and Physical Planning. In 1993 and 1997, the 1992 Irrigation Policy was amended to promote stakeholder participation, decentralization, privatization, and economic pricing. While progress has been made in IMT, development of micro water rights, and water pricing, many more reform tasks are incomplete, including regional cooperation with India to harness its irrigation and hydropower potential.

Water institution reform in *Bangladesh* has several challenges, especially in light of the poverty reduction role of water sector, frequent flood-related damages, and health hazards of arsenic water and poor drainage (Alam 1997; Rahman 1998; Bangladesh Water Development Board 2000; Nishat and Faisal 2000). Recent legal initiatives (e.g., the Environmental Conservation Act of 1995 and the Environmental Pollution Control Ordinance of 1997) are related more to water quality and floods than to water allocation and management, while those on the policy and administrative fronts address allocational and management aspects. For instance, the National Water Management Policy of 1999 takes an intersectoral perspective and streamlines water administration. The National Water Council is the chief policy body; the Ministry of Water Resources is the main executive agency for water resources management; and the Water Resources Planning Organization prepares and updates water sector plans. Since Bangladesh is located in the drainage basin of several international rivers, its institutional reform initiatives entail an international dimension. The

1996 Ganges water-sharing agreement between India and Bangladesh has provided a partial framework for joint water management between these two countries. With this agreement, the Joint Rivers Commission, which has dealt with water-sharing problems between the two countries in the past, has become still more important in dealing with daily problem solving, data sharing, and overall coordination.

Southeast Asia Region

Water sector reforms in *China* are closely linked to the economic liberalization programs initiated since the early 1980s. The 1988 water law, passed after a decade of consultations, has strengthened both water administration and water policy (The People's Republic of China (PRC) 1988). Considering water as the people's property, the law distinguishes the state's management and allocation rights from the people's use rights. It advocates water permits and full cost recovery, stipulates the basin as the basic management unit, and mandates the formulation of national, regional, and sectoral water plans. Despite a centralized political system, water sector management is quite decentralized.[14] The 1997 Law on Flood Control and National Policy on Pollution Control and Aquatic Protection address flooding and pollution.[15] The State Water Industry Policy of 1997 is unique for a socialist country as it allows private investment in the water sector (PRC 1997: 1). To create the institutional framework necessary to translate these policies into reality, the Ministry of Water Resources (MOWR) has prepared the Master Plan of the Water Law and Regulation System as well as the Water Legal System Construction (Ke Lidan 1997: 642, 645). Water-drawing permits are already being issued, and the institutional structures needed to support permit-based water allocation are expected to be in place by 2010.

The water sector and its institutional arrangements in *Cambodia* have to be viewed in the light of three aspects: the country's recovery from war and related political disturbances, transition from a command economy to a market-based economy, and its location in the Mekong River Basin, the main international basin in Southeast Asia. For political economy reasons, Cambodia's outdated water institutional arrangements are changing slowly (Royal Government of Cambodia 1996; Sisovann 1997; Sina 1998, 1999). The Environmental Protection and Natural Resources Law of 1996 is only tangentially related to the main water sector concerns. As to the water administration, the Ministry of Environment – established in the aftermath of 1993 elections – has primary responsibility for water resources management. However, with the creation of new investment laws and the initiation of five-year development plans, reform prospects are bright both in general and in water sector. Since water-related objectives are the focus of the 1996–2000 plan, efforts are being made to develop water law and water policy and to strengthen water administration. Since water-related decisions of up-stream countries of the Mekong River affect its water sector, Cambodia needs regional cooperation to better utilize its water resources potential. Considering the critical role of the regional institution, the Mekong River Committee, institutional reforms in Cambodia are to be crafted within the basin-based institutional arrangements.

Water management in *Thailand* is constrained by a heavy dose of centralization, a supply-driven approach, subsidy syndrome, and outdated institutions, but the situation has been changing since 1992 (Thai Delegation 1996; Jarayabhand, Sokultanjaroenchai and, Tongdhamachart, 1998; Aekaraj and Chevapraset 1999; Pattanee 2000; Molle 2001). Thailand lacks a comprehensive water law, but a draft water law is being prepared by the National Water Resources Committee, chaired by the prime minister. This law is expected to rectify weak spots in the legal framework for water management. Government policy lacks clear guidance in many areas, including water pricing, demand management, investment priorities, and information and technology application. The situation becomes further complicated, as nine national committees and more than 30 government agencies in nine ministries work in the policy and administrative arenas. Despite a somewhat bleak situation for water volume management, some progress has been made on water quality, both at the macro and micro levels, since the enactment of National Environmental Quality Act (1992) and the establishment of the Wastewater Management Authority (1995). Recently, policy has shifted noticeably toward a basin approach, demand-management strategies including allocation and pricing, and decentralization including user participation and private sector involvement.

Indonesia's archipelago nature complicates water management, but the country has taken steps to strengthen its water sector and management institutions (Indonesian Delegation 1996; Sutardi 1997; Ismaji 1998; Sosongko 1999; World Bank 1999a). Since water can be a limiting factor when withdrawals exceed an estimated 20 percent of water potential, allocation and management are a constant challenge. During the first water development plan (1969–93), water policies were formulated within the framework of Water Law 11/1974. As part of cost-recovery policy, Indonesia also promoted IMT in public irrigation systems. The initiatives undertaken to address water quality in 1982 include the Water Quality Management and Regulation Policy, the Clean River Program, and the creation of the National Environmental Agency. For administration purposes, Indonesia's 5,600 river basins are grouped into 73 river territories. The second water development plan (1994–2019) aims to strengthen water resources infrastructure and institutions. It adopted an integrated approach for water planning and management, especially within a basin framework. Indonesia still faces outstanding reform tasks, such as streamlining water administration including the creation of river basin structures, promoting private participation, and strengthening allocation mechanisms including the use of economic instruments and creation of water rights.

South Korea, like many other Southeast Asian countries, has to contend with severe water shortages and floods due to uneven rainfall patterns and poor water quality due to sedimentation and industrial pollution. As a response to these problems, the water management institutions of South Korea are changing, but not at the expected pace (Shim 1996; Ham 1997; Hee 1998; Kwun 2000). The legal framework for water management is defined by the River Act, Multipurpose Dam Act, Natural Disaster Prevention Act, Public Water Surface Area Management Act, and Water Quality Preservation Act. The Ministry of Construction and Transportation is the chief water management body. The Water Resources Bureau is responsible for policy preparation and coordination, but the Water Resources Corporation actually plans, develops, manages, and regulates dams in South Korea. The Ministry of Environment manages water quality aspects through direct control as well as economic instruments. The Ministry of Home Affairs, responsible for water supply, has recently launched a five-year comprehensive Plan for Clean Water Supply in collaboration with other ministries and agencies noted above. South Korea has prepared plans to create the institutional structures needed to manage surface and subsurface water and promote water conservation through water pricing, water reuse, and water-saving technologies.

The water sector in *Laos* is marked by its monsoon dependence, linkages with forest management, underutilization of hydropower and irrigation potential (less than 2 percent and 20 percent, respectively), significance of the Mekong River Basin (with 38 percent share in total basin flow), and quality impairment from sedimentation. Water institutional reforms are still closer to proposals than initiatives, but a few definite steps have been taken (Rasphone 1996; Souvannabouth 1997; Souk 1998, 1999). There are some water-related policies at subsectoral and regional levels, but Laos does not have a national water resources policy. Similarly, while water-related provisions are scattered in the 1991 Constitution, the Water Law of 1996 was the first law devoted exclusively to water. This law provides a framework for a basin-based intersectoral approach to water management and applies water quality criteria for ecosystem protection. However, the law still needs clarification through appropriate decrees from relevant ministries. On the policy front, issues such as water licensing, water pricing, community participation, private sector partnership, and regional cooperation figure prominently in the legal and policy dialogues. On the administrative front, the multiplicity of administrative entities and absence of a national water master plan create serious problems for administrative and technical coordination. Since Laos is a member of the Mekong River Committee, its water sector could also benefit from international cooperation.

The water sector and its institutional arrangements in *Vietnam* are affected by problems common to the Indo-China Peninsula as well as by those that are specific to the country's own political past and economic future. These problems include the syndrome of scarcity–flood-water quality, monsoon pattern and topography, past political events involving prolonged war and internal conflicts, and people's economic aspirations (World Bank 1995, 1999b; Su 1996, 1998; World Bank, et al. 1996; Nam 1997; Nguyen 1999; Tu 2000). While the 1992 Constitution provides the overall legislative and administrative framework for water resource management, the Water Resources Law of 1999 defines more specific legal provisions, including the license and permit systems, and monitoring and enforcement mechanisms. For water quality, the National Law on Environmental Protection of 1993 was enacted. The Ministry of Water Resources was dismantled and its functions given to the Ministry of Agriculture and Rural Development, and the Ministry of Planning. Other ministries related to construction and urban development, planning and investment, environment, and energy also have an influence on the water sector. Water management at the local level shows significant decentralization as local committees of users maintain and manage both irrigation and water supply schemes. However, extensive reforms are still needed on both the policy and administrative fronts as the legal provisions on water volume and quality have yet to be translated into operational policies, and fragmented regulatory and enforcement mechanisms continue to impede implementation.

The water sector in *Myanmar*, a country under Junta military council, faces not only physical challenges – seasonal and spatial water scarcity, periodic floods, and sediment-induced poor water quality – but also underdeveloped institutional arrangements (Myint, Kyaw, and Thwin 1996; Myint 1997; Wai and Thein 1998; Economic Intelligence Unit 2000a). A stronger linkage between water resources and forests requires an environmental perspective on water management. Activities related to irrigation, floods, and drainage do not effectively address emerging concerns nor are they being articulated within an integrated perspective. With the formation of the National Commission of Environmental Affairs in 1990, environmental and water quality legislation came into being. On the policy front, subsidies, absence of economic instruments, and top-down approaches remain the predominant features. The main government agencies involved in water resource management include the Irrigation Department, Utilization Department (lift irrigation), General Affairs Department (water supply and sanitation), and Myanmar Electric Power Enterprise (hydropower generation), and Inland Water Transport (river navigation). Although the Irrigation Department takes the lead role in the water sector, it does not have the mechanisms needed to coordinate the rest of the agencies. The water sector also lacks skilled personnel and suffers because of the unbalanced functional specialization and disciplinary backgrounds of the personnel who are available.

Oceania Region

Water institutions in *Australia*, though more mature than in most other countries, are still undergoing changes partly to reflect changing resource realities and partly through deliberate reforms effected since the late 1980s (Musgrave 1997: 17). The Water Reform Agreement signed in 1994 by the Council of Australian Governments proposes additional institutional initiatives to improve water quality, refine water-rights system and water allocation procedures, institute independent review of water prices, and promote community participation. Since compliance with these policies entails attractive federal money, most states have prepared time-bound action plans for implementing these aspects. The agreement reached by the Murray–Darling Basin Ministerial Council in 1995 for putting a collective cap on water extraction is a unique interstate initiative to control water stress and water salinity within the basin (see later).[16] Apart from national, state, and regional efforts, there have been some noteworthy developments at subsectoral levels. Trends toward corporatization and privatization are seen in both the urban sector (e.g., Hunter Water in 1991 and Sydney Water in 1994) and in the irrigation sector (e.g., in the Murray Irrigation Area and Coleambally and Murrumbidgee Irrigation Area since 1997) (Department of Land and Water Conservation 1997: 8). These changes further enhance the role of economic instruments and market-based water allocation procedures while also improving the physical health and sustainability of the water sector in Australia.

The evolution of water institutions in *New Zealand* reflects the four phases of its water sector development policy: flood control in the 1940s, pollution control in the 1950s, irrigation and power development in the 1960s and 1970s, and environmental aspects in the 1980s (Farley and Simon 1996; Scrimgeour 1997). The legal framework for water management in New Zealand is defined largely by the Soil Conservation and Rivers Control Act (1941), Water and Soil Conservation Act (1967), and Resource Management Act (1991). On the administrative side, water management responsibilities were shifted from the Ministry of Works and Development to the Ministry for the Environment in the early 1990s. A recent change with a fundamental effect on the irrigation sector was the sale of 52 public irrigation projects to private owners during 1998–2000. While New Zealand's water problems are less serious than those found in some Asian and African countries, it still has it own challenges, especially in intersectoral allocation between economic and ecological needs, groundwater volume and quality, the political economy of water management, and the application of science and technology. The

National Agenda for Sustainable Water Management, agreed in 1999, suggested the necessary processes and mechanisms for tackling many of these challenges (Ministry for the Environment 1999).

The water sector and its institutional arrangement in the *Philippines* – an archipelago like Indonesia – are evincing some noteworthy changes (Philippines Delegation 1996; World Bank 1996; Sosa 1997; Rivera and Sosa 1998; Baltazar 1999; United Nations 1999a). The institutional framework for integrated water resources management, established in the 1970s, placed the Philippines ahead of many countries at a similar stage of development. The Water Code of 1976, as enforced by the National Water Resources Board, provides the guiding framework for about 20 public agencies and 10 government departments dealing with water. The National Irrigation Administration is a key agency, as it mobilizes 80 percent of the total water resources to irrigation districts. Water quality monitoring and groundwater regulations are the responsibility of the Department of Environment and Natural Resources. To ensure coordination among the agencies dealing with water quality, the Water Crisis Commission was created under the National Water Crisis Act of 1995. For management purposes, the country is divided into 12 hydrology-based water regions. In addition to progress in IMT policy, the privatization of water supply systems in Manila and other urban areas has been successful due to both legislative (Executive Order 311; Republic Act 7718) and financial (Presidential Decree 198) support. However, these subsectoral initiatives, though successful as a process, have not yet appreciably improved performance. Besides, from an overall management perspective, despite notable institutional initiatives, many gaps (e.g., weak information system, enforcement, and operational coordination) persist in the Philippine water sector.

SELECTED BEST PRACTICES

Before unraveling the common trends and general patterns underlying the nature and direction of institutional changes observed across countries, some best-practice cases should be identified. Though isolated and context-specific, these cases illustrate healthy practices that can strengthen the institutional basis for improvements in water allocation, financing, and management. These cases have a policy value as they help in unraveling the general principles underlying success stories.

Mexico offers three best practices: the IMT, the formation of RBOs, and the water permit registry. The IMT in Mexico is exemplary for its speed and coverage as well as for the extent of other supportive legal and administrative changes effected both during and after IMT. While the Mexican case supports the big-bang approach to IMT, it also underlines the critical roles of other factors, such as macroeconomic compulsion, political will, and farmers' cooperation. Unlike the IMT program initiated by the national government, the initiatives for basin organizations came from the provincial governments under an unprecedented threat of pollution and groundwater depletion within the basins concerned. The water permit registry, as the record of all quantified permits for surface and subsurface water in the country, maintains the technical basis for the emergence and growth of water markets.

Chile offers three major sets of best practices. The first set consists of practices that facilitate market-based water allocation, such as transferable water use rights, registry of water rights, multitiered WUAs, and administratively enforced third-party protection. The second set, supporting project viability, consists of a clear demarcation of responsibility between water administration and users, where project construction is conditional on users' prior payment commitment (also seen in Nepal, Spain, and a few other countries), and the mandatory formation of WUAs right up to the project level. The third set, capable of improving the performance of the urban water sector, consists of debureaucratization and privatization of urban water supply agencies, full-cost pricing with protection of poor consumers through demand rather than supply-side subsidies, and the mandatory requirement to treat urban sewage to protect water quality.

The most remarkable of the best practices in *Brazil* is the region- and sector-specific water strategy that sets regional and sectoral priorities in terms of their susceptibility to water volume and quality problems. Other best practices include the program of 'water democratization' to promote user participation, the system of basin-level organizations, such as the Watershed Committees, to strengthen basin development, and interstate mechanisms, such as the Water Resources Councils, to promote federal–state coordination in water management.

Best practices in *Spain* are observed both at the macro and micro levels. At the macro level, the most notable one is the role played by RBOs in interregional water transfers and intersectoral water allocations. This practice demonstrates that RBOs can function as a potential administrative framework for promoting market-based solutions to interregional and intersectoral water allocation problems. At the subsectoral level is the practice of encouraging urban water supply agencies to be autonomous and financially self-dependent (e.g., Canal Isabel II in Madrid). Local-level best practices include the traditional community-based water allocation systems operating in Valencia and the water markets in the Canary Islands.[17]

Best practices in *Morocco* – mostly at the subsectoral level – include the granting of autonomy to public urban water supply agencies and the privatization of urban water supply in cities such as Casablanca. Similarly, the use of a revolving loan fund for urban users to install water meters and retrofit water appliances is an innovative way of making users self-finance urban water conservation. The RBOs in Morocco are unique, as they are based more on projects than on the river systems, and hence their boundaries are defined by both hydrology and demand areas. In addition, since they are managed by agricultural agencies, they serve as an organizational means of integrating water delivery with the provision of farm inputs.

Some of the most exemplary best-practice cases of water reuse and involvement of user groups in the operation of domestic supply are seen in *Tunisia*, one of the pioneering countries in wastewater reuse. Tunisia uses 100 mcum of treated wastewater for irrigation, and this volume is expected to triple by 2010. Tunisia involves user associations extensively in the operation and management of local drinking water schemes. In fact, these associations account for more than 60 percent of all WUAs in Tunisia.

Egypt also illustrates water reuse-related best practice, as about 30 percent of the irrigation water in the Nile Delta area is reused. Although this practice improves use efficiency and minimizes drainage problems, it also has all the negative consequences of increased salinity and other water quality problems. The lesson of this case is that, since good practices are not necessarily the best from every angle, care has to be exercised when attempting to generalize them.

Israel is known for its extensive application of water-saving technologies and judicious choice of water-conserving cropping systems. Israel's three-part progressive tariff for irrigation water is also unique as a water-pricing practice. Other best practices include the proposal for selective privatization of water administration and the increasing emphasis on water recycling and reuse.

The outstanding best practice of *South Africa* relates to its water law, especially a modern legal framework that it is creating for a market-oriented water sector. The water-pricing policy is also noteworthy for its scope, covering not only O&M and capital costs but also the costs of water management, conservation, and research. Other best practices include the emphasis on catchment management, conflict resolution through natural resource courts, and extensive application of sprinkler and drip technologies. The Vaal River Basin – with extensively interconnected storage and both-way water movement facilities – is an interesting case of an engineering basis for balancing demand and supply over time and space. Best practices in the urban sector include the reliance on demand management techniques including multitiered water pricing, retrofitting, and water education (e.g., Hermanus, a coastal tourist town in Western Cape province).

The best practices of *Sri Lanka* include its IMT program, the recent piloting of a share-based and farmer-managed irrigation water company, and its cascade system of water use. Although IMT in Sri Lanka is less extensive than in Mexico, it is notable for promoting WUAs as multipurpose agencies involved not only in water allocation and cost recovery but also in farm-input delivery. Piloting a water company concept is in line with the declared policy of irrigation privatization and management decentralization. The cascade system of water use, where the unused water flowing from the upper reaches of the system is used and reused several times before the water reaches the sea, results in a system-level physical water use efficiency of up to 80 percent.

Despite its limited institutional initiatives at the national level, *India* has some best practices at the state and local levels. Among them are the institutional reforms initiated under the Water Resources Consolidation Projects in states such as Andhra Pradesh, Orissa, and Tamil Nadu. Other best practices include the creation of autonomous corporations in Gujarat, Karnataka, and Maharashtra to mobilize public funds and the initiative of Andhra Pradesh and Maharashtra to solicit corporate investments in the water sector. Best practices at the local level cover the community-managed Pani Panchayat (Water Council) system and the cooperative river-based lift irrigation schemes in Maharashtra, and the groundwater markets in Gujarat, Uttar Pradesh, Tamil Nadu, and West Bengal (Saleth 1998).

Australia's best practices include permit-based volumetric water allocation, transferable permits, and user-oriented public agencies but with effective regulatory capabilities. These practices provide the necessary institutional framework for realizing the cap program to reduce water extraction to its 1993–94 volume in the Murray–Darling Basin. The Murray–Darling RBO is one of the most successful interstate water management organizations in the world. Another unique feature is the role played by the Independent Pricing and Regulatory Tribunal in regulating urban and rural water prices. In the urban sector, best practices include granting autonomy to water supply agencies (e.g., Sydney Waters) and involving private companies in water provision (e.g., Adelaide, South Australia).

The legal distinction between the regulatory and allocative functions of the state as well as between users' rights and payment obligations is an important legal best practice in *China*. While such a distinction is also found in the water laws of Chile, Brazil, Israel, Mexico, South Africa, Spain, and Sudan, it is the clearest in the Chinese law. This legal feature and the policy-level demarcation of the operational spheres of public and commercial entities within the water sector made explicit in the 1997 Water Industry Policy are the key ingredients for an efficient water institution. Despite their bureaucratic linkages with the MOWR, the water conservancy commissions are also an interesting form of RBO to promote further administrative decentralization within the water sector.

Privatization can also be considered a best practice, especially when viewed purely from an economic rather than from an ideological perspective. Many countries have initiated privatization both in the urban sector (e.g., Argentina, Brazil, Mexico, Morocco, Philippines, Portugal, and the United Kingdom) and in the irrigation sector (e.g., Argentina, Australia, and New Zealand).[18] While privatization policies, especially in the urban sector, are common in many countries, the *United Kingdom* is the only country to have developed a systematic framework for regulating private supply agencies, thereby ensuring some balance between private incentives and public interests. Just like the United States, the United Kingdom is also distinguished for its effective arrangements for public hearing and conflict resolution.

An interesting legal best practice in *Italy* relates to the legal provisions for identifying and protecting environmentally vulnerable zones (e.g., nitrate vulnerable areas and sensitive areas for eutrophication). This provision was made to comply with the EC water framework directives. Another legal best practice, observed in *Portugal*, relates to the legal definition of 'water domain' and its implication for integrated resource management. Since *water domain* is defined as water bodies including the strips of land along their borders, this concept can facilitate an integrated approach to both water and land resources management. Another of Portugal's best practices relates to the stipulation that the proceeds of water and pollution charges must remain in the water sector and be used for river basin development. Since this practice can enable users to see the direct connection between payment and service, it has a bearing on users' willingness to pay and comply.

Several best-practice cases of water quality management are seen in the *Philippines*. Water quality has nonetheless improved markedly since the creation of the Water Crisis Commission and the River Rehabilitation Secretariats in each of the 40 most polluted rivers and with the active involvement of all the stakeholders. The rehabilitation of the Pasig River is the best example. A somewhat similar best practice is seen in *Thailand*, where a major long-term project to clean up 359 rivers of major importance has substantially improved water quality. Although the full impacts of the project are yet to be measured, the case of Chao Phraya Basin shows what can be achieved with a comprehensive and participatory approach to water quality management.

COMMON TRENDS AND PATTERNS

Although our country-specific review of the water sector features, institutional arrangements, and reform initiatives is brief, cross-country comparison does give a feel for the nature, status, and direction of ongoing changes in the global water sector. As physical, financial, and ecological constraints limit the relevance of supply-side solutions, countries are now trying their best, within their political economy constraints, to set right the institutional foundation necessary to promote demand-side solutions. While institutional reforms differ across countries in terms of their coverage and effectiveness, they evince remarkable similarity in terms of their thrust and direction. These similarities include the increasing importance assigned to market-based allocation, decentralization and privatization, integrated water resource management, and economic viability and physical sustainability.

From Water Development to Water Allocation

The paradigmatic shift from water development to water allocation requires a radical reorientation of water institutions. The challenge lies not so much in enacting allocation-oriented water laws and policies as in building an allocation-oriented organizational structure out of an outmoded water administration with insufficient skills and resources. Unlike the development era, characterized by a bureaucratic and closed-loop decision structure where political and engineering considerations predominate, the allocation era demands an open and participatory decision process where economic issues take priority and a premium is set for consensual procedures and outcomes. Some countries (e.g., Australia and Chile) and regions such as California and Colorado in the United States already have the capability to meet the challenges of the allocation paradigm. They have not only the tradition of distinguishing allocation functions from development functions within water administration but also the institutional ingredients to support water markets as an allocation mechanism. Similarly, despite their focus on water quality and other environmental dimensions, countries such as the United Kingdom and France have also developed relatively sophisticated institutional arrangements to manage their water sectors. While countries such as Spain and China can develop their institutional potential faster, others have to go a long way to create the necessary institutions for ushering their water sector into the allocation paradigm.

Toward Decentralization and Privatization

The dominant trend toward decentralization – a key factor to accelerate the transition to the allocation paradigm – is an unmistakable feature of the water sector worldwide. Countries have begun to recognize the functional distinction between the decentralized arrangements needed for user participation and centralized mechanisms needed for coordination and enforcement. The key feature of the ongoing process of decentralization, evident at both the sectoral and subsectoral levels, is the importance assigned to RBOs, IMT, and utility-type bodies in the urban water sector. RBOs share a common conceptual basis, though called by different names in different countries (e.g., Watershed Committees in Brazil, Water Conservancy Commissions in China, Basin Councils in Mexico, and Hydrogeological Federations in Spain).

In the context of RBOs and other regionally decentralized arrangements, two caveats must be recognized. First, regionalization may not automatically ensure a decentralized system of decisionmaking as some RBOs of the past (e.g., the Tennessee Valley Authority) are often considered centralized organizations. And, second, decentralization also requires some form of centralized mechanism to ensure both coordination and conflict resolution. The key to this centralization–decentralization dilemma lies in carefully crafting the institutional arrangements at different geographical levels so as to achieve both local flexibility and regional coordination in water use decisions. Only within such a framework can RBOs and other regionally decentralized management mechanisms function as an effective organizational basis both for pursuing integrated water resource management and for resolving interregional and intersectoral water conflicts.

IMT, the program for transferring the managerial responsibilities, including cost recovery and system maintenance, to legalized WUAs, is the main mode of decentralization within the irrigation sector. IMT is extensive in Mexico, Sri Lanka, Tunisia, Turkey, and the Philippines and is picking up in countries such as India, Morocco, Indonesia, and Pakistan. While China has a tradition of involving communities in lower level irrigation management, Australia and western parts of the United States have arrangements such as irrigation districts where farmers have far greater and more direct managerial and financial responsibilities. In Spain, the proposal to grant full autonomy to basin organizations is likely to advance the process of decentralization still further.

Decentralization within the urban water sector occurs via the emergence of autonomous and financially self-dependent utility-type organizations for the delivery of urban water services. Instances of such companies can be found in many countries. Although China has no such utilities at present, the 1997 Water Industry Policy aims to create them. In Australia, Chile, Mexico, Morocco, the Philippines, and Argentina, urban water sector decentralization has also taken the form of privatization. While privatization and decentralization are advanced in countries with relatively privatized water sectors (Australia, Chile, France, the United Kingdom, Argentina, and New Zealand), even countries such as China and India, with a bureaucratic water sector, are actively exploring ways of tapping private financial, managerial, and technical resources for water development and management.

Despite some striking examples of privatization initiatives in the irrigation sector (e.g., the United Kingdom, Australia, Argentina, and New Zealand), the initiatives observed in the water sector of the sample countries are confined mainly to the economically attractive and technically viable segments of the water sector such as urban water supply, sanitation, and desalinization. Since the private sector cannot be expected to take up 'public good' water activities (e.g., flood control), the public sector will continue to be important in these water-related activities. Thus, although privatization and other decentralization initiatives minimize the role of bureaucracy, they cannot eliminate the role of government. Nor is such elimination desirable in view of the need for both the regulatory and the enabling functions that the state apparatus has to perform in the new context. Since the privatization process can be instrumental not only in strengthening complementarity but also in rekindling a spirit of healthy competition between the public and private sectors, it adds a new institutional dimension to water resource management.

Toward Integrated Water Resource Management

All countries are committed to integrated water resource management, but their institutional arrangements underpinning this approach are quite different. Most countries have policy organs (e.g., water resource councils or stakeholder bodies) to facilitate an integrated perspective on the water sector. However, not all of them have developed a regionally and sectorally disaggregated national water plan. Australia, Israel, Mexico, Spain, and some other countries already have a national water plan. China, Brazil, Morocco, South Africa, Sri Lanka, and others have a mandate to develop such a plan under recently enacted or proposed water laws. Soon India will also have a national water plan. Although these water plans neither require nor lead to any institutional changes, they provide the necessary technical framework to promote an integrated perspective on water sector issues. The translation of such an integrated perspective into practice will entail significant institutional changes.

In an effort to eliminate prevailing sectoral bias and to incorporate environmental issues within water management, many countries are reorganizing their water administration, moving water from the agriculture and power ministries to the environment or natural resources ministries.[19] Countries such as Australia have had water within the overall portfolio for natural resources from the start, whereas Brazil, Mexico, Spain, Morocco, and others have only recently moved water matters to the environment ministry. Another administrative attempt is the integration of most water-related functions within one organization (e.g., Brazil and Indian states such as Tamil Nadu and Orissa). There is also a growing tendency among countries (e.g., China, France, South Africa, and Sri Lanka) to incorporate watershed and catchment management considerations within basin management plans.

Toward Financial Viability and Physical Sustainability

Countries unanimously agree that a phased improvement in cost recovery is the first step toward salvaging the water sector from financial crisis and physical degeneration. While the full recovery of O&M costs is the stated objective in all countries, countries such as Australia and Chile have gone a step ahead of others by trying annuity-based capital cost recovery. South Africa is attempting to recover the costs involved in water conservation, management and research as well. But the basic problem persists, as subsidies continue even in countries such as Australia, Chile, and Israel. Improved financial health can facilitate the physical health of water distribution and drainage infrastructure, but the physical sustainability of the water sector cannot be ensured without controlling pollution and other water quality problems. The common approach in this respect involves water quality grading, quality standards, and pollution control regulations. All the sample countries grade their water in terms of quality defined by chemical properties and usability status. Although most countries have provisions for a pollution permit system, they are at different stages of implementation. Australia and Israel as well as most EU countries enforce strict quality standards. Other countries lack the necessary institutional mechanisms and political will to make much headway on pollution. Nevertheless, policy-level awareness of water pollution and its health and environmental effects is evident in all countries.

FACTORS MOTIVATING INSTITUTIONAL CHANGE

Institutional initiatives in the global water sector, though similar in thrust and direction, are different in origin and motivation as well as in their ability to initiate and sustain the reform process. Our cross-country review suggests that institutional changes within the water sector occur due to both endogenous factors (e.g., water scarcity, performance deterioration, and financial nonviability) and exogenous factors (e.g., macroeconomic crisis, political reform, international agreements, natural calamities, and technological progress).

While water crisis was the underlying factor motivating reforms in most contexts, the proximate or immediate factors triggering institutional changes came from elsewhere in the economy. For instance, the macroeconomic crisis of the late 1980s was the motive force for IMT in Mexico and the current reform debates in India. In South Africa, water sector reform is an important part of the ongoing process of economic and political reconstruction. Similarly, in Chile, China, and Brazil, since water sector reforms have benefited from the synergetic influences of their political and economic liberalization policies, the reforms are an integral part of an economywide liberalization program. In Spain and Portugal, water sector reforms are a key component of the transition from a controlled system to a liberalized one and the subsequent obligations of membership in the European Union. In countries such as Sri Lanka, India, Pakistan, and Morocco, international lending agencies (e.g., the World Bank and the Asian Development Bank) and technical organizations (e.g., IWWI and FAO) are also catalyzing institutional changes within the water sector.

Although all countries are committed to reforming their water institutions, they are at different stages in terms of the extent and effectiveness of institutional reforms. This is an outcome of the gap between their intentions and requirements and their willingness and capabilities. Political economy constraints and inability to win the confidence and cooperation of users also limit the impact of reforms already undertaken. As a result, except for a few countries where powerful economic pressure and political commitment played a key role, institutional reforms in most countries consist mainly of statements of intention, ceremonial changes or cosmetic adjustments.

Our comparative review, despite its brevity and conciseness, allows tentative placement of countries within the spectrum of water institutional change as visualized in our stage-based conception of the process. Countries such as Australia, Chile, the United Kingdom, and France, as well as regions such as California and Colorado in the United States, are in an advanced, though not an ideal, stage where the institutional changes initiated have begun to yield substantial performance gains. In these countries and regions, the institutional reforms are also irreversible and sustainable. Israel, with its technologically advanced and economically sensitive water sector, may well be ahead of most other countries when its reform proposals take practical shape. Although Mexico, Sri Lanka, Portugal, and New Zealand have made good progress in reforming their irrigation sector, they have not yet made similar progress in other water subsectors. These and other similarly placed countries can be considered in the third stage, where institutional reforms, both procedural and substantive in nature, are gradually reaching maturity. As a result, performance gains of perceptible magnitude are still to be realized.

Spain, followed by China, also has the organizational potential as well as the water law and water sector reform proposals to strengthen its water institutions. Morocco is also favorably placed in terms of its macro level institutional reforms and its partial success in reforming the urban water sector and promoting IMT and basin-based integrated approach in the irrigation sector. Although Brazil shows considerable political commitment followed up by concrete actions in the form of water law enactment and administrative reorganization, the country is still constrained by the constitutional division of water sector responsibilities between the federal and state governments. Although India's progress on water sector reform is slow at the national level, it has made good progress at the state and local levels. Most of the remaining countries, despite sector-specific progress by some (e.g., Thailand, the Philippines, and Tunisia), are still at the interface between the first and second stages where perceptional changes toward reforms are either becoming more pronounced or being articulated in the political sphere. But every country in the world is contemplating water institutional reform in one form or another.

IMPLICATIONS FOR INSTITUTIONAL TRANSACTION COST THEORY

Our evaluation of institutional changes in the global water sector, though based on a small cross-country sample, has pertinent implications for institutional economics theory as well as for national and international strategies for promoting institutional change in the water sector. The mere occurrence of institutional changes in most countries can be taken as observational evidence that the opportunity costs of institutional change are growing and could soon surpass the corresponding transaction costs in many countries. The fact that institutional changes are not uniform – either across institutional components or across water subsectors – suggests that both opportunity costs and transaction costs vary considerably by context.

The variations in the extent and coverage of institutional reform across countries provide evidence for the powerful effects that factors both endogenous and exogenous to the water sector have on the opportunity and transaction costs of institutional change in the water sector. These factors act together to raise the opportunity costs of institutional change, reduce the corresponding transaction costs, and create a pro-reform climate. Since some of these factors also capture the political economy imperatives, wherever the opportunity cost is high enough to counter the political transaction costs and path-dependency constraints, actual institutional changes occur or are initiated. Depending upon the endurance of such costs in the reckoning of policymakers, government administrators, and the general public, the changes initiated are sustained and translated in observable performance improvement over time. When this happens, institutional changes reach the take-off stage as performance gains can silence the remaining opposition and provide a stream of resources to deepen the reform process. As path dependency begins to work in favor of reform, it ensures the irreversibility of the reform process.

Our cross-country review also provides information on the internal dynamics of institutional change. The experience of Australia, California, Chile, the United Kingdom, and France confirms that earlier reforms reduce the transaction costs of subsequent reforms. Though not reported in our country-specific review, there is also evidence of strong institutional linkages. For instance, the effects that the creation of financially independent corporate entities (e.g., Tunisia, Namibia, and Portugal) has on pricing policy provide evidence of the linkage between administrative reform and policy reform. The synergy effects from exogenous factors and the scale-related effects of institutional interlinkages clearly suggest that countries with only partial reforms at present could deepen their institutional reforms faster and with less financial cost and political opposition.

As transaction costs decline and political balance improves along the institutional change continuum, a logically linked sequential reform strategy should be pursued. Priorities should be set for reform in the water subsectors and institutional components in terms of their performance impact, facilitative roles for downstream reforms, and political acceptability. Such a strategy also affords a political economic advantage, as it can be used to create the pro-reform political coalition necessary to support and sustain the reform process. A strategy designed to exploit synergies from institutional interlinkages and from exogenous factors with proper timing, packaging, and sequencing has a better chance of success with the least cost and political opposition. While the rationale of and need for such a reform strategy are clear, the main policy question still has to be answered: How can an effective strategy for institutional reform be identified, incorporating all the design principles, including priorities for institutions, sequencing, packaging, and timing? We will try to provide some answers to this and related questions – both from an analytical and an empirical perspective – in the ensuing chapters.

NOTES

1. The endogenous factors include water scarcity, water conflicts, financial and physical deterioration of water infrastructure, and operational inefficiency of water institutions. The exogenous factors include economic development, demographic growth, technical progress, economic and political reforms, international commitments, social values and ethos, and natural disasters such as floods and droughts.
2. For instance, with the institution of transferable water rights, the prospects for other institutional aspects such as conflict resolution and water markets increase due to the linkages that the transaction costs of the latter two institutional aspects have with those of the water-rights system.
3. The scale economies in transaction costs emerge from the fact that the cost of transacting water institutional changes is lower when water sector reform is part of overall, countrywide economic reform and political reconstruction than it would be otherwise. This also shows how institutional changes within the water sector are linked to exogenous changes elsewhere in the economy.
4. The summary reflects the features of the water management systems in England and Wales, but some features are common to the systems in Scotland and Northern Ireland.
5. Crop diversification programs alone cannot meet this challenge. As water markets can be a part of the solution in such situations (Garrido 1997), deliberate policies and legal provisions are needed to facilitate their emergence and growth.
6. If this wetland area is managed appropriately, an estimated 10 bcum – about 40 percent of the present total water potential – could be added annually to Sudan's water resource.
7. For instance, the ambitious project for diverting water from the Okavango – a river shared with Angola and Botswana – to avert water shortage in the Namibian capital Windhoek, has been shelved due to Botswana's objection. Now, Namibia is in the final stages of awarding a contract for a desalinization plant in South Africa to meet the water needs of its coastal towns.
8. Mekorot operates the National Water Carrier – the pipeline system moving water from Lake Galilee to the Negev desert. It is now entering areas such as urban water retail, sewage treatment, and desalination.
9. This firm, the official water planner for 20 years, has been privatized as an engineering consulting outfit.

10.   Since the introduction of the block-rate system, water wastage has declined in all sectors, and water productivity has increased by more than 250 percent in agriculture and 80 percent in industry.

11.   As a result of a government policy of promoting women-run WUAs since 1995, 249 of these are now in operation, in addition to 149 other women-run organizations in rural areas (MEA 1997).

12.   A new NWP is due for approval. Though almost a repeat of the earlier policy, the new one has more emphasis on private sector participation in irrigation financing and management.

13.   Funds from the public are mobilized through state-guaranteed long-term water bonds issued by semiautonomous agencies. Such agencies include the Narmada Valley Development Authority created by Gujarat state and the Krishna Valley Development Corporation floated by Karnataka state.

14.   For instance, 77 percent of all water projects in China are managed at the county level. The remaining (intercounty and interprovincial) projects are managed either at provincial level or by the Ministry of Water Resources or its regional organs, the Water Conservancy Commissions (Ke Lidan 1997: 655).

15.   While a tenth of China – with half the population and two-thirds of agricultural and industrial output – suffers from periodic floods, more than 600 cities – mainly in the economically important north – suffer from perpetual water shortage. Water pollution and its health hazards threaten 436 of China's 532 monitored rivers.

16.   It is normally difficult to reverse current water use to 1993–94 volumes, but strong political commitment and the system for volumetric water allocation across regions, sectors, and individuals tend to enhance the prospects of realizing the target.

17.   The Valencia system, beginning with the Arab invasion of Spain, is known for an almost quantitative interfarm water allocation effected without any water meters. Although institutions and technologies are complementary, the Valencia case, where social organization is substituted for water-measuring technology, suggests that there is an economically relevant margin within which institutions and technologies can be substitutes.

18.   The extent of irrigation privatization is significant in both Argentina and New Zealand. In Argentina, private companies operate a hundred multipurpose dams with a total storage capacity of about 160 bcum under long-term license. In New Zealand, private groups operate 52 irrigation projects.

19.   The feeling is emerging among a few experts that the movement of water into environment and other related ministries itself causes a new bias due to the increasingly constraining role of environmental concerns, which can lead to single-purpose planning centered around environment and ecology instead of producing the integrated approach desired.

8. Institution–performance linkages: evidence and evaluation

Chapter 7 provides anecdotal and descriptive evidence for some of the more explicit linkages between institutional aspects and their performance implications as observed in one or more sample countries. Although the more subtle linkages evident in the process of institution–performance interaction are not covered, Chapter 7 provides ample theoretical reasoning and observational evidence for the relative role of endogenous and exogenous factors in water institutional reforms in the light of transaction cost and political economy considerations. This evidence and the discussion of country-specific and cross-country trends and patterns in water challenges and institutional responses provide the necessary background for the interpretation of results and analysis presented here. The present chapter is the most critical part of our study, as it brings together the theoretical issues and observational evidence bearing upon the empirical results so as to highlight their strategic value and policy implications.

EMPIRICAL EVALUATION: APPROACH AND FRAMEWORK

For a better analysis of the results and appreciation of their implications, we must first clarify our approach and framework within which the three sets of models specified in Chapter 5 are empirically estimated and evaluated. The approach allows us to identify the estimation techniques and procedures that are appropriate for different models, whereas the evaluation framework enables us to indicate the way the models are estimated and their results are presented and evaluated. We have adopted two approaches for the estimation of the three models. These are the single equation approach involving the Ordinary Least Squares (OLS) technique and the system or the simultaneous equation approach involving the Three-Stage Least Squares (3-SLS) technique. Since these estimation techniques and procedures vary across models, we must know the implications of their assumptions for our analysis. Understanding the way the models are estimated and the results are presented is equally important. These aspects are discussed below.

Econometric Approaches

As we know, the two approaches used for estimating the models have different assumptions regarding the nature of the econometric relationships evident or postulated among the equations being estimated. The single equation approach assumes that the equations are separate with no linkages among them whereas the system approach assumes that the equations are structurally nested either with sequential or simultaneous linkages. The two approaches also suggest different econometric techniques and estimation procedures. While the single equation approach requires the reliance on the OLS technique, the system approach underlines the need for advanced econometric methods involving either an instrumental variable, Two-Stage Least Squares (2-SLS), or 3-SLS techniques. Of the three techniques that can be used for estimation under the system approach, we opted to use the 3-SLS in view of its superior econometric features.[1] Given these approaches and the nature of the three sets of models specified in Chapter 5, it is natural for the econometric approaches and, hence, the estimation techniques and procedures, to vary across models.

Since Model A has just a single equation, it is estimated with the single equation approach and its underlying OLS technique. In contrast, in view of the sequential linkages evident among the 10 equations in Model B, estimating them as a single system using the 3-SLS technique will be more realistic. Purposively, however, these equations are also estimated with the single equation approach and the OLS technique. The specific reason for estimating Model B under both approaches is to contrast its performance and thereby provide some econometric evidence for the existence of sequential linkages among institutional and performance variables that have so far been demonstrated only analytically (Figure 5.3). To extend the comparative analysis of model performance under different estimation techniques, the performances of Model B under the OLS and 3-SLS techniques are also compared with the performance of Model A. In this case, the comparison is confined to three equations, [B6], [B7], and [B8], as Model A has no counterparts for the remaining equations of Model B that characterize different layers of institutional interlinkages and institution–performance linkages.

Evaluation Framework

Having described the approaches used for the estimation of different models, let us also note a few relevant aspects pertaining to the estimation, presentation, and evaluation of the empirical results. All the equations in the three models specified in Chapter 5 are generic in that they show only the relationship between their respective dependent and independent variables without any explicit indication of the exact functional form of the relationships. Although these equations can be estimated with a variety of functional forms, in our estimation exercise we have adopted a simple linear form for all the equations.[2] With a simple linear form, all the equations are also estimated with a constant term for the express purpose of capturing the important effects of excluded variables, especially those capturing exogenous factors such as socioeconomic, political, demographic, and ecological factors.[3] Given such a functional specification for their equations, all the models are estimated with the applicable technique and procedures using the latest version of the popularly used econometric software package known as SHAZAM (Version 8.0).

A few words should also be said about the presentation and evaluation of the results. Since all the models we are estimating are large either in terms of the number of variables or equations, or in terms of both, they cannot be presented in a single table. Thus, for presentational convenience, estimated results for all the models are reported in two related tables (8.1a and 8.1b). As to the evaluation of results, although we apply only the normally used econometric tests, for additional clarity we need to state them explicitly. Specifically, the relative statistical significance of the estimated coefficients of the variables is evaluated based on their t-ratios at the significance levels of 10 percent and 20 percent. Although it is a convention to use the significance level of 10 percent, we relax it to 20 percent to identify the relatively more significant among the insignificant variables at the conventional level. The explanatory power of the OLS equations is evaluated using the R-Square (R^2) and that of 3-SLS is evaluated both in terms of System R^2 and the Likelihood Ratio test.[4] Since our data set is based on cross-sectional information, the econometric problem of heteroskedasticity may arise.[5] To make sure that this problem does not lead to biased estimates, we use the Breusch–Pagan test statistic. Although this statistic is reported only for the 3-SLS results, since it pertains to the econometric properties of the data set, it applies equally to other contexts including the OLS results.

To add clarity to our discussion on the institution–performance linkages, it is useful to recall at this stage the analytical categorization of various layers of institution–performance interaction that we made in Chapter 5. For analytical convenience, the linkages among institutional aspects within each of the three institutional components are denoted as intra-institutional linkages whereas the same among those across institutional components are denoted as interinstitutional linkages. Both intra- and interinstitutional linkages form part of the institutional linkages. The other layers pertain to performance linkages where the performance of the water institution is related to the performance of its three components, and that of the water sector is related to the performance of the water institution. These institutional and performance layers are sequentially nested and form part of the overall process of institution–performance interaction. With these

explanatory and technical preliminaries on the approach and evaluation framework, we are ready to present and analyze the empirical results of the models,
focusing especially on the evidence they provide for the existence and significance of the institutional and performance linkages.

EVIDENCE FOR INSTITUTION–PERFORMANCE LINKAGES

We have been discussing all along the strategic significance and performance
implications of the institutional interlinkages and institution–performance
linkages inherent in the process of institution–performance interaction both in
general and in water sector contexts. While the theoretical and conceptual
basis for these linkages was provided in Chapters 2 and 4, a detailed analytical exposition of the same was shown in Chapter 5 (Figure 5.3). Some descriptive and anecdotal evidence for some of these linkages, as observed in one or
more of our sample countries, was also given in Chapter 7. With the empirical
information and the identified sets of models, we can now provide the most
direct evidence – both for the existence of these linkages and for their performance implications – that is feasible within the current state of information.
The evidence for institutional and performance linkages can be shown from a
comparison of the OLS results of both Models A and B with the 3-SLS results
of Model B, as presented in Tables 8.1a and 8.1b.

To understand the rationale and basis for these comparisons, let us recall
here the different assumptions and modeling properties on which the three sets
of results are based. Model A, with a single equation, presents the conventional conception of institution–performance interaction by postulating water
sector performance as a simple and direct function of a set of 21 variables
representing various law, policy, and administration-related institutional
aspects. Thus, unlike Model B, it neither recognizes the institutional and
performance linkages as represented by equations [B1] to [B5] nor distinguishes the direct effects of institutional aspects from their indirect effects
channeled through water institution and its components as characterized by
equations [B9] and [B10]. As a result, Model A does not have these seven critical equations characterizing various layers of linkages evident within the
process of institution–performance interaction. Although Model B, which
includes these seven equations, clearly recognizes the institutional and performance linkages, when it is estimated with the OLS technique, it assumes away
the sequentially nested nature of the 10 equations. As a result, the OLS version
of Model B, unlike its 3-SLS version, could neither capture the performance
implications of the institutional linkages nor distinguish their direct effects
from their indirect effects.

Table 8.1a Comparing estimates for Models A and B with different assumptions on the nature of institution–performance interaction in the water sector

Equations	Dependent variables	Independent variables	Model A (one single OLS)		Model B			
					As separate OLS		As 3-SLS	
			Coefficient[a]	t-ratio	Coefficient[a]	t-ratio	Coefficient[a]	t-ratio
[1]	LCRMEE	LPRSRF	–	–	0.047	0.314	0.079	0.556
		PGPIUP	–	–	**0.252**	3.287	**0.246**	3.481
		POPAWE	–	–	-0.015	-0.120	0.096	0.880
		ABALFS	–	–	**0.793**	1.763	**0.822**	2.212
		AARINF	–	–	*0.169*	1.601	*0.122*	1.408
		AEXTST	–	–	0.124	1.054	*0.141*	1.303
		Constant	–	–	**2.305**	2.383	**1.818**	2.085
[2]	PIRSWE	LPRSRF	–	–	**0.225**	1.636	**0.209**	1.686
		LCRMEE	–	–	**0.200**	2.367	**0.698**	3.633
		PGPIUP	–	–	-0.003	-0.040	*-0.139*	-1.557
		AEXTST	–	–	**0.260**	2.506	**0.299**	3.025
		Constant	–	–	0.495	0.729	**-1.750**	-2.025
[3]	PCOREC	LPRSRF	–	–	*-0.063*	-1.457	**-0.070**	-1.833
		PGPIUP	–	–	0.024	1.084	*0.024*	1.297
		POPAWE	–	–	0.013	0.364	-0.018	-0.593
		AIBDWP	–	–	**0.386**	2.675	**0.265**	2.153
		Constant	–	–	**2.132**	9.124	**2.358**	11.750
[4]	ASBUDC	AIBDWP	–	–	0.588	0.840	**1.485**	2.008
		PCOREC	–	–	-0.310	-0.722	**-3.426**	-3.590
		PGPIPP	–	–	-0.061	-0.619	-0.022	-0.233
		PGPIUP	–	–	0.117	1.086	*0.155*	1.463
		Constant	–	–	**3.760**	3.634	**10.178**	5.111

Table 8.1a continued

Equations	Dependent variables	Independent variables	Model A (one single OLS)		Model B			
					As separate OLS		As 3-SLS	
			Coefficient[a]	t-ratio	Coefficient[a]	t-ratio	Coefficient[a]	t-ratio
[5]	LACPRE	LPRSRF	–	–	–0.073	–0.494	**0.200**	1.292
		LOEPRV	–	–	**0.349**	3.976	**0.289**	3.600
		PCOREC	–	–	**0.538**	1.801	**3.814**	6.499
		POELWL	–	–	**0.247**	2.591	**0.208**	2.486
		AACCME	–	–	0.043	0.495	–0.021	–0.278
		Constant	–	–	0.200	0.215	**–7.036**	–4.769

Notes: [a]Coefficients in **bold** are significant at 10 percent or better whereas coefficients in ***bold and italic*** are significant at 20 percent. Since Model A does not recognize institutional interlinkages, it does not have the coefficients for the five equations [1] to [5].

– Not applicable because the one-equation OLS estimate does not capture the linkages represented by equations [1] to [5].

192

Table 8.1b Comparing estimates for Models A and B with different assumptions on the nature of institution–performance interaction in the water sector

Equations	Dependent variables	Independent variables	Model A (one single OLS)		Model B As separate OLS		Model B As 3-SLS	
			Coefficient[a]	t-ratio	Coefficient[a]	t-ratio	Coefficient[a]	t-ratio
[6]	LOEFWL	LTRWSA	0.472	1.713	0.476	1.366	0.259	0.730
		LPRSRF	-0.006	-0.066	0.097	0.906	0.095	0.853
		LCRMEE	-0.008	-0.151	0.242	3.518	0.321	1.489
		LACPRE	-0.006	-0.106	-0.012	-0.164	0.241	1.173
		LINTRE	-0.008	-0.216	0.125	2.490	0.093	1.779
		LOECEN	-0.039	-0.948	0.122	2.211	0.076	1.462
		LOEPRV	0.030	0.571	0.184	2.711	0.066	0.790
		Constant	–	–	1.809	3.152	1.256	1.556
[7]	POEFWP	PPSCRL	-0.122	-1.565	-0.159	-1.603	-0.107	-1.189
		PCOREC	0.184	1.053	0.675	3.182	1.523	3.241
		PIRSWE	0.120	2.205	0.040	0.616	0.783	5.278
		PGPIPP	-0.020	-0.480	-0.086	-1.730	-0.103	-2.265
		PGPIUP	-0.043	-0.993	0.096	1.744	0.062	0.977
		POPAWE	-0.013	-0.182	0.075	0.833	0.053	0.590
		POELWL	0.093	1.63	0.389	5.754	0.179	2.605
		Constant	–	–	0.934	1.262	-2.067	-1.977

Table 8.1b   continued

Equations	Dependent variables	Independent variables	Model A (one single OLS)		Model B — As separate OLS		Model B — As 3-SLS	
			Coefficient[a]	t-ratio	Coefficient[a]	t-ratio	Coefficient[a]	t-ratio
[8]	AOEFWA	AORGBA	-0.074	-0.909	-0.033	-0.330	0.035	0.359
		ABALES	**0.718**	2.924	**1.046**	3.514	**1.062**	3.827
		AIBDWP	0.273	1.003	0.141	0.423	0.121	0.383
		ASBUDC	*-0.054*	-1.476	-0.015	-0.339	0.149	1.098
		AACCME	-0.062	-1.239	-0.018	-0.294	-0.030	-0.481
		AARINF	**0.205**	3.463	**0.252**	3.538	**0.226**	3.126
		AEXTST	**0.171**	2.372	**0.403**	4.975	**0.356**	4.661
		Constant	–	–	**1.142**	2.099	0.841	1.188
[9]	WIPOEV	LOEFWL	–	–	**0.148**	1.767	**0.371**	2.484
		POEFWP	–	–	**0.217**	2.420	-0.072	-0.415
		AOEFWA	–	–	**0.377**	4.568	**0.622**	4.188
		Constant	–	–	**1.881**	4.020	***0.840***	1.304
[10]	WSPOEV	WIPOEV	–	–	**0.383**	6.737	**0.843**	7.355
		POPAWE	–	–	-0.053	-0.888	-0.063	-1.149
		ASBUDC	–	–	**-0.062**	-2.015	**-0.132**	-1.570
		PCOREC	–	–	-0.067	-0.437	***-0.450***	-1.278
		AARINF	–	–	**0.183**	3.588	**0.098**	1.934
		AEXTST	–	–	**0.155**	2.717	0.041	0.672
		Constant	–	–	**1.886**	3.630	**1.537**	1.972
		Constant	**2.783**	4.427				
	R²/System R²		0.517		– _b		0.765	

Notes: [a]Coefficients in **bold** are significant at 10 percent or better whereas coefficients in ***bold and italic*** are significant only at 20 percent. Since Model A does not recognize either the performance linkages among institutional components or the direct effect of some institutional factors on water sector performance, it does not have the coefficients for equations [9] and [10].
The R² for the OLS estimation of equations [1] to [10] are respectively 0.14, 0.10, 0.10, 0.26, 0.19, 0.33, 0.36, 0.43, 0.37, and 0.52.
[b] Not applicable because the one-equation OLS estimation does not capture the linkages represented by equations [6] to [10].

194

The performance differences between Model A and the OLS and 3-SLS versions of Model B are directly linked to their varying assumptions regarding the nature of institutional linkages and their performance implications. A carefully performed comparison of their results could, therefore, indicate which model or version is consistent with our empirical information. This could then be the basis for establishing the evidence for both the existence and performance contributions of the linkages. The comparison proceeds in two stages. In the first stage, the OLS results of Models A and B are compared to show the importance of explicitly recognizing and modeling some of the most important institutional and performance linkages. In the second stage, the OLS and 3-SLS results of Model B are compared to show the necessity of estimating the equations together as a system when institutional and performance synergies are present and the direct effects of institutional factors are distinguishable from their indirect effects. While the comparison in the first stage provides the necessary evidence for the existence of institutional and performance linkages, that in the second stage adds evidence for their performance contributions.

Evidence for the Existence of Linkages

To provide evidence for the existence of institutional and performance linkages, we first exploit the particular feature that distinguishes Model A from Model B: the absence of the seven linkage equations ([B1] to [B5], [B9], and [B10]) in the former but their presence in the latter. Thus, when the estimates for these equations are significant in the OLS results of Model B, we can take that as empirical evidence for the existence of the linkages they represent. At the same time, we also compare the relative significance of the 21 variables (in equations [6] to [8] in Table 8.1b) common to both models. In the first stage of comparison involving the OLS results of both models, we focus on two aspects. The first aspect of comparison is related to the significance of the variables in the seven linkage equations excluded in Model A but included in Model B. The second aspect of comparison is related to the number of statistically significant variables among those common to both models. Thus, we can empirically establish the existence of the institutional and performance linkages when the following two conditions are satisfied. First, the statistical significance of the variables in equations [B1] to [B5], [B9], and [B10] is stronger in Model B than in Model A. Second, the number of statistically significant variables (excluding the constant term) in equations [6], [7], and [8] is greater for the OLS results for Model B than for Model A. The first condition is both necessary and sufficient to establish the existence of institutional and performance linkages. In contrast, the second condition is only a necessary condition, as it aims to show only that the OLS performance of Model B is as good as that of Model A.

As we reflect on these two conditions with the OLS results of both models presented in Tables 8.1a and 8.1b, we can easily verify that both conditions are indeed satisfied but with two notable exceptions. First, since none of the variables is significant in equation [4], the institutional linkage postulated here seems to be unimportant. Second, in the particular context of equation [8], contrary to the second condition, the number of significant variables identified by the OLS results of Model A exceeds that of Model B. These exceptions are not serious, however, as we consider the following facts. As can be seen from Table 8.1a, equation [4] is insignificant only when it is estimated as a separate OLS equation but not when estimated as a part of the 3-SLS equation system. The second condition that failed in equation [8] is not so critical, as it forms only a part of the necessary condition. Third, taking all 21 variables together, the total number of statistically significant variables identified by the OLS results of Model B (12) is still larger than that of Model A (eight). Finally, comparing the absolute magnitude of the coefficients of the statistically significant variables common to both models, we find that those associated with Model B are larger in almost every case.[6] In view of these facts, we can safely conclude that all the linkages postulated are very important and, as we will see, they also contribute significantly to the overall performance of both water institution and water sector.

Evidence for the Performance Implications of Linkages

The second stage of comparison involving the OLS and 3-SLS results of Model B is still more important, as it enables us to provide evidence for the significant performance implications of the institutional and performance linkages. As noted, although Model B explicitly recognizes these critical linkages, when its equations are estimated as separate relations within an OLS framework, it also fails equally to capture the performance implications of institutional and performance synergies flowing among the equations both directly and indirectly. Since such a failure means an underestimation of the performance impact of the institutional and performance variables, the OLS results cannot reveal the full and realistic picture of the process of institution–performance interaction. In contrast, when Model B is estimated by considering all 10 of its equations together within a system framework, the results will be more realistic and reliable as they capture the sequentially nested characteristics of the equations. As a result, the performance implications of the institutional linkages can be more accurately evaluated and the direct and indirect effects of institutional variables on water sector performance can be more clearly distinguished.

The second-stage comparison of the OLS and 3-SLS results for Model B also focuses on some of the same aspects considered in the first-stage comparison, especially the relative size and significance of the coefficients of both the institutional and performance variables in the system. There is, however, an additional aspect pertaining to the relative explanatory power of the OLS and 3-SLS versions of the model in question. Specifically, the evidence for both the existence and the significant performance contributions of the institutional and performance linkages can be established when the following three conditions are satisfied. First, the number of statistically significant variables (excluding the constant) identified by the 3-SLS results is the same or larger than that identified by the OLS results for most equations. Second, the absolute magnitude of the coefficients of the linkage variables (the dependent variables in equations [1] to [9] that enter as independent variables in other equations) obtained in the case of 3-SLS results is larger than that obtained in the OLS results. And, finally, when the explanatory power of the 3-SLS results, as indicated by its R^2, is larger than that of the OLS results.

By applying these conditions to the results in Tables 8.1a and 8.1b, we find that the total number of statistically significant variables identified by the 3-SLS results of Model B (34) exceeds that identified by its OLS counterpart (31). Most noteworthy is the fact that, in the case of the first five equations representing institutional interlinkages, the 3-SLS results not only identify the same set of variables (11) identified as significant by the OLS results but also identify seven additional variables as significant. This result, and the fact that equation [4], shown to be insignificant by the OLS results, turns out to be significant under the 3-SLS results, shows the effects of the nested structure among all the equations. For instance, even though the linkage variable *ASBUDC* (seriousness of budget constraint) is not significant in equation [8], it is highly significant in equation [10]. This result suggests that while its indirect effect on water sector performance via *AOEFWA* (overall performance of the water administration) is insignificant, its direct effect on the ultimate performance variable *WSPOEV* (overall performance of the water sector) is very important. But, the linkage variable *PCOREC* (cost-recovery status), despite the dissipation of its effects due to the insignificance of other variables in the linkage chain (e.g., *POEFWP* [overall effectiveness of water policy] in equation [9]), has significant effects on *WSPOEV*. These effects of *PCOREC* are channeled both indirectly, through its effects on *ASBUDC* (via equation [4]), and directly in terms of its effects in equation [10]. Similarly, although the linkage variable *LCRMEE* (effectiveness of conflict-resolution mechanisms) does not have any direct effects, it has substantial indirect effects on sector performance via *LOEFWL* (overall performance of water law).

We can also see many instances of the multifarious effects of even nonlinkage variables such as *PGPIUP* (effectiveness of user participation policy), *ABALFS* (balance in functional specialization), *AARINF* (information adequacy), and *AEXTST* (extensiveness of science and technology application).

While the effects of *PGPIUP* are channeled only indirectly through the direct and indirect effects of the linkage variables *LCRMEE*, *PCOREC*, and *ASBUDC*, those of *AARINF* and *AEXTST* are channeled both indirectly via the linkage variables *LCRMEE* and *AOEFWA* and directly in terms of its proxy role in equation [10]. However, some of the effects of the linkage variables as well as others in the linkage equations become dissipated mainly due to the insignificance of *POEFWP* in equation [9]. Although *POEFWP* is insignificant, a number of policy-related institutional variables (e.g., *PCOREC* and *PGPIUP*) do have substantial effects on institutional and sectoral performance, both directly and indirectly. This means, among other things, that the effects of some of the policy-related institutional variables are channeled more through other variables than through *POEFWP*. In this sense, it is more accurate to say that it is the transmission of the effects of policy variables via other variables that leads to the insignificance of *POEFWP* rather than that the latter causes dissipation of the effects of the former.[7]

In view of their sequential linkages as well as the multifarious nature of both their direct and indirect effects, the significance of some variables naturally varies across the estimation procedures. Since the 3-SLS estimation aims to maximize the performance of the total system rather than that of any single equation, some variables with significant effects in the context of one equation will usually become insignificant from the perspective of the equation system. As the effects of some variables are either captured, moderated, or preempted by some other variables within the system, the difference in the number of significant variables identified by the two versions of Model B is itself an indication of the significance of institutional and performance linkages. From this perspective, therefore, the smaller number of significant variables identified by the 3-SLS results in equations [6], [7], and [9] does not represent a serious repudiation of the performance implications of the linkages.

While the number of significant variables is only a necessary condition in the context of the present comparison, the sufficient condition for demonstrating the performance contributions of institutional linkages is related to the absolute magnitude of the coefficients of the significant variables. The rationale for using this condition as evidence for the performance implications of institutional linkages comes from the following simple fact. In the presence of strong institution–performance linkages, the coefficients of most variables, especially those capturing the linkages, are likely to be large if they either benefit from positive institutional and performance synergy or remain strong enough to withstand the negative effects of other related variables in the system. Otherwise, for reasons contrary to those stated above, either the size of the coefficient will be smaller or the variable itself becomes insignificant. As can be verified from Tables 8.1a and 8.1b, of the 34 statistically significant variables under the 3-SLS results, 21 have coefficients that are substantially larger and more significant than their OLS counterparts. In contrast, of the 31 statistically significant variables under the OLS results, only 17 have coefficients that are larger and more significant than their 3-SLS counterparts.

What is more important from the perspective of the performance significance of institutional linkages is the size of the coefficients associated with the linkage variables; that is, the dependent variables in the first nine equations that enter as independent variables in other equations. As can be seen, all linkage variables indeed have larger and more significant coefficients. Instances in this respect can be seen by comparing the coefficients of *LCRMEE* in equations [2] and [3] and *PCOREC* in equations [4], [5], [7], and [10]. But, the coefficient of *WIPOEV* – the most important of all the linkage variables because it captures the overall effects of institutional and performance linkages and transmits them ultimately to water sector performance – provides the most dramatic instances of all that are evident in Tables 8.1a and 8.1b. While the size of the coefficient for this important linkage variable is 0.843 in the 3-SLS results, it is only 0.383 in the OLS results. This is the most direct evidence that we can provide for the consistency of the system version of Model B within our empirical context. This evidence also supports the existence and significant performance contributions of the institutional and performance linkages in reality. This is supported further by the fact that the System R^2 for the 3-SLS results is far higher than that obtained for the OLS results of Model A, suggesting that the 3-SLS version of Model B fits the empirical data far better than its OLS counterpart.

EVALUATION OF INSTITUTION–PERFORMANCE LINKAGES

Providing evidence for the existence and performance implications of institutional linkages, though very important from the perspective of our objectives, is only a part of the story. The other but critical part of the story pertains to the evaluation of the relative importance of institutional variables and identification of the most significant institutional aspects in terms of the magnitude of their performance impact. In this evaluation, our focus is on the system version of Model B, which has been shown to be consistent not only with our theoretical discussion and analytical description but also with our empirical data. Thus, our evaluation is now confined to the 3-SLS results reported in Tables 8.1a and 8.1b with a focus on the relative role and policy implications of institutional aspects in different equations representing various layers in the process of institution–performance interaction. The analysis of the relative role of institutional aspects is obviously based on the size, direction, and statistical significance of the coefficients for the variables represented by them in different equations.

At this stage, let us recall the distinctions and the structural linkages evident among the three subsets of equations in Model B. The first subset – containing equations [1] to [5] – captures the institutional linkages across institutional components. In other words, it captures the relationships that some of the law-related institutional aspects have with policy and administration-related institutional aspects, and vice versa. In contrast, the second subset containing equations [6] to [8] captures the linkages only within each of the three institutional components. That is, it characterizes the relationship that the legal, policy, and administrative components of the water institution have with their respective institutional aspects. The third subset contains only equation [9] and [10]. Equation [9] represents the relationship that water institution performance has with the performance of its three institutional components. It captures the effects transmitted not only by equations [6] to [8] but also by the first five equations and represents the performance linkages within water institution. Equation [10] captures the relationship that water sector performance, the ultimate dependent variable in the system, has with water institution performance as well as with some other institutional variables entering as proxies capturing certain economywide conditions and policy trends.

Although the three subsets of equations are distinct, as they capture different facets of institution–performance interaction, they do have a sequentially nested structure. Thus, when they are estimated together as a system, as we did with the system version of Model B, the effects of institutional interlinkages captured by the first set of five equations ([1] to [5]) are transmitted to the next set of three equations ([6] to [8]). The second set of equations, in turn, transmits both its own effects and the effects of the first set of equations to equation [9], which then captures these effects of institutional components and institutional aspects and transmits them ultimately to water sector performance in equation [10]. Besides their indirect effects routed through water institution performance, some of the institutional aspects also have direct effects on water sector performance, though as proxies for some general condition related to policy, finance, information, and technology.

The distinctions and structural linkages among the three subsets of equations are made not only to facilitate understanding of the relative role and significance of the institutional factors but also to provide a useful analytical framework for a more organized evaluation of the institutional and performance linkages. This framework structures our ensuing evaluation into three parts: interinstitutional linkages (equations [1] to [5]), intra-institutional linkages (equations [6] to [8]), and institution–performance linkages (equations [9] and [10]). The first and second subsets of equations, both focused only on institutional linkages, should be distinguished. The first subset deals with institutional linkages across three water institutional components (interinstitutional linkages); the second subset deals with the institutional linkages within each of the three institutional components (intra-institutional linkages). The third subset of equations, of course, represents the institution–performance linkages. However, in view of the structural linkages among all the equations within the system, their categorization into subsets is made only for analytical convenience. Thus, as we evaluate the relative role of institutional aspects in all three subsets of equations, we will highlight their interactions within the sequentially nested structure by distinguishing the direct and indirect effects of these aspects on the performance of water institution, its components, and water sector.

Interinstitutional Linkages

The relative role of institutional aspects in various layers of interinstitutional linkages can be evaluated from the 3-SLS results for the first five equations reported in Tables 8.1a and 8.1b. Taking the first among these five linkages, we find that the effectiveness of conflict-resolution mechanisms (*LCRMEE*) is strongly influenced by the positive and statistically significant effects of four of the six variables representing various legal, policy, and administrative aspects. The significant variables are that the policy variable representing the effectiveness of user participation policy (*PGPIUP*) and the three administrative variables representing, respectively, balance in functional specialization (*ABALFS*), information adequacy (*AARINF*), and extensiveness of science and technology application (*AEXTST*). Of these four institutional aspects, *ABALFS*, followed by *PGPIUP*, have a more dominant effect than the other two. In any case, the results are understandable because a functionally balanced water administration and an active user participation policy, coupled with better technology and information, could considerably improve the effectiveness of conflict-resolution mechanisms.

Equation [2] represents the institutional interlinkage that the effectiveness of intersectoral and regional water transfer policy (*PIRSWE*) has with two legal variables, one policy variable, and one administrative variable. The results show that all four variables are statistically significant, suggesting clearly the dependence of the effectiveness of the policy-related institutional aspect on other legal, policy, and administrative aspects. These variables, listed in terms of their relative importance, are: *LCRMEE*, *AEXTST*, the legally specified water-rights format (*LPRSRF*), and *PGPIUP*. All of these except *PGPIUP* also have positive effects. The dominant positive effect of *LCRMEE* is very significant from the perspective of institutional linkages. Since it is a variable linking equation [1] with [2], it transmits the effects of all the significant variables that affected it in equation [1]. Thus, both *AEXTST* and *PGPIUP* affect water transfer policy directly due to their effects in equation [2] and indirectly through their effects on *LCRMEE*.

The indirect effect of *PGPIUP* is positive. However, its direct effect is negative. The opposing effect of this institutional aspect is consistent with intuition, as an effective user participation policy and, hence, user participation, could enhance the effectiveness of water transfer policy through its contribution to conflict resolution. But, user participation could also have a constraining influence on water transfer policy, which could favor users in one sector or region over the others.[8] The significant positive effects of *LCRMEE* and *LPRSRF*, however, suggest that more effective legal arrangements for conflict resolution and property rights in water could considerably improve the effectiveness and prospects of water transfer policy. These two legal institutional aspects could also be used to counter the negative effects of *PGPIUP*, as user opposition is less likely if there is an effective water-rights system to protect individual water shares and a conflict-resolution arrangement to compensate for any loss caused by water transfer.

Equation [3] shows the nature of the relationship that the policy-related institutional aspect of cost-recovery status (*PCOREC*) has with one law-related institutional aspect, two policy-related institutional aspects, and one administration-related institutional aspect. These variables are: *LPRSRF*, *PGPIUP*, effects of other policies on water policy (*POPAWE*), and the existence of an independent water-pricing body (*AIBDWP*). According to the estimated results, all variables but *POPAWE* are significant. Among the three significant variables, *AIBDWP* and *PGPIUP* have positive effects; *LPRSRF* has a negative effect. The positive effect of both *AIBDWP* and *PGPIUP* on cost-recovery status is understandable, as the existence of an independent water-pricing body could imply the likelihood of frequent revisions in water rates, and user participation could contribute to a better recovery of water charges. Of these two, however, *AIBDWP* has a larger and more significant effect than *PGPIUP*. This result has important implications for designing institutional arrangements for cost recovery, as it shows that the institutional aspect related to water rate determination and revision is more important than that related to the recovery of water charges.[9]

The negative effect of *LPRSRF* on cost recovery suggests that, as water rights become increasingly private, the effectiveness of cost recovery declines. While this result seems counterintuitive on the surface, it has some plausible theoretical and practical consistency. The explanation for this result can be both optimistic and theoretic as well as pessimistic and realistic. The optimistic version is based on the theoretical reasoning that, with a clear and private water-rights system, the significance of price-based periodic recovery of water charges declines as the one-time, annual, full-cost payment for water rights would be paid before water use (e.g., water rights-based irrigation companies). The pessimistic but realistic version is based on the reasoning that, despite variations in the water-rights format, cost recovery is either poor or partial in most cases.

The institutional interlinkage of the administration-related institutional aspect *ASBUDC*, representing the seriousness of the budget constraint, with four other institutional aspects is characterized in equation [4]. The result shows that, except for the variable representing the effectiveness of private sector promotion policy (*PGPIPP*), the other three variables have a significant relationship with *ASBUDC*. These variables, stated in terms of their relative significance, are *PCOREC*, *AIBDWP*, and *PGPIUP*. Of them, *PCOREC* has a negative effect; the other two have positive effects. Since the variable *ASBUDC* is formulated in a negative sense (i.e., seriousness of budget constraint), the positive coefficients of its independent variables will mean negative effects, and vice versa. Thus, the negative coefficient of *PCOREC* actually implies the positive fact that effective cost recovery reduces the seriousness of the budget constraint. Because this variable is the linkage variable, it also transmits the effects of all the significant variables in equation [3]. The relationship can also be interpreted in a different way: that is, the seriousness of the budget constraint also provides a policy compulsion to improve cost recovery. In fact, it is this interpretation that accurately explains the positive coefficients of both *AIBDWP* and *PGPIUP*. Thus, the seriousness of the budget constraint leads to the necessity of an independent water-pricing body and effective user participation policy but not the other way around. For it would lead to an inconsistent explanation that the existence of a water-pricing body and an effective user participation policy exacerbate the seriousness of the budget constraint. The mere existence of a water-pricing body and the creation of effective user participation have not yet had a significant budgetary impact. The insignificance of the *PGPIPP* can be explained by the fact that institutional constraints still limit the private sector's role in most countries.

The last of the five equations capturing interinstitutional linkages postulates the legal aspects of the effectiveness of accountability provisions (*LACPRE*) as a function of two each of legal and policy aspects and one administrative aspect. These aspects are: *LPRSRF*, effectiveness of legal provisions for privatization (*LOEPRV*), *PCOREC*, effectiveness of law–policy linkages (*POELWL*), and effectiveness of administrative accountability (*AACCME*). All the variables capturing these aspects, except the one related to the administrative aspect, have a significant positive effect on the effectiveness of the legal provisions for accountability. Of these four variables, the linkage variable *PCOREC*, which also transmits the effects of all the significant variables in equation [3] into the present equation, has the largest influence. *LPRSRF* has both a direct effect and an indirect effect via the linkage variable *PCOREC*.

The positive effects of *PCOREC* and *LPRSRF* are understandable in view of the direct relationship that cost recovery and the water-rights system have with accountability, but the positive effects of the other two variables need an explanation. The direct positive effect of *LOEPRV* is due to the fact that effective legal provisions for private sector participation are likely to be associated with good legal provisions for accountability, one of the legal conditions necessary for private sector participation. Moreover, when the legal provisions for privatization become effective and actually induce private involvement in the water sector, it also helps to tighten the accountability of water sector officials and water users.[10] The positive effect of *POELWL* is due to the fact that strong operational linkages between water law and water policy are likely to contribute to the practical application of the accountability provisions. This is because effective law–policy linkages mean that there will be adequate legal provisions and organizational mechanisms for achieving accountability goals.

Intra-institutional Linkages

Since the intra-institutional linkages deal with the institutional linkages within each of the three water institution components, they show how the overall performance of these components is affected by their respective institutional aspects. But, as noted in the context of equations [1] to [5], some of these institutional aspects are also affected by their counterparts both within and outside a given institutional component. As a result, the intra-institutional linkages to be evaluated below are also affected by the interinstitutional linkages discussed above. With this fact in mind, the intra-institutional linkages can be evaluated by considering the results for equations [6] to [8]. These equations capture the relationship that the overall performance of each of the three components of water institution (water law, water policy, and water administration) has with its constituent institutional aspects. Taking each of these equations, let us identify the relative role of institutional aspects and also highlight the effects of the interinstitutional linkages transmitted by some of these institutional aspects into the three intra-institutional relationships.

Water law performance: relative role of legal aspects
As seen in Table 8.1b, equation [6] postulates the overall performance of the legal component of water institution as a function of seven legal aspects. In terms of the statistical significance of the estimated coefficients of this equation, only three of the seven legal aspects considered are significant and all have a positive effect. These variables – given in the order of their relative importance (as indicated by the absolute size of their coefficients) – are: *LCRMEE*, degree of integration within water law (*LINTRE*), and centralization tendency within water law (*LOECEN*). Since *LCRMEE*, with the dominant positive effect on water law performance, is a linkage variable (equation [1]), it transmits not only its own effects but also the positive effects of

PGPIUP, *ABALFS*, and *AARINF*. As a result, the performance of water law is influenced not only by its own legal aspects but also, equally, by the policy aspect related to user participation and by the administrative aspects related to functional specialization and information adequacy.

Unlike *LCRMEE*, *LACPRE*, which is also a linkage variable (equation [5]), is not significant. Therefore, neither its own effects nor the effects of the significant legal and policy aspects that it has captured in equation [5] could be transmitted.[11] As a result, the significant indirect effects of both *LPRSRF* and *LOEPRV* – which are insignificant in the present equation, suggesting the absence of their direct effect on water law performance – could not be transmitted.[12] The performance of the water law component, therefore, depends on the direct effects of three legal aspects (*LCRMEE*, *LINTRE*, and *LOECEN*) and the indirect effects of one policy aspect (*PGPIUP*) and two administrative aspects (*ABALFS* and *AARINF*). All of these, however, have positive effects. While the positive effect of the variables other than *LOECEN* is perfectly understandable, that of *LOECEN* seems to be inconsistent with the current emphasis on decentralization. The key to understanding its positive effects lies in the fact that a dose of centralization at both the legal and administrative levels is itself necessary to promote the decentralization process and to ensure efficient coordination and conflict resolution.[13] Thus, as per our empirical results, an effective conflict-resolution provision (reinforced by user participation, balanced functional specialization, and adequate information), legal integration, and a dose of centralization are the major factors likely to improve the performance of water law.

Water policy performance: relative role of policy aspects
The relative role of the seven policy aspects in determining the overall performance of water policy can be evaluated from the results pertaining to equation [7] in Table 8.1b. Of the seven policy variables considered, only four are statistically significant. These policy variables – listed in the order of the absolute magnitude of their coefficients – are: *PCOREC*, *PIRSWE*, *POELWL*, and *PGPIPP*, representing, respectively, the cost-recovery status, effectiveness of water transfer policy, strength of law–policy linkage, and effectiveness of privatization policy. Of these four significant policy aspects, all but *PGPIPP* have positive effects on water policy performance, suggesting the intuitively consistent result that effective cost recovery and water transfer policies and strong law–policy linkages improve the overall performance of water policy. The negative effect of *PGPIPP*, representing the effectiveness of private sector promotion policies, is equally consistent as we interpret it within the context of the two-way flow of effects between water policy and its constituent policy aspects. Since it is the failure of past water policies that prompts current policy efforts to enhance private participation in financing, maintenance, and

management, poor water policy performance often leads to more effective privatization policies. It is in this sense that the negative coefficient of *PGPIPP* needs to be interpreted.

PCOREC and *PIRSWE*, with stronger effects than the other two significant policy aspects, are also the linkage variables capturing and transmitting the effects of other legal, policy, and administrative aspects from equations [2] and [3], respectively. Since *PIRSWE* is also a function of yet another law-related linkage variable, *LCRMEE*, it captures and transmits the effects from equation [1] as well. As we can see from equations [1] to [3], the two policy-related linkage variables capture the effects of six institutional aspects: *LPRSRF, PGPIUP, AEXTST, AARINF, AIBDWP,* and *ABALFS*. Since *PCOREC* and *PIRSWE* capture and transmit the indirect effects of these institutional aspects into equation [7], the legal and administrative aspects also affect the overall performance of water policy, though indirectly. They are the legal aspect of water rights as well as the administrative aspects of technology application, information adequacy, existence of an independent water-pricing body, and balanced functional specialization. *PGPIUP*, which is insignificant in equation [7], suggesting the absence of its direct effect, has significant indirect effects on water policy performance through both the linkage variables: *PIRSWE* and *PCOREC*. Glancing at the institutional aspects indirectly affecting water policy performance, the administrative aspects have a major influence, which is consistent with the critical dependence of water policy performance on the effectiveness of the administrative arrangements needed to put policy into practice.

Water administration performance: relative role of administrative aspects

How the performance of water administration is affected by the relative role and significance of its seven institutional aspects can be evaluated from equation [8]. According to the results in Table 8.1b, of these seven administration-related institutional aspects, only three are significant. These significant aspects – listed in the order of the absolute size of their coefficients – are: *ABALFS, AEXTST,* and *AARINF*. As we have seen in the context of previous equations, these three administrative aspects also have substantial indirect effects on the performance of both water law and water policy due to their significant impact on the linkage variables *LCRMEE* and *PIRSWE* in equations [1] and [2], respectively. All three administrative aspects have a positive coefficient, suggesting clearly that water administration performance can be enhanced by creating a staffing pattern with a broad-based functional specialization, extending science and technology application into critical areas of planning and management, and improving the information basis of water sector.[14]

Among the insignificant variables in equation [8], the most noteworthy is the linkage variable *ASBUDC*. Although this variable has no effect on the performance of water administration, as we will see below, it has a significant direct effect on water sector performance. Similarly, *AIBDWP*, another insignificant variable in the present equation, has significant indirect effects not only on water administration performance via *ASBUDC* (equation [4]), but also on water policy performance via the linkage variable *PCOREC* (equation [3]). The other insignificant variables – *AORGBA* and *AACCME*, representing, respectively, the spatial organization of water administration and effectiveness of administrative accountability provisions – suggest that, with better technology, information, and functional specialization, these administrative aspects would probably become less important. Besides its implications for the scope of institutional substitutability, this result also shows how the limitations associated with some institutional aspects can be overcome, especially through information and communication technologies.

Institution–Performance Linkages

The focus of our analysis so far has been on the relative role of institutional aspects in institutional linkages both within and across the three components of water institution. Now, our focus shifts to the evaluation of the same in the context of institution–performance linkages, but still paying attention to the relative effects of institutional aspects on institutional linkages. It is the strength of those linkages, as determined by the direct and indirect effects of institutional aspects, that determines water institution performance and affects water sector performance. This is clear from the way the relationships between institutional aspects, institutional linkages, and the performance of the water institution and the water sector are structured and modeled in the system version of Model B. Just as the first five equations are nested with the next three equations ([6] to [8]), so are the equations [6] to [8] linked with the last two equations ([9] to [10]). Since equations [9] and [10] represent, respectively, the penultimate and ultimate layers of institution–performance interaction, they provide a unified context for evaluating the ultimate performance impacts of institutional aspects as routed through the layers of institutional linkages represented by equations [1] to [8].

Water institution performance: relative role of institutional aspects
Equation [9] evaluates the relationship that water institution performance has with the performance of its three components. In Table 8.1b, the performance levels of both water law and water administration have a positive and significant effect on the overall performance of water institutions. In contrast, the performance of water policy has a negative and insignificant effect. Of the two

significant institutional components, the effect of water administration component is much stronger, almost twice as strong as water law component. This is
understandable because, as noted, water administration has a pivotal role in
translating, enforcing, and monitoring the legal provision at the grass-roots
level. From this angle as well as from the fact that water policy in many
contexts is essentially a political economy representation of water law, the
insignificance of water policy is also understandable.

Since all three variables in equation [9] are linkage variables, the nature and
significance of their effects also have implications for the effects of the institutional aspects captured either directly in equations [6] to [8] or indirectly in
equations [1] to [5]. From this perspective, therefore, the overall performance
of the water institution depends ultimately on both the direct and the indirect
effects of institutional aspects that together determine the individual performance of both water law and water administration. The institutional aspects
playing a significant role in determining water institution performance can be
identified from equations [1] to [8]. These aspects include three legal aspects
(*LCRMEE*, *LINTRE*, and *LOECEN*), one policy aspect (*PGPIUP*) and three
administrative aspects (*ABALFS*, *AARINF*, and *AEXTST*). As can be noted
from equations [6] and [8], while the direct and indirect effects of the first four
aspects are captured and transmitted by water law performance, those of the
last three aspects are captured and transmitted by water administration performance.

Although water policy performance has no significant effect on water
institution performance, one of the policy aspects does have some indirect
effects via the linkage variable *LCRMEE*. Thus, from the perspective of water
institution performance, the most important and significant institutional
aspects are: effective conflict-resolution provisions, legal integration, a
healthy dose of centralization within water law, user participation policy,
balanced functional specialization, adequate information, and technology
application. Because water administration performance has a stronger effect
on water institution performance, among these institutional aspects, those
related to water administration are more important than the others. This fact
is reinforced by the results in equations [1] and [6] that the linkage variable
LCRMEE, with its dominant effect on water law performance, is itself
affected by the indirect effects of three of the administrative aspects listed
above.

Water sector performance: relative role of institutional aspects

The performance linkage between water institution and water sector can be
evaluated using the estimated results for equation [10] reported in Table 8.1b.
This equation specifies water sector performance as a function of water institution performance and five other institutional aspects used as proxies such

as: policy bias against the water sector: (*POPAWE*), fiscal status (*ASBUDC*), cost-recovery commitment (*PCOREC*), and information and technology status (*AARINF* and *AEXTST*). It captures both direct and indirect effects of the institutional aspects routed through a variety of channels and various layers of institutional and performance linkages as well as these proxy variables. Only four of these six factors are found to have significant effects on the overall performance of the water sector. Listed in the order of their relative importance, they are: water institution performance, cost-recovery commitment, fiscal health, and information status.

Water institution performance and information status have an understandable positive effect. Cost-recovery commitment and fiscal health have a negative effect requiring some explanation. The institutional aspect of the seriousness of the budget constraint is used as a proxy for poor fiscal health of the economy on the following reasoning. A serious budget constraint for water administration means more than poor financial performance within the sector, because it can be a result of a cut in the budget allocated to the water sector due to the economy's poor fiscal health. Viewed in this light, the negative coefficient of *ASBUDC* means that serious budget constraint impels improvements in water sector performance. This can happen in a variety of ways, such as the selection of a few projects for fast implementation, improved cost recovery, active promotion of user and private sector participation, staff reduction, and other similar economy measures. The negative effect of *PCOREC*, considered here a proxy for the government's general cost-recovery commitment, can imply the following. Either there is a vast gap between the commitment and its translation into practice, especially in the context of the water sector, or poor water sector performance remains the motivating force for improving cost recovery within the water sector.

Returning to water institution performance, the most significant and dominant factor affecting water sector performance, the results confirm strongly the role of institutional linkages in improving water sector performance. Since water institution performance is the ultimate linkage variable in the system, it captures both the direct and indirect effects of institutional aspects flowing through all the previous equations and transmits them finally to water sector performance. As a result, all the institutional aspects that affected water institution performance also affect water sector performance indirectly while some of the institutional aspects such as *PCOREC* and *ASBUDC* affect it directly in their capacity as proxies. Since these proxies are also the linkage variables, they bring to bear the effects of the significant institutional aspects represented in equations [3] and [4]. These institutional aspects are: *LPRSRF*, *PGPIUP*, and *AIBDWP*, representing, respectively, the water-rights format, effectiveness of user participation policy, and the existence of an independent water-pricing body.

Taking these institutional aspects together with those affecting water institution performance, the most important institutional aspects having either a direct, indirect, or mixed effect on water sector performance can be listed by distinguishing the way their effects are channeled. The institutional aspects affecting water sector performance via water institution performance are effective conflict-resolution provisions, legal integration, a healthy dose of centralization within water law, user participation policy, balanced functional specialization, adequate information, and technology application. Those affecting water sector performance directly as proxies are: cost-recovery status and seriousness of budget constraint. The institutional aspects affecting water sector performance indirectly through the direct effects of the proxy variables are: water-rights format, effectiveness of user participation policy, and existence of an independent water-pricing body. Thus, the overall performance of the water sector depends on the multifarious effects of four legal aspects (*LCRMEE*, *LINTRE*, *LOECEN*, and *LPRSRF*), two policy aspects (*PCOREC* and *PGPIUP*), and five administrative aspects (*ABALFS*, *ASBUDC*, *AEXTST*, *AARINF*, and *AIBDWP*). These results are very much in line with the attention that these and related institutional aspects are receiving in the ongoing debate on water sector reform, both nationally and globally.

EMPIRICAL RESULTS: VALIDITY AND RAMIFICATIONS

The preceding analysis of the empirical results provides considerable insights into the relative role and significance of institutional aspects both at a given layer and in the whole process of institution–performance interaction within water sector. While identifying the significant institutional aspects and institutional linkages, we have also seen their insignificant counterparts. Specifically, the five insignificant institutional aspects are: *LTRWSA*, *PPSCRI*, *AORGBA*, *POPAWE*, and *AACCME*. The first three of these aspects appear in only one equation; the other two appear in more than one equation, but do not have a significant effect in any of them. Of the nine linkage variables (the dependent variables in equations [1] to [9]), two (*LACPRE* and *POEFWP*) are insignificant, thereby causing the insignificance of three more institutional aspects (*LOEPRV*, *POELWL*, and *PGPIPP*) with significant indirect effect as well as one linkage variable (*PIRSWE*) with significant direct effect. Thus, with the exception of these 10 institutional aspects and three linkage equations, the remaining 11 institutional aspects and six linkage equations have very significant effects on the overall performance of the water sector, both directly and indirectly, through a variety of channels. These results, though illuminating our comprehension of institution–performance interaction, raise a few serious questions. Is this result reliable and robust enough for universal generalization?

How are they influenced by the role of exogenous factors characterizing the general socioeconomic, demographic, and resource environment within which the process of institution–performance interaction occurs? And, more importantly, what are their ramifications for practical policy, especially for institutional design and reform strategy?

Validity and Robustness

The results show convincingly that the model capturing the institution–performance linkages fits the data well and is therefore consistent with empirical reality. As we will see in the next chapter, in terms of the values of χ^2 and the Breusch–Pagan test statistic (Table 9.1b and 9.2b), the estimated results also seem to be free from the bias caused by noises such as autocorrelation and heteroskedasticity. The set of institutional aspects identified as having dominant effects on both water institution and water sector performance is also in consonance with the current thinking and recent reform initiatives – both proposed and ongoing – of many national governments and international funding and technical agencies. While our results are certainly empirically valid, econometrically reliable, and intuitively consistent, we still need to verify their robustness and sensitivity. The robustness of the model and its results can be verified by evaluating them in various contexts, each defined by certain distinct characteristics endogenous to the sample itself. These characteristics are related to sample size, respondents' subject specialization, and the reform status of sample countries. These endogenous characteristics can be used to categorize the sample into groups, each of which can then be used as a distinct context for the estimation and evaluation of the system version of Model B. In addition to its role in verifying the robustness of the model, this exercise could also provide additional insights and further empirical support.

While the robustness of the model and its results can be evaluated using certain characteristics endogenous to the sample, their sensitivity can be evaluated by considering the influence of the exogenous factors. Since the constant term in all the equations in Model B captures the combined effects of these factors, its sign, magnitude, and statistical significance can indicate both the direction and the intensity of the combined effects of the general socioeconomic, political, legal, and resource environment on the process of institution–performance interaction. The constant terms also capture the effects of the excluded institutional aspects as well as those included but with insignificant effects. Given the intricate linkages among institutional aspects, the effects of some aspects may either be captured by or mixed with others.[15] As we see from the results presented in Tables 8.1a and 8.1b, the constant term in all equations except equation [8] is highly significant, suggesting the significance of the combined effects of the exogenous factors as well as the excluded and insignificant institutional aspects. Although it is negative and significant in equations [2] and [7], it is positive and highly significant in the case of the most important equations.

The positive effect of the constant term, especially in equations [9] and [10], suggests clearly the intrinsic synergy that the process of institution–performance interaction can derive from the general environment, now strongly oriented toward reform. As a matter of fact, considering the relative size of the coefficients, the constant terms capturing the general environment have a much stronger effect on water sector performance than the variable capturing the overall performance of water institution.[16] However, the constant term that indicates the direction and significance of only the combined effects of the exogenous and other factors can help neither in distinguishing the effects of the exogenous factors from others nor in evaluating the relative individual effects of the exogenous factors. We also recognize that the individual effects of the exogenous factors can neither be incorporated into Model B nor be evaluated directly within a system framework due to the already noted data and technical problems. But, we can evaluate their effects indirectly by estimating the nine equations in Model C. From this extraneous analysis, we can show only the relative effects of a selected set of exogenous factors on the nine main variables related to the performance of both water institution and water sector, but cannot demonstrate how the individual effects are captured by the institutional and performance variables in the system. The exercise of testing the robustness of Model B directly and evaluating the sensitivity of the model variables indirectly is carried out in Chapter 9.

Ramifications for Practical Policy

The unique empirical evidence we have provided for the existence and performance significance of institutional linkages offers a new perspective on the process of institution–performance interaction both in general and in water sector contexts. In particular, we have shown the strategic role of the linkage variables in capturing the effects of the significant institutional aspects on various layers of intra- and interinstitutional linkages and transmitting them ultimately into the two layers of institution–performance linkages. From this exercise, we have not only distinguished direct from indirect effects but also indicated various channels through which these indirect effects are transmitted to influence sequentially the performance of institutional components, the water institution, and the water sector.

With the quantification of various layers of linkages and the identification of the channels of impact transmission, we can quantitatively trace channels through which the effects of a marginal change in institutional aspects are transmitted to water sector performance. As we trace out all the institutional routes through which institutional aspects transmit their impact, we can also evaluate the relative performance impact of a marginal change in each of the institutional aspects and identify the relative significance of various impact-transmission channels. For instance, the following is what we mean by impact-transmission channels and their underlying institutional routes or chains. A change in *PGPIUP* affects first *LCRMEE* (in equation [1]), which in turn affects *LOEFWL* (in equation [6]), which in turn affects *WIPOEV* (in equation [9]), which ultimately affects *WSPOEV* (in equation [10]). Thus, *LCRMEE–LOEFWL–WIPOEV* forms an impact-transmission channel between *PGPIUP* and *WSPOEV* and thus represents an institutional route or chain. Similarly, a change in *PGPIUP* also creates effects through other channels, some of which are significant (e.g., *PCOREC* and *PCOREC–ASBUDC*), while others are not (e.g., *PCOREC–LACPRE–LOEFWL–WIPOEV* and *PIRSWE–POEFWP–WIPOEV*). We will formalize and evaluate all such institutional chains in Chapter 10.

Since the identification and evaluation of the institutional chains and their impact-transmission channels enable us to rank institutional aspects in terms of the extensiveness of their institutional linkages and the intensity of their impact transmission, they are very valuable for deriving institutional design and implementation principles, including institutional sequencing and packaging. With the delineation of the institutional routes or chains through which the impact transmission occurs, both the weak and strong links that either obstruct or promote the process of impact transmission can be identified. All this information is of key value for designing institutional reform programs, as it provides a basis for evaluating alternative sequencing and packaging of institutional aspects in terms of their relative performance impact. This information is also indispensable for setting priorities and targeting strategic institutional aspects and the institutional routes of their impact transmission. The strategic significance of this tracing exercise for designing institutional reforms, complete with sequencing, packaging, and timing, and scaling, is elaborated and numerically demonstrated in Chapter 10. Although we do not have enough numerical information to deal with the issue of timing and scaling, we will also address this critical issue based on both the observational evidence discussed in Chapter 7 and inferences from the regression results for Model C, to be discussed in Chapter 9.

NOTES

1. When there are sequential linkages among equations, as in the present context, the 3-SLS technique provides unbiased and consistent estimates with Maximum Likelihood Estimation characteristics. Moreover, this technique is also more convenient for tracing how the effects of a marginal change in one variable in an equation spread throughout the system.
2. While it is both possible and desirable to experiment with quadratic and other nonlinear forms, either with logarithmic transformation or with interactive terms, problems such as the

existence of a large number of zero values and a large, though countable, number of inter-active variables present serious technical constraints for such experiment.

3. The effects that some of these factors have on performance evaluation can also be evaluated more explicitly with the help of the nine equations in Model C. The constant terms in the equations in this model could, in fact, capture the effects of other exogenous factors that are not included due to data limitations.

4. While R^2 shows the explanatory power of all the variables within an equation, System R^2 evaluates the explanatory power of all the equations estimated together as a system. The Likelihood Ratio test is also an index of the explanatory power of the model as it is based on the difference between the maximum likelihood that is estimated with the restriction that all coefficients in the model are zero and the same estimated without that restriction (Kennedy 1987: 58–9).

5. Simply put, this problem is due to the relationship between the magnitude of the indepen-dent variables and their residuals (i.e., the difference between their actual and estimated values). Specifically, it exists whenever the absolute magnitude of the residuals is related to the independent variable such that the former is small (large) for lower (higher) values of the latter. If, in contrast, the absolute magnitude of the residuals is, more or less, the same regardless of the values of the independent variables, the problem is absent. This can be econometrically verified with the Breusch–Pagan test statistics having a chi-square (χ^2) distribution for large samples (Kennedy 1987: 96–8).

6. The comparison of both the number and magnitude of the coefficients of the 21 variables common to both models may look unrealistic because the dependent variables with which they are related in the two models are different. However, our conclusion is still valid because it is based on comparison of the same set of coefficients with that obtained in the 3-SLS results of Model B, which captures both direct and indirect effects. While the size and significance of coefficients cannot be used to test the fit of the models, as far as they reflect the effects of linkages and synergy, they can be used as an indicator of the realistic nature of different model formulations.

7. Dissipation means only that the effects are not captured by any other variables. It does not mean that the effects are lost, because they are implicitly captured by the system. In this sense, a variable is insignificant only in the context of a given equation but not so in the context of the total system.

8. Since the irrigation sector has a dominant share in water use in most contexts, intersectoral water transfers are likely to adversely affect the share of the irrigation sector, and interre-gional water transfers have a similar effect in the region from which water is transferred. Because user participation policy is confined mainly to the irrigation sector, the adverse effects of either kind of transfer are likely to face strong opposition from user groups.

9. This result is a clear contradiction to the current policies pursued by national governments and international donor and funding agencies in many developing countries, focused more on institutional aspects related to recovery such as water user associations (WUAs) than on the institutional aspect related to pricing and rate revision. While the institutional aspect of WUAs is important, as it facilitates and paves the way for other institutional aspects (e.g., conflict resolution as shown in equation [1]), the priority assigned to this aspect is due more to the political economy constraint for reforming pricing-related institutional aspects. For more details on the institutional issues surrounding water pricing within a political economy perspective, see Dinar (2000).

10. Private sector participation is advocated as much for this healthy effect on accountability as for its financial and technical contributions (Saleth 1999).

11. The insignificance of *LACPRE* – appearing as a linkage variable only in equation [6] – means that its effects as well as the effects of other institutional aspects, which it captured in equa-tion [5], could not be transmitted anywhere in the system. Since both its individual and acquired effects are dissipated, the institutional linkage represented by equation [5] remains very loosely connected with the system. This does not mean that this equation should be elim-inated, as it still implicitly contributes to the performance of the whole system and provides an important instance of impact dissipation within institution–performance interaction. As we shall see in the context of equation [9], this applies equally to equation [7] as well.

12. Although the legal aspect *LPRSRF* has no direct effect on water law performance and its indirect effect on the same becomes dissipated due to the insignificance of *LACPRE*, it still has significant impact on water sector performance due to its indirect effects via *PCOREC* in equation [3].

13. The ultimate solution to the centralization–decentralization dilemma lies not in opting for one or the other, but in their optimal blending through institutional means. Thus, with carefully crafted institutional arrangements, structured at different geographical and decision-making levels, both local flexibility and regional coordination can be achieved in water use decisions. Only within such a framework can spatially decentralized arrangements such as the RBOs function as an effective organizational basis both for pursuing integrated water resource management and for resolving interregional and intersectoral water conflicts.

14. This result is consistent with current priorities on the technical agendas of many national governments and international funding agencies. It also provides clear justification for additional investment in these key technical areas, indispensable for strengthening the planning and implementation capabilities of water administration.

15. Such a possibility indicates the practical difficulties of isolating the effects of some of the individual law-, policy-, and administration-related institutional aspects, even when the water institution is decomposed with still finer analytical details. This applies especially to water administration, where more accurate analytical decomposition is difficult and the effects of most administrative aspects are too intertwined to isolate.

16. This is understandable in view of the positive role of many developments occurring both within and outside the water sector. These developments include the resurgence of democratic forms of government that favor decentralization and participation, the increasing water scarcity that motivates many unconventional solutions (e.g., water markets), and technical progress that enables more accurate measurement and monitoring. Since these developments foster a pro-reform climate, their synergetic impulses can be exploited through proper design, sequencing, and timing of the strategy for institutional reforms within the water sector.

9. Institution–performance linkages: robustness and contextuality

The analysis of empirical results in the preceding chapter has provided us with rich insights into the process of institution–performance interaction within the water sector. It enables us to identify the most significant institutional aspects and show how their effects – both direct and indirect – are being channeled through various layers of institutional and performance linkages to be transmitted ultimately to water sector performance. The empirical knowledge on the relative significance of institutional aspects and their impact-transmission channels is invaluable for designing reform packages, including setting and sequencing institutional priorities, based on their linkage roles and relative performance impacts. The policy value of the empirical results, however, depends critically on their reliability and credibility as evaluated in terms of their robustness with changing contexts and their sensitivity to factors both endogenous and exogenous to our sample and estimation contexts. The main objective of this chapter is to evaluate the robustness and sensitivity of the results derived and discussed in previous chapter and to establish, thereby, their dependability as an empirical basis for designing generic reform packages, to be attempted in the next chapter.

EVALUATING ROBUSTNESS AND SENSITIVITY: CONTEXT AND APPROACH

The robustness and sensitivity aspects can be evaluated by comparing the results discussed in Chapter 8 with those obtained in different estimation contexts. These estimation contexts are defined by certain distinct characteristics endogenous to our sample, such as sample size, respondents' disciplinary backgrounds, and the reform status of sample countries. In other words, by categorizing our sample into subsets in terms of these endogenous characteristics and comparing the results of the system version of Model B across these subsamples, much can be learned about the robustness and sensitivity of the results to contextual variations. In addition to its role in evaluating the robustness properties of the results across sample size groups, this exercise can enable us to understand the sensitivity of the results to internal and contextual factors such as disciplinary bias, ideological domination, and regional configuration.

This comparative analysis can also provide some indirect idea about the sensitivity of the results to exogenous factors such as demographic status, development stage, and resource conditions that together define the overall environment within which the process of institution–performance interaction occurs within the water sector. But, it is of little help in explicitly evaluating the sensitivity of the results to these exogenous factors, as informational and methodological constraints do not permit incorporation of these exogenous factors directly within the system framework of Model B. The sensitivity of the results to these exogenous factors can, however, be evaluated indirectly in terms of their influence on the subjective evaluation of nine performance variables within the framework of Model C. With these points in mind, let us now describe briefly the estimation contexts as well as the evaluation approach and criteria that we use to evaluate the robustness and sensitivity of the results reported in Chapter 8.

Estimation Contexts

The estimation contexts are defined in terms of three key features – sample size, subject specialization of experts, and reform status of sample countries – which can be used to categorize our sample into subgroups. Since the context defined by sample size allows us to estimate the model with three different sample sizes – 43, 84, and 127 (denoted as sample contexts I, II, and III, respectively) – it can help us in evaluating the robustness of the results obtained with different sample sizes. In addition to its role in evaluating the robustness of the model and its estimated coefficients, this context captures the role of yet another interesting dimension. The sample size variations also correspond to the variations in survey phase and geographic focus (Table 6.2). For instance, sample context I includes the responses from the first survey phase, focused predominantly on South Asia, China, Australia, and South America. Sample context II corresponds to the second and third phases of the survey, with a major focus on Southeast Asia and Europe. Sample context III, covering all three surveys, provides an overall global perspective. The estimation and comparison of the results from the system version of Model B within these three sample contexts could, therefore, be useful for judging the sensitivity of the results to variations in sample size and geographic focus.[1]

The estimation context defined by the disciplinary backgrounds of sample experts is based on the categorization of the sample into two, more or less, equal groups: engineers (61 responses) and social scientists (66 responses). Thus, engineers account for 48 percent of the responses and social scientists account for the remaining 52 percent. Although the first group consists almost entirely of engineers, it also includes two experts with hydrological and geological backgrounds. Similarly, the second group, consisting mostly of economists (32 percent), also includes experts with other social science disciplines (16 percent) and legal backgrounds (4 percent). As noted in Chapter 6, however, this categorization does not imply any strict departmentalization of the respondents' knowledge base, as they have considerable transdisciplinary understanding gained through interaction and experience. The categorization is intended essentially to capture the effects that differences in the personal preference, theoretical orientation, and ideological predilections of these two subgroups have on their subjective evaluation of institution–performance interaction and hence, on the estimated results. Thus, by comparing the results of the system version of Model B obtained for the two sample groups, we can see whether there is any group-specific pattern in the configuration of statistically significant institutional and performance variables.

The estimation context defined by the reform status of sample countries is based on the classification of sample responses into two groups: those from countries recently undergoing water sector reforms (71 responses) and those from other countries (56 responses).[2] Since the reform environment and subjective perception are interrelated, the evaluation of institution–performance interaction by respondents from countries that have undertaken substantial reforms in recent years is likely to be different from the same evaluation by respondents from other countries. The comparison of model results across the two country groups can, therefore, capture the effects of area-specific differences in the evaluation process. Specifically, the difference in the relative magnitude and statistical significance of model coefficients obtained for the two samples could provide valuable information about differences in the configurations of institutional variables receiving attention in the two sets of countries. The comparison could also indicate region-specific differences in the nature and role of exogenous factors affecting both the perception and the reality of institution–performance linkages. Moreover, we can also expect institutional and performance linkages to be stronger in reform countries than in others.

While the robustness of the results and their sensitivity to internal and contextual factors are evaluated by comparing the 3-SLS results of Model B across the three estimation contexts noted above, their sensitivity to exogenous factors is inferred through an analysis of both the simple and stepwise OLS results of Model C. Since the nine equations of Model C postulate each of the nine performance variables as dependent on the same set of 12 variables representing some major economic, demographic, environmental, and institutional variables, their estimation can provide information on the relative direction, magnitude, and significance of the exogenous factors on performance evaluation. From this exercise, we can understand the relative effects of exogenous factors on the subjective process of performance evaluation and thereby infer the potential for their direct impact on the performance of both water institution and water sector.

Approach and Focus

The main approach for evaluating the consistency and reliability of the results discussed in Chapter 8 involves a comparison of the 3-SLS results of Model B related to the all-sample context with those related to various subsample contexts described above. The sets of context-specific results will also be compared among themselves to isolate area- and group-specific differences in the influence of factors endogenous and contextual to the sample.[3] This comparative analysis will focus on the size, direction, and significance of the coefficients of all the variables in Model B obtained under the three estimation contexts. The purpose of evaluation at this stage is fourfold. The first objective is to identify the most robust variables, those with significant coefficients in all contexts, and contrast them with the contextual ones. The second is to compare the size and direction of the coefficient pertaining to both the robust and the contextual variables and show the variations in their relative significance across contexts. The third is to identify some of the reasons for the contextual differences in the behavior of institutional variables and to identify caveats, if any, for the general results discussed in Chapter 8. The last is to explain the overall implications of the robustness of institutional variables for the relative significance of various layers of institutional and performance linkages, as well as for the scope of convergence in perceptual evaluation.

We recognize that our evaluation of both the robustness and sensitivity properties of the results is only relative and indicative rather than absolute and exhaustive. This is because the contexts considered here are just a few among many possible ones.[4] Nevertheless, by comparing the 3-SLS results of Model B under various subsample contexts, additional insights can be gained into the relative significance, linkage effects, and the contextual properties of institutional aspects. In addition to its role in evaluating the robustness and sensitivity of the results, the estimation exercise in various contexts and perspectives can also enrich our evaluation framework, thereby maximizing our understanding of the robustness, sensitivity, and contextual properties of the process of institution–performance interaction. Specifically, the comparative analysis of context-specific results with those obtained in the all-sample context helps not only to identify exceptions and caveats to the general pattern in the behavior of institutional aspects but also to indicate the extent of convergence in perceptional evaluation.

The sensitivity of the results to exogenous factors is evaluated indirectly, based on inferences derived from a comparison of the estimated results of the

nine equations of Model C under both the simple and stepwise OLS procedures. Model C is estimated using only the secondary data described in
Chapter 6. It is equally possible to conceive some sequential relationships
among the nine equations of Model C. For instance, as we follow the specification of equations [C1] to [C9], we see that equations [C1], [C2], and [C3]
can be linked with equation [C4] in the sense that the dependent variables in
the first three equations can enter as independent variables in equation [C4].
Similarly, equations [C5], [C6], [C7], and [C8] can also be linked with equation [C9] as the dependent variables in those four equations are basically the
four performance components of the dependent variable in equation [C9]. It
would be interesting to estimate Model C with a system perspective, but serious technical reasons have prevented us from doing so. Since the independent
variables in all nine equations of the model are the same, a major econometric
problem of identification prevents us from estimating the equations with a
system approach.[5] As a result, the only approach feasible for estimating the
equations in Model C is the single-equation approach and hence, they are all
estimated with the OLS technique.

Although Model C is estimated with a single-equation approach, we have
used both the simple and stepwise procedures of the OLS technique. The
simple procedure includes all 12 independent variables in Model C, regardless
of their explanatory power and statistical significance, but identifies the most
significant among them. In contrast, the stepwise procedure considers one
variable at a time and includes only those remaining significant at a specified
probability level, in our case this level is 20 percent. Thus, the stepwise procedure helps identify the most effective combination of independent variables
that explains the variations in the performance variables. The purpose of
comparing Model C results under the two different OLS procedures is
twofold. The first objective is to find out whether the explanatory power and
relative significance are different when all the variables are taken together and
when only the most significant subset among the 12 variables is used. The
second objective is to see whether the set of statistically significant variables
identified by one procedure is different from that identified by the other procedure. The latter aspect is crucial because the relative effect of each variable is
highly sensitive to the variables with which it is combined in an equation.[6]
Although this sensitivity implies the econometric problem of multicollinear-
ity, it shows the interesting phenomenon of linkages among exogenous factors
that together define the overall environment for institution–performance interaction. Since this exercise could help us identify the most effective combination of independent variables in each equation, it could provide valuable
insights into the individual and joint effects of the exogenous factors on
performance evaluation and, by induction, on the performance of water institution and water sector.

ROBUSTNESS OF RESULTS

Since robustness relates to the sensitivity of results to variations in sample size, this property can be evaluated by comparing the 3-SLS results obtained in three contexts defined by different sample sizes. As noted already, since the sample size variations also coincide with a change in the configuration of sample countries, the comparison can also shed light on the effects of regional differences in water sector concerns and institutional challenges. The sample-specific results are reported in Tables 9.1a and 9.1b. The main purpose of comparing these sample-specific results is to test the durability and reliability of the all-sample results – especially the relative significance of institutional variables and their configurations – reported in Chapter 8 when sample size and regional coverage vary. From this comparison, some insights can be gained into the four key aspects. These aspects are: robustness and contextuality of institutional variables, variations in their relative significance, causes and caveats for the robustness properties and relative significance, and implications for institutional and performance linkages and for their perceptional evaluation.

Robustness and Contextuality

Let us focus first on the most robust of the institutional variables included in the first five equations representing various layers of institutional interlinkages. In equation [1], capturing the effects of interinstitutional linkages on the effectiveness of conflict-resolution mechanisms *(LCRMEE)*, the only significant variable in all the three sampling contexts is the one representing the institutional aspect of user participation policy *(PGPIUP)*. While the variable representing the impact of other policies affecting water policy *(POPAWE)* is uniformly insignificant, the other institutional variables are significant in either sampling context I or III. Of the four institutional variables included in equation [2], only two are robust with significant coefficients in all sampling contexts. They are the water-rights format *(LPRSRF)* and extensiveness of science and technology application *(AEXTST)*. This means that these two institutional aspects have a more durable role in determining the effectiveness of water transfer policy *(PIRSWE)*, irrespective of sampling variations. The other two institutional aspects representing *LCRMEE* and *PGPIUP*, though insignificant in sampling context II, are significant in the other two sampling contexts. It is also clear in equation [2] that the behavior of all four variables in sampling context I remains consistent with that observed in context III representing the all-sample case, although there are considerable differences in the magnitude of their coefficients across these two sampling contexts.

The consistent behavior of institutional variables across sampling contexts

Table 9.1a. Institution–performance interaction in the water sector: effects of sample size and country coverage

(3-SLS Estimates of Model B)

Equations	Dependent variables	Independent variables	I (Sample 1–43)		II (Sample 44–127)		III (Sample 1–127)	
			coefficient[a]	t-ratio	coefficient[a]	t-ratio	coefficient[a]	t-ratio
[1]	LCRMEE	LPRSRF	−0.129	−0.791	0.496	2.108	0.079	0.556
		PGPIUP	0.316	2.523	0.182	2.111	0.246	3.481
		POPAWE	0.137	0.846	−0.038	−0.262	0.096	0.880
		ABALFS	1.357	2.441	0.132	0.250	0.822	2.212
		AARINF	0.015	0.128	0.130	0.962	0.122	1.408
		AEXTST	−0.007	−0.046	0.234	1.662	0.141	1.303
		Constant	2.522	1.757	1.810	1.594	1.818	2.085
[2]	PIRSWE	LPRSRF	0.457	2.307	0.405	2.467	0.209	1.686
		LCRMEE	1.350	5.438	−0.094	−0.614	0.698	3.633
		PGPIUP	−0.364	−2.118	0.016	0.188	−0.139	−1.557
		AEXTST	0.230	1.274	0.587	5.833	0.299	3.025
		Constant	−4.019	−2.738	−0.008	−0.011	−1.750	−2.025
[3]	PCOREC	LPRSRF	−0.096	−2.032	−0.052	−0.858	−0.070	−1.833
		PGPIUP	0.065	1.837	−0.004	−0.157	0.024	1.297
		POPAWE	−0.003	−0.055	0.031	0.766	−0.018	−0.593
		AIBDWP	0.815	4.087	0.105	0.639	0.265	2.153
		Constant	1.894	5.151	2.221	8.719	2.358	11.750

[4]	ASBUDC	AIBDWP	**2.922**	2.462	*1.119*	1.266	**1.485**	2.008
		PCOREC	**-3.713**	-3.814	*-2.322*	-2.126	**-3.426**	-3.590
		PGPIPP	-0.136	-0.925	0.034	0.287	-0.022	-0.233
		PGPIUP	*0.244*	1.291	0.123	0.989	*0.155*	1.463
		Constant	**10.265**	5.254	**7.694**	3.143	**10.178**	5.111
[5]	LACPRE	LPRSRF	**0.039**	0.249	0.095	0.392	*0.200*	1.292
		LOEPRV	**0.394**	3.140	**0.230**	2.031	**0.289**	3.600
		PCOREC	**1.363**	2.549	**2.588**	3.129	**3.814**	6.499
		POELWL	**0.248**	1.626	*0.130*	1.338	**0.208**	2.486
		AACCME	*0.171*	1.466	-0.093	-1.085	-0.021	-0.278
		Constant	**-2.962**	-1.938	**-3.108**	-1.598	**-7.036**	-4.769

Note: [a] Coefficients in **bold** are significant at 10 percent or better whereas coefficients in ***bold and italic*** are significant at 20 percent.

Table 9.1b. *Institution–performance interaction in the water sector: effects of sample size and country coverage*

(3-SLS Estimates of Model B)

Equations	Dependent variables	Independent variables	I (Sample 1–43)		II (Sample 44–127)		III (Sample 1–127)	
			coefficient[a]	t-ratio	coefficient[a]	t-ratio	coefficient[a]	t-ratio
[6]	LOEFWL	LTRWSA	**1.222**	2.443	0.054	0.117	0.259	0.730
		LPRSRF	**0.190**	1.969	−0.050	−0.226	0.095	0.853
		LCRMEE	**0.327**	2.179	0.241	1.176	**0.321**	1.489
		LACPRE	−0.114	−0.631	**0.749**	2.934	0.241	1.173
		LINTRE	**0.171**	2.630	−0.019	−0.256	**0.093**	1.779
		LOECEN	−0.036	−0.495	**0.223**	3.166	**0.076**	1.462
		LOEPRV	**0.212**	1.700	−0.079	−0.710	0.066	0.790
		Constant	**1.669**	1.892	0.266	0.280	**1.256**	1.556
[7]	POEFWP	PPSCRI	**−0.248**	−2.545	−0.043	−0.300	−0.107	−1.189
		PCOREC	**1.024**	2.830	**2.363**	3.727	**1.523**	3.241
		PIRSWE	**0.180**	1.753	**0.526**	2.109	**0.783**	5.278
		PGPIPP	**−0.152**	−2.366	−0.066	−1.238	**−0.103**	−2.265
		PGPIUP	−0.021	−0.258	**0.129**	1.644	0.062	0.977
		POPAWE	0.080	0.726	−0.002	−0.019	0.053	0.590
		POELWL	**0.415**	4.633	0.118	1.189	**0.179**	2.605
		Constant	0.914	0.811	**−3.433**	−2.736	**−2.067**	−1.977

224

		Model 1		Model 2		Model 3	
[8]	AOEFWA						
	AORGBA	-0.049	-0.246	0.053	0.538	0.035	0.359
	ABALFS	*0.941*	1.422	**0.952**	3.573	**1.062**	3.827
	AIBDWP	0.773	1.179	0.126	0.371	0.121	0.383
	ASBUDC	0.161	0.826	-0.056	-0.509	0.149	1.098
	AACCME	-0.139	-0.857	0.056	1.107	-0.030	-0.481
	AARINF	0.082	0.631	**0.258**	3.060	**0.226**	3.126
	AEXTST	**0.363**	2.077	**0.364**	4.188	**0.356**	4.661
	Constant	*1.904*	1.425	**1.070**	1.701	0.841	1.188
[9]	WIPOEV						
	LOEFWL	0.762	3.347	-0.056	-0.403	**0.371**	2.484
	POEFWP	-0.158	-0.678	*-0.272*	-1.529	-0.072	-0.415
	AOEFWA	0.276	1.999	**1.095**	5.917	*0.622*	4.188
	Constant	1.051	1.204	**1.480**	2.339	*0.840*	1.304
[10]	WSPOEV						
	WIPOEV	**0.786**	6.256	**0.399**	3.054	**0.843**	7.355
	POPAWE	*-0.139*	-1.543	-0.066	-0.922	-0.063	-1.149
	ASBUDC	-0.043	-0.633	0.002	0.021	*-0.132*	-1.570
	PCOREC	0.046	0.155	*0.605*	1.335	*-0.450*	-1.278
	AARINF	0.053	0.854	**0.205**	2.588	**0.098**	1.934
	AEXTST	0.002	0.023	**0.139**	1.617	0.041	0.672
	Constant	*1.297*	1.301	0.065	0.067	**1.537**	1.972
System R^2		0.884		0.797		0.765	
χ^2		92.694		134.090		183.850	
Breusch–Pagan test		75.554		174.640		230.710	
Sample size		43		84		127	

Note: [a] Coefficients in **bold** are significant at 10 percent or better whereas coefficients in ***bold and italic*** are significant at 20 percent.

225

I and III in equation [2] can also be observed in the context of both equations [3] and [4]. Notably, in the particular case of equation [3], since none of the institutional variables is significant in sampling context II, the institutional interlinkage captured by the equation itself seems to be contextual in nature. In contrast, two robust and context-independent variables in equation [4] have a more durable and consistent effect on the linkage variable capturing the seriousness of budget constraint (*ASBUDC*). They are the institutional variables representing, respectively, the presence of an independent water-pricing body (*AIBDWP*) and cost-recovery status (*PCOREC*). *PCOREC* is also a linkage variable in equation [2], which, as noted above, not only has no robust variables across the sampling contexts but also has no significant institutional variables in sampling context II. Of the remaining two institutional aspects in equation [4], the variable representing the effectiveness of user participation policy (*PGPIUP*) is significant across all sampling contexts except II whereas the variable representing the institutional aspect of the effectiveness of private sector promotion policy (*PGPIPP*) remains insignificant, irrespective of the sampling context.

Of the five institutional variables in equation [5], three variables – *PCOREC*, *LOEPRV*, representing the effectiveness of legal provisions for private participation, and *POELWL*, representing the overall water law–water policy linkages – are robust with consistent behavior across sample contexts. In contrast, the remaining two institutional variables – *LPRSRF* and *AACCME*, representing respectively property-rights format and the effectiveness of administrative provisions for accountability – are contextual. The effects of these two contextual variables, unlike the three robust variables noted above, on the effectiveness of the legal provisions on accountability (*LACPRE*) are, therefore, sensitive to sample size variations and regional coverage. Although the institutional variables in equation [6] show some consistency in their behavior, none is robust enough for behavioral consistency across all three sample contexts. Of the seven institutional variables in this equation, three (*LTRWSA*, representing the legal treatment of water from difference sources, *LACPRE*, and *LOEPRV*) are more contextual, as they are significant in only one sample context. *LPRSRF*, which is robust in equation [2] and significant in two of the three sample contexts in equations [3] and [5], turns out to be insignificant here in all three sample contexts. By and large, all the law-related institutional aspects are contextual in their effects on the overall effectiveness of water law (*LOEFWL*).

Of the seven institutional variables in equation [7], only *PCOREC* and *PIRSWE* are robust; the others are contextual in terms of their effect on the overall effectiveness of water policy (*POEFWP*). Both the robust variables are also linkage variables, bringing with them the effects of interinstitutional linkages captured respectively in equations [2] and [3]. Of the contextual variables, *PGPIPP* and *POELWL*, though insignificant in sample context II, show consistency in terms of their significance in the other two sample contexts. Turning now to equation [8], of the seven institutional variables determining the overall effectiveness of water administration (*AOEFWA*), only two are robust: those representing, respectively, the administrative aspects of balanced functional specialization (*ABALFS*) and extensiveness of science and technology application (*AEXTST*). The variable representing the institutional aspect of information adequacy within water administration (*AARINF*) is significant in two of the three sample contexts; the rest of the variables are uniformly insignificant.

Only one variable is robust and consistent in equation [9] – *AOEFWA*. The other two variables, *LOEFWL* and *POEFWP*, are significant in only one or two sample contexts. Among the latter, although *LOEFWL* is not significant in sample context II, its behavior is consistent in the other two sample contexts. *AOEFWA*, followed by *LOEFWL*, seems to have a more consistent effect on the overall performance of water institution (*WIPOEV*) than does *POEFWP*. Coming to the last equation, only one variable, *WIPOEV*, has a robust and consistent effect on the overall performance of the water sector (*WSPOEV*). The rest of the variables remain essentially contextual. Although *PCOREC* and *AARINF* are significant in two sample contexts, their behavior is not consistent due to differences in the magnitude and direction of their impact.

From an overall perspective, it is clear from Tables 9.1a and 9.1b that, of the 25 institutional and performance variables in the model (excluding the ultimate dependent variable *WSPOEV*) – covering 16 exogenous and nine endogenous variables – only 12 variables are robust. Of the robust ones, four are linkage or endogenous variables (*PCOREC*, *PIRSWE*, *AOEWA*, and *WIPOEV*) and eight are exogenous variables (*LPRSRF*, *LOEPRV*, *POELWL*, *PGPIUP*, *AIBDWP*, *ABALFS*, *AARINF*, and *AEXTST*). However, the robustness of these variables is also context specific, as some of the variables that are robust in one equation are not in other equation(s). For instance, *PGPIUP* is robust in equation [1] but not in four other equations where it enters as an exogenous or independent variable. Similarly, *LPRSRF* remains a robust variable in equation [2], but the endogenous or linkage variable *PCOREC*, the most robust as an independent variable in equations [4], [5], and [7], becomes contextual in equation [10]. In view of the contextual nature of even the robust variables, the robustness properties of individual institutional aspects need not always be a sufficient condition to ensure the robustness of the institutional and performance linkages that these variables capture and transmit.

Consistency and Caveats

We have distinguished the robust variables from the contextual ones mainly in terms of their uniform statistical significance across sample contexts. More important, however, is testing the sensitivity of the magnitude and direction of their coefficients to sampling variations. Specifically, we would like to know whether sampling variations lead to a change in the relative importance and behavior of the institutional variables in each equation. The evaluation of the robustness properties of institutional aspects shows that their relative influence, as evaluated in terms of the size of their coefficients, varies considerably across sample contexts. Sensitivity in the behavior of institutional aspects to sample size variations is clear from our comparisons of the coefficient size and sign of each institutional aspect in all equations across sample contexts. This result is not unexpected, though the comparison does yield a few distinct and interesting patterns with considerable implications for the relative importance of the institutional linkages as well as for the overall reliability of our model. Let us now deal with each of these patterns.

Relative significance of institutional aspects

Although the relative sizes of the coefficients associated with institutional aspects vary across sample contexts, there is a notable consistency in the relative importance and direction of the impact of institutional aspects, as evaluated by the absolute size and sign of their coefficients, in most of the equations. This consistency is particularly remarkable, as the institutional aspect having the dominant effect is the same across sample contexts in most equations. This consistency, together with the robustness properties of institutional aspects, indicates that the relative importance of institutional variables in various layers of institutional and performance linkages is largely free from sample size variations. This is an important result, as it provides significant evidence for the overall robustness of our model of institution–performance interaction. As we will see, however, this result is not free from exceptions and caveats.

While emphasizing the overall consistency in the relative importance of institutional aspects across sample contexts, let us also identify some notable exceptions that provide the basis for identifying a few caveats to the general pattern. These caveats are more important in sample context II and, to some extent, in sample context I. For instance, in equation [1], the institutional variable *LPRSRF*, which is insignificant in sample contexts I and III, becomes the most dominant variable in sample context II. The relative importance of institutional variables in equation [3] is fairly consistent across sample contexts I and III whereas none of them is significant in sample context II. This means that the layer of institutional linkages characterized by equation [3] itself seems to be largely irrelevant in this particular context. In contrast, equation [6] displays considerable inconsistency in the relative importance of institutional aspects across sample contexts, with each context showing a different institutional aspect as dominant.

In equation [9], although sample contexts I and III identify the same institutional aspects as significant, they diverge in terms of the relative importance of these significant variables. *LOEFWL* has the dominant effect in sample context I; *AOEFWA* has that distinction in sample context III. While *AOEFWA* remains the dominant institutional aspect in sample contexts II and III, sample context II, unlike the other two sample contexts, identifies *POEFWP* as the next most important institutional variable. This means that, among the three water institutional components, the relative importance of the water law and water policy components remains more contextual than the water administration component. Similarly, in equation [10], the most critical component of the system, *WIPOEV* remains consistently the most dominant institutional variable affecting the overall performance of water sector, but the relative importance of the remaining variables shows considerable variations across sample contexts.

As noted already, an analysis of the relative significance, robustness, and consistency of institutional aspects across sample contexts provides valuable insights for designing and implementing institutional reform packages. The exceptions and caveats to the general pattern provide equally valuable information for ensuring that the institutional reform package addresses location-specific concerns and problems. From the evaluation of the robustness properties of institutional aspects and consistency in their relative significance, some of the critical institutional components can be identified for enhancing the overall performance of the water institution and the water sector in most contexts. From the perspective of developing institutional reform packages, these key components will form the nucleus around which other context-specific components can be built to enhance the effectiveness of the reform package in addressing both general as well as contextual and location-specific problems and concerns. The exceptions and caveats, in fact, help in identifying the additional institutional components necessary to ensure flexibility and location specificity in reform packages.

Relative strength of institution–performance linkages

Comparing the results of sample contexts I and II, we see that the size of the coefficients associated with most of the institutional aspects in almost all equations is larger in sample context I than in sample context II. This is also true in terms of the number of significant institutional aspects in most equations. It is an important indication that linkages among institutional aspects and their performance implications are much stronger in sample context I than in sample context II. This important result is basically an outcome of the difference in the country coverage and geographical focus of the two sample contexts. As seen from Table 6.2, sample context I includes responses mainly from South Asia including China, North and South America, Australia, and the Middle East. In these regions, water sector is dominated by heavy irrigation demand, water scarcity, and associated social and political problems. In contrast, sample context II covers responses mostly from Europe and Southeast Asia, where, by and large, the water sector is affected more by water quality and flood-related problems than by any acute water scarcity.

As seen from Table 6.1, the countries covered by the two sets of samples display a distinct pattern in key features of their water sectors. For instance, the average water withdrawal per capita of countries covered by sample I (5,600 cum) is lower than that (6,500 cum) of those covered by sample II. Although sample I covers only 11 countries, their irrigated area (131 mha) exceeds the same (47 mha) in the 28 additional countries covered by sample II. The total annual water demand of countries covered by sample I is about 554 bcum whereas that of the additional countries covered by sample II is only 182 bcum. But, the two sets of countries are different not merely in their resource endowments and equally also in their demographic and socioeconomic conditions. For instance, sample I countries have a combined population of 3.05 billion with an average population density of 71 persons per sqkm. The additional countries covered in sample II have a combined population of only 1.35 billion with an average population density of 51 persons per sqkm. Moreover, sample I countries have many more people (588 million) living below the poverty line than do the countries added in sample II (212 million).

Demographic and socioeconomic pressures on the water sector are clearly more acute in sample I countries than those added in sample II. That is why the institutional linkages and their implications for water sector performance are stronger in sample I, but get weaker as countries with less severe problems are added in sample II. By the same token, the perception of institution–performance linkages is much stronger among experts in the first set than in the second. This is the main reason for the differential results observed in the two sample contexts. The implication is that, although water institutional reforms are equally necessary in both sets of countries, the sample I countries consider them much more important for water sector performance than those added in sample II. That also explains why most of the recently observed institutional changes in the water sector (described in Chapter 7) are concentrated in the 11 countries covered in the first sample.

Implications for Overall Reliability

Concerning the overall implications of the observed consistency as well as variations in the sample-specific results, the configurations of robust variables in most equations across sample contexts I and II are distinct. This distinct pattern implies that the institution–performance linkages are stronger in the sample I context than in the sample II context. Such a differential pattern in the configuration of robust variables and their implications for institution–performance linkages are also explained in terms of the distinct pattern in the features of the water sector in countries covered by the first two sample contexts. The comparison of the size of the coefficients of robust institutions across sample contexts I and II reveals another interesting aspect with considerable implications for the relative significance and performance of various layers of institutional linkages. Namely, the size of the coefficients of robust variables is larger for sample I than for sample II in all equations except [7], [8], and [9]. These exceptions imply three inter-related aspects.

First, interinstitutional linkages are stronger than intra-institutional link-ages in the context of sample I. In contrast, intra-institutional linkages are stronger than their interinstitutional counterparts in the context of sample II. Second, while interinstitutional linkages in sample I are stronger than those observed in sample II, intra-institutional linkages in the second set are stronger than in the first set. Finally, but more importantly, in light of the two points noted above and the relative size of the coefficients associated with *WIPOEV* in equation [10], the relative performance implications of intra- and interinsti-tutional linkages can be inferred. As the coefficient of *WIPOEV* – the ultimate linkage variable that captures the impacts transmitted through various layers of institutional linkages – is larger for sample I, the interinstitutional linkages, as captured by the first five equations, seem to be more important than intra-institutional linkages in determining the overall performance of the water sector.

These results, together with the exceptions and caveats previously noted, suggest a clear need for regionally differentiated institutional reform poli-cies. Institutional reform should focus on strengthening intra-institutional linkages in sample I countries but on strengthening interinstitutional link-ages in sample II countries. Regionally differentiated strategies do not, however, mean that the importance of universally relevant institutional aspects should be underestimated or neglected. We have identified such institutional aspects in our evaluation of the robustness properties of the results. That evaluation also provides some key insights into the robustness properties of various layers of institutional linkages characterized by differ-ent equations. As can be seen from Tables 9.1a and 9.1b, with the exception of the layers of institutional linkages represented by equations [1], [3], and [6], all the layers are robust and more durable. This means that the results on the relative significance of institutional aspects and their performance implications (discussed in Chapter 8) are more reliable and amenable to generalization. The exceptions mentioned above, however, signal some important caveats about the contextuality of some of the layers of institu-tional linkages.

SENSITIVITY OF RESULTS: ROLE OF DISCIPLINARY BIAS

The evaluation of the sensitivity of results to sample size variation has provided us with some interesting insights into their stability and consistency properties. But, for a firmer conclusion in this respect, we have to ask how sensitive the results are to two other aspects endogenous to our sample: the subject backgrounds of the sample experts and the reform status of sample countries. The influence of the experts' disciplinary backgrounds and subject specializations is evaluated by categorizing the respondents into two groups: engineers and social scientists. The model has to be evaluated in this context to see whether the frequently mentioned disciplinary divide in water sector leads to any noticeable differences in the perception of institution–performance linkages. By comparing the results across the expert groups, we can discover whether there are any group-specific differences in the importance assigned to different institutional aspects.

Based on this evaluation, it is also possible to know whether the 'disciplinary divide' in the water sector affects the choice of institutional configurations and their implications for institution–performance linkages. One obvious but general hypothesis in this respect is that engineers are likely to emphasize engineering and administration-related institutional aspects, whereas social scientists tend to underline economic and market-related institutional aspects. If the experts display some uniformity or convergence in their evaluation of institution–performance linkages, the alternative to the above-stated hypothesis will be true. In other words, the discipline-induced bias in the preference of institutional aspects can be expected to be either minimal or absent. The possibility of this bias will receive a special attention as we attempt a comparative evaluation of the group-specific results.

Disciplinary Background and Subjective Perception

Since the subjective perception of the sample experts about current and alternative institutional arrangements is the information basis of our estimated results, these results will reflect the effects of both the objective and subjective factors affecting experts' perceptional evaluation. One of the most important factors that can powerfully influence the process of subjective evaluation is related to norms. These norms depend upon many social, cultural, and legal factors (see Sjostrand 1995: 24), but they are also shaped by educational curricula and professional affiliations (DiMaggio and Powell 1983). Thus, there can be a distinct pattern in the perception of the relative importance of institutional aspects and their configurations among groups with a similar disciplinary background. However, mobility and interaction among individuals often lead to a 'flow of norms between contexts' and generate a 'continuous stream of experiences and ideas across previously unlinked or relatively autonomous settings' (Sjostrand 1995: 40). This means that, despite a basic difference in the discipline-based norms across individuals, an increasing sense of empathy and inclination for accommodation can lead to convergence in their subjective perception of institutional arrangements.

The empirical validity of this proposition about disciplinary bias can be evaluated using the estimated results for engineers and social scientists (Tables 9.2a and 9.2b). These tables also provide the corresponding results for the all-sample context so that we can also evaluate the consistency of the group-specific results with the overall pattern. While this consistency aspect will be dealt with later, let us first consider the convergence properties of the group-specific results by focusing on the nature and extent of convergence in the evaluation observed between the expert groups. As we did in the context of our evaluation of the robustness of results, we will evaluate the convergence properties of group-specific results in terms of the size, significance, and direction of the coefficients associated with the institutional and performance variables in various equations. The objectives of this evaluation are twofold. The first is to see how far the expert groups converge or diverge in their evaluation of the relative significance of institutional and performance variables in different equations and to highlight the extent of convergence observed in the configuration and relative ordering of institutional aspects between the expert groups. The second is to show how the convergence noted above relates to the group-specific evaluation of the relative strength of various layers of institution–performance linkages and to indicate their implications for institutional design and implementation.

Convergence in Institution–Performance Evaluation

The issue of convergence in institution–performance evaluation between the two groups of experts can be evaluated better by considering each of the equations representing a particular layer of institution–performance interaction. To begin with, in equation [1], although there is a difference in the number of significant institutional variables between the expert groups, there is agreement on the significance of effective user participation policy (*PGPIUP*) and effective legal mechanisms for conflict resolution (*LCRMEE*). But, there is also a difference between the two groups in terms of the relative importance of institutional aspects as a balanced functional specialization (*ABALFS*), considered not at all significant by engineers but highly significant by social scientists. Moreover, from the perception of social scientists, *ABALFS* also has a much larger effect than *PGPIUP*. In equation [2], the expert groups agree on the importance of two institutional aspects, *LCRMEE* and *AEXTST*, representing

Table 9.2a. Institution–performance interaction in the water sector: effects of disciplinary background of sample experts

(3-SLS Estimates of Model B)

Equations	Dependent variables	Independent variables	Engineers		Social scientists		All sample	
			coefficient[a]	t-ratio	coefficient[a]	t-ratio	coefficient[a]	t-ratio
[1]	LCRMEE	LPRSRF	0.183	0.868	0.069	0.363	0.079	0.556
		PGPIUP	0.296	3.053	0.150	1.540	0.246	3.481
		POPAWE	−0.012	−0.074	0.154	1.074	0.096	0.880
		ABALFS	0.501	0.894	1.065	2.004	0.822	2.212
		AARINF	0.100	0.733	0.114	0.975	0.122	1.408
		AEXTST	0.117	0.617	0.162	1.235	0.141	1.303
		Constant	2.545	1.809	1.581	1.394	1.818	2.085
[2]	PIRSWE	LPRSRF	0.147	0.736	0.318	1.884	0.209	1.686
		LCRMEE	0.696	2.728	0.764	3.533	0.698	3.633
		PGPIUP	−0.121	−0.882	−0.128	−1.271	−0.139	−1.557
		AEXTST	0.368	1.969	0.220	1.845	0.299	−1.557
		Constant	−2.077	−1.422	−1.946	−1.992	−1.750	−2.025
[3]	PCOREC	LPRSRE	−0.009	−0.178	−0.105	−1.840	−0.070	−1.833
		PGPIUP	0.014	0.568	0.029	0.973	0.024	1.297
		POPAWE	−0.101	−2.288	0.075	1.643	−0.018	−0.593
		AIBDWP	0.154	0.995	0.445	2.292	0.265	2.153
		Constant	2.734	9.877	1.879	6.247	2.358	11.750

[4]	ASBUDC	AIBDWP	**1.544**	1.719	0.332	0.315	**1.485**	2.008
		PCOREC	**-1.647**	-1.625	**-1.906**	-1.841	**-3.426**	-3.590
		PGPIPP	-0.027	-0.233	0.032	0.230	-0.022	-0.233
		PGPIUP	0.052	0.397	0.179	1.221	*0.155*	1.463
		Constant	**6.681**	2.956	**6.662**	3.152	**10.178**	5.111
[5]	LACPRE	LPRSRF	0.186	0.880	-0.009	-0.051	*0.200*	1.292
		LOEPRV	**0.422**	3.644	**0.312**	2.975	**0.289**	3.600
		PCOREC	**2.882**	3.662	**1.562**	2.652	**3.814**	6.499
		POELWL	-0.076	-0.574	**0.415**	3.656	**0.208**	2.486
		AACCME	**0.290**	2.491	-0.111	-1.078	-0.021	-0.278
		Constant	**-5.417**	-2.583	**-2.316**	-1.632	**-7.036**	-4.769

Note: [a] Coefficients in **bold** are significant at 10 percent or better whereas coefficients in ***bold and italic*** are significant at 20 percent.

Table 9.2b. Institution–performance interaction in the water sector: effects of disciplinary background of sample experts

(3-SLS Estimates of Model B)

Equations	Dependent variables	Independent variables	Engineers		Social scientists		All sample	
			coefficient[a]	t-ratio	coefficient[a]	t-ratio	coefficient[a]	t-ratio
[6]	LOEFWL	LTRWSA	-0.200	0.398	**0.868**	1.996	0.259	0.730
		LPRSRF	0.092	0.639	0.133	0.960	0.095	0.853
		LCRMEE	**0.488**	2.446	**0.357**	1.647	**0.321**	1.489
		LACPRE	-0.153	-0.740	0.093	0.473	0.241	1.173
		LINTRE	0.012	0.162	**0.198**	3.035	**0.093**	1.779
		LOECEN	**0.175**	2.332	0.002	0.041	**0.076**	1.462
		LOEPRV	**0.246**	2.326	0.061	0.662	0.066	0.790
		Constant	1.248	1.177	*1.367*	1.562	*1.256*	1.556
[7]	POEFWP	PPSCRI	-0.076	-0.548	-0.077	-0.684	-0.107	-1.189
		PCOREC	*0.891*	1.399	*1.578*	3.089	*1.523*	3.241
		PIRSWE	**0.638**	3.019	**0.278**	1.971	**0.783**	5.278
		PGPIPP	**-0.109**	-1.628	*-0.087*	-1.373	**-0.103**	-2.265
		PGPIUP	0.071	0.836	*0.099*	1.375	0.062	0.977
		POPAWE	**0.247**	1.734	-0.072	-0.596	0.053	0.590
		POELWL	0.101	0.975	**0.395**	4.385	**0.179**	2.605
		Constant	-0.818	-0.439	**-1.464**	-1.519	**-2.067**	-1.977

236

			Coef.	t	Coef.	t	Coef.	t
[8]	AOEFWA	AORGBA	**0.319**	2.210	-0.159	-1.227	0.035	0.359
		ABALFS	**0.854**	2.203	**1.355**	3.603	**1.062**	3.827
		AIBDWP	**-1.059**	-2.273	**0.774**	1.793	0.121	0.383
		ASBUDC	**0.547**	3.523	0.174	1.068	0.149	1.098
		AACCME	0.060	-0.789	-0.017	-0.206	-0.030	-0.481
		AARINF	**0.289**	2.757	**0.159**	1.637	**0.226**	3.126
		AEXTST	**0.408**	3.413	**0.390**	3.940	**0.356**	4.661
		Constant	-1.281	-1.039	*1.067*	1.330	0.841	1.188
[9]	WIPOEV	LOEFWL	**0.412**	2.612	**0.402**	2.193	**0.371**	2.484
		POEFWP	**-0.358**	-1.762	0.108	0.571	-0.072	-0.415
		AOEFWA	**0.647**	3.813	**0.543**	2.905	**0.622**	4.188
		Constant	**1.961**	2.116	0.152	0.192	*0.840*	1.304
[10]	WSPOEV	WIPOEV	**0.875**	6.158	**0.854**	6.731	**0.843**	7.355
		POPAWE	-0.078	-0.891	-0.104	-1.170	-0.063	-1.149
		ASBUDC	0.012	0.158	*-0.211*	-1.597	**-0.132**	-1.570
		PCOREC	-0.097	-0.244	-0.107	-0.230	**-0.450**	-1.278
		AARINF	**0.209**	3.266	0.004	0.058	**0.098**	1.934
		AEXTST	-0.072	-0.851	0.084	1.029	0.041	0.672
		Constant	-0.218	-0.194	**1.712**	1.800	**1.537**	1.972
System R^2			0.783		0.888		0.765	
χ^2			93.127		144.550		183.850	
Breusch–Pagan test			153.830		102.640		230.710	
Sample size			61		66		127	

Note: [a] Coefficients in **bold** are significant at 10 percent or better whereas coefficients in ***bold and italic*** are significant at 20 percent.

237

the extensiveness of science and technology application. There is further agreement about the dominant role played by *LCRMEE*, which is actually a linkage variable transferring the effects from equation [1]. But, perceptions diverge as to the next most important institutional aspect, because social scientists rank water-rights format (*LPRSRF*) whereas engineers consider *AEXTST* as the next most important institutional variable.

The group-specific differences in the configuration and ordering of institutional variables can also be seen in equation [3]. Here, engineers consider the variable representing the effects of other sectoral policies on water policy (*POPAWE*) as the only institutional aspect affecting cost-recovery status (*PCOREC*). But, social scientists, though agreeing on the importance of *POPAWE*, consider two additional institutional variables to be also important: *LPRSRF* and *AIBDWP*, representing the existence of an independent water-pricing body. In fact, for the social scientists, these additional variables are more important than *POPAWE* in determining cost-recovery status. Moreover, although both groups agree on the importance of *POPAWE*, they differ fundamentally in terms of the direction of its effects. Engineers believe it has a negative effect on cost-recovery status; social scientists, a positive effect. In the case of the institutional interlinkage characterized by equation [4], the expert groups agree that better cost-recovery status can reduce the seriousness of the budget constraint (*ASBUDC*). But engineers, unlike social scientists, consider also an additional institutional aspect, *AIBDWP* as another important factor with a positive role. A similar pattern can be seen in the context of equation [5] except that there is convergence on the importance of two institutional aspects, but divergence about the role of an additional institutional aspect, identified by each group. Although the expert groups disagree on the configuration and relative importance of the institutional aspects, they still agree on the dominant role of the linkage variable *PCOREC*.

Turning now to the group-specific differences in the configuration and relative importance of institutional aspects in equations characterizing intra-institutional linkages, the results for equation [6] in Table 9.2b show considerable divergence in the perceptional evaluation of the two groups. Of the three institutional aspects identified as important by each group, all but the linkage variable *LCRMEE* are highly group-specific. The engineers consider the centralization tendency in water law (*LOECEN*) and the effectiveness of legal provisions for privatization (*LOEPRV*) as the two other important variables. In contrast, the social scientists consider unified legal treatment of different water sources (*LTRWSA*) and internal consistency within water law (*LINTRE*) as the other two important variables. In addition, since the social scientists consider *LTRWSA* as the dominant institutional aspect determining the overall effectiveness of water law (*LOEFWL*), group-specific differences in institutional configuration also involve different sets of priorities for institutional aspects.

In contrast to a predominantly divergent tendency in their group-specific evaluation of equation [6], the expert groups display a highly convergent tendency in their evaluation of both equations [7] and [8]. In equation [7], although the social scientists identify five institutional aspects as important against only four identified by the engineers, both groups agree on the important role played by three institutional aspects in determining the overall effectiveness of water policy (*POEFWP*). The three institutional aspects are *PCOREC*, effectiveness of water transfer policies (*PIRSWE*), and effectiveness of private sector promotion policy (*PGPIPP*). However, the divergence is restricted to *POPAWE* (emphasized only by the engineers), and *PGPIUP* and *POELWL* (both underlined only by the social scientists). These additional institutional variables identified by the two groups, however, alter the relative importance and priority of even the institutional aspects on which there is agreement. While both groups agree on the dominant role of *PCOREC*, they differ in terms of the relative importance assigned to all the other significant institutional aspects.

In equation [8], the engineers, who agree with all four institutional variables identified as important by the social scientists, stress the importance of two additional variables in determining the overall effectiveness of water administration (*AOEFWA*). The four institutional aspects eliciting convergence are *ABALFS*, *AIBDWP*, *AEXTST*, and *AARINF*, and the two additional institutional aspects identified only by the engineers are the organizational basis of water administration (*AORGBA*) and *ASBUDC*. Despite a greater degree of convergence in the evaluation of equation [8] by expert groups, they have different priorities for the institutional aspects. For instance, engineers assign top priority to *AIBDWP*, then to *ABALFS*, *ASBUDC*, *AEXTST*, and *AARINF*. The social scientists give priority to *ABALFS*, then to *AIBDWP*, *AEXTST*, and *AARINF*. Notwithstanding the differences in the ordering of institutional aspects, the expert groups largely agree on the configuration of institutional aspects remaining significant in equation [8]. Turning now to the last two equations, capturing the performance implications of institutional interlinkages, equation [9], unlike equation [8], shows convergence in priorities but a slight change in the configuration of the institutional components. Both groups agree that *AOEFWA*, followed by *LOEFWL*, has the dominant role, but the engineers, unlike the social scientists, believe *POEFWP* is also important for determining the overall effectiveness of the water institution (*WIPOEV*).[7] In equation [10], both groups agree on the dominant role played by *WIPOEV* in determining the overall performance of the water sector (*WSPOEV*). However, they disagree on the role of the additional institutional variable – *AARINF* for the engineers, *ASBUDC* for the social scientists.

Overall, the configuration of institutional aspects identified by both groups is consistent in all equations except [3] and [6]. But, the group-specific differences in the ordering of even the commonly agreed institutional aspects in the case of most equations suggest that the expert groups disagree on the relative importance of institutional aspects. This means that agreement on the role of the institutional aspects is necessary but insufficient for convergence on the relative significance of institutional aspects. For instance, the social scientists assign greater importance to *LTRWSA*, *LPRSRF*, *LINTRE*, and *POELWL* whereas the engineers focus on *LOECEN*, *LOEPRV*, *AORGBA*, and *AACCME*. Thus, the social scientists seem to give high importance to legal aspects, especially those related to water rights, internally consistent water law, and legally consistent water policy. But, the engineers value more the role of centralized water law, private sector participation, organizational character of water administration, and administrative accountability. This differential pattern of institutional aspects identified by the two groups can be interpreted as evidence for the presence of disciplinary bias in institution–performance evaluation. Considering the degree of consistency on the role and significance of many key institutional aspects, however, we can conclude that the disciplinary bias is restricted more to micro details than to macro thrust and focus. The presence of macro convergence in the face of micro divergence can be shown still more clearly from the group-specific pattern in the relative importance assigned to various layers of institution–performance interaction.

Relative Significance of Institution–Performance Layers

As a direct consequence of the group-specific differences in the relative significance of institutional aspects, there is also a difference in the relative importance assigned to both the direct and linkage roles of some institutional aspects. For instance, although the expert groups agree on the importance of the linkage roles of *PGPIUP* in equation [1] and *POPAWE* in equation [3], they disagree on the importance of their direct roles in equation [7]. Similarly, although both groups recognize the importance of *ASBUDC* in the context of different equations, they disagree in terms of the routes though which its effects are transmitted to water sector performance. While the engineers consider its effects to be transmitted indirectly via *AOEFWA* in equations [8] and [9], the social scientists underline its direct effects (as a proxy for the overall fiscal health of the country) on water sector performance in equation [10]. Likewise, the social scientists consider the interinstitutional linkage effects of *AIBDWP* to be transmitted mainly through *PCOREC* in equation [3] whereas the engineers consider the transmission channel to be *ASBUDC* in equation [4]. Furthermore, although both groups recognize the intra-institutional linkage effects of *AIBDWP* in equation [8], they disagree on the direction of its effects. Similar disagreement on the direction of effects can also be seen in the case of *POPAWE* in equation [3].

Apart from the differences in perception on the layers or channels through which the effects of some of the institutional aspects are transmitted, the groups also differ in terms of the composition of these effects. For instance, as per the engineers' evaluation, the linkage variable *LCRMEE*, which transfers the interinstitutional effects from equation [1] to [2], brings with it only the effects of *PGPIUP*. But, in terms of the social scientists' evaluation, it transmits the effects of both *PGPIUP* and *ABALFS*. In the perception of the social scientists, the linkage effects of *ABALFS* take precedence over those of *PGPIUP*. Similarly, the engineers' evaluation shows that the linkage variable *PCOREC* in equation [4] transfers the effects of only *POPAWE* from equation [3]. However, from the social scientists' perspective, *PCOREC* transfers the effects not only of *POPAWE* but also of both *AIBDWP* and *LPRSRF*. Similar group-specific differences in the composition of effects can also be seen in the context of other linkage variables such as *LOEFWL* and *AOEFWA*, which transfer, respectively, the intra- and interinstitutional effects from equations [6] and [8] to equation [9].

It is the group-specific differences in the relative importance of transmission channels and in the composition of the transmitted effects that explain the variations in the size, significance, and direction of the coefficients associated with various institutional variables in different equations. Although this pattern appears to indicate the effects of disciplinary bias, we need to reckon the general agreement among the expert groups on the role and relative importance of many other institutional aspects. Such an agreement, in fact, suggests that the group-specific differences observed in the relative role, significance, and linkage effects of institutional aspects need not be interpreted as an outcome of any group-specific subjective bias, but rather as an outcome of genuine differences in the experts' technical backgrounds and objective considerations. Even if there is any subjective bias or partisan tendency due to disciplinary bias, it is likely to be confined to the lower echelons of the layers of institution–performance interaction.

Our results provide some support for the increasing convergence at higher layers of institution–performance interaction. For instance, in relating the size of the coefficient associated with the most important linkage variables in equations [9] and [10] with that in the rest of the equations, we find an interesting pattern with considerable implications for perceptional convergence. The group-specific differences in the size of the coefficients of the most important institutional variables decline as we move up to the higher layers of institution–performance linkages. This can easily be verified by noting how close is the size of the group-specific coefficients associated with *LOEFWL* and *AOEFWA* in equation [9] and *WIPOEV* in equation [10]. This is not the case with the coefficients of most institutional aspects – both convergent and divergent – in other equations (Tables 9.2a and 9.2b). This result suggests that the expert groups differ more in their evaluation of the relative strength of intra- and interinstitutional linkages than in their evaluation of the strength of the over-all linkage between water institution and water sector performance. In other words, as we have noted already, the divergence is confined more to details and particulars than to the main thrust and focus.

CONTEXTUALITY OF RESULTS: ROLE OF REFORM ENVIRONMENT

As per our subjective theory of institutional change outlined in Chapter 4, it is the convergence in the perception of the need for institutional change that initi-ates the process of change. But, institutional change also plays a major role in reinforcing and sustaining convergence in perception.[8] Just as the growing consensus on the perception of institution–performance linkages determines the nature and direction of institutional change, so too does the reform envi-ronment in reinforcing convergence in subjective perception. It is this rein-forced convergence in perception that sustains the process of institutional change. In other words, in an advanced and mature stage of institutional change, the change process has some in-built mechanisms for sustaining itself. If this is true, we can expect the various layers of institution–performance link-ages observed in the context of reform countries to be stronger than those observed in other countries. This important aspect will receive a special atten-tion during our comparative evaluation of the results across country groups.

The influence of the overall reform environment on subjective perception, and hence, on institution–performance interaction, is evaluated by comparing the results of the system version of Model B for two country groups, defined in terms of the presence or absence of significant institutional reforms within the water sector. Since the subjective perception and reform environment are intri-cately linked in a two-way relationship, the evaluation of the process of insti-tution–performance interaction by experts in reform countries is likely to be different from the same evaluation by their counterparts in other countries. Such evaluation differences obviously lead to area-specific differences both in the configuration and ordering of institutional aspects as well as in the nature and strength of institutional and performance linkages. We also expect that the area-specific pattern of evaluation is more pronounced and powerful enough to transcend the discipline-based group-specific differences among the expert groups both within and across country groups. What effects the interface between reform environment and subjective evaluation has on the configura-tion of institutional aspects and the nature of their linkages can be evaluated by comparing the country-group results. The area-specific results, together with the all-sample results, are presented in Tables 9.3a and 9.3b. In our evaluation of the results across country groups, we will focus on both the convergence in

Table 9.3a. Institution–performance interaction in the water sector: effects of the reform status of sample countries

(3-SLS Estimates of Model B)

Equations	Dependent variables	Independent variables	Reform countries		Other countries		All sample	
			coefficient[a]	t-ratio	coefficient[a]	t-ratio	coefficient[a]	t-ratio
[1]	LCRMEE	LPRSRF	0.030	0.158	0.250	1.166	0.079	0.556
		PGPIUP	**0.235**	2.540	**0.247**	2.433	**0.246**	3.481
		POPAWE	-0.052	-0.350	**0.291**	2.026	0.096	0.880
		ABALFS	0.388	0.862	**1.203**	2.238	**0.822**	2.212
		AARINF	0.114	1.005	0.084	0.724	*0.122*	1.408
		AEXTST	*0.273*	1.656	-0.012	-0.086	*0.141*	1.303
		Constant	**2.555**	2.064	1.010	0.853	**1.818**	2.085
[2]	PIRSWE	LPRSRF	*0.229*	1.364	0.112	0.544	**0.209**	1.686
		LCRMEE	**0.644**	2.792	**0.740**	3.140	**0.698**	3.633
		PGPIUP	-0.096	-0.782	-0.104	-0.879	*-0.139*	-1.557
		AEXTST	*0.217*	1.366	**0.332**	2.628	**0.299**	3.025
		Constant	-1.186	-0.952	**-2.143**	-2.040	**-1.750**	-2.025
[3]	PCOREC	LPRSRF	-0.022	-0.482	*-0.087*	-1.333	*-0.070*	-1.833
		PGPIUP	0.016	0.687	0.016	0.490	*0.024*	1.297
		POPAWE	*-0.097*	-2.364	**0.080**	1.651	-0.018	-0.593
		AIBDWP	*0.218*	1.468	*0.323*	1.530	**0.265**	2.153
		Constant	**2.696**	10.700	**1.905**	5.797	**2.358**	11.750

Table 9.3a. continued

(3-SLS Estimates of Model B)

Equations	Dependent variables	Independent variables	Reform countries		Other countries		All sample	
			coefficient[a]	t-ratio	coefficient[a]	t-ratio	coefficient[a]	t-ratio
[4]	ASBUDC	AIBDWP	**1.828**	1.977	0.477	0.428	**1.485**	2.008
		PCOREC	**-3.434**	-3.449	-1.165	-1.070	**-3.426**	-3.590
		PGPIPP	-0.094	-0.770	0.106	0.772	-0.022	-0.233
		PGPIUP	0.077	0.552	0.101	0.701	*0.155*	1.463
		Constant	**10.807**	5.170	**4.835**	2.044	**10.178**	5.111
[5]	LACPRE	LPRSRF	0.155	0.831	0.051	0.225	*0.200*	1.292
		LOEPRV	**0.365**	3.287	**0.335**	2.908	**0.289**	3.600
		PCOREC	**3.505**	5.281	**1.638**	2.450	**3.814**	6.499
		POELWL	-0.005	-0.044	**0.383**	3.196	**0.208**	2.486
		AACCME	*0.169*	1.661	-0.096	-0.876	-0.021	-0.278
		Constant	**-6.172**	-3.672	***-2.613***	-1.481	**-7.036**	-4.769

Note: [a] Coefficients in **bold** are significant at 10 percent or better whereas coefficients in ***bold and italic*** are significant at 20 percent.

244

Table 9.3b. Institution–performance interaction in the water sector: effects of the reform status of sample countries

(3-SLS Estimates of Model B)

Equations	Dependent variables	Independent variables	Reform countries		Other countries		All sample	
			coefficient[a]	t-ratio	coefficient[a]	t-ratio	coefficient[a]	t-ratio
[6]	LOEFWL	LTRWSA	-0.234	-0.452	0.753	1.653	0.259	0.730
		LPRSRF	0.154	1.120	0.173	0.912	0.095	0.853
		LCRMEE	0.544	2.032	0.094	0.435	0.321	1.489
		LACPRE	-0.064	-0.279	0.478	1.971	0.241	1.173
		LINTRE	-0.002	-0.024	0.189	2.429	0.093	1.779
		LOECEN	0.170	2.410	0.044	0.622	0.076	1.462
		LOEPRV	0.248	2.371	-0.066	-0.564	0.066	0.790
		Constant	0.313	0.269	1.511	1.626	1.256	1.556
[7]	POEFWP	PPSCRI	-0.145	-1.209	-0.082	-0.639	-0.107	-1.189
		PCOREC	1.368	2.699	1.803	2.962	1.523	3.241
		PIRSWE	1.010	5.117	0.368	2.347	0.783	5.278
		PGPIPP	-0.100	-1.751	-0.086	-1.252	-0.103	-2.265
		PGPIUP	0.047	0.543	0.100	1.247	0.062	0.977
		POPAWE	0.289	2.186	-0.170	-1.222	0.053	0.590
		POELWL	0.078	0.918	0.392	3.895	0.179	2.605
		Constant	-3.093	-1.999	-1.655	-1.400	-2.067	-1.977
[8]	AOEFWA	AORGBA	0.230	1.533	-0.208	-1.284	0.035	0.359
		ABALFS	1.106	3.200	0.949	2.041	1.062	3.827
		AIBDWP	-0.520	-1.260	0.758	1.367	0.121	0.383
		ASBUDC	0.206	1.484	0.476	2.420	0.149	1.098
		AACCME	-0.014	-0.191	0.011	1.117	-0.030	-0.481
		AARINF	0.282	2.904	0.219	1.710	0.226	3.126
		AEXTST	0.356	3.132	0.353	2.772	0.356	4.661
		Constant	-0.193	-0.163	0.205	0.232	0.841	1.188

Table 9.3b. continued

(3-SLS Estimates of Model B)

Equations	Dependent variables	Independent variables	Reform countries		Other countries		All sample	
			coefficient[a]	t-ratio	coefficient[a]	t-ratio	coefficient[a]	t-ratio
[9]	WIPOEV	LOEFWL	**0.278**	1.629	**0.421**	2.220	**0.371**	2.484
		POEFWP	-0.024	-0.110	0.076	0.400	-0.072	-0.415
		AOEFWA	**0.402**	2.638	**0.541**	2.728	**0.622**	4.188
		Constant	**2.319**	2.882	0.157	0.190	***0.840***	1.304
[10]	WSPOEV	WIPOEV	**0.896**	6.407	**0.676**	4.680	**0.843**	7.355
		POPAWE	***-0.119***	-1.418	-0.081	-0.850	-0.063	-1.149
		ASBUDC	-0.060	-0.967	0.017	0.136	***-0.132***	-1.570
		PCOREC	-0.171	-0.468	0.059	0.110	***-0.450***	-1.278
		AARINF	**0.228**	3.925	0.079	0.728	**0.098**	1.934
		AEXTST	-0.048	-0.617	0.073	0.790	0.041	0.672
		Constant	0.093	0.098	1.065	1.105	**1.537**	1.972
System R^2			0.797		0.898		0.765	
χ^2			113.080		128.080		183.850	
Breusch–Pagan test			170.110		98.0260		230.710	
Sample size			71		56		127	

Note: [a] Coefficients in **bold** are significant at 10 percent or better whereas coefficients in ***bold and italic*** are significant at 20 percent.

246

institutional configurations and the relative significance of various layers of institution–performance linkages.

Variations in Institutional Configuration and Relative Significance

Across the country groups, the institutional variables showing consistent behavior in terms of significance in one or more equations are: *LCRMEE, LOEPRV, PCOREC, PIRSWE, PGPIUP, PGPIPP, POPAWE, AIBDWP, AORGBA, ABALFS, ASBUDC, AARINF,* and *AEXTST.* All these variables except *POPAWE, AORGBA,* and *AIBDWP* also exhibit consistent behavior in terms of the direction of effects. However, the consistency in the significance and direction of their effect is not uniform across equations, suggesting the presence of region-specific differences in the nature of institution–performance linkages. For instance, the administration-related institutional aspect *AIBDWP* that remains significant for both country groups in equations [3] and [8] is significant only for the reform countries in equation [4]. This institutional aspect, with a positive effect in equations [3] and [4] for both groups, has, however, a negative effect in equation [8] for the reform group. Similarly, the policy-related institutional aspect *PCOREC,* significant with a positive sign for both regions in equations [5] and [7], becomes significant only for the reform regions in equation [4], that too, with a negative effect. While other institutional variables in the remaining equations also display a similar kind of area-specific differential pattern, the particular behavior of the policy-related institutional aspect *POPAWE* requires a closer examination in view of its dual role both as an institutional aspect and as a proxy for the overall policy environment.

Although *POPAWE* is significant in the context of the interinstitutional linkage represented by equation [3] for both areas, it has a negative effect in the case of reform countries, but has a positive effect for other countries. That is, other sectoral policies unfavorably affect cost recovery in reform countries, but favorably affect them in other countries. In contrast, in the context of both the intra-institutional linkage represented by equation [7] and the institution–performance linkage represented by equation [10], the same institutional variable is significant only in reform countries. It has a positive effect in equation [7], but a negative effect in the context of the equation [10]. This result seems paradoxical, as it suggests that, in the particular context of reform countries, the other sectoral policies with a positive effect on the overall performance of water policy have an unfavorable effect on the overall performance of water sector. This paradox can be explained partly by the dual role of *POPAWE* – as a policy-related institutional aspect and as a proxy for a general policy bias against the water sector – and partly by the two-way flow of effects already discussed in several other contexts.[9]

Apart from the 13 distinct institutional variables that are significant for both country groups in one or more equations, there are also area-specific sets of additional institutional aspects. These additional institutional variables for reform countries (excluding those included in the 13 variables listed above) are: *LPRSRF, LOECEN, PGPIPP, AACCME,* and *AARINF.* Those for other countries are: *LPRSRF, LTRWSA, LACPRE, LINTRE,* and *POELWL.* Although *LPRSRF* is included in the set of additional institutional variables for both groups, there is a notable difference, as it is significant with a positive effect for reform countries in equation [2], but has a significant negative effect for other countries in the context of equation [3]. This law-related institutional aspect remains insignificant for both groups in equation [6]. Thus, the significance and direction of its effects differ both across groups and across institutional layers. In any case, layer-specific differences in the behavior of common variables as well as area-specific differences in the set of additional variables suggest that the constellations of institutional aspects underlying the process of institution–performance interaction differ significantly across country groups.

Variations in the Relative Strength of Institutional Layers

As to the nature and relative strength of institutional interlinkages, since all equations except [4] and [6] have at least one institutional variable common to both country groups, the institutional and performance linkages represented by them are considered equally important in both contexts. However, the absence of consistency in the set of significant institutional aspects across country groups for equations [4] and [6] suggests a marked area-specific difference in the nature and strength of the institutional linkages represented by these equations. The fact that none of the institutional variables in equation [4] is significant for other countries lacking significant institutional reforms suggests that the institutional interlinkages represented as well as captured by this equation seem to be irrelevant in the context of these countries. As a direct consequence of the irrelevance of equation [4], the linkage effects transmitted by *PCOREC* from equation [3] have also become nullified. In contrast, the linkage effects among the institutional aspects within equation [4] and between equations [3] and [4] are both strong and effective in the context of reform countries. As a result, *ASBUDC* – the linkage variable in equation [4] entering as an independent variable in equation [8] – captures and transmits the effects of more institutional aspects in reform countries than in other countries. In reform countries, unlike in their counterparts, therefore, the relatively stronger interinstitutional linkages also contribute to stronger intra-institutional linkages, with considerable performance implications.[10]

The inconsistent set of significant institutional aspects for equation [6] across country groups adds yet another dimension to the area-specific differential pattern concerning the nature of institution–performance linkages. In this equation, representing the effects of law-related institutional aspects on *LOEFWL*, *LCRMEE* is significant for reform countries, whereas *LACPRE* is significant for the non-reform countries. Thus, in the case of reform countries, *LOEFWL* captures the effects transmitted through the institutional layer represented by equation [1]. But, in the context of other countries, it captures the effects being transmitted through the institutional layer represented by equation [5]. Since equation [5] is also linked with equation [3] through *PCOREC*, *LOEFWL*, in the context of non-reform countries, also captures indirectly the institutional layer represented by equation [3]. This distinct pattern in the layers of linkages being captured by *LOEFWL* in equation [6] has a direct bearing on the nature and strength of the performance linkages represented by equation [9] for the two country groups.

Even in the case of equations other than [4] and [6] with one or more institutional aspects significant for both groups of countries, there are also area-specific differences in the additional institutional variables. This fact suggests that there are also some distinct patterns in the institutional configurations defining various layers of institution–performance interaction across the country groups. From an overall perspective, these distinct patterns appear to be more pronounced in the context of interinstitutional linkages represented by the first five equations than in the context of intra-institutional linkages characterized by the next four equations. This is consistent with our observation that group- and area-specific differences are confined mostly to the lower echelons of institution–performance linkages, but diminish as we move up to higher levels of linkages.

Since we have hypothesized that the institution–performance linkages will be stronger in the reform countries, it is useful to compare the size of the coefficients of the institutional variables considered significant in both areas. For the system as a whole, there are 18 cases where there is consistency in terms of the significance of the institutional aspects (Tables 9.3a and 9.3b).[11] While the coefficients in nine of these cases are larger for the reform countries, those in the remaining nine cases are larger for the other countries. Although the size of the coefficients of the institutional variables in the context of reform countries is lower in half of the cases, the institution–performance linkages here can still be considered stronger than those linkages in other countries in view of the following two results. First, the number of significant institutional variables observed for reform countries is the same as or greater than that observed for other countries in all but equation [5]. Second, the size of the coefficient of *WIPOEV*, the ultimate linkage variable, is far larger for reform countries than for others, suggesting larger performance implications associated with stronger institutional linkages.

Institution–performance linkages are clearly stronger in reform areas, and this perception precipitates reform in the first place. While the same rationale can be used to explain the absence or inadequacy of recent reforms in nonreform countries, there are also additional reasons linked with resource-related and political economic conditions. Most of the countries lacking recent reforms are well endowed with water resources (e.g., those in Southeast Asia). Although others (e.g., France, Germany, and the United Kingdom) do not have volume-related scarcity issues, they have undertaken significant reforms in the past to address water quality and intersectoral allocation issues. In still other countries (e.g., in North and East Africa), the absence of reforms relates more to political economy constraints than to the absence of perceived needs and pressures for reform. The interactive effects of these three factors explain the absence or inadequacy of reforms, despite a high degree of consensus on the nature and configuration of institutional aspects. The message is clear that the general consensus on the need, nature, and thrust of institutional change, though necessary, cannot be effective enough to initiate reform without strong socioeconomic and political pressures. In many cases, these pressures have played a critical role in shaping and strengthening consensus and coalitions for institutional reforms (Chapter 7).

The region-specific differences in institutional configurations and their implications for institutional and performance linkages also suggest some interesting aspects related to both the motivation and thrust of perceived institutional change. In a more generic interpretation of our results, the financial deterioration within the water sector, caused by poor cost recovery and represented by the seriousness of budget constraint, has been a major factor motivating institutional change in many reform countries. Since the financial performance of the water sector is also affected by other sectoral policies, especially those related to agriculture, and by macroeconomic policy, the critical role of these policies cannot be underestimated. Apart from the seriousness of water conflicts stemming from increasing water scarcity, macroeconomic reform has been a major factor behind water sector reform initiatives in most countries. The investment crunch caused by fiscal crisis has forced many countries to look for avenues for mobilizing resources within the water sector and to seek additional resources from the private sector (Chapter 7). In view of the intricate role played by the financial and policy aspects, the sample experts in reform countries have put major emphasis on the institutional linkages involving these aspects.

As the configuration of institutional aspects identified in the context of reform countries suggests, there is greater emphasis on cost recovery, conflict resolution, organizational structures, administrative accountability, user involvement, and private sector participation. Although the reform process in most of these countries tends toward decentralization and market orientation, there is also an overall thrust on a centralized system of water law, as decentralization cannot succeed without a dose of centralization. In contrast, in countries without recent reforms, more emphasis has been placed on an integrated approach to water resources, legal aspects of accountability, aligning water policy with water law, and policy aspects related to intersectoral and regional water transfers. This configuration of institutional aspects observed in the nonreform countries is understandable as they face water quality and water allocation problems rather than water scarcity and water development as the major sectoral challenges. In addition, since many of these countries (especially in Europe) also have comprehensive water laws, the major thrust here is to integrate and strengthen the law–policy linkages in water sector.

ROLE OF EXOGENOUS FACTORS IN PERFORMANCE EVALUATION

We have shown how exogenous factors such as economic and political reform, demographic condition, resource endowment, and even natural calamities have played a catalytic role in inducing water sector reforms in many sample countries (Chapter 7). We have also seen some evidence of exogenous influences while explaining the differential perception and evaluation of institution–performance linkages across country groups. This evidence is, however, rather inductive and indirect. It is also too general and qualitative to be convincing, as we are unable to show either the magnitude or the relative importance of the effects of these exogenous factors. But, we can provide some more specific and quantitative, though still indirect, evidence of the relative role and significance of exogenous factors on perceptional evaluation and thereby infer their possible effects on our results related to institution–performance interaction. This we attempt by using the regression results for Model C. Model C explicitly relates the performance variables – pertaining to both water institution and water sector – with a common set of 12 exogenous variables representing various socioeconomic, demographic, institutional, and resource-related aspects (Chapter 5).

Since the performance variables are perceptional in nature and exogenous variables are actually observed, Model C provides a framework for directly capturing a major segment of the interface between the subjective evaluation of institution–performance interaction and the objective reality of the general environment within which the process of interaction evolves. The estimated results for Model C can, therefore, enable us to quantitatively evaluate the relative effects of the exogenous factors on the subjective evaluation of performance components. Since we have estimated all the equations in Model C under both the simple and stepwise OLS procedures, we can also distinguish the individual effects of the exogenous factors from their joint effects and show, thereby, how their relative significance and configurations vary across performance components. As noted, the configurations of exogenous factors identified for various equations of Model C can enable us to delineate the subset of exogenous factors jointly having a dominant effect on various performance variables. Since this subset defines together a given objective environment within which the subjective evaluation is performed, it can identify the most robust and prominent components of the institutional environment affecting the perceptional evaluation of different layers of institution–performance interaction.

Although the effects of the exogenous factors on the subjective perception of all the institutional variables included in Model B can be evaluated, we confine our attention to their effects on the perceptional evaluation of only five performance-related variables. These are the four variables representing the overall performance of the water institution and the performance of its three components and the one variable representing the overall performance of water sector. Although Model B includes only the variable representing the overall performance of water sector, we also consider the influence of exogenous factors on its four main dimensions: physical, financial, economic, and equity performance. Since we want to demonstrate here the relative role and significance of exogenous factors both individually and jointly, this selective focus does not imply any limitation of our analysis. As we could see from Model B (Chapter 5), since the variables representing water institutional and sectoral performance enter into equations representing higher level linkages, the focus on them can help in understanding the kinds of effects that the exogenous factors have on the evaluation of the most important layers of institution–performance interaction. This exercise can allow inferences on the effects of these factors on the evaluation of other layers in the system.

Effects on the Evaluation of Institutional Performance

The nature and extent of exogenous influence on the evaluation of the four variables representing institutional performance can be inferred from the regression results for the first four equations of Model C. The simple and stepwise OLS estimates for these equations are presented in Table 9.4a. Considering first the effects of exogenous variables on the evaluation of the overall performance of the water institution (*WIPOEV*), we can see from simple OLS results that only three of the 12 exogenous variables have a significant effect on *WIPOEV*. These three variables – all having a positive effect – in the order of their importance are GNP per capita (*GNPPPC*), index of food production (*FPIIND*), and population density (*POPDEN*). The configuration of the exogenous variables having significant effects on *WIPOEV*, however, changes with the stepwise estimates. In this case, the four significant variables, in the order of their significance, are Environmental Regulatory Regime Index (*ENVRRI*), *GNPPPC*, decadal change in urban population (*DCUPOP*), and *POPDEN*. Since the stepwise estimates identify the subset among the exogenous variables having together the dominant effect on the dependent variable, the individual and joint

Table 9.4a. Influence of exogenous variables on the perceptional evaluation of institutional performance

(Simple OLS estimates of Model C)

Independent variables	Equation numbers/Dependent variables							
	[C1]/LOEFWL		[C2]/POEFWP		[C3]/AOEFWA		[C4]/WIPOEV	
	coefficient[a]	t-ratio	coefficient[a]	t-ratio	coefficient[a]	t-ratio	coefficient[a]	t-ratio
GNPPPC	**0.111**	1.715	**0.145**	1.910	**0.102**	1.498	**0.114**	1.511
POPDEN	-0.002	-1.248	0.002	1.084	**0.002**	1.335	**0.003**	1.613
DCUPOP	-0.007	-0.229	-0.028	-0.747	-0.038	-1.118	-0.045	-1.196
FWATWC	-0.001	-0.791	0.000	-0.141	0.000	-0.005	0.000	-0.553
PWATAG	0.011	0.787	0.021	1.258	0.002	0.137	0.009	0.540
ALANDC	**-1.394**	-2.325	-0.110	-0.155	**-1.013**	-1.601	-0.116	-0.165
FPIIND	0.028	1.227	0.032	1.209	**0.043**	1.804	**0.038**	1.446
EXPEDU	0.101	0.636	0.188	1.004	**0.242**	1.440	0.225	1.204
GININD	-0.001	-0.046	0.026	0.702	-0.025	-0.749	-0.007	-0.179
NCNATW	0.019	0.404	**-0.132**	-2.441	-0.030	-0.619	0.020	0.377
ENVRRI	**0.708**	2.218	-0.276	-0.734	0.351	1.042	0.223	0.595
ININCR	0.016	0.862	-0.010	-0.461	0.007	0.375	0.010	0.462
Constant	0.053	0.015	-2.500	-0.577	-1.448	-0.373	-2.106	-0.489
R^2	0.541		0.437		0.544		0.445	

253

Table 9.4a. continued

(Stepwise OLS estimates of Model C)

Independent variables	Equation numbers/Dependent variables							
	[C1]/LOEFWL		[C2]/POEFWP		[C3]/AOEFWA		[C4]/WIPOEV	
	coefficient[a]	t-ratio	coefficient[a]	t-ratio	coefficient[a]	t-ratio	coefficient[a]	t-ratio
GNPPPC	–	–	0.112	2.392	0.106	3.684	0.076	2.572
POPDEN	-0.002	-1.635	–	–	–	–	0.002	1.331
DCUPOP	–	–	–	–	-0.044	-1.417	-0.058	-1.758
FWATWC	–	–	–	–	–	–	–	–
PWATAG	–	–	0.023	1.721	–	–	–	–
ALANDC	-0.892	-1.898	–	–	-0.943	-1.897	–	–
FPIIND	–	–	–	–	–	–	–	–
EXPEDU	–	–	–	–	–	–	–	–
GININD	–	–	–	–	–	–	–	–
NCNATW	–	–	-0.107	-2.535	–	–	–	–
ENVRRI	0.869	3.326	–	–	0.486	1.691	0.417	1.351
ININCR	0.026	2.937	–	–	–	–	–	–
Constant	4.586	7.959	2.579	1.923	4.439	9.449	4.858	9.378
R^2	0.465		0.364		0.444		0.367	

Notes: [a] In the case of simple OLS estimates, coefficients in **bold** are significant at 20 percent or better. In the case of stepwise OLS estimates, all the variables with reported coefficients are significant at 20 percent or better.
– Automatically excluded by the stepwise estimation process.

254

variations in these four exogenous variables account for most of the variations in *WIPOEV*.[12]

ENVRRI, *GNPPPC*, and *FPIIND* move directly; DCUPOP moves inversely with economic development.[13] In view of their association and concurrent changes with the process of development, the exogenous factors themselves are related. This fact, taken with the relative magnitude and direction of the effects of variables identified by both the simple and stepwise OLS procedures, implies that the economic, technical, institutional, and demographic changes associated with the development process have a positive influence on the performance of water institution. It can also be inferred that the exogenous factors associated with the development process enhance water institution performance mainly through their favorable effects on the economy wide institutional density and linkages. This is actually the corollary of the established fact that water institution benefits from autonomous changes in the overall institutional environment as induced by various factors associated with economic development.

Turning now to the nature of the relationship between exogenous variables and the component-specific performance of water institution, the most immediate aspect to note is that the configurations of exogenous factors identified as significant by both estimation procedures vary considerably across water institution components. In the case of simple OLS results, while *GNPPPC* has a uniform positive effect on the performance of all three water institution components, it has a dominant effect only on the effectiveness of water policy (*POEFWP*). The exogenous factor that most strongly influences the overall effectiveness of water law (*LOEFWL*) is per capita arable land (*ALANDC*) followed by *ENVRRI*.[14] *ALANDC* has a negative effect, whereas *ENVRRI* has a positive effect. The dominant role of these two variables also remains unchanged across the estimation procedures. The negative effect of *ALANDC* suggests, in fact, the positive association of resource scarcity and land inequity with legal performance. The positive effect of *ENVRRI* is understandable as effective regulatory regimes also imply effective legal systems. In general terms, the performance of water law is affected not only by the effectiveness of its constituent legal aspects but also by resource scarcity and by the effectiveness of institutional and regulatory arrangements in related sectors.

As to the effects of exogenous variables on the performance of water policy, only two of the 12 are significant as per the simple OLS estimates but three are significant as per the stepwise estimates. While *GNPPPC* and the proportion of natural capital in national wealth (*NCNATW*) are significant under both estimates, the proportion of water withdrawal for agriculture (*PWATAG*) is significant only under the stepwise estimates. *GNPPPC* has the expected positive effect on *POEFWP*, suggesting that the overall performance of water policy will improve with economic development. *NCNATW* has a negative effect, implying a poor water policy performance in countries where natural capital accounts for a greater share of their total wealth. This result is consistent with intuition, because water policy usually performs poorly in areas with a better resource endowment, as indicated by a higher value of *NCNATW*. This fact also implies a direct association between resource scarcity and water policy performance. However, the positive coefficient associated with *PWATAG* in stepwise results is inconsistent with reality, because the performance of water policy is often poor when the water sector is dominated by irrigation demand and water policy becomes subservient to agricultural policies.

According to simple OLS results, the overall effectiveness of water administration (*AOEFWA*) is influenced by five exogenous variables. These variables, listed in the order of their impact, are *ALANDC*, *EXPEDU*, *GNPPPC*, *FPIIND*, and *POPDEN*. As in the case of *LOEFWL*, *ALANDC* dominates with a negative effect, suggesting that the socioeconomic values of effective water administration increase with resource scarcity as reflected by per capita arable land. Since such pressure occurs more frequently in developing countries than in other areas, the negative effect of *ALANDC* also suggests the positive influence of economic development on the performance of water administration. This is supported further by the positive effect of *GNPPPC* and the proportion of GNP spent on education (*EXPEDU*), both of which vary directly with economic growth and development. The effective combination of exogenous variables, as identified by the stepwise procedure, consists of only four variables. But, it includes only two of the five variables mentioned above, *ALANDC* and *GNPPPC*. The other two variables in the combination are *DCUPOP* and *ENVRRI*. While *DCUPOP* has a negative effect, indicating that water administrations in areas with a recent surge in urbanization perform less efficiently than water administrations in other areas, *ENVRRI* has a positive and the second most dominant effect, supporting our earlier argument. That is, an effective regulatory regime implies not just an effective legal system but also an efficient administrative apparatus.

Effects on the Evaluation of Water Sector Performance

The configuration and relative influence of exogenous variables in the context of the overall and dimension-specific performance of water sector can be evaluated by estimating the remaining five equations of Model C. The simple and stepwise OLS estimates for these equations are presented in Table 9.4b. Considering first the simple OLS results, showing how the individual variations in each of the exogenous factors affects the evaluation of sectoral performance, we find that only three factors have a significant effect on the overall performance of the water sector (*WSPOEV*). They are *GNPPPC*, *NCNATW*, and *FPIIND*. In the stepwise estimates, accounting for the effects of both the individual and joint variations of the exogenous variables on *WSPOEV*, *GNPPPC* and *NCNATW* continue to have a dominant role. However, the

Table 9.4b Influence of exogenous variables on the perceptional evaluation of water sector performance

(Simple OLS estimates of Model C)

Independent variables	Equation numbers/Dependent variables									
	[C5]/WSPPHY		[C6]/WSPFIN		[C7]/WSPECO		[C8]/WSPEQU		[C9]/WSPOEV	
	coefficient[a]	t-ratio	coefficient[a]	t-ratio	coefficient[a]	t-ratio	coefficient[a]	t-ratio	coefficient[a]	t-ratio
GNPPPC	0.050	0.673	**0.178**	2.606	0.080	0.985	0.081	0.978	**0.097**	**1.429**
POPDEN	0.002	1.018	0.001	0.915	**0.003**	1.484	0.001	0.614	0.002	1.136
DCUPOP	**-0.067**	-1.822	-0.040	-1.197	-0.007	-0.177	-0.039	-0.938	-0.038	-1.138
FWATWC	0.000	0.023	**-0.001**	-1.641	**-0.001**	-1.339	0.000	-0.473	-0.001	-0.948
PWATAG	0.007	0.419	0.012	0.802	-0.005	-0.298	0.013	0.730	0.007	0.450
ALANDC	0.187	0.270	**-1.130**	-1.780	-0.395	-0.526	-0.341	-0.443	-0.420	-0.664
FPIIND	0.014	0.552	**0.058**	2.438	**0.054**	1.916	0.028	0.988	**0.039**	**1.633**
EXPEDU	0.088	0.476	0.185	1.091	0.163	0.812	0.030	0.147	0.117	0.690
GININD	0.024	0.669	0.018	0.553	0.030	0.766	-0.032	-0.786	0.010	0.309
NCNATW	**-0.103**	-1.905	-0.012	-0.249	-0.030	-0.505	**-0.137**	-2.265	**-0.071**	**-1.425**
ENVRRI	-0.089	-0.238	-0.013	-0.039	-0.408	-1.010	**-0.680**	-1.640	-0.297	-0.875
ININCR	0.003	0.148	0.016	0.796	**0.041**	1.670	0.019	0.742	0.020	0.963
Constant	2.075	0.491	**-5.334**	-1.375	-5.884	-1.282	1.900	0.403	-1.809	-0.468
R^2	0.377		0.601		0.513		0.473		0.488	

Table 9.4b continued

(Stepwise OLS estimates of Model C)

Independent variables	Equation numbers/Dependent variables									
	[C5]/WSPPHY		[C6]/WSPFIN		[C7]/WSPECO		[C8]/WSPEQU		[C9]/WSPOEV	
	coefficient[a]	t-ratio	coefficient[a]	t-ratio	coefficient[a]	t-ratio	coefficient[a]	t-ratio	coefficient[a]	t-ratio
GNPPPC	–	–	0.195	5.618	–	–	–	–	0.066	2.258
POPDEN	–	–	–	–	–	–	–	–	–	–
DCUPOP	-0.077	-2.646	-0.001	-1.561	–	–	-0.050	-1.444	-0.041	-1.365
FWATWC	–	–	–	–	-0.001	-1.554	–	–	–	–
PWATAG	–	–	–	–	–	–	–	–	–	–
ALANDC	–	–	-1.383	-2.576	–	–	–	–	–	–
FPIIND	–	–	0.052	2.675	–	–	–	–	–	–
EXPEDU	–	–	0.204	1.613	–	–	–	–	–	–
GININD	–	–	–	–	–	–	-0.044	-1.340	–	–
NCNATW	-0.114	-3.293	–	–	–	–	-0.157	-3.723	-0.073	-1.846
ENVRRI	–	–	–	–	–	–	-0.501	-1.511	–	–
ININCR	–	–	–	–	0.054	4.906	–	–	–	–
Constant	6.791	16.100	-2.874	-1.095	2.023	3.138	8.787	7.094	5.334	7.957
R^2	0.313		0.536		0.402		0.391		0.384	

Note: [a] In the case of simple OLS estimates, coefficients in **bold** are significant at 20 percent or better. In the case of stepwise OLS estimates, all the variables with reported coefficients are significant at 20 percent or better.
– Automatically excluded by the stepwise estimation process as insignificant.

configuration of exogenous factors that jointly explain the variations in *WSPOEV* now includes *DCUPOP* instead of *FPIIND*. The direction of the effects of the dominant variables shows that economic development has a positive effect on the overall performance of water sector, whereas better endowment of natural resources has a negative effect.

Turning now to the relative significance of exogenous factors on the dimension-specific performance of water sector, regardless of the estimation procedure, the physical performance of water sector (*WSPPHY*) is affected only by *NCNATW* and *DCUPOP*. These variables also have the expected negative effect, suggesting the kind of role that natural resource endowment and urbanization play in the physical dimension of water sector performance. According to OLS estimates, four exogenous factors have a significant effect on the financial dimension of water sector performance (*WSPFIN*). In the order of their impact, they are *ALANDC*, *GNPPPC*, *FPIIND*, and freshwater withdrawal per capita (*FWATWC*). The configuration of exogenous factors having a joint impact on *WSPFIN* includes not only these four variables but also the education variable *EXPEDU*, which has the second most dominant impact on financial performance. The positive effects of *GNPPPC*, *FPIIND*, and *EXPEDU* suggest the direct association of financial performance with economic development and agricultural prosperity. The negative effects of *ALANDC* and *FWATWC* underline the positive effect of resource scarcity on the financial dimension of water sector performance.

The simple OLS results indicate that the economic dimension of water sector performance (*WSPECO*) is affected by four exogenous variables: *FPIIND*, *ININCR*, *POPDEN*, and *FWATWC*. Considering their direction of effect, the result is consistent with expectations, as agricultural prosperity, international economic rating, demographic pressure, and water scarcity all have a positive impact on the economic performance of water sector. However, the stepwise estimates indicate that individual and joint variations in only two of these four factors – *ININCR* and *FWATWC* – explain the variations in the economic performance of water sector. In any case, given the positive association between *ININCR* and countries' overall economic performance, this result again underlines the dominant role that economic development and resource scarcity play in influencing the economic dimension of water sector performance.

The equity dimension of water sector performance (*WSPEQU*) is affected by two exogenous factors, *ENVRRI* and *NCNATW*, capturing, respectively, the effectiveness of regulatory institutions and composition of national wealth. The negative effects of both factors suggest that the equity performance of water sector is likely to be higher in areas with more effective regulatory arrangements but a lesser share of natural capital in their total wealth. Besides these factors, the configuration of exogenous factors identified by the stepwise procedure as having the dominant joint effect on equity performance also includes *GININD* and *DCUPOP*. The negative effect of *GININD* indicates that the overall inequity in the economy also spills into the water sector.

Despite its simplicity and crude nature, the evaluation of the configurations and relative significance of the exogenous factors affecting the performance of water institutions, water sector, and their components provides some useful insights into the nature and pattern of exogenous influence on the subjective evaluation of institution–performance interaction. Generally, factors associated with economic development, regulatory institutions, and education have a positive influence, as they generate some autonomous changes in the institutional sphere to which the water institution is not an exception. In view of the phenomenon of institutional creation and thickening usually associated with the development process, institutional linkages are strengthened, thereby contributing to improved institutional performance. Demographic changes, resource scarcity, and increasing socioeconomic inequity have a similar effect, as they enhance the economic value of effective institutional arrangements in every sector, including water. From this perspective, therefore, the evaluation of institution–performance interaction – both in general and in the water sector – cannot be isolated from the overall socioeconomic, demographic, institutional, and resource-related environment. As implied in our evaluation of the relative impact of the exogenous factors, the subjective process of institution–performance evaluation should have captured most of the exogenous influences from the general environment.

ALL-SAMPLE RESULTS: CONSISTENCY AND RELIABILITY

Having evaluated the effects of factors both endogenous and exogenous to our sample and evaluation contexts, we now have a good idea of the consistency and reliability of the all-sample results. Since the process of institution–performance interaction is evaluated not directly in terms of observed information but only indirectly in terms of the subjective perception of such interaction, the analysis of our model results across sample contexts has enabled us to make some inferences about the convergence and stability properties of the results. As these properties are pivotal to support and supplement the conclusions derived in Chapter 8 and to support the exercise on institutional priority setting, sequencing, and packaging to be attempted in Chapter 10, let us review and recapitulate them at this stage. According to our analysis of the robustness properties, with some notable caveats, the behavior of institutional aspects and their implications for institution–performance linkages have shown considerable stability and consistency in the face of sample size variations. In addition to the overall robustness and consistency in the behavior of institutional aspects and the relevance and significance of institution–performance linkages, three other important factors support the reliability of the all-sample results presented in Chapter 8.

First, in comparison to results obtained in subsample contexts, the all-sample results show the same or more institutional variables to be significant in almost every equation. This means that the institutional and performance linkages that are characterized by different equations in Model B become stronger with the enlargement of sample size, expertise mix, and country coverage. Second, the all-sample results balance differences or extremities in the behavior of institutional aspects observed in subsample contexts. While subsample results are valuable for identifying useful caveats and understanding the role of context-specific factors, the all-sample context, with its normalizing property, helps to identify generic features in both institutional configurations and institution–performance linkages. Finally, the all-sample results also display some superior econometric properties. Although R^2 declines marginally with an increase in sample size, both the χ^2 and Breusch–Pagan test statistics improve tremendously with sample size. The behavior of the latter two statistics suggests that the results from the all-sample context become increasingly free of the noises from both autocorrelation and heteroskedasticity.

The influence of disciplinary bias and ideological aspects, though strong at the individual layers of institutional and performance linkages, weakens from an overall or macro perspective of the process of institution–performance interaction. The effects of group- and area-specific bias at the micro levels as well as its remaining vestiges at the macro level can be reduced considerably by increasing the number of experts and countries and by performing the evaluation from a general rather than a group-specific perspective. This implies that the results from the all-sample context are likely to be bias free and will provide a more reliable picture of the nature and strength of institution–performance linkages. As we can see from Tables 9.2a and 9.2b, the all-sample results have removed the extremes observed in group-specific results and provided a more balanced and generalizable evaluation of institution–performance interaction. Instances of normalization properties in the all-sample context are *POPAWE* in equation [3] and *AIBDWP* in equation [8] – both with a differential sign across expert groups and becoming insignificant in the all-sample context. Similarly, as we can see from Tables 9.3a and 9.3b, the all-sample results also exclude the institutional variables that have different signs across country groups (e.g., *POPAWE* in equation [3], and *AORGBA* and *AIBDWP* in equation [8]). The set of significant institutional aspects in the all-sample results, therefore, excludes those with inconsistent behavior and lacking agreement about their significance.

The set of institutional aspects that are significant in the all-sample context evince or gain consistent behavior and elicit or attain perceptional consensus. Thus, for instance, this set does not include all the institutional aspects that are identified as significant only by one expert or country group, but does include those considered insignificant by both expert and country groups. For more specific instance, we can see that in equation [5] of Table 9.2a, while engineers and social scientists consider three institutional variables significant, the all-sample context shows four significant institutional variables. Of these four variables, *LOEPRV* and *PCOREC* are considered significant by both groups; *POELWL* is considered significant only by the social scientists. In contrast, the last of the four variables, *LPRSRF*, is considered insignificant by both groups. While the set of significant institutional variables in the all-sample context includes *POELWL*, identified as significant by the social scientists, it excludes *AACCME*, identified as significant by the engineers. These and other similar instances in Tables 9.2a, 9.2b, 9.3a, and 9.3b suggest that the all-sample results highlight only the institutional variables with enough agreement and consistent behavior.

An institutional variable that may be insignificant in a group-specific context can become significant when enough experts consider it to be significant.[15] Thus, with an enlarged and diverse sample, the scope for convergence and consensus on the perception of institution–performance linkages will increase, together with the overall reliability and credibility of the results. This ability to capture the overall consensus on the role and behavior of institutional aspects makes the all-sample results realistic, reliable, and generalizable. In view of these properties, the all-sample results can be a reasonable basis for understanding the nature of the process of institution–performance interaction from a global perspective. At the same time, the exceptions and caveats that emerged from subsample contexts provide valuable insights that allow us to understand the local and contextual aspects of the same process. In this sense, the area- and group-specific analysis both supports and qualifies our conclusions in Chapter 8 about the process of institution–performance interaction both in general and in water sector contexts.

NOTES

1. Incorporating the effects of variations in geographic focus or country coverage into the evaluation process is valuable for bringing some additional insights into the role that regional configurations – with the corresponding configuration of endogenous and exogenous factors – play in the evaluation of institution–performance interaction.
2. The reform status-based classification of countries is based on literature review (Saleth and Dinar 1999a and 2000) as well as on our own subjective considerations as to the extent and depth of recently observed reform initiatives based on interaction with key water experts in sample countries. Note that this classification is based only in terms of water sector reforms undertaken in the 1990s. As a result, the 'other countries' include not only those with no reform but also those with significant reforms in the 1980s (e.g., the United Kingdom, France, and the Philippines).
3. Although the two expert groups and two country groups themselves define four different sample contexts, the focus here is not on the role of sample size variations but on the influence of endogenous factors, such as disciplinary background and reform environment, on subjective perception, and hence, on the regression results.

4. For instance, many more sample contexts can be defined by categorizing the sample in terms of both endogenous and exogenous factors such as profession and age of experts as well as development status, demographic features, and water resource endowment of sample countries.

5. The identification condition requires that the number of exogenous variables excluded from any equation must be at least equal to the number of endogenous variables minus one. Unlike the equations in Model B, none of those in Model C can satisfy this condition, and hence, could not be econometrically identified or estimated. For details, see Johnston (1984: 250–55).

6. Under the stepwise procedure, unlike its simple OLS counterpart, the variations in the dependent variables are explained not only by the individual variations in each independent variable but also by their joint variations. Although this fact makes the stepwise estimates biased, it also shows how well the stepwise procedure exploits the available information on the relationship between all the variables in an equation. For details, see Kennedy (1987: 77–9).

7. The coefficient associated with *POEFWP* is negative for engineers. The reasons for this inverse relationship of *POEFWP* with *WIPOEV* have been explained in Chapter 8 using the argument based on the two-way flow of effects between these performance variables. Thus, instead of viewing a more effective water policy as negatively affecting the overall performance of water institutions, poor performance of water institutions can realistically be seen as creating a compulsion for a more effective water policy.

8. This fact does not involve any circular reasoning, as it is the initial convergence in perception that leads to institutional change, which, in turn, plays a major role in reinforcing the initial consensus needed to sustain the already initiated process of institutional change.

9. This paradox can also be interpreted in light of two other facts. First, since the positive effects of *POPAWE* in equation [7] are indirect, the insignificance of the linkage variable *POEFWP* in equation [9] nullifies them. Second, its indirect negative effects in equation [3], though partially lost due to the insignificance of a few variables in the linkage chain, are captured by others (e.g., *ASBUDC*) and are reflected in equation [9] via equation [8]. These residual and indirect negative effects are further reinforced by the direct negative effects in equation [10]. In other words, the negative effects of *POPAWE* are dominant and reflect implicitly the effects of poor cost recovery and the resultant budget constraint, even when both the direct and the indirect effects of the institutional variables capturing these aspects are insignificant (e.g., *PCOREC* and *ASBUDC* in equation [10]).

10. For instance, in the case of reform countries, *ASBUDC* not only has a direct effect but also brings the effects of equations [3] and [4] to bear upon equation [8]. In contrast, in the case of other countries, this variable has a direct effect only in equation [8].

11. These 18 cases include the 15 cases of single and multiple occurrence of the 13 variables (listed earlier) in equations [1] to [8] and the three performance variables (*LOEFWL*, *AOEFWA*, and *WIPOEV*) in equations [9] and [10].

12. The R^2 for simple OLS shows that all 12 variables together explain only 45 percent of the variations in *WIPOEV*. The R^2 for the stepwise OLS shows, on the other hand, that just these four variables explain 37 percent of the variations. The stepwise procedure, unlike that based on simple OLS, takes into account both the individual and joint effects of the significant independent variables, hence, it has greater explanatory power. While this results in econometric bias, it does capture the explanatory power of the economically relevant linkages among independent variables.

13. As a point of clarification, the direction of the relationship between *ENVRRI* and economic development is explained by the fact that, since development enhances the value of the environment, an economic necessity emerges for an effective regulatory regime to protect the environment. Similarly, the inverse relationship between *DCUPOP* and development can be understood by comparing the level and change in urban population between the developed and developing countries.

14. In the stepwise estimates, *GNPPPC* becomes insignificant, possibly due to the overpowering influence of two other significant variables, the international credit rating index (*ININCR*) and *ENVRRI*, both of which have a strong positive association with *GNPPPC*.

15. On similar reasoning, an institutional aspect that is significant (insignificant) for a group can become insignificant (significant) if the number of experts considering it to be insignificant (significant) in both groups is more (less) than those considering it to be significant (insignificant) in a single group.

10. Institutional sequencing and packaging

Our analysis in the two previous chapters shows that our model of institution–performance interaction, cast within a simultaneous equation framework, is resilient and its empirical results in different estimation contexts are robust and reliable. The analytical and empirical strength of our approach allows us to take the analysis to its next logical level, which is still more insightful from both theoretical and policy perspectives. The initial focus of our analysis was mainly on the relative role and significance of institutional aspects, based on their local effects within a given equation. Attention then shifted to the formalization of various layers of institution–performance linkages, utilizing the relationship among variables across equations within the simultaneous system framework. The evaluation of the local effects of institutional variables within different equations and the strength of institutional intra- and interlinkages provides a basis for understanding the systemwide institutional and performance impacts of a marginal change associated with a variable in any given equation within the system. This chapter attempts to evaluate the nature, pattern, and implications of such systemwide impacts initiated by local changes in the institutional variables and to address some key issues surrounding institutional design and reform implementation both in general and in water sector contexts.

With the quantification of different layers of linkages among institutional and performance variables, we can now trace quantitatively the multifarious routes through which the effects of a marginal change in an institutional variable are transmitted and reflected ultimately on water sector performance. By tracing all the routes of impact transmission associated with a change in each of the institutional variables that are amenable to deliberate policy intervention, we can numerically evaluate them in terms of their relative performance contributions. The insights from such an evaluation exercise are invaluable both for understanding the inner dynamics of the process of institution–performance interaction and for addressing the practical issues of institutional priority setting, sequencing, and packaging as well as reform timing, spacing, and scaling. The value of the tracing exercise for designing and implementing both generic and context-specific institutional reform programs is illustrated in this chapter with empirically derived numerical results from the estimation of the system version of Model B.

APPROACH AND FRAMEWORK

To facilitate an appreciation of the way the results are derived, presented, and interpreted, let us begin by specifying first the approach used to trace all the impact-transmission channels and the framework used to evaluate their relative performance contributions.

Tracing the Impact-Transmission Channels

The approach used to trace all the impact-transmission channels is simple and straightforward. Of the 26 institutional and performance variables in the system, only 16 institutional variables (those enclosed within ovals in Figure 5.3) are truly exogenous to the model.[1] Only these exogenous institutional variables are amenable to deliberate policy intervention. Our tracing exercise focuses only on the effects of marginal change in each of these 16 institutional variables. Given the estimated coefficients for the 16 exogenous variables as well as those for other variables within the interlinked equation system, we trace all the channels through which the effects of these institutional variables are transmitted through the system. These impact transmission channels are easy to identify in Figure 5.1 by following the arrows originating from each exogenous variable and ending finally with *WSPOEV*, the ultimate dependent variable of the system. Having identified all these channels, we then characterize each of them by the number and configuration of institutional and performance variables involved in their impact transmission.

As we trace all the routes through which the effects of the 16 exogenous variables are transmitted to *WSPOEV*, we can identify 63 distinct impact-transmission channels,[2] each described by its underlying linkage chain. These channels and their linkage chains characterize different layers of institution–performance linkages (discussed extensively in the two previous chapters) and are defined by varying numbers and configurations of exogenous and en route variables. The en route variables are essentially endogenous or linkage variables that lie between an exogenous variable and the ultimate dependent variable of the system. Table 10.1 depicts these channels, their linkage chains and en route variables, and the set of equations through which they operate. Of the 63 channels, 15 are associated with five law-related exogenous variables, 25 are associated with five policy-related exogenous variables, and 23 are associated with six administration-related exogenous variables. The number of impact-transmission channels differs across exogenous variables, as does the number of en route variables across the impact-transmission channels. Of the 16 institutional variables, the policy-related institutional variable of *PGPIUP* has the highest number of impact-transmission channels (11). This is followed by the exogenous variables *LPRSRF* with

10 transmission channels and *POPAWE* and *AIBDWP*, each with eight transmission channels.

The number of impact-transmission channels associated with each exogenous variable is indicative of the level and intensity of their linkage with others
within the system. But, the number of en route variables associated with each
impact-transmission channel is indicative of the length of the linkage chain and
has implications for the speed and effectiveness of impact transmission. Despite
the fact that they enter as independent variables in one or more equations in the
simultaneous system, all the en route variables are essentially endogenous in
nature, conveying only the effects initiated by changes in the 16 exogenous variables across the equation system. The number of en route variables also distinguishes the direct effects from the indirect effects of institutional variables. The
direct effects involve no en route variables, as they are transmitted directly to
WSPOEV, whereas the indirect effects are transmitted via one or more en route
variable. As can be seen in Table 10.1, only three of the 63 channels have direct
effects, but all the remaining channels convey indirect effects with en route variables ranging from 1 to 4. The frequency distribution of the channels in terms of
their en route variables shows that there are more channels having two and three
(each with 20) variables than those having one (with seven) and four (with 13)
variables. A longer chain of en route variables means the indirect effects are
transmitted through many institution–performance variables. They are prone to
both distortions and delays because their ultimate strength depends on the effectiveness of the en route variables taken both individually and collectively.

Evaluating the Impact-Transmission Channels

Having traced all the impact-transmission channels associated with each
exogenous variable, the next step is to quantify the impact transmitted and
then rank them in terms of their relative performance significance. To calculate the relative level of impact transmitted by various channels, we rely on the
following procedure. First, we partially differentiate the relevant equations of
the system version of Model B with respect to each of the 16 exogenous variables. Since some of these variables appear in more than one equation and
some also affect the endogenous variables appearing as exogenous variables
in other equations, the differentiation process leads to different sets of differential chains. The mathematical representation of these sets of differential
chains associated with all the exogenous variables is given in Appendix C. The
differential chains listed in Appendix C are basically the mathematical analog
for all 63 channels listed in Table 10.1.

After identifying all the differential chains, calculating the value of the
impact transmitted by each channel is straightforward in terms of the value(s)
of the partial differential(s) associated with it. As can be seen in Appendix C,

Table 10.1 Impact-transmission channels and linkage chains associated with 16 exogenous variables

No.		Impact-transmission channels/Linkage chains	En route variables	Equations transmitting the impact
1	LINTRE	LOEFWL WIPOEV WSPOEV	2	[6] [9] [10]
2	LOECEN	LOEFWL WIPOEV WSPOEV	2	[6] [9] [10]
3	LOEPRV	LACPRE LOEFWL WIPOEV WSPOEV	3	[5] [6] [9] [10]
4		LOEFWL WIPOEV WSPOEV	2	[6] [9] [10]
5	LPRSRF	LACPRE LOEFWL WIPOEV WSPOEV	3	[5] [6] [9] [10]
6		LCRMEE LOEFWL WIPOEV WSPOEV	3	[1] [6] [9] [10]
7		LOEFWL WIPOEV WSPOEV	2	[6] [9] [10]
8		PCOREC ASBUDC AOEFWA WIPOEV WSPOEV	4	[3] [4] [8] [9] [10]
9		PCOREC ASBUDC WSPOEV	2	[3] [4] [10]
10		PCOREC LACPRE LOEFWL WIPOEV WSPOEV	4	[3] [5] [6] [9] [10]
11		PCOREC POEFWP WIPOEV WSPOEV	3	[3] [7] [9] [10]
12		PCOREC WSPOEV	1	[3] [10]
13		LCRMEE PIRSWE POEFWP WIPOEV WSPOEV	4	[1] [2] [7] [9] [10]
14		PIRSWE POEFWP WIPOEV WSPOEV	3	[2] [7] [9] [10]
15	LTRWSA	LOEFWL WIPOEV WSPOEV	2	[6] [9] [10]
16	PGPIPP	ASBUDC AOEFWA WIPOEV WSPOEV	3	[4] [8] [9] [10]
17		ASBUDC WSPOEV	1	[4] [10]
18		POEFWP WIPOEV WSPOEV	2	[7] [9] [10]
19	PGPTUP	ASBUDC AOEFWA WIPOEV WSPOEV	3	[4] [8] [9] [10]
20		ASBUDC WSPOEV	1	[4] [10]
21		LCRMEE LOEFWL WIPOEV WSPOEV	3	[1] [6] [9] [10]
22		PCOREC ASBUDC AOEFWA WIPOEV	3	[3] [4] [8] [9]
23		PCOREC ASBUDC WSPOEV	2	[3] [4] [10]
24		PCOREC LACPRE LOEFWL WIPOEV WSPOEV	4	[3] [5] [6] [9] [10]
25		PCOREC POEFWP WIPOEV WSPOEV	3	[3] [7] [9] [10]
26		PCOREC WSPOEV	1	[3] [10]
27		LCRMEE PIRSWE POEFWP WIPOEV WSPOEV	4	[1] [2] [7] [9] [10]
28		PIRSWE POEFWP WIPOEV WSPOEV	3	[2] [7] [9] [10]
29		POEFWP WIPOEV WSPOEV	2	[7] [9] [10]
30	POELWL	LACPRE LOEFWL WIPOEV WSPOEV	3	[5] [6] [9] [10]
31		POEFWP WIPOEV WSPOEV	2	[7] [9] [10]

Table 10.1   *continued*

No.		Impact-transmission channels/Linkage chains	En route variables	Equations transmitting the impact
32	POPAWE	LCRMEE LOEFWEL WIPOEV WSPOEV	3	[1] [6] [9] [10]
33		PCOREC ASBUDC AOEFWA WIPOEV WSPOEV	4	[3] [4] [8] [9] [10]
34		PCOREC ASBUDC WSPOEV	2	[3] [4] [10]
35		PCOREC POEFWP WIPOEV WSPOEV	3	[3] [7] [9] [10]
36		PCOREC WSPOEV	1	[3] [10]
37		LCRMEE PIRSWE POEFWP WIPOEV WSPOEV	4	[1] [2] [7] [9] [10]
38		POEFWP WIPOEV WSPOEV	2	[7] [9] [10]
39		WSPOEV	0	[10]
40	PPSCRI	POEFWP WIPOEV WSPOEV	2	[7] [9] [10]
41	AACCME	AOEFWA WIPOEV WSPOEV	2	[8] [9] [10]
42	AARINF	LACPRE LOEFWL WIPOEV WSPOEV	3	[5] [6] [9] [10]
43		AOEFWA WIPOEV WSPOEV	2	[8] [9] [10]
44		LCRMEE LOEFWL WIPOEV WSPOEV	3	[1] [6] [9] [10]
45		LCRMEE PIRSWE POEFWP WIPOEV WSPOEV	4	[1] [2] [7] [9] [10]
46		WSPOEV	0	[10]
47	ABALFS	AOEFWA WIPOEV WSPOEV	2	[8] [9] [10]
48		LCRMEE LOEFWL WIPOEV WSPOEV	3	[1] [6] [9] [10]
49		LCRMEE PIRSWE POEFWP WIPOEV WSPOEV	4	[1] [2] [7] [9] [10]
50	AEXTST	AOEFWA WIPOEV WSPOEV	2	[8] [9] [10]
51		LCRMEE LOEFWL WIPOEV WSPOEV	3	[1] [6] [9] [10]
52		LCRMEE PIRSWE POEFWP WIPOEV WSPOEV	4	[1] [2] [7] [9] [10]
53		PIRSWE POEFWP WIPOEV WSPOEV	3	[2] [7] [9] [10]
54		WSPOEV	0	[10]
55	AIBDWP	AEOFWA WIPOEV WSPOEV	2	[8] [9] [10]
56		ASBUDC AOEFWA WIPOEV WSPOEV	3	[4] [8] [9] [10]
57		ASBUDC WSPOEV	1	[4] [10]
58		PCOREC ASBUDC AOEFWA WIPOEV WSPOEV	4	[3] [4] [8] [9] [10]
59		PCOREC ASBUDC WSPOEV	2	[3] [4] [10]
60		PCOREC LACPRE LOEFWL WIPOEV WSPOEV	4	[3] [5] [6] [9] [10]
61		PCOREC POEFWP WIPOEV WSPOEV	3	[3] [7] [9] [10]
62		PCOREC WSPOEV	1	[3] [10]
63	AORGBA	AOEFWA WIPOEV WSPOEV	2	[8] [9] [10]

the value of the impact transmitted by the channels involving direct effects is the value of the partial differential of equation [10] with respect to the relevant exogenous variable. The value of the partial differentials in these cases is nothing but the coefficient for the concerned exogenous variables in equation [10]. In contrast, the value of impact being transmitted by the channels involving indirect effects is the product of the partial differentials of relevant equations with respect to relevant exogenous and endogenous variables. Again, the product of the partial differentials in these cases is actually the product of the coefficients for the exogenous and en route variables in the relevant linkage chains.

Since the indirect effects transmitted by the channels are calculated as a product of the coefficients of the variables in their linkage chains, both the number of variables and the size of their coefficients play a key role in determining the relative level of impact transmission. Thus, when the linkage chains are lengthy and most coefficients have a value of less than one, the level of impact transmission can be lower than in contrary cases.[3] However, this does not necessarily mean that the channels having direct effects with no en route variable will invariably have a larger value than those having lengthy linkage chains and variables with fractional values. The value of the impact transmitted by an individual channel can be lower when its linkage chain is lengthy and its variables have fractional coefficients. But, the total impact due to a change in an exogenous variable can still be larger when its effects are transmitted through more channels. This is because the total impact due to a marginal change in an exogenous variable is the sum of the values associated with all its impact-transmission channels. This is why we consider more important, from the perspective of both institution building and performance improvement, to promote exogenous variables having more intricate linkages with other variables and linkage chains with variables having larger coefficients.

While both the nature and implications of the procedure used to quantify the level of impact transmitted by various channels are clear, we need to be careful about the kinds of coefficients used for impact quantification. Although the estimated coefficients of Model B can be directly used to quantify the value of various impact-transmission channels, they are likely to bias the evaluation of the relative significance of the channels. The bias originates in variations in both the exogenous and endogenous variables in the system not only in terms of the sign and significance of their coefficients but also in terms of the value of their mean and standard deviation. To correct for the bias emanating from these variations, we have to standardize the coefficients. There are two econometric approaches to standardizing the coefficients. The first involves the use of the concept of *elasticity at means*, wherein the coefficient of an independent variable is multiplied by the ratio of its mean value to the mean value of the dependent variable in question. The other approach involves the concept of *standardized coefficients*, wherein the coefficient of the independent variable is weighted by the ratio of its standard deviation to the standard deviation of the dependent variable. While the former approach adjusts the coefficients for their relative levels, the latter approach adjusts the coefficients for their relative variability. Since we are interested in comparing how a marginal change in different independent variables alters the value of their dependent variable, adjusting the coefficients for their variability makes more sense than adjusting them for their mean levels.[4] That is why we use standardized coefficients to calculate the value of various impact-transmission channels.

To correct for the possible bias from variations in the signs of coefficients, we use the absolute value of the coefficients for the following three reasons. First, as argued in several places in Chapters 8 and 9, the negative coefficients in many cases are indicative only of a positive effect.[5] Second, since most of the channels involve indirect effects with values obtained by multiplying the relevant coefficients of variables in the linkage chains, sign differences will not allow any clear inference about the direction of the aggregate impact being transmitted.[6] Third, in light of the two points just noted, magnitude is more important than direction when comparing the relative levels of impacts transmitted by different channels. On these grounds, we use only the absolute values of the coefficients to calculate the magnitude of impact transmitted by different channels.

Instead of viewing the bias due to variations in the significance of coefficients as a problem, we consider it as an opportunity to illustrate why some of the impact-transmission channels become insignificant and how this fact can be exploited to determine the thrust of institutional reform programs. Our approach involves a comparison of the values of the impact-transmission channels calculated using all the coefficients with the values obtained using only the significant coefficients. It is important to recognize that in the calculation involving only the significant coefficients, the values of the impact-transmission channels will be positive only when all the variables of their underlying linkage chains have a significant coefficient. Otherwise, their values will be zero. The zero value for the ineffective channels is due to the fact that, if one or more variables in the linkage chain have insignificant coefficients, the variables in question fail to convey even the effects of other significant variables therein.

The evaluation of the relative impact transmission by channels is used to derive policy inferences related to institutional priority setting, sequencing, and packaging. Given the value and significance of the channels, the significant or effective impact-transmission channels can be distinguished from their insignificant or ineffective counterparts. Such a distinction can serve two very important purposes. The first is to indicate the magnitude of performance loss caused by the insignificance of some of the institutional and performance variables. The second is to identify the channels and the underlying variables that suffer from the problem of such insignificance. From the perspective of institutional reform, these channels with one or more insignificant variables should receive priority. The comparative analysis of the impact-transmission channels will identify these channels and use them to show how their performance impact can be enhanced by targeting the reform effort on the insignificant institutional and performance variables involved. Some additional aspects are also involved, especially those related to institutional priority sequencing, and packaging as well as timing and scale of institutional reform. Since they can be better appreciated after the comparative analysis of the channels, the discussion on them is reserved for a later section.

There are too many impact-transmission channels to present them all within a single table. For presentational convenience, we break the tables into three parts, each giving information on the channels related, respectively, to the law-, policy-, and administration-related institutional variables. The relative performance contributions of the individual impact-transmission channels associated with the exogenous variables are evaluated both in the all-sample context as well as in the context of two country groups defined by their recent reform status. The evaluation across country groups is a check for the robustness and contextuality of the all-sample results and to see the influence of recent reform initiatives. Within this analytical framework, first we evaluate the relative proportion of the impact transmitted by various channels associated with each exogenous variable and then consider the total impact transmitted by all the exogenous variables. With these observations on our approach and evaluation framework, let us now begin with the analysis of the results.

RELATIVE SHARE OF TRANSMISSION CHANNELS: OVERALL PERSPECTIVE

The relative importance of each channel is evaluated in terms of the magnitude and share of its impact transmission relative to others, both within each of the three channel groups (law, policy, and administration-related channels) and across all 63 channels. The values of the impact being transmitted by the channels are calculated using first all the coefficients, irrespective of their significance, as well as using those that are only significant. In presenting the results (see tables), the significant channels (those having significant coefficients for all their linkage variables) are distinguished by values in bold type. In addition to the value of impact transmission, the relative shares of the channels in total impact obtained both at the level of each of the three channel groups and at the level of all 63 channels are also calculated to allow their ranking and facilitate comparison. With these observations, all the tables that show the relative importance and significance of the channels in different contexts (all-sample, reform countries, and other countries) will become self-explanatory.

Relative Importance of Law-Related Channels

Table 10.2a shows the value, relative share, and rank of 15 impact-transmission channels associated with the five law-related exogenous variables. Most of the channels are associated with *LPRSRF*, representing the legal aspect of property-rights format. As we consider their values as calculated using all the coefficients, these channels have lower individual values and shares than the channels associated with *LINTRE*, *LOECEN*, and *LOEPRV*, representing, respectively, the three law-related institutional aspects of internal consistency, centralization tendency, and privatization provisions within water law. However, since *LPRSRF* has 10 channels as against others with just two or fewer, it has a larger impact than all the other law-related exogenous variables. Specifically, these 10 channels together account for about 44 percent of the impact transmitted by the law-related channels and about 8 percent of the impact transmitted by all 63 channels. But, taken together, the first four channels associated with *LINTRE*, *LOECEN*, and *LOEPRV* still dominate, with a combined share of more than 50 percent of the total impact transmitted through all the law-related channels and close to 9 percent of the impact transmitted through all 63 channels.

If we consider the channels in terms of their values calculated using only the significant coefficients, only four become significant. They are the two single channels associated, respectively, with *LINTRE* and *LOECEN* and two of the 10 channels associated with *LPRSRF*. These significant channels account for only 44 percent of the total impact in the context of law-related channels and 8 percent of the total impact in the context of all 63 channels. The impact of *LPRSRF*, which has a larger share when calculated with all the coefficients, has only the second largest share when evaluated with the significant coefficients. This clearly suggests that, although exogenous variables with more channels have stronger institutional and performance linkages, they do not necessarily produce a stronger performance impact. Much depends not only on the strength and effectiveness of the channels, as reflected by the magnitude and significance of the coefficients related to the variables in their linkage chains, but also on the possibility of strengthening some of the key channels through suitable reform. Thus, for instance, if it is possible to strengthen the two channels associated with *LOEPRV* as well as some of the channels of *LPRSRF* with relatively larger shares of impact, the relative importance and significance of both the channels and exogenous variables can be altered through policy means. The information in Table 10.2a can therefore

Table 10.2a *Law-related channels: relative share and significance of impact in all-sample context*

No.	Channel	Linkage chains					Value	Share (percent)		Rank	
								Within law	Overall	Within law	Overall
1	LINTRE	LOEFWL	WIPOEV	WSPOEV			**0.061**	**17.43**	**3.09**	**1**	**7**
2	LOECEN	LOEFWL	WIPOEV	WSPOEV			**0.043**	**12.20**	**2.17**	**2**	**10**
3	LOEPRV	LACPRE	LOEFWL	WIPOEV	WSPOEV		0.036	10.21	1.81	3	13
4		LOEFWL	WIPOEV	WSPOEV			0.034	9.64	1.71	4	14
5	LPRSRF	LACPRE	LOEFWL	WIPOEV	WSPOEV		0.014	3.98	0.71	10	39
6		LCRMEE	LOEFWL	WIPOEV	WSPOEV		0.007	2.09	0.37	12	50
7		LOEFWL	WIPOEV	WSPOEV			0.027	7.78	1.38	6	21
8		PCOREC	ASBUDC	AOEFWA	WIPOEV	WSPOEV	0.017	4.96	0.88	10	34
9		PCOREC	ASBUDC	WSPOEV	WSPOEV		**0.022**	**6.17**	**1.10**	**8**	**27**
10		PCOREC	LACPRE	LOEFWL	WIPOEV	WSPOEV	0.019	5.32	0.94	9	32
11		PCOREC	POEFWP	WIPOEV	WSPOEV		0.006	1.71	0.30	14	53
12		PCOREC	WSPOEV				**0.029**	**8.32**	**1.48**	**5**	**20**
13		LCRMEE	PIRSWE	POEFWP	WIPOEV	WSPOEV	0.002	0.69	0.12	15	63
14		PIRSWE	POEFWP	WIPOEV	WSPOEV		0.009	2.64	0.47	13	46
15	LTRWSA	LOEFWL	WIPOEV	WSPOEV			0.024	6.85	1.22	7	25
Subtotal	All coefficients						0.350	100.00	17.75		
	Only significant coefficients						0.154	44.12	7.83		

273

Table 10.2b   Policy-related channels: relative share and significance of impact in all-sample context

No.		Impact-transmission channels/Linkage chains	Value	Share (percent) Within policy	Share (percent) Overall	Rank Within policy	Rank Overall
16	PGPIPP	ASBUDC AOEFWA WIPOEV WSPOEV	0.003	0.83	0.17	24	60
17		ASBUDC WSPOEV WIPOEV	0.006	1.40	0.29	19	54
18		POEFWP WIPOEV WSPOEV	0.012	3.00	0.62	12	41
19	PGPIUP	ASBUDC AOEFWA WIPOEV WSPOEV	0.022	5.26	1.10	6	26
20		ASBUDC WSPOEV WSPOEV	**0.036**	**8.88**	**1.85**	**3**	**12**
21		LCRMEE LOEFWL WIPOEV WSPOEV	**0.044**	**10.74**	**2.24**	**2**	**9**
22		PCOREC ASBUDC AOEFWA WIPOEV	0.012	2.85	0.59	14	43
23		PCOREC ASBUDC WSPOEV WSPOEV	**0.020**	**4.81**	**1.00**	**7**	**29**
24		PCOREC LACPRE LOEFWL WIPOEV WSPOEV	0.013	3.05	0.64	11	40
25		PCOREC POEFWP WIPOEV WSPOEV	0.004	0.98	0.20	22	58
26		PCOREC WSPOEV WSPOEV	**0.020**	**4.78**	**0.99**	**8**	**30**
27		LCRMEE PIRSWE POEFWP WIPOEV WSPOEV	0.015	3.57	0.74	10	38
28		PIRSWE POEFWP WIPOEV WSPOEV	0.012	2.88	0.60	13	42
29		POEFWP WIPOEV WSPOEV	0.007	1.65	0.34	18	51
30	POELWL	LACPRE LOEFWL WIPOEV WSPOEV	0.024	5.84	1.22	5	24
31		POEFWP WIPOEV WSPOEV	0.017	4.07	0.85	9	37
32	POPAWE	LCRMEE LOEFWL WIPOEV WSPOEV	0.010	2.53	0.53	15	44
33		PCOREC ASBUDC AOEFWA WIPOEV	0.005	1.26	0.26	20	56
34		PCOREC ASBUDC WSPOEV WSPOEV	0.009	2.13	0.44	16	47
35		PCOREC POEFWP WIPOEV	0.003	0.75	0.16	25	61
36		PCOREC WSPOEV WIPOEV	0.009	2.12	0.44	17	48
37		LCRMEE PIRSWE POEFWP WIPOEV	0.003	0.84	0.17	23	59
38		POEFWP WIPOEV WSPOEV	0.004	0.99	0.21	21	57
39		WSPOEV WIPOEV	0.068	16.57	3.45	1	6
40	PPSCRI	POEFWP WIPOEV WSPOEV	0.034	8.22	1.71	4	15
Subtotal		All coefficients	0.410	100.00	20.83		
		Only significant coefficients	0.120	29.21	6.08		

be used to identify the channels and the variables in their linkage chains that should receive priority in an institutional reform program.

Relative Importance of Policy-Related Channels

The relative roles and significance of the policy-related impact-transmission channels can be evaluated from Table 10.2b, giving their values, shares, and ranks. Of the 25 channels associated with five policy-related exogenous variables, 11 are related to *PGPIUP*, representing the effectiveness of user participation policy, and eight are related to *POPAWE*, representing other general and sectoral policies affecting water policies. In terms of the values calculated with all the coefficients, the 11 channels associated with *PGPIUP* jointly account for about 50 percent of the total impact transmitted by all the 25 policy-related channels. But, they account for only about 10 percent of the total impact transmitted by all 63 channels. The corresponding figures associated with *POPAWE* are 27 percent and 6 percent. When evaluated on the basis of significant coefficients only, only four of the 25 channels become relevant and all these four channels are related to *PGPIUP*. The significant channels account for only 29 percent of the total impact transmitted by all policy-related channels.

Although the policy-related channels have a larger impact than the law-related channels, in terms of the value of significant channels, the latter channels, as a group, do far better than the former. The reason is not difficult to find. Among all the policy-related channels, some channels have a larger impact, but they are insignificant. A number of channels exhibit this property, but the most important one is *POPAWE–WSPOEV*, which conveys the direct effects of other sectoral policies on water sector performance. This channel has the largest share, both among the channels associated with *POPAWE* (about 62 percent) and among all policy-related channels (17 percent). If institutional reform is designed to effect changes in other sectoral policies in a way that makes this channel (and other related channels) significant and effective, water sector performance could be enhanced by 4 to 6 percent. Since this kind of reform effort is also likely to create favorable changes in all channels involving *POPAWE*, the performance impact of such reform could still be far larger.

The insignificance of a larger number of policy-related channels is consistent with the stronger role of legal and administrative performance that we obtained in the context of Chapter 8 and evaluated further in Chapter 9. But the information in Table 10.2b adds another insight. As can be seen from the four channels with a significant and larger impact, the variable *PGPIUP* has stronger direct and indirect linkages with legal and administrative aspects through en-route variables such as *PCOREC*, representing cost-recovery status. It also has an influence on *LCRMEE* and *LACPRE*, representing, respectively, the legal aspects of the efficacy conflict-resolution mechanisms and accountability provisions, as well as on

ASBUDC, representing the administrative aspects of the seriousness of the budget constraint. This provides some evidence that, although the water policy may not have any significant effect on the performance of the water institution, and hence, water sector performance, some of the policy-related variables do have a key role in indirectly strengthening the performance contributions of both the water law and water administration components of water institution.

Relative Importance of Administration-Related Channels

The values, shares, and ranks of 23 administration-related channels are listed in Table 10.2c. These channels are associated with six exogenous variables related to water administration. These channels account for 61 percent of the total impact of all 63 channels calculated from all the coefficients and 52 percent of the total impact calculated using only the significant coefficients. Their largest combined share of the total impact suggests that these administration-related channels are more important for performance improvement than their law- and policy-related counterparts. Moreover, unlike the case of law- and policy-related exogenous variables, four of the six administration-related exogenous variables have two or more significant channels. While the number of significant channels is four each in the case of law- and policy-related channels, it is 10 in the case of administration-related channels. The 10 significant channels account together for 84 percent of the total impact of all 23 administration-related channels calculated with all the coefficients. This means that most of the significant channels also have a larger magnitude and share of performance impact not only within the context of Table 10.2c but also across Tables 10.2a, 10.2b, and 10.2c. This result suggests clearly the dominant role of the channels associated with administration-related exogenous variables, as a group, in determining the overall institutional and sectoral performance.

The administration-related channels with larger and more significant impact are associated with the four variables: *AEXTST*, *AARINF*, *ABALFS*, and *AIBDWP*. These variables represent, respectively, the extent of science and technology application, adequacy and relevance of information, balanced functional specialization, and existence of an independent water-pricing body. *AEXTST*, with four of its five channels significant, has the largest share (20 percent) of the total impact of all administration-related channels, irrespective of whether the impact is calculated with all or only significant coefficients. Although *AIBDWP* has more channels than other administration-related exogenous variables, its share of the impact is still lower than the shares of *AEXTST*, *AARINF*, and *ABALFS* with far fewer channels. This suggests, once again, that the magnitude and share of their impact may not necessarily be related to the number of channels associated with the exogenous variables. In any case, all four exogenous variables noted above have a larger share of impact than all the law- and policy-related exogenous variables.

Table 10.2c Administration-related channels: relative share and significance of impact in all-sample context

No.		Impact-transmission channels/Linkage chains					Value	Share (percent)		Rank	
								Within administration	Overall	Within administration	Overall
41	AACCME	AOEFWA	WIPOEV	WSPOEV			0.025	2.08	1.28	13	23
42		LACPRE	LOEFWL	WIPOEV			0.002	0.20	0.12	23	62
43	AARINF	AOEFWA	WIPOEV	WSPOEV			**0.164**	**13.53**	**8.31**	**3**	**3**
44		LCRMEE	LOEFWL	WIPOEV	WSPOEV		0.017	1.39	0.86	18	**36**
45		LCRMEE	PIRSWE	POEFWP	WSPOEV		0.006	0.46	0.28	22	25
46		WSPOEV					**0.136**	**11.24**	**6.91**	**4**	**4**
47	ABALFS	AOEFWA	WIPOEV	WSPOEV			**0.176**	**14.54**	**8.93**	**2**	**2**
48		LCRMEE	LOEFWL	WIPOEV	WSPOEV		0.026	2.14	1.32	12	**22**
49		LCRMEE	PIRSWE	POEFWP	WIPOEV	WSPOEV	0.009	0.71	0.44	20	49
50	AEXTST	AOEFWA	WIPOEV	WSPOEV			**0.234**	**19.37**	**11.90**	**1**	**1**
51		LCRMEE	LOEFWL	WIPOEV	WSPOEV		0.018	1.46	0.90	16	**33**
52		LCRMEE	PIRSWE	POEFWP	WIPOEV	WSPOEV	**0.031**	**2.56**	**1.57**	**11**	**19**
53		PIRSWE	POEFWP	WIPOEV	WSPOEV		**0.101**	**8.36**	**5.13**	**5**	**5**
54		WSPOEV					0.041	3.39	2.08	7	11
55	AIBDWP	AOEFWA	WIPOEV	WSPOEV			0.017	1.40	0.86	17	35
56		ASBUDC	AOEFWA	WIPOEV			0.032	2.63	1.62	10	18
57		ASBUDC	WSPOEV	WSPOEV			**0.540**	**4.44**	**2.73**	**6**	**8**
58		PCOREC	ASBUDC	WIPOEV	WSPOEV		0.019	1.60	0.98	15	31
59		PCOREC	ASBUDC	WSPOEV			**0.033**	**2.71**	**1.66**	**8**	**16**
60		PCOREC	LACPRE	LOEFWL	WSPOEV		0.021	1.72	1.06	14	28
61		PCOREC	POEFWP	WIPOEV			0.007	0.55	0.34	21	52
62		PCOREC	WSPOEV	WSPOEV			**0.033**	**2.69**	**1.65**	**9**	**17**
63	AORGBA	AOEFWA	WIPOEV	WSPOEV			0.010	0.81	0.49	19	45
Subtotal	All coefficients						1.209	100.00	61.41		
	Only significant coefficients						1.021	84.44	51.86		
Grand total	All coefficients						1.969	–[a]	100.00		
	Only significant coefficients						1.295	–[a]	65.78		

Note: [a] Grand total is for all 63 channels reported in Tables 10.2a, 10.2b, and 10.2c.

As we move through the variables in the linkage chains associated with all the significant channels reported in Tables 10.2a and 10.2b, we find that the effects of administration-related exogenous variables are also transmitted through law- and policy-related institutional and performance variables. This clearly suggests that administrative reforms have a larger performance impact mainly in view of their implications not only for administrative performance but also for the performance of water law and policy. The results provide strong evidence for giving administrative aspects a top priority in institutional reform programs. Specifically, the immediate priority should be on the application of science and technology, strengthening the information base, broadening the disciplinary background of personnel, and creating an independent water-pricing body. Interestingly, these administrative reforms are politically neutral and also have extensive forward and backward linkages conducive for promoting both immediate and long-term institutional and sectoral performance. These reforms require larger investments than, say, mere policy declarations, but in view of their role in improving the capability and outlook of water administration, they can initiate both an immediate and a long-term flow of benefits far greater than the initial investment costs.

RELATIVE SHARE OF TRANSMISSION CHANNELS: ROLE OF RECENT REFORMS

The role of recently undertaken reforms in determining the relative share and significance of different channels associated with the exogenous variables can be evaluated by comparing the results obtained for reform countries with those obtained for other countries. As we did in the all-sample context, the results are presented and analyzed by distinguishing the channels in terms of their association with law-, policy-, and administration-related exogenous variables. The analysis is based on a comparison of the relative impact shares of the channels in total impact within each of the three channel groups as well as contrasting the same across the two country groups.

Relative Importance of Law-Related Channels

Table 10.3a depicts the value, relative share, and rank of the 15 channels associated with the five law-related exogenous variables as obtained in the context of reform countries and other countries. The most immediate aspect to note is that the behavior of the channels in terms of the relative size and significance of their impact shows an entirely different pattern across the two country groups. Both the channels that are significant and their relative share in total impact are different across the country groups. For instance, the single channels associated

Table 10.3a Law-related channels: relative share and significance of impact across country groups

No.	Impact-transmission channels/linkage chains	Reform areas					Other areas				
		Value	Share (percent)		Rank		Value	Share (percent)		Rank	
			Within law	Overall	Within law	Overall		Within law	Overall	Within law	Overall
1	LINTRE LOEFWL WIPOEV WSPOEV	0.001	0.33	0.05	13	58	**0.103**	**27.58**	**6.13**	**1**	**5**
2	LOECEN LOEFWL WIPOEV WSPOEV	**0.083**	**28.84**	**4.46**	**2**	**7**	0.020	5.38	1.20	6	20
3	LOEPRV LACPRE LOEFWL WIPOEV WSPOEV	0.010	3.60	0.56	5	31	**0.067**	**17.97**	**3.99**	**2**	**10**
4	LPRSRF LOEFWL WIPOEV WSPOEV	**0.111**	**38.33**	**5.93**	**1**	**6**	0.028	7.37	1.64	5	17
5	LPRSRF LACPRE LOEFWL WIPOEV WSPOEV	0.003	0.87	0.13	11	51	0.006	1.48	0.33	10	38
6	LCRMEE LOEFWL WIPOEV WSPOEV	0.004	1.39	0.21	8	45	0.005	1.45	0.32	11	39
7	LOEFWL WIPOEV WSPOEV	0.039	13.60	2.10	3	14	0.040	10.63	2.36	4	14
8	PCOREC ASBUDC AOEFWA	0.006	1.91	0.29	6	40	0.014	3.79	0.84	8	27
9	PCOREC ASBUDC WSPOEV	0.003	0.90	0.14	10	50	0.001	0.29	0.07	15	61
10	PCOREC LACPRE LOEFWL WIPOEV WSPOEV	0.001	0.42	0.06	12	57	**0.016**	**4.17**	**0.93**	**7**	**26**
11	PCOREC POEFWP WIPOEV WSPOEV	0.001	0.22	0.03	14	61	0.006	1.72	0.38	9	35
12	PCOREC WSPOEV	0.004	1.28	0.20	9	48	0.004	1.09	0.24	12	47
13	LCRMEE PIRSWE POEFWP WIPOEV WSPOEV	0.000	0.14	0.02	15	62	0.003	0.75	0.17	13	52
14	PIRSWE POEFWP WIPOEV WSPOEV	0.005	1.74	0.27	7	42	0.002	0.45	0.10	14	57
15	LTRWSA LOEFWL WIPOEV WSPOEV	0.019	6.45	1.00	4	22	**0.059**	**15.87**	**3.53**	**3**	**12**
Subtotal	All coefficients	0.289	100.00	15.46			0.374	100.00	22.23		
	Only significant coefficients	0.194	67.16	10.38			0.245	65.60	14.58		

279

with both *LINTRE* and *LTRWSA* that are insignificant with only a marginal impact in the context of reform countries are significant with substantial impact in the context of other countries. While none of the channels associated with *LPRSRF* is significant in the context of reform countries, the one that transmits the effects of property rights via cost recovery and legal provisions for accountability is significant with a considerable share in the total impact transmitted by all law-related channels.

Of the two channels associated with *LOEPRE*, the first one, which transmits its effects indirectly via the variable representing the effectiveness of the legal provisions for accountability, is significant in the context of other countries. In the context of the reform countries, the significant channel is the second one, which transmits the effects of privatization policy directly to overall performance of water law. This channel accounts for the largest share of the total impact transmitted by all law-related channels. The total impact of the law-related channels – calculated either with all the coefficients or with only the significant among them – is far lower in the context of reform countries than in other countries. Similarly, there are only two significant channels in the context of reform countries, but four in the context of other countries. These results give an impression that the law-related exogenous variables play a major role in countries lacking institutional reforms. The relative size and significance of the impact of the channels observed in non-reform countries also suggest that law-related institutional aspects such as internal consistency, effective accountability provisions, and integrated treatment of water sources remain the key reform issues.

Since the countries that have recently undertaken substantial institutional reform also have a relatively mature water sector, their major focus is on privatization and adding a dose of centralization to their water laws. Although only two of the 15 channels are significant in the case of these reform countries, they account for 67 percent (as compared with the case of other countries with four significant channels accounting for 66 percent) of the total impact observed in the context of Table 10.3a. However, both country groups still have a considerable scope for enhancing institutional and sectoral performance by strengthening some of the channels, especially the third one, associated with *LPRSRF*. Although the institutional reforms related to property rights have substantial forward linkages, they also require the prior creation of a strong institutional and technical foundation. Since the reform countries either have or could create most of the institutional and technical prerequisites, property-rights reforms are more likely and effective in these countries than in others.

Relative Importance of Policy-Related Channels

The value, share, and rank of the 25 channels associated with the five policy-related exogenous variables obtained in the context of the two country groups

Table 10.3b Policy-related channels: relative share and significance of impact across country groups

No.		Impact-transmission channels/linkage chains	Reform areas Value	Reform Share (percent) Within policy	Reform Share (percent) Overall	Reform Rank Within policy	Reform Rank Overall	Other areas Value	Other Share (percent) Within policy	Other Share (percent) Overall	Other Rank Within policy	Other Rank Overall
16	PGPIPP	ASBUDC AOEFWA WIPOEV WSPOEV	0.015	3.58	0.78	7	26	0.033	8.80	1.96	3	15
17		ASBUDC WSPOEV	0.012	2.88	0.62	8	28	0.003	0.86	0.19	19	48
18		POEFWP WIPOEV WSPOEV	0.004	1.10	0.24	18	44	0.008	2.11	0.47	12	33
19	PGPIUP	ASBUDC AOEFWA WIPOEV WSPOEV	0.011	2.70	0.58	9	30	0.029	7.63	1.70	4	16
20		ASBUDC WSPOEV	0.009	2.17	0.47	10	33	0.003	0.75	0.17	21	53
21		LCRMEE LOEFWL WIPOEV WSPOEV	**0.062**	**15.26**	**3.31**	**2**	**8**	0.011	2.87	0.64	8	28
22		PCOREC ASBUDC AOEFWA WIPOEV	0.008	1.90	0.41	12	35	0.005	1.40	0.31	15	40
23		PCOREC ASBUDC WSPOEV	0.006	1.52	0.33	16	39	0.001	0.14	0.03	25	63
24		PCOREC LACPRE LOEFWL WIPOEV WSPOEV	0.002	0.42	0.09	22	56	0.006	1.54	0.34	13	36
25		PCOREC POEFWP WIPOEV WSPOEV	0.001	0.22	0.05	23	59	0.002	0.63	0.14	22	54
26		PCOREC WSPOEV	0.005	1.27	0.28	17	41	0.002	0.40	0.09	24	60
27		LCRMEE PIRSWE POEFWP WIPOEV WSPOEV	0.006	1.56	0.34	15	38	0.006	1.49	0.33	14	37
28		PIRSWE POEFWP WIPOEV WSPOEV	0.004	0.99	0.21	19	46	0.003	0.84	0.19	20	49
29		POEFWP WIPOEV WSPOEV	0.002	0.48	0.11	21	53	0.008	2.21	0.49	11	32
30	POELWL	LACPRE LOEFWL WIPOEV WSPOEV	0.000	0.03	0.01	25	63	**0.070**	**18.75**	**4.18**	**2**	**9**
31		POEFWP WIPOEV WSPOEV	0.003	0.69	0.15	20	49	0.027	7.20	1.60	5	18
32	POPAWE	LCRMEE LOEFWL WIPOEV WSPOEV	0.008	1.86	0.40	13	36	0.008	2.23	0.50	10	31
33		PCOREC ASBUDC AOEFWA WIPOEV WSPOEV	**0.027**	**6.60**	**1.43**	**4**	**17**	0.017	4.62	1.03	7	23
34		PCOREC ASBUDC WSPOEV	0.021	5.30	1.15	5	19	0.002	0.45	0.10	23	56
35		PCOREC POEFWP WIPOEV WSPOEV	0.008	2.03	0.44	11	34	0.005	1.28	0.28	17	43
36		PCOREC WSPOEV	0.018	4.43	0.96	6	23	0.005	1.33	0.30	16	42
37		LCRMEE PIRSWE POEFWP WIPOEV WSPOEV	0.001	0.19	0.04	24	60	0.004	1.16	0.26	18	46
38		POEFWP WIPOEV WSPOEV	0.007	1.64	0.36	14	37	0.009	2.48	0.55	9	29
39		WSPOEV	**0.129**	**31.82**	**6.90**	**1**	**5**	0.087	23.20	5.17	1	8
40	PPSCRI	POEFWP WIPOEV WSPOEV	0.038	9.36	2.03	3	15	0.021	5.65	1.26	6	19
Subtotal		All coefficients	0.405	100.00	21.68			0.375	100.00	22.28		
		Only significant coefficients	0.218	53.69	11.64			0.070	18.75	4.18		

are given in Table 10.3b. When the impact of these channels is calculated with all the coefficients, those associated with *POPAWE*, representing the impact of other sectoral policies on water policy, have the largest share in the case of both country groups. But, their share in the context of reform countries (54 percent) is much larger than the share (37 percent) found in other countries. Although *PGPIUP*, representing the effectiveness of user participation policy, has more channels than other exogenous variables, it has only the second largest share in reform countries (28 percent) and the third largest share in other countries (20 percent). The two channels associated with *POELWL*, representing the overall linkages between water law and water policy, have only a marginal share for reform countries, but have the second largest share in the context of other countries (26 percent). The combined share of the three channels associated with *PGPIPP*, representing the effectiveness of private sector promotion policy, is also larger in other countries (12 percent) than in reform countries (6 percent).

Considering the impact of channels in terms of only the significant coefficients, of the 25 channels, three are significant in reform countries but only one is significant in other countries. Within these three significant channels, we can also identify the variations in the sources and patterns of impact transmission. The channel capturing the impact of other sectoral policies directly on water sector performance has the largest share (32 percent). The channel that conveys the performance effects of user participation policy through conflict resolution and legal performance has the next largest share (15 percent), and the channel that transmits the indirect effects of other sectoral policies via cost recovery and budget constraint has a 7 percent share. This suggests that the two key factors for performance in reform countries are the effectiveness of user participation policy and the impact of other sectoral policies. This is understandable as farm sector policies in most contexts negatively affect cost recovery (due to subsidized water rates) and contribute to budget constraint (due to poor recovery and lower budgetary allocation). We have indeed observed this phenomenon in several of our sample countries.

In non-reform countries, the only significant channel is related to law–policy linkages, and it suggests the major role that effective law–policy linkages can play in improving the overall performance of water law and water policy, especially by strengthening the legal aspects of accountability. The channel related to accountability aspects has a 19 percent share in the total impact of all policy-related channels and 4 percent of the total impact of all 63 channels. The insignificance of the remaining channels for both country groups does not mean that the exogenous variables associated with them are of no consequence. The ineffectiveness of the remaining channels is essentially due to the insignificance of one or more of the en route variables underlying these channels. If this bottleneck were to be eliminated by targeting the reform on the institutional aspects represented by these en-route variables underlying the channels with a substantial but insignificant share of total impact, the performance contributions of the remaining channels could be enhanced considerably. Since only 19 percent of the total impact transmitted by all policy-related channels is significant in non-reform countries, the magnitude of the reform task in the sphere of water policy is far greater in these countries than in reform countries.

In non-reform countries, reform should focus on the variables underlying the insignificant channels with a substantial share in the total impact of all policy-related channels. As we screen all insignificant policy-related channels for reform countries, we can identify six channels with a share of 4 percent or more. These are the two channels associated with *POPAWE*, with a combined impact share of 28 percent, and one channel each related, respectively, to *PGPIPP* (9 percent), *PGPIUP* (8 percent), *POELWL* (7 percent), and *PPSCRI* (6 percent). The configuration and sequencing of variables in the linkage chains underlying these channels provide the basis for deciding institutional priorities within the reform program targeting the policy sphere in countries lacking recent reforms. Although the significant channels have a 54 percent share in the total impact of policy-related channels in reform countries, these countries also need other types of reforms to enhance and consolidate the performance gains already achieved. In this respect, the reform countries can focus on the four currently insignificant channels with an individual share of 4 percent or more but a combined share of about 24 percent. They are the two channels associated with *POPAWE* and one each associated with *PGPIPP* and *PPSCRI*.

Relative Importance of Administration-Related Channels

The relative level and share of the impact transmitted by the 23 channels associated with six administration-related exogenous variables obtained across country groups are given in Table 10.3c. Irrespective of country group, the administration-related channels, as a group, are far more critical than their legal and policy counterparts for enhancing the performance of both water institution and water sector. Together, they account for a predominant share of the total impact transmitted by all 63 channels. However, the share of these channels is much higher in reform countries (63 percent) than in other countries (56 percent). The gap between the country groups in terms of the share of significant channels is wider still: 51 percent in reform countries but only 37 percent in other countries. Most of the administration-related channels with a larger share of the impact are also significant in both country groups, and all the exogenous variables with the exception of *AACCME*, representing the effectiveness of administrative accountability, have at least one significant channel.

Of the channels associated with each exogenous variable across country groups, among reform countries those associated with *AARINF* account for the largest share (40 percent) and those associated with *AEXTST* have the second

Table 10.3c Administration-related channels: relative share and significance of impact across country groups

No.	Impact-transmission channels/linkage chains	Reform areas Value	Reform Share (percent) Within admin.	Reform Share (percent) Overall	Reform Rank Within admin.	Reform Rank Overall	Other areas Value	Other Share (percent) Within admin.	Other Share (percent) Overall	Other Rank Within admin.	Other Rank Overall
41 AACCME	AOEFWA WIPOEV WSPOEV	0.009	0.75	0.47	18	32	0.005	0.55	0.31	15	41
42	LACPRE LOEFWL WIPOEV WSPOEV	0.005	0.41	0.26	19	43	0.018	1.93	1.07	10	22
43 AARINF	AOEFWA WIPOEV WSPOEV	**0.136**	**11.58**	**7.28**	**3**	**3**	**0.111**	**11.91**	**6.61**	**3**	**3**
44	LCRMEE LOEFWL WIPOEV	0.021	1.75	1.10	12	20	0.003	0.33	0.18	19	51
45	LCRMEE PIRSWE WIPOEV WSPOEV	0.002	0.18	0.11	21	52	0.002	0.17	0.10	21	58
46	WSPOEV	**0.307**	**26.12**	**16.42**	**1**	**1**	0.110	11.78	6.54	4	4
47 ABALFS	AOEFWA WIPOEV WSPOEV	**0.135**	**11.50**	**7.23**	**4**	**4**	**0.099**	**10.61**	**5.89**	**5**	**6**
48	LCRMEE LOEFWL WIPOEV	0.018	1.51	0.95	14	24	0.009	0.98	0.54	13	30
49	LCRMEE PIRSWE POEFWP WIPOEV	0.002	0.15	0.10	23	55	0.005	0.51	0.28	16	44
50 AEXTST	AOEFWA WIPOEV WSPOEV	**0.149**	**12.69**	**7.98**	**2**	**2**	**0.172**	**18.40**	**10.21**	**1**	**1**
51	LCRMEE LOEFWL WIPOEV	0.020	1.69	1.06	13	21	0.001	0.12	0.06	23	62
52	LCRMEE PIRSWE POEFWP WSPOEV	0.025	2.14	1.34	11	18	0.003	0.33	0.19	18	50
53	PIRSWE POEFWP WIPOEV	**0.052**	**4.41**	**2.77**	**8**	**12**	**0.117**	**12.53**	**6.95**	**2**	**2**
54	WSPOEV	0.056	4.76	2.99	7	11	0.097	10.39	5.76	6	7
55 AIBDWP	AOEFWA WIPOEV WSPOEV	**0.057**	**4.88**	**3.07**	**6**	**10**	**0.067**	**7.14**	**3.96**	**7**	**11**
56	ASBUDC AOEFWA WIPOEV	**0.041**	**3.53**	**2.22**	**9**	**13**	0.020	2.13	1.18	9	21
57	ASBUDC WSPOEV	0.033	2.83	1.78	10	16	0.002	0.21	0.12	20	55
58	PCOREC ASBUDC AOEFWA WIPOEV	**0.017**	**1.44**	**0.90**	**15**	**25**	0.016	1.68	0.93	12	25
59	PCOREC ASBUDC WSPOEV	0.014	1.15	0.72	16	27	0.002	0.16	0.09	22	59
60	PCOREC LACPRE LOEFWL WIPOEV	0.004	0.32	0.20	20	47	**0.017**	**1.85**	**1.03**	**11**	**24**
61	PCOREC POEFWP WIPOEV WSPOEV	0.002	0.16	0.10	22	54	0.007	0.76	0.42	14	34
62	PCOREC WSPOEV	0.011	0.96	0.61	17	29	0.005	0.48	0.27	17	45
63 AORGBA	AOEFWA WIPOEV WSPOEV	**0.060**	**5.10**	**3.21**	**5**	**9**	**0.047**	**5.03**	**2.79**	**8**	**13**
Subtotal All coefficients		1.18	100.00	62.86			0.934	100.00	55.49		
Only significant coefficients		0.95	81.24	51.07			0.630	67.47	37.44		
Grand total All coefficients		1.870	[a]	100.00			1.683	[a]	100.00		
Only significant coefficients		1.367	[a]	73.09			0.946	[a]	56.20		

Note: [a] Grand total is for all the 63 channels reported in Tables 10.3a, 10.3b and 10.3c.

largest share (26 percent). In non-reform countries, however, the channels associated with *AEXTST* have the largest share (42 percent) and those associated with *AARINF* display the second largest share (24 percent). The relative shares of the remaining channels except those associated with *ABALFS* remain more or less the same across country groups. The share of the channels associated with *AIBDWP*, representing the existence of an independent water-pricing body (around 15 percent), and those associated with *AORGBA*, representing the geographical basis of water organization (around 5 percent), remain consistent across country groups. However, *ABALFS*, representing the level of balance in functional specialization within water administration, has a considerably larger share in reform countries (13 percent) than in other countries (8 percent).

The administration-related exogenous variables, except those with a dominant share of total impact, display a somewhat similar pattern of behavior across country groups. But, most of the country-specific variations actually lie both in the relative share, and in the number and configuration, of linkage chains underlying the significant channels. For instance, as we compare the linkage chains underlying the significant channels associated with *AIBDWP* across country groups, the impact of this variable in reform countries is conveyed mainly through cost recovery (*PCOREC*), budget constraint (*ASBUDC*), and the overall performance of water administration (*AOEFWA*). In contrast, in nonreform countries, although the effects of *AIBDWP*, as conveyed through *AOEFWA*, are dominant, they are further conveyed through *PCOREC*, legal provisions for accountability (*LACPRE*), and the overall performance of water law (*LOEFWL*).

Similarly, the channel conveying the direct performance effects of the adequacy and relevance of information (*AARINF*) has the largest impact (26 percent) in reform countries. In the case of other countries, however, *AARINF* has a substantial but insignificant share (12 percent). Although both the significant channels associated with the exogenous variable *AEXTST*, representing the extent of science and technology application within water administration, are important in both country groups, they have, however, a larger share in other countries than in reform countries. As noted, the channel conveying the indirect effects of *AEXTST* via the performance of water administration has, in fact, the largest impact in non-reform countries.

RELATIVE IMPORTANCE OF EXOGENOUS VARIABLES

The relative value and share of various channels discussed in the previous section provide an idea of the possible role and significance of the exogenous variables with which those channels are associated. A closer evaluation of the relative role and significance of the exogenous variables in terms of their share in total impact calculated using both all and only significant coefficients is, however, essential to identify the institutional aspects that should receive priority within an institutional reform program. Since the channels associated with a given exogenous variable only transmit the impact due to a marginal change in that variable, the sum of the impact transmitted by these channels represents the total or systemwide impact of the marginal change in that exogenous variable. The relative importance of the exogenous variables depends on three aspects: the number of impact-transmission channels, the length of the linkage chains underlying these channels, and the size of the coefficients for the variables in the linkage chains. Thus, an exogenous variable having more channels with shorter linkage chains and larger coefficients for the variables in the linkage chains is likely to have a larger share of impact than another having fewer channels with longer linkage chains and smaller coefficients for their en-route variables. The relative importance of an exogenous variable depends not only on the sum of the magnitude of its impact but also on how significant is such impact. The significance of impact of an exogenous variable is reflected by the sum of the impact being transmitted by its significant channels.

Overall Perspective

The all-sample results pertaining to the values and relative shares of the 16 exogenous variables are given in Table 10.4a. The number of all and significant channels associated with each of the exogenous variables can also be seen in the table. As we consider the performance impact calculated using all the coefficients, *AEXTST* has the dominant share of performance impact (22 percent), followed by *AARINF* (16 percent), *AIBDWP* (11 percent), *ABALFS* (11 percent), and *PGPIUP* (10 percent). Of the remaining exogenous variables, those with a notable share of performance impact are *LPRSRF* (8 percent) and *POPAWE* (6 percent). Although the most dominant of the exogenous variables are related mostly to administration-related institutional aspects, as we have noted in the previous section, all of them have powerful effects also on law- and policy-related institutional and performance variables operating in the linkage chains underlying their impact-transmission channels.

Even when we consider the performance impact in terms of only the significant channels, the top five exogenous variables listed above, once again, fare far better than the others. Notably, the share of the impact associated with all these variables has improved despite the lower impact and the insignificance of some of their channels. In any case, *AEXTST*, once again, has the top share of performance impact (30 percent), followed by *AARINF* (24 percent), *ABALFS* (16 percent), *PGPIUP* (9 percent), and *AIBDWP* (9 percent). Of the remaining exogenous variables, the three legal variables (*LINTRE*, *LOECEN*, and *LPRSRF*) show a significant positive contribution as they have at least one

Table 10.4a Exogenous variables: relative share and significance of impact in all-sample context

No.	Exogenous variables	All coefficients				Only significant coefficients			
		Channel	Value	Share	Rank	Channel	Value	Share	Rank
1	*LINTRE*	1	0.061	3.09	9	1	0.061	4.71	6
2	*LOECEN*	1	0.042	2.17	10	1	0.043	3.29	8
3	*LOEPRV*	2	0.069	3.50	8	–	–	–	–
4	*LPRSRF*	10	0.153	7.75	6	2	0.051	3.91	7
5	*LTRWSA*	1	0.024	1.22	14	–	–	–	–
6	*PGPIPP*	3	0.021	1.09	15	–	–	–	–
7	*PGPIUP*	11	0.203	10.30	5	4	0.120	9.26	4
8	*POELWL*	2	0.041	2.07	11	–	–	–	–
9	*POPAWE*	8	0.112	5.67	7	–	–	–	–
10	*PPSCRI*	1	0.034	1.71	12	–	–	–	–
11	*AACCME*	2	0.028	1.40	13	–	–	–	–
12	*AARINF*	4	0.322	16.36	2	3	0.317	24.45	2
13	*ABALFS*	3	0.210	10.69	4	2	0.201	15.53	3
14	*AEXTST*	5	0.425	21.59	1	4	0.384	29.67	1
15	*AIBDWP*	8	0.215	10.90	3	3	0.119	9.19	5
16	*AORGBA*	1	0.010	0.50	16	–	–	–	–
Total		63	1.969	100.00	–	20	1.295	100.00	–

Note: Not calculated for non-significant variables for obvious reasons.

significant channel. Notably, these three law-related exogenous variables have a combined share of about 12 percent. Among all the variables having two or more significant channels, the proportion of insignificant channels is high for *LPRSRF*, *PGPIUP*, and *AIBDWP*. However, eight of the 16 exogenous variables have a zero value as their en-route variables in impact–transmission channels are ineffective in transmitting the impact of these exogenous variables.

Effects of Reform Status of Countries

The evaluation of the relative role and significance of the exogenous variables in the all-sample context clearly identify the institutional aspects that should receive priority within an institutional reform program for a generic context. However, the robustness of the results should be checked by performing the same evaluation in the context of country groups defined in terms of their recent reform status. Such an evaluation has the additional benefit of highlighting the kinds of effects that recent institutional reforms have on the relative role and significance of the exogenous variables. Table 10.4b gives the comparative picture of the level, share, and significance of the impact of exogenous variables across the country groups. The exogenous variables display some noteworthy differences in terms of their value, relative share, and rank. While *AARINF* has the largest share in the case of reform countries, *AEXTST* has that distinction in other countries. The three variables that are next in line of importance (*POPAWE*, *AIBDWP*, and *ABALFS*) show a somewhat consistent behavior across the country groups. *PGPIUP*, which had the fifth largest share in the all-sample context, has the seventh largest share in reform countries but the tenth largest share in other countries. In contrast, *POPAWE*, which had the seventh largest share in the all-sample context, has the third largest share in the context of both country groups.

Despite variations in their values, relative shares, and ranks, most of the variables identified as having the top shares in the all-sample context retain their relative importance, irrespective of the reform status of countries. This is true even when the relative importance of the exogenous variables is considered in terms of the performance contributions of only their significant channels. There are, however, differences in the significance of the performance contributions of a number of variables. While six institutional variables remain consistently significant in both country groups, others show inconsistency. For instance, *POPAWE*, *LOECEN*, and *PGPIUP* have the third, seventh, and eighth rank, respectively, in reform countries, but all become insignificant in the context of other countries. In contrast, *LINTRE*, *POELWL*, *LTRWSA*, and *LPRSRF* have the third, sixth, eighth, and tenth rank, respectively, for other countries, but they become insignificant for the reform countries. This suggests that, although there is considerable consistency in the relative importance and

Table 10.4b   Exogenous variables: relative share and significance of impact across country groups

No.	Exogenous variables	All coefficients							Only significant coefficients							
		Reform countries				Other countries			Reform countries				Other countries			
		Channels[a]	Value	Share	Rank	Value	Share	Rank	Channels	Value	Share	Rank	Channels	Value	Share	Rank
1	LINTRE	1	0.001	0.05	16	0.103	6.13	6	–	–	–	–	1	0.103	10.91	3
2	LOECEN	1	0.083	4.46	8	0.020	1.20	16	1	0.083	6.10	7	–	–	–	–
3	LOEPRV	2	0.121	6.47	6	0.095	5.64	9	1	0.111	8.11	6	1	0.067	7.11	7
4	LPRSRF	10	0.065	3.47	9	0.097	5.74	8	–	–	–	–	1	0.016	1.65	10
5	LTRWSA	1	0.019	1.00	13	0.059	3.53	11	–	–	–	–	1	0.059	6.28	8
6	PGIPIPP	3	0.031	1.64	12	0.044	2.62	13	–	–	–	–	–	–	–	–
7	PGPIUP	11	0.115	6.17	7	0.075	4.43	10	1	0.062	4.53	8	–	–	–	–
8	POELWL	2	0.003	0.16	15	0.097	5.78	7	–	–	–	–	1	0.070	7.43	6
9	POPAWE	8	0.218	11.68	3	0.138	8.19	3	2	0.156	11.40	3	–	–	–	–
10	PPSCRI	1	0.038	2.03	11	0.021	1.26	15	–	–	–	–	–	–	–	–
11	AACCME	2	0.014	0.73	14	0.023	1.38	14	–	–	–	–	–	–	–	–
12	AARINF	4	0.466	24.91	1	0.226	13.43	2	2	0.443	32.42	1	1	0.111	11.76	2
13	ABALFS	3	0.155	8.29	5	0.113	6.71	5	1	0.135	9.89	4	1	0.099	10.47	4
14	AEXTST	5	0.302	16.15	2	0.390	23.17	1	2	0.201	14.71	2	2	0.289	30.54	1
15	AIBDWP	8	0.179	6.90	4	0.135	8.00	4	3	0.116	8.46	5	2	0.084	8.88	5
16	AORGBA	1	0.060	3.21	10	0.047	2.79	12	1	0.060	4.39	9	1	0.047	4.97	9
	Total	63	1.870	100.00	–	1.683	100.00	–	14	1.367	100.00	–	12	0.946	100.00	–

Note: [a] In the 'all-coefficient' case, the number of channels remain obviously the same for Reform countries and Other countries.
– Not calculated for nonsignificant variables.

289

significance of the variables at the top of the performance impact scale, there are notable differences at the bottom.

Since most of the variables at the top, which have larger and significant performance contributions, show consistent behavior across country groups, the performance impact of country-specific variations in the behavior of variables with smaller and insignificant contributions is likely to be lower. This does not mean, however, that institutional reform undertaken in the reform countries has no effect on the relative performance of the institutional variables. As we can see from Table 10.4b, the performance impact of all six variables showing consistency in their significance is substantially higher in the reform countries than in their counterparts, except for *AEXTST*, where the converse is true. This suggests that, although there is a remarkable consistency in the relative importance and significance of the most important institutional variables, there are substantial differences in their absolute contributions. These differences are likely to be an outcome of the recent institutional reforms.

IMPLICATIONS FOR INSTITUTIONAL DESIGN

The comparative analysis of the impact-transmission channels and exogenous variables in terms of their relative impact share and significance in different estimation contexts has some major implications for reform design and implementation, especially for institutional priority setting, sequencing, and packaging. To appreciate these implications, let us recall the basic logic of our evaluation method and empirical approach. We consider the relative size and significance of the coefficients associated with various institutional and performance variables, and hence, the relative share and significance of different impact-transmission channels, as a quantitative representation of the level and intensity of consensus among the sample experts. Because this consensus represents convergence on both the perception of present reality and the expectation of future changes, the results can be interpreted as a joint outcome of what has happened and what is expected to happen in institution-performance interaction within water sector. Thus, the relative shares of the channels and exogenous variables in total impact can be viewed as a consensual estimation of their actual and expected contributions. With this perspective, we can now identify some of the most important implications of our results for institutional priority setting, sequencing, and packaging as well as reform timing, speed, and scale.

Linkage Length and Impact Transmission

The relation between the number of en route variables and the impact level of the channels can be quantified by correlating the two. Since the impact level of the channels shows some notable variations, depending upon whether it is calculated in the all-sample context or for country groups defined in terms of their recent reform status, we have attempted the correlation exercise in all three contexts. The respective correlation coefficients obtained in the all-sample, reform countries, and other countries are: –0.332, –0.454, and –0.330.[7] The negative but low value of the correlation coefficient obtained in all three cases suggests that, while channels with more en-route variables can have a lower value, this is not necessarily always true. However, a larger value of the correlation coefficient for the reform regions suggests that longer chains are likely to contribute less than smaller chains. This fact provides some support, though weak and indirect, to our hypothesis pertaining to the characteristics of the recent reform process and its impact pattern in the reform countries. The reform process, by and large, directly affects water sector performance more than institutional performance. This means that performance gains realized in the reform countries cannot be sustained unless the reform is taken to the next stage and focuses on institutional strengthening by concentrating on the longer chains characterizing institutional thickening and interlinkages.

One of the main results is that the channels with larger and more direct effects are likely to help improve institutional functioning, and hence, water sector performance. Larger chains, though good for institutional strengthening and thickening, may not lead to any immediate impact on water sector performance for two reasons. First, in the case of channels involving longer institutional chains, the initial effect of a change in the exogenous variables (which, by nature, are also policy or instrumental variables) may be moderated or distorted by the weakness or inefficiency of the en-route variables. Second, the role of time is also implicit, as some or all of the en-route variables may need differential time to capture and transmit the effects of an initial change in the exogenous variables. For instance, the performance impact of property rights on conflict resolution may take more time than, say, its effects on use efficiency. On the other hand, institutional aspects related to the application of science and technology and information may be faster. The relative significance and larger performance contributions of channels related to these variables observed in all three contexts provide some evidence for this fact.

From the perspective of designing institutional reform, the two factors noted above point to yet another important aspect – namely, performance impact can be enhanced not only by sequencing and packaging but also by giving special attention to the time-related dynamics of both institutional change and its performance impact. Thus, changing just one institutional component or aspect will not improve performance without concurrent changes also in other related institutional components or aspects. This does not necessarily mean that the reform program should be neither all-encompassing nor simultaneous to the point of swamping the reform agency's financial and implementation capabilities. The key is to identify the institutional chains that have the most dominant and immediate effect and target them for reform. But, because the channels involving lower and slower performance impact are also essential to sustain the operational capacity of water institutions, institutional variables have to be packaged to include both those with a large and immediate performance impact and those with lower and slower impact. While the fast-acting reforms have the tactical role of retaining economic and political relevance by bringing immediate and noticeable performance returns, the slower-acting reforms are critical to ensure long-term sustainability of institutional reform through a gradual but concerted effort to strengthen institutional linkages.

Institutional Priority Setting, Sequencing, and Packaging

In terms of the relative share and significance of their impact, the impact-transmission channels can be grouped into four categories: those with large and significant impact, those with large but insignificant impact, those with smaller and significant impact, and those with smaller and insignificant impact. The number, sequence, and configuration of variables in the linkage chains underlying the first two categories of the channel provide invaluable information for designing the reform package, complete with institutional priority, sequencing, and packaging. Based on the nature of the variables, we can also derive insights as to the time that the impact transmission may take. From this perspective, a generic reform package can be identified from the relative share and significance of the channels evaluated in the all-sample context. Such a package can, of course, be specialized by utilizing similar information obtained in the context of country groups. The inference on institutional priority is based on the relative size and significance of the impact-transmission channels, whereas the inference on sequencing and packaging is based on the order and configuration of the variables in their underlying linkage chains.

From the perspective of institutional priority setting, a clear message comes from our comparative analysis of impact-transmission channels. The setting of priorities for the exogenous variables is straightforward given the intensity of their institutional linkages as reflected by the number of their impact-transmission channels, and the relative magnitude and share of their performance impact. The results are unequivocal for giving top priority to the application of science and technology, building a strong information base, creating an independent water-pricing body, broadening functional specialization within the water administration, and formulating an effective user participation policy. Although most of the channels transmitting the impact of the first three institutional aspects listed above are significant, there is also an issue of sequencing not only among these three aspects but also between these and other institutional aspects. For instance, science and technology application is a critical first step toward building an information base, which can enhance the effectiveness of water pricing. Similarly, an efficiently functioning network of water user associations (WUAs) at various levels is a precondition for an effective property-rights arrangement. Delineation of property rights and establishing WUAs together make up the critical institutional condition to promote such institutional aspects as cost recovery, accountability, conflict resolution, and negotiated water transfers.

From the standpoint of institutional packaging and sequencing, special attention should be given to balanced functional specialization, user participation policy, and property-rights format because most of their channels are insignificant. The focus here should be on strengthening the variables in the linkage chains underlying the channels that transmit the larger share of their impact. The variables underlying these channels and others with similar properties should form part of the constellation of institutional aspects to be covered within the reform package. Since the insignificant channels are an indication of weak or dormant linkages among the variables in the linkage chains, they can be strengthened only by adopting a package approach suitable for simultaneous reform in several related institutional and performance variables. Our comparative analysis of the channels in different contexts provides ample information for designing the right reform package to strengthen some of the channels that are currently insignificant, but have considerable potentials for enhancing institutional and sectoral performance.

Having discussed the issue of priorities and sequencing, we must recognize that the channels are categorized into law-, policy-, and administration-related channels mainly for analytical and presentational convenience. As we have seen, the impacts transmitted by these channels transcend this categorization through the strong institutional and performance linkages evident both within and across the legal, policy, and administration components of water institutions. These linkages are formalized by the variables in the linkage chains underlying various impact-transmission channels. For instance, some of the law-related channels have policy- and administration-related variables in their linkage chains. Similarly, the policy- and administration-related channels have legal variables in their linkage chains.

As per our results, the administration-related channels are more important than other channels, as they account for 61 percent of the total impact calculated from all the coefficients and 52 percent of the impact calculated using only the significant coefficients. Their significance for the overall performance of both water institution and water sector stems from their importance in determining the performance of not only water administration but also that of water policy and water law. However, the dominant share of administration-related channels underlines the fact that the implementation-related institutional aspects are more critical for performance improvement than legal prescriptions and policy statements. This also opens up the issue of choice between a poor law–policy regime implemented well and a better law–policy regime implemented poorly.

Strengthening Impact-Transmission Channels

We have argued that the impact-transmission channels must be strengthened for enhancing the performance contributions of significant channels and turning the insignificant channels into significant ones. How can this be done? Many significant channels also have the largest shares, whereas most insignificant channels have low and marginal shares. Such a direct association between the size and significance of the impact transmitted by the channels has important implications. Since experts and policymakers assign a premium to channels and associated exogenous variables with larger institutional and sectoral performance impacts, these channels are likely to be significant and remain at the top of the priority hierarchy. Thus, when institutional reform improves the performance contribution of one or more institutional aspects, their larger performance impact itself ensures the significance of the channels in which they operate.

By targeting the institutional and performance variables underlying both the significant channels with lower values and their insignificant counterparts with higher values, their relative importance and significance can be improved. Thus, both the level and effectiveness of the impact transmitted by some of the selected channels can be enhanced through institutional strengthening. But, the issue is how to do this in the operational context of a reform program. The results of the comparative analysis of impact-transmission channels presented here provide some answers. The comparative analysis enables us to identify and prioritize the channels that need strengthening. The linkage chains underlying these prioritized channels provide information on both configuring and sequencing the institutional and performance variables to be targeted for strengthening. Given the relative contribution of these variables, as indicated by the size and significance of their coefficients in the relevant equations of Model B (Chapter 9), the variables can also be ranked for a focused reform attempt.

Before illustrating the reasons for and the practical means of institutional strengthening, a few words are in order to identify the channels and the variables to be given priority. Our empirical results enable us to establish priorities among channels only in terms of their relative share and significance of impact. But, other considerations, especially pertaining to the relative significance of their long-term impact on institutional strengthening and performance improvement, are beyond our present model of institution–performance interaction. In view of the futuristic aspects and location specificity of these considerations, they can be addressed only on a case-by-case basis, giving due weight to factors such as local conditions, reform stage, and reformers' expectations.[8] Since the channels with lengthy linkage chains have the best potential for strengthening institutional linkages, they should receive high priority. Similarly, the institutional and performance variables figuring in the linkage chains of more channels deserve priority over others mainly because any successful effort to reform them will strengthen all the channels in which they appear.

Most of the issues on setting priorities for channels and variables within an institutional strengthening program could be made more transparent with the following illustration. Consider, for instance, the policy-related channel *PGPIUP–LCRMEE–LOEFWL–WIPOEV–WSPOEV* with a share of just 2.23 percent of the total impact transmitted by all 63 channels. Although this channel is significant, with a ninth largest share, its impact is low because the coefficients associated with the exogenous variable *PGPIUP* as well as the two en-route variables *LCRMEE* and *LOEFWL* are lower (Tables 8.1a and 8.1b). Under this condition, the impact transmitted by the channel will improve if the performance contributions of both the exogenous variable and the two en-route variables are improved. However, the performance contributions of a marginal change in the institutional aspect of *PGPIUP* cannot be realized fully as long as the two en-route variables remain weak in the linkage chain. In this sense, institutional strengthening is a precondition even for reform in the exogenous variables. With institutional strengthening and improved performance contributions (higher value for the coefficients) of the en-route variables, the total impact and the relative share of the channels will also change.

The impact-transmission capabilities of the en route variables can be improved by enhancing the value of their coefficient. How can we do this? This question can be answered by referring to the results reported in Table 8.1. *LCRMEE*, the dependent variable in equation [1] but independent variable in equation [6], is significantly affected not only by *PGPIUP* but also by three other institutional variables: *ABALFS*, *AARINF*, and *AEXTST*. Since all these three variables are also exogenous variables amenable to policy intervention, a change in one or more of them can positively affect *LCRMEE* in equation [1].[9] Within the simultaneous equation system, such a positive impact is likely to improve the coefficient of *LCRMEE* in equation [6]. This, in turn, will have repercussions on *LOEFWL*, the dependent variable in equation [6] but independent variable in equation [9]. In a similar fashion, the coefficient of *LOEFWL* in equation [9] can also be improved by changing other significant legal aspects such as *LINTRE* and *LOECEN*. The systemic impact of a change in one or more variables in different equations will also strengthen the linkage chains underlying all the other channels involving the en-route variables as well as those affecting or being affected by these en-route variables. It is precisely for this reason we argue that preference has to be given to institutional variables, which are involved in more channels.

Priority and Performance: Role of Recent Reforms

From an overall perspective, the comparison of the relative level and share of
the impact of all channels across country groups reveals a few notable facts.
First, while the impact of the law-related channels is higher in the other countries, the impacts of policy- and administration-related channels are higher in
the reform countries. This means that the consensus on the relative importance
of the legal dimensions of institutional reform is stronger in other countries
than in the reform countries. This also suggests that although the recent institutional changes observed in reform countries have a major thrust on the
policy and administrative dimensions, further progress in these spheres is
viewed to be constrained by a lack of sufficient legal reforms. Second, as we
consider the share of the significant channels in total impact, the reform countries have a larger share than other countries both within and across the law-,
policy-, and administration-related channels. This is a clear indication that
institutional linkages and their performance implications are stronger in the
reform countries as compared to other countries.

   Although the configurations and priorities of policy-related reforms are
more or less the same across country groups, there are considerable differences in the thrust, scale, and effectiveness of the initiated reforms. Since the
reform countries have already undertaken significant reforms in various water
institution components, further institutional reforms, involving both substantial and marginal changes, are likely to be more effective and less costly in
view of the upstream and downstream linkages created by the reforms already
undertaken. As a result, the impact of the reforms on institutional and sectoral
performance is likely to be faster and more effective in the reform countries
than in other countries. From the perspective of institutional hierarchy, since
information application usually follows the application of science and technology, the dominant role of *AARINF* in reform countries suggests that these
countries should have already made substantial progress in *AEXTST*. Although
there is only a marginal variation in the number of significant channels
between the country groups (14 for reform countries and 12 for other countries), the overall share of significant channels in total impact is far higher in
reform countries (73 percent) than in other countries (56 percent). This result
suggests the following four important and interrelated aspects.

   First, in reform countries, unlike other countries, most of the channels with
a larger share of total impact are significant. This means that the reform
program in countries lacking recent reforms should target variables in the linkage chains underlying the insignificant channels with a larger share. Second,
the substantially higher share of significant channels in reform countries is
essentially due to the stronger institutional linkages possibly achieved through
their recent institutional reforms. Third, although the insignificant channels

are many, they have only a small share of the total impact even in reform countries. Since this means that most of the total impact comes from only a few channels, the extent of institutional linkages contributed by recent reforms appears to be low due either to slower development of these linkages or limited institutional coverage of reforms. To enhance their institutional and sectoral performance, the reform countries have to concentrate more on intensifying their reform by concentrating on the already significant as well as the currently insignificant channels. Fourth, in some of the reform countries with a mature water sector, additional performance benefits can most likely be obtained only with a substantial and more intense reform effort. This does not apply to countries lacking recent reform or in the early stage of institutional reform, where performance gains can be substantial even with a smaller dose of reform. The intuition here is that performance return that increases in the initial stages of reform could decrease in later stages of reform.

The nature of the impact generated by recent reform is manifested in the fact that the impact-transmission channels in reform countries have a far higher level of total impact and that a larger part of this impact is significant. The minimal difference in the number of significant channels and significant variables among the two country groups suggests another important aspect – namely that the larger performance impact in reform countries is due more to the larger contributions of the exogenous variables through their direct impact than to their indirect impact through the strengthening of institutional linkages. If institutional linkages were strengthened, the number of significant channels would have been far higher in reform countries than in other countries. For the nature and thrust of future institutional reform, especially in reform countries, this fact implies that, to ensure the sustainability of the performance impact of the recently undertaken reforms, reform program has to move to its next stage, focusing on strengthening the linkages among key institutional aspects. Although efforts to reform institutional linkages are likely to yield no or low immediate performance impact, they will pave the way for more durable long-term benefits in both institutional and sectoral performance.

Scale and Timing in Institutional Reform

In addition to the issues of priority and sequencing, our analysis also highlights equally important aspects related to reform implementation such as the timing, spacing, scale, and dose of reform effort. The larger impact conveyed by the significant channels suggests the issue of scale in reform effort. That is, since the variables associated with these channels produce a larger impact, both institutional and sectoral performance can be enhanced by involving these variables in a larger reform effort. The scale of effort also has a time dimension, as the additional reform effort can be undertaken either simultaneously or sequentially with an appropriate time gap between and spacing of reform components. The issue of when, how and where to make the additional reform effort, however, depends on whether the performance impact associated with an exogenous variable is substantial or marginal, whether such impact is immediate or delayed, and whether the institutional linkages of the variable is strong or weak. Since the speed of impact transmission depends on the nature and configuration of variables in the linkage chains, the final answer to the issue of scale and timing requires the evaluation of all channels to consider specifically their immediate and long-term implications for institutional strengthening and performance improvement.

While our estimation is based on the assumption of linear effect of all variables, in reality the effects of some of the institutional variables are subject to either increasing or decreasing return on scale. Information on the scale aspects therefore has to be derived outside the context of our model. From our general knowledge of the reform process, the nature of the institutional and performance effects can be understood from the extent of reform already undertaken in a given institutional sphere, the extent of upstream and downstream linkages of the institutional aspect in question, and the extent of supportive reforms in related spheres. All these aspects also depend on country-specific considerations. Usually, the nature of the effects associated with each of the key institutional aspects can be understood, based on careful thinking and detailed observations in a given context. For instance, the performance impact of an additional unit of reform effort in user participation policy can be evaluated for a given region after a detailed review of its institutional linkages, the extent of reforms in related areas, and observations on current and past performance of this policy. The evaluation can be based both on observed data (e.g., extent of cost recovery and level of O&M expenditures) and anecdotal and case study-based information (e.g., role of WUAs in decisionmaking and basin arrangements).

Although the linear specification of our model does not allow us to have any direct information on the issue of scale involved in the effects of exogenous variables, it does provide some idea of the scale aspects involved in the transmission of their effects. The scale aspects involved in impact transmission can be addressed in terms of the size of the coefficients associated with the en-route variables. When all the coefficients of the en-route variables have a value of less than one, it means that the effects of the exogenous variables will be transmitted less than proportionately. In contrast, when all the en route variables have coefficients with values greater than one, the transmission of the effects of a variable will be more than proportionate. However, since the en-route variables in many contexts are likely to have mixed values for their coefficients (some with fractional values and others with values greater than one), the ultimate scale of the impact transmission of a channel will depend upon the size configuration of the coefficients of its en-route variables. Based on the values of all channels – each with a different number and configuration of en-route variables – obtained in different estimation contexts, we can see that the scale of their impact transmission is characterized by a diminishing trend due mainly to the lower values associated with their fractional coefficients. Since the issue of scale related to the impact-transmission process is as important as the same related to the effects of the exogenous variables, the impact-transmission channels have to be strengthened to make the underlying coefficients larger and more significant.

Role of Time in Effecting Reform and Realizing Impact

From the perspective of designing institutional reform packages, the relative performance impact of exogenous variables and their channels suggests a clear choice between the exogenous variables with fewer channels but larger impact and those with more channels and smaller impact. The choice is not as easy as it seems, however, because of the intervening role of institutional amenability to reform, political feasibility, and the time dimension involved in effecting institutional strengthening and realizing their impact-transmission potential. Although these issues cannot be addressed directly within our analytical framework, where the time dimension is not explicitly incorporated, our results provide some basis for deriving useful inferences and hypotheses on this count. For instance, the choice naturally tilts toward variables such as *LINTRE* and *LOECEN* in view of their stronger and more significant performance impact as well as their amenability to reform with less political resistance. Although the reforms needed to enhance the internal consistency and privatization provisions within law may be politically easier and quicker, they take time to mature and yield observable performance impact.

In contrast, although political difficulties will considerably delay property-rights reform, once such reforms are undertaken their performance impact will be faster. In addition, with property-rights reforms in place, institutional reforms in related spheres can become easier. Such a facilitative role for downstream reforms is critical for reducing the total transaction cost of the overall reform program. More importantly, since property-rights reforms have intricate linkages with use efficiency, accountability, conflict resolution, cost recovery, and water transfers, once they are in place, they are likely to contribute as much to the process of long-term institutional thickening as to immediate performance contributions. Such a process is indispensable to lay the foundation for institutional sustainability and long-term performance improvement. These considerations assign greater priority to variables with stronger institutional and performance linkages such as *LPRSRF*, notwithstanding their political and technical constraints and lower immediate performance contributions. Nevertheless, the choice between institutional aspects with a scope for quicker reform but delayed impact and those with difficult reforms but faster impact is still a difficult one. The difficulty can be resolved through a tradeoff between immediate performance benefits and long-term institutional and performance gains. The institutional reform program should be designed in such a way as to account for these tradeoffs with appropriate priority setting, sequencing, and packaging of institutional aspects. Reform implementation aspects such as timing, spacing, and scale are also valuable for their strategic roles in overcoming political, technical, and resource constraints for institutional reform.

NOTES

1. Although some of the remaining 10 variables appear as independent variables in one or more equations, they are still dependent on the behavior of different subsets of only these 16 exogenous variables.

2. This list includes the channels conveying the direct effects of *POPAWE*, *AEXTST*, and *AARINF* in equation [10]. But, it excludes the two channels involving the direct effects of *PCOREC* and *ASBUDC* – included as proxies for general cost-recovery policy and fiscal health – in the same equation because they are actually the endogenous variables in equations [3] and [4], respectively.

3. The size of the coefficient associated with the en-route variables is indicative of their transmission ability. Thus, when the coefficient of an en route variable has a value of less than one, it means that the impact transmission is less than proportionate due to institutional distortion and dilution. When there are more en-route variables in the chains and all have fractional coefficients, they can dilute an even larger and more than proportionate impact of the exogenous variable involved.

4. Besides the justification in terms of our interest in the variability rather than the level of a variable, an additional factor specifically requires the use of standardized coefficients instead of elasticity at mean values. This factor relates to the potential bias in using the ratio of means as a weighting factor when the model variables vary in terms of their unit of measurement. Such a bias will be at its minimum when the ratio of standard deviations is used as the weighting factor.

5. This is partly because of the negative way in which some of the variables (e.g., *ASBUDC* capturing the seriousness of budget constraint) are formulated and partly because institutional constraints, though negative in format, will actually have a positive performance effect. In addition, there is also the argument based on two-way flow of effects noted in Chapter 8. According to this argument, a negative association between *PCOREC* and *WSPOEV*, for instance, should not be interpreted as an inverse relation between cost recovery and water sector performance, but as an indication that poor performance in the water sector is generating pressures to improve cost recovery.

6. For instance, one negative coefficient in the case of a channel involving more than two variables can make the value of the impact negative whereas two negative coefficients can make the same positive. While this is mathematically correct, from the perspective of evaluating the direction of the impact flow, the result can be complicated and confusing.

7. We have attempted the correlation exercise to see how the values of all channels obtained in different estimation contexts are related. In this attempt, we correlated the values of the channels obtained in the all-sample context of with those for the two country groups (reform and nonreform countries), and the two expert groups (engineers and social scientists). The correlation coefficient for reform countries is 0.763; for other countries, 0.816. The slightly higher coefficient in the latter context suggests that the values of the channels obtained in the all-sample context are closer to those obtained in other countries than to those obtained

in reform countries. The correlation coefficient between reform countries and engineers is 0.834; between other countries and engineers, 0.686. In contrast, the correlation coefficient between reform countries and social scientists is 0.474; between other countries and social scientists, 0.825. The high correlation between the values of channels in reform (other) countries and that for engineers (social scientists) suggests that, while the sample in reform countries is dominated by the engineers' perception, the sample in other countries is dominated by the social scientists' perception. This is why we have excluded the comparative analysis of the channels across the expert groups.

8. For countries at the reform threshold, strategic considerations require priority for channels involving direct effects, as they can yield the quick performance returns needed to counter political resistance and consolidate performance gains. In contrast, in countries at an advanced stage of reform, sustainability considerations require priority for channels conveying indirect effects through lengthy linkage chains, as they can deepen the process of institutional thickening so crucial to ensure the resilience and sustainability of the reform process.

9. Because *ABALFS* has the largest magnitude of effect of the four significant variables in the equation under consideration, this variable deserves priority over others in reform efforts for institutional strengthening, especially in the case of developing countries.

11. Conclusions with implications for theory and policy

The main thrust of institutional change within the water sector is to enhance the capabilities and increase the readiness of policymakers to solve current and future water challenges. Given this thrust, the major goals of institutional initiatives in the water sector are transparent. These goals are to: treat water as an economic good, strengthen allocation capabilities, increase reliance on market forces, revive the payment culture, ensure financial self-sufficiency, promote decentralized decision structures, and encourage the use of modern technology and information inputs. Institutional reform of the magnitude required to achieve these goals is a daunting challenge in most countries with outdated and poorly functioning water institutions. The economic and resource-related rationale for the thrust and objectives of institutional change, as described above, are well understood. But, the issue of how to effect water institutional change within the constraints and opportunities of political economy continue to remain elusive to both researchers and policymakers.

The identification of a strategy for water institutional reform with minimum transaction costs and maximum political acceptability requires sharp understanding of the analytical and operational linkages among the components of water institutions and their ultimate impact on water sector performance. A better appreciation of the mechanics of institution–performance interaction in the water sector also requires a broader and more integrated conception of water institutions to capture both the effects of the exogenous factors constituting the institutional environment for such interaction and the influence emanating from prior, concurrent, and subsequent reforms elsewhere in the economy. Current knowledge enables this causative chain of changes to be traced, including their nature and direction. But, current methodologies and available information do not permit a rigorous evaluation of the performance implications of institutional linkages inherent in the process of institution–performance interaction. This is a serious gap in both institutional economics theory and in water sector policy. It is this knowledge gap that has provided both the motivation and justification for the present study. Our venture into this uncharted course of policy research has succeeded in breaking new ground, both in terms of analytical, methodological, and empirical innovations and in terms of contributions to theory and policy. But, these contributions are not without their caveats and limitations.

ANALYTICAL AND METHODOLOGICAL CONTRIBUTIONS

By providing an entirely new perspective on the inner dynamics of the process of institution–performance interaction, this study makes some important contributions in terms of its analytical approach, evaluation methodology, empirical findings, and policy insights. The importance of these contributions to institutional economics in general and water institutional economics in particular is discussed below.

Analytical Framework

The analytical framework of this study is unique, as it is based on a detailed, yet manageable, decomposition of water institutions and water sector performance and on the characterization of the analytical and operational linkages among various components within a 'pattern model.' This study, for the first time, makes a detailed analytical decomposition of a broadly conceived concept of water institution that covers all the major legal, policy, and administrative or organizational aspects both within and outside the strict confines of the conventionally defined water sector. The term 'water institution' is decomposed into three broad components: water law, water policy, and water administration or organization. Each of these institutional components is again decomposed to identify their constituent institutional aspects. These institutional aspects cover not only those having a direct bearing on water sector but also those capturing the legal, policy, and administrative influences emanating especially from the agricultural, environmental, and fiscal sectors. In a similar vein, the performance of the water sector – considered to cover all water subsectors – is also decomposed in terms of its physical, financial, economic, and equity dimensions. The institutional structure is distinguished from the institutional environment as defined by the social-, political-, economic-, and resource-related exogenous factors so as to highlight the influence of these factors on the institutional and sectoral performance.

A still finer decomposition is possible. For analytical and operational convenience, however, the aspect-based decomposition approach underlying our 'institutional decomposition and analysis' framework concentrates on the policywise most important institutional aspects. The rudiments of this framework were developed in our earlier work (Saleth and Dinar 1999b); further refinements were inspired by its close resemblance with the rule-based decomposition approach underlying the 'institutional analysis and development' framework of E. Ostrom and her co-workers (E. Ostrom 1986, 1990, 1999; E. Ostrom, Gardner, and Walker 1994). The close resemblance between the two frameworks cannot, however, distract us from some fundamental differences between them, especially at the application stage. For instance, the rule-based decomposition, though captures the properties of individual rules, cannot capture some significant macro features shared by two or more rules (e.g., integration or consistency among legal rules or linkages between law and policy dimensions) or their performance implications. In this sense, the aspect-based decomposition stretches beyond the rule-based perspective.

Our decomposition attempt is also less abstract and more amenable to analytical exposition and empirical translation. By focusing on the internal structure and dynamics of institutions, it demonstrates not only the intricate linkages evident both within and across the institutional components but also their implications for institutional and sectoral performance. While interest in the structure of and linkages within institutions is as old as institutional economics itself, empirical studies on this important aspect are rare. It is here that our study makes its mark. Taking institutional decomposition into the empirical realm, it sheds light on the inner dynamics of the process of institution–performance interaction by demonstrating the performance implications of institutional linkages as well as the strategic roles of the general institutional environment as defined by exogenous factors such as the socioeconomic, political, legal, and resource-related aspects.

Subjective Theory and Stage-Based Perspective of Institutional Change

Despite the growth of theoretical and empirical literature in institutional economics, dark and gray spots persist and they remain as a frontier area for further research in institutional economics. One area relates to the overestimation of the role of information and the concurrent underestimation of the role of the software that people use for interpreting information. Information alone cannot reduce uncertainties in human interaction, as individuals interpret identical information differently. Since the differences originate from the differences in subjective perception or in the mental models of individuals, the need for a 'mental model approach' is inevitable to reconstruct the 'software' that people use to process information. Another gap relates to the need to evaluate the central role played by individuals as 'agents of chance' in the process of institutional change. Although the critical role of the individual is repeatedly underlined in institutional economics, there is hardly any systematic attempt to investigate that role, especially within an empirical context. Since the roles of individuals can be evaluated fully only with the incorporation of their subjective perception into the formal model, these two gray areas in institutional economics are interrelated.

This study addresses these two interrelated gaps not only by incorporating the roles of subjective perception of individuals into the formal model but also by making these roles as the heart of its evaluation methodology and empirical framework. The analytical vehicle used for their formal incorporation in the evaluation framework is the stage-based perspective underlying our subjective theory of institutional change. The central role played by the subjective perception of the agents of change can be demonstrated by identifying four distinct stages in the process of institution–performance interaction. They are: perception change, political translation and articulation of such perception change, institutional changes of a procedural nature followed by institutional changes of a substantive nature, and actual performance impact. Perception change that pervades through these four stages assigns key role for individuals as the agents of change, reflects the effects of the tension between existing institutions and sources of change, and provides clues about the nature and direction of institutional change.

Perception change, though subjective in nature, is not independent of objective phenomena such as impending water scarcity, prevalent fiscal crisis, emerging success stories, and even natural disasters. Factors such as ideologies do influence the mental model of individuals, but economic factors, especially the expected benefit and its share, play an equally powerful role in the mental construct of desirable institutions. Transaction costs – both economic and political – remain a key force both in the cognitive and observed phases of the process of institutional change. The political process of reform and bargaining strengths of groups are also equally important. Our stage-based conception of institutional change, therefore, integrates the roles of agents of change, their subjective perception, interest group considerations, and the transaction cost approach within a unified framework. In contrast to the literature, which has ignored the insightful first stage, our study highlights and elaborates on the centrality of the mind change of individuals – not just in the first stage but equally also in the remaining stages of the institutional change process. A careful evaluation of the first stage of institutional change is very important, as it can provide insights on the perception of causal linkages evident in the process of institution–performance interaction, the extent of consensus on preferred institutional configurations, and the likely nature and direction of institutional change. In this sense, perception and its convergence allow us to see the nature and intensity of underlying demand for institutional change. Perceptional evaluation is also inevitable, even in the remaining stages, in view of the vast time gap between stages and the difficulty of observing actual institutional changes and measuring their performance impacts. Besides its ability to highlight the role that individuals play as agents of change, the subjective theory also enables us to integrate the transaction cost and political economy approaches with the subjective perception of key players.

Innovative Empirical Context

The subjective theory and the stage-based perspective of institutional change are used for two purposes. First, they are used as an analytical framework for integrating a number of important but less addressed issues in institutional economics. Second, they are used to justify the logic behind the empirical context relied on here for the evaluation of institution–performance interaction. It is the central roles played by agents of change and their subjective perception within the stage-based perspective of institutional change that, in fact, rationalize and justify our empirical context. Although our study extends and refines the empirical tradition of using perception-based data for institutional analysis, it justifies the legitimacy of the empirical approach not in terms of the unavailability of objective data but in terms of its consistency with institutional and political economy theories. The inherently subjective nature of institutions and the centrality of subjective perception in institutional change, in fact, warrant subjective information much more than observed data.

In addition to these strong theoretical and analytical justifications, there are also equally important practical justifications for our reliance on judgmental evaluation and its validity as an empirical basis for evaluating institutional change. The inevitability of subjective information is underlined by a few powerful facts. Subjective information, unlike observed data capturing past and static situations, can tap the accumulated wisdom of key players, capture their expectations and futuristic considerations, and synthesize different types of information (objective data, subjective observation, and expected trend). Besides its ability to internalize some difficult-to-measure concepts such as performance, efficiency, and equity, subjective evaluation can also capture the effects of objective factors such as water scarcity and economic development and individual-specific subjective factors such as disciplinary orientation and ideological predilections.

Relying on this empirical approach, the information on all relevant institutional and performance variables derived from our decomposition exercise is obtained by administering a structured questionnaire to a sample of key players in the water sector of several countries. The sample consists of 127 water sector experts with diverse backgrounds and experience from 43 countries and regions, representing different continents, development stages, reform status, and resource conditions. While stressing the theoretical consistency and practical advantages of our empirical approach, we recognize that the quality of information is sensitive to asset specificity, bounded rationality, and information impactedness conditions. The survey approach helps to capture the special knowledge of water sector experts as derived from their practical experience, understanding, and proximity to various layers of decisionmaking. The carefully designed survey instrument minimizes the cognitive and communication limitations imposed by bounded rationality and information impactedness and facilitates a more efficient and less biased information transfer. In an important sense, our approach of eliciting perceptional information through the survey instrument is similar in spirit to the contingent valuation approach used to elicit values in missing market situations and delphi approach used to evaluate uncertain events. The theoretical consistenty and practical advantages of our approach involving carefully designed survey instrument and large and diverse sample, helps to ensure that the information obtained is representative and reliable. This has been confirmed, in fact, by the intuitively consistent empirical results.

Pluralistic Methodology

Because institutions are entities operating in the interface between law, policy, and administration, their evaluation requires a multidisciplinary approach involving multiple methodologies. Since we attempt to evaluate water institutional structures and their performance impacts from both macro and disaggregated perspectives, our approach combines the relevant elements from various traditions of institutional theory and analysis. Our methodological framework allows us to combine a multipronged empirical analysis combining a descriptive cross-country analysis of recent institutional changes, anecdotal and theoretical support for institutional and performance linkages, and rigorous quantitative analysis of institution–performance interaction based on econometric estimation using perception-based information. While the cross-country analysis is inherently descriptive, it relies on an institutional transaction cost approach and a political economy perspective to explain the nature and direction of ongoing institutional changes across sample countries.

Anecdotal evidences of institutional and performance linkages are derived mainly from our cross-country review of sectoral features and institutional reforms observed in the global water sector, but some theoretical reasoning and intuitive explanations are also given to support the existence and significance of institutional linkages and their performance contributions. The quantitative analysis is based on a unique model of institution–performance interaction that takes a systemic perspective of the interaction process and mimics the way this process is perceived in the minds of key players in the water sector. While the cross-country analysis highlights the role that factors, both internal and external to the water sector, play in motivating water institutional changes, the relative influence of some exogenous factors is also quantitatively evaluated using both perceptional and observed data. Since this exercise relates perception-based performance variables to observation-based secondary data on some exogenous variables, it also provides useful insights into the influence of exogenous factors on subjective perceptions of institutional and sectoral performance. Despite the pluralistic nature of our methodology, the central approach underlying the multi-pronged empirical analysis is invariant. Since we evaluate the performance implications of the internal structural features of water institution mainly from a macro perspective, our approach is positive rather than normative.

Modeling Institution–Performance Interaction

The review of the literature on institutional evaluation shows how different is our attempt in terms of its detailed modeling of the institution–performance interaction in the water sector. As noted, it translates and mimics the mental process of evaluation. Utilizing the decomposition exercise, defining a set of variables to capture the status, nature, or performance of key institutional and performance aspects, and focusing on a few critical layers of institutional and performance linkages, we have modeled the process of institution–performance interaction under alternative perspectives. The conventional conception of institution–performance interaction is represented in a single-equation model that postulates water sector performance as a simple and direct function of various law-, policy-, and administration-related institutional aspects. In contrast, the more realistic conception of the interaction process is modeled by a system of 10 interlinked equations to distinguish various layers evident in the process of institution–performance interaction and explicitly recognize the existence of sequential linkages among them. By contrasting the empirical performance of these two models, we have provided econometric evidence for the existence and performance significance of institutional linkages. Similarly, by evaluating the system model under different disaggregated contexts, we have also provided evidence for the robustness and sensitivity in the behavior of the institutional aspects, their linkage, and their performance implications.

In fact, the methodological superiority and policy relevance of the system approach go far beyond its ability to provide evidence for the existence and performance significance of the institutional linkages. With the quantification of different layers of institutional and performance linkages, the simultaneous equation system provides a framework to systematically isolate and quantitatively trace the multifarious routes through which the effects of a marginal change in an institutional variable are transmitted and ultimately reflected in water institutional and sectoral performance. These routes or impact-transmission channels, in fact, characterize the micro chains operating beneath the main layers of institution–performance interaction and can be defined by the number and configuration of en-route variables that lie between the institutional variable being changed and the ultimate dependent variable in the system. These impact-transmission channels, associated with all the institutional variables that are amenable to deliberate policy intervention, are identified and quantitatively evaluated in terms of their relative length, significance, and performance contributions. The insights from this evaluation exercise are used to understand the inner dynamics of the process of institution–performance interaction and to address the practical issues of priority setting, sequencing, and packaging as well as scale and timing, so critical for designing and implementing institutional reform programs.

The analytical mismatch between subjective information and objective data prevents us from directly incorporating the exogenous effects from economic, social, political, and resource-related factors into our model of institution–performance interaction, but their effects are still accounted for within our evaluation. The inclusion of a constant term in all the equations of the system can help capture the effects of exogenous factors. But, this technique does not help us to understand their relative significance or distinguish their influence from those of other excluded institutional variables. As a result, the individual and joint influences of the exogenous factors are evaluated in terms of a separate and independent model that explicitly postulates the performance variables as a function of a selected set of exogenous variables. Since the performance variables are perception based and the exogenous variables are derived from observed data on economic, demographic, institutional, and resource-related aspects, this exercise also helps us to evaluate the interface between the subjective perception of institution–performance interaction and the objective reality of the institutional environment within which such interaction occurs.

IMPLICATIONS FOR THEORY AND POLICY

The theoretical significance and policy relevance of our study emerge mainly from its detailed empirical results on institution–performance interaction. This section provides a summary of the major results and highlights some of their key implications for institutional theory and water sector policy.

Existence and Performance Significance of Institutional Linkages

In addition to the analytical exposition of institutional and performance linkages, our study provides strong econometric evidence of the existence of institutional linkages and their performance implications. Specifically, the evidence for the existence and performance significance of the institutional linkages is established by contrasting the empirical performance of different models of institution–performance interaction, each with different assumptions about institutional and performance linkages. According to our empirical results, the system model with an explicit recognition of these linkages evinces a far better statistical and econometric performance in various estimation contexts. Since such a superior performance means that the model is consistent with the data and remains robust, the institutional and performance linkages incorporated in the model are consistent with reality. This is an important result, as it opens up an entirely new way of looking at the process of institution–performance interaction and calls for a different approach to initiate and sustain institutional reform both in general and in water sector contexts. What this means for practical policy is the fact that the institutional linkages can be strategically used to counter technical and political constraints for institutional reforms.

Relative Role and Significance of Institutional Aspects

The empirical results provide us with ample insights into the relative role and significance of institutional aspects in determining the performance of water institutions and water sector. Considering first the institutional aspects that influence the performance of water institutional components, the overall performance of water law depends on the direct effects of three legal aspects: effectiveness of conflict-resolution provisions, legal integration, and centralization tendency within water law. It also depends on the indirect effects of one policy aspect (effectiveness of user participation policy) and two administrative aspects (balanced functional specialization and information adequacy). All six aspects have a positive effect on legal performance. The overall performance of water policy, on the other hand, depends on the direct effects of four policy aspects: cost-recovery status, effectiveness of water transfer policy, strength of law–policy linkage, and effectiveness of privatization policy. The positive effect of the first three policy aspects suggests the intuitively consistent result that better cost recovery, effective water transfer policies, and stronger law–policy linkages improve the overall performance of water policy. Water policy performance also depends on the indirect effects of one legal aspect (water-rights format), one policy aspect (effectiveness of user participation policy), and four administrative aspects (technology application, information adequacy, existence of an independent water-pricing body, and balanced functional specialization). Considering the direction and magnitude of the effects of the four administrative aspects listed above, it is clear that the ultimate performance of water policy depends critically on the effectiveness of the administrative arrangements necessary to translate the policy into practice.

The overall performance of water administration depends only on the direct effects of three institutional aspects: balanced functional specialization, technology application, and information adequacy. The positive effects of these three administrative aspects suggest that a staffing pattern with broad-based functional specialization, application of science and technology in critical areas of planning and management, and a strong water information base can jointly enhance water administration performance. This result is very much in conformity with the current priority that the above listed aspects receive in the policy agenda of many national governments and international funding agencies on their technical agendas. It also provides a clear justification for additional investment in these key technical areas indispensable for strengthening the planning and implementation capabilities of water administration. The insignificance of administrative aspects such as the spatial features of water organization and the effectiveness of administrative provisions for accountability suggests that with improved technology, information, and functional specialization, these administrative aspects may become less important. This fact also implies the scope for institutional substitution.

From an overall perspective, since water institution performance hinges more on the performance of its administrative and legal components, it depends indirectly on all the institutional aspects that determine the performance of these two institutional components. The most important and significant institutional aspects determining water institution performance are: effective conflict-resolution provisions, legal integration, a healthy dose of centralization within water law, user participation policy, balanced functional specialization, adequate information, and technology application. Since water institution performance is the main factor affecting the ultimate performance of the water sector, all the institutional aspects affecting the former also determine the latter indirectly. Besides these institutional aspects with indirect effects via water institution performance, water sector performance is also affected by the direct effects of two institutional aspects serving as proxies: cost-recovery status and seriousness of the budget constraint. Three other aspects affect water sector performance indirectly through the direct effects of the proxy variables. They are water-rights format, effectiveness of user participation policy, and existence of an independent water-pricing body. Thus, the overall performance of the water sector depends on the multifarious effects of four legal aspects, two policy aspects, and five administrative aspects. The institutional aspects identified as having the dominant effect on institutional and sectoral performance are consistent with the attention that they are receiving in the ongoing debate on water sector reform at both the national and global levels.

Robustness and Sensitivity

The behavioral robustness and sensitivity of the institutional aspects are evaluated in terms of the consistency of the sign, size, and significance of their coefficients across three sample sizes, two expert groups (engineers and social scientists), and two country groups (reform countries and others). Of the 25 institutional and performance variables included in our model, only 12 are robust. Of the robust variables, four are linkage or endogenous variables and eight are independent or exogenous variables. These linkage variables are: cost-recovery status, effectiveness of intersectoral water transfers, overall performance of the water administration, and overall performance of water institution. The exogenous or independent variables are: water-rights format, legal provisions for privatization, law–policy linkages, user participation policy, existence of an independent water-pricing body, balanced functional specialization, information adequacy, and technology application. Since the robustness properties of some of these variables are also layer specific in the sense that they are robust in one equation but not so in other equation(s), the robustness of individual institutional aspects, though necessary, is not sufficient to ensure the robustness of the institutional and performance linkages.

While the behavioral sensitivity of institutional aspects to sample size variations is not an unexpected result, the comparison does yield a few distinct patterns with considerable implications both for the relative significance of the institutional linkages and for the overall reliability of our model. Although the absolute size of the coefficients associated with most institutional aspects varies across sample contexts, there is a remarkable degree of consistency in the size and the direction of their impact in most equations. This consistency, together with the robustness properties of institutional aspects, indicates that the relative importance of the institutional variables – in various layers of institutional and performance linkages – is largely free from sample size variations. As to the robustness of the 10 layers of institutional and performance linkages, our results show that seven are robust with consistent behavior across estimation contexts. The inconsistent behavior of institutional aspects and layers of linkages provides equally valuable information for tailoring the institutional reform package to address location-specific issues. From the perspective of reform design, the robust institutional aspects will form the nucleus around which other context-specific aspects can be built to enhance the effectiveness and flexibility of the reform package.

The distinct pattern in the configuration and performance significance of institutional aspects observed among the two sample size contexts – each covering countries with differential water scarcity and sectoral concerns – sheds light on the effects that the general institutional environment has on the process of institution–performance interaction. For instance, the coefficients associated with most of the institutional aspects are much larger and more significant for the subsample covering mainly countries facing severe water scarcity than for the subsample covering countries where water quality and floods, rather than water scarcity, are the major problems. Since this result implies a stronger perception of institution–performance linkages among experts in countries facing water scarcity than in other countries, it provides evidence for the effect of water scarcity on the subjective perception of institutional performance. Still more interesting is the spatial pattern in the relative strength of intra- and interinstitutional linkages. For instance, interinstitutional linkages are stronger than intra-institutional linkages in countries facing water scarcity whereas the reverse is true for other countries. Comparing these two linkage categories across the two country groups, we find, however, that interinstitutional linkages (intra-institutional linkages) are stronger (weaker) in water-scarce countries than in others. The spatial patterns of institutional linkages and performance impact imply that the linkages across institutional components are more important for performance than the linkages within the institutional components.

Perceptional Convergence

From an overall perspective, the results obtained in the context of the two expert groups (engineers and social scientists) suggest a general consistency in the configuration of institutional aspects identified by both groups. But, the group-specific differences in the ordering of even the commonly agreed institutional aspects suggest that the expert groups disagree on institutional ranking and priority. This means that perceptional convergence on the role of institutional aspects, though necessary, is not sufficient for consensus on their relative priority and significance. The social scientists generally give considerable importance to legal aspects, especially those related to water rights, internally consistent water law, and a legally consistent water policy. The engineers attach greater significance to a relatively centralized water law, private sector participation, organizational aspects, and administrative accountability. Considering the degree of consistency on the role and significance of many key institutional aspects, however, we can conclude that the disciplinary bias is restricted more to micro details than to macro thrust.

The presence of macro convergence in the face of micro divergence is illustrated still more clearly by group-specific patterns related to the importance of various layers of institution–performance interaction. For instance, while the experts agree on the importance of an effective user participation policy, other sectoral policies affecting water policy, and seriousness of the budget constraint, they differ only in terms of their perception of the layers through which the effects are transmitted. Thus, the group-specific differences in the relative importance of transmission channels and in the composition of transmitted effects need not be viewed as an outcome of disciplinary bias among experts but as an outcome of genuine differences in their technical understanding. Notably, these group-specific differences are confined mostly to the lower echelons of the layers of institution–performance interaction, but the degree of convergence among expert groups increases as they move to the evaluation of the higher layers of the interaction process.

Role of Reform Environment

The influence of the reform environment on the strength and performance impact of the institutional aspects and their linkages is evaluated by comparing the results obtained in the context of two country groups defined in terms of their recent reform status. According to our subjective theory and stage-based perspective of institutional change, increasing convergence in the perception of the need for institutional change among key players both initiates and fosters the process of institutional change. The effectiveness and sustainability of the initiated change, however, depend on whether the perceptional convergence is powerful enough to create a pro-reform climate and political realignment, exploit scale economies, and circumvent path-dependency constraints. In view of the critical role of other factors, perceptional convergence, though necessary, is not enough to initiate institutional change of any substantial magnitude. Since it is the presence of both the necessary and sufficient conditions that explains the reform initiatives, it is logical to expect the layers of institution–performance linkages observed in reform countries to be stronger than those in other countries. This expectation is strongly supported by our empirical results. The institutional linkages are not only stronger but their performance impacts are also more pronounced in reform countries than in other countries.

Despite the differential strength of institution–performance linkages across country groups, there is considerable convergence in the behavior of some institutional aspects. The institutional variables showing consistent behavior across country groups are: effective legal provisions for conflict resolution and privatization, cost-recovery status, effective policies for water transfer, user participation, and private sector involvement, influence of other sectoral policies affecting water policy, existence of an independent water-pricing body, organizational basis of water administration, balanced functional specialization, seriousness of the budget constraint, adequate information, and technology application. While countries lacking recent reforms underline the same set of institutional aspects, the implied consensus could not result in actual reforms mainly due to the countervailing influence of resource- and political economy-related factors. Most of the countries lacking recent reforms also have well endowed water resources (e.g., those in Southeast Asia). Although some other countries (e.g., France, Germany, and the United Kingdom) do not have any volume-related scarcity issues, they have undertaken significant reforms in the past to address water quality and intersectoral allocation issues. In still other countries (e.g., those in North and East Africa), the absence of reforms is related more to political economy constraints than to the lack of consensus for change. The message is clear that the general consensus on the need, nature, and thrust of institutional change, though necessary, is not sufficient to initiate and sustain reforms, especially in the absence of strong socioeconomic and political pressures for change.

The convergence on the role of institutional aspects also coexists with notable divergence about their relative significance. For instance, the reform countries emphasize cost recovery, conflict resolution, organizational structures, administrative accountability, user involvement, and private sector participation.

Although the reform process in most of these countries tends toward decentralization and market orientation, there is an overall thrust on a centralized system of water law, as decentralization cannot succeed without a dose of centralization, especially in the legal domain. In contrast, in countries lacking recent reforms, the emphasis is more on an integrated approach to water resources, legal aspects of accountability, aligning water policy closely with water law, and policy aspects related to intersectoral and regional water transfers. This difference in the configurations of institutional aspects observed in the two country groups is, in a sense, indicative of their being at different stages of the reform process. A closer look at the institutional aspects receiving attention in the two country groups shows that the reform countries are dealing with those institutional aspects with more immediate performance implications. In contrast, other countries are focusing either on preliminary institutional issues with no or little direct performance significance or higher level institutional issues with strong implications for institutional strengthening, but low or no implications for secoral performance. This fact explains why institution–performance linkages are stronger in reform countries than in other countries.

As expected, spatial differences in the nature and strength of institution–performance linkages are the direct outcome of country group-specific variations in the configurations of institutional aspects that define various layers of institution–performance interaction. From an overall perspective, however, these distinct patterns are more pronounced in the context of interinstitutional linkages than in the context of intra-institutional linkages. This finding reinforces our earlier observation that the expert and country group-specific differences are confined mostly to the lower echelons of institution–performance linkages, but diminish as we move up to higher levels of linkages. The region-specific differences in institutional configurations and their implications for institution–performance linkages also suggest some interesting aspects related to both the motivation and thrust of perceived institutional changes. As per a more generic interpretation of our results, the financial deterioration within the water sector caused by poor cost recovery and represented by the seriousness of the budget constraint has been a major factor motivating institutional change in many reform countries. Since the financial performance of the water sector is also affected by other policies such as the agricultural and, especially macroeconomic policies, the critical role of the effects of these policies should not be underestimated.

Exogenous Influence on Perceptional Evaluation

The significant positive effect that the constant term has in most contexts suggests the synergy that the institution–performance interaction can derive from the general socioeconomic, political, legal, and resource-related environment. In view of this synergy within the general institutional environment, a given level of reform effort or institutional change is likely to lead to a faster and more than proportionate change in water sector performance. Although this is an encouraging sign, to exploit such synergy in the process of reform the relative roles of most, if not all, components of the institutional environment must be understood. For this purpose, we estimated the institutional and sectoral performance variables derived from perceptional information as a function of some of the exogenous variables derived from observed data on economic, demographic, institutional, and resource-related aspects. Despite its simplicity and crude nature, this estimation exercise allowed us to understand the relative significance and configurations of exogenous factors affecting the performance of water institution, water sector, and their components. Since the performance variables are perceptional and the exogenous variables are observed, this exercise also allowed us to derive some useful insights into the nature and pattern of exogenous influence on the subjective evaluation of institution–performance interaction.

Generally, factors associated with economic development, regulatory effectiveness, and education have a positive influence, as they are capable to generate some autonomous changes in the institutional sphere, including water institutions. In view of the phenomena of institutional creation and thickening usually associated with the development process, institutional linkages are strengthened, thereby contributing to improved institutional performance. This supports the acknowledged fact that institutional performance benefits from autonomous changes in the overall institutional environment as induced by various factors associated with economic development. Notably, the negative effects of demographic changes, resource scarcity, and increasing socio-economic inequity tend to enhance the economic value of effective institutional arrangements in all sectors including water. From this perspective, therefore, the evaluation of institution–performance interaction, both in general and in water sector contexts, cannot be isolated from the overall socioeconomic, demographic, institutional, and resource-related environment. In fact, as implied in our evaluation of the relative impact of the exogenous factors, the subjective process of institution–performance evaluation should have captured a large part of the exogenous influence from the general environment.

Convergence and Stability of Results

Although the process of institution–performance interaction is evaluated only indirectly in terms of the perception-based results, the analysis of these results across sample contexts allows us to infer their convergence and stability properties. First, in comparison to results obtained in various subsample contexts, the all-sample results show the same or more institutional variables to be significant in almost every equation. This means that institutional and performance linkages become stronger with the enlargement of sample size, expertise mix, and country coverage. Second, the all-sample results also tend to balance differences or extremities in the behavior of institutional aspects observed in subsample contexts. However, the subsample results are valuable in identifying useful caveats and understanding, thereby, the role of context-specific factors. But, the all-sample context, with its normalizing properties, helps to identify generic features both in institutional configuration and in institution–performance linkages.

The influence of disciplinary bias and ideological aspects is strong at the level of individual layers of institutional and performance linkages, but it tends to become weak from an overall or macro perspective of the process of institution–performance interaction. The effects of the group- and area-specific bias at the micro level as well as its remaining vestiges at the macro level are reduced considerably as the number of experts and countries increases and the evaluation is performed from a general rather than from a context-specific perspective. This implies that the results from the all-sample context are relatively bias free and provide a more reliable and generic picture on the nature and strength of institution–performance linkages. The all-sample results remove the extremities observed in group-specific results and provide a more balanced and generalizable evaluation of institution–performance interaction. With an enlarged and diverse sample, the scope for convergence and consensus on the reality of institution–performance linkages increases as does the overall reliability and credibility of the results and their theoretical and policy implications.

IMPLICATIONS FOR REFORM DESIGN AND IMPLEMENTATION

As we compare the independent institutional variables and their impact-transmission channels in terms of their relative importance and significance in different estimation contexts, we gain considerable insight into institutional design and implementation issues, especially those related to institutional priority setting, sequencing, and packaging as well as reform timing and scaling. To appreciate the implications of this comparative analysis, a fact that underpins our evaluation method and empirical approach should be recognized. That is, the relative size and significance of the coefficients associated with different variables, and hence, the relative share and significance of different channels, are viewed as a quantitative representation of the overall consensus among the opinionmakers in global water sector. Since such consensus is not only on the perception of present reality but also on the expectation of future change, the results can be interpreted as a representation of both what has happened and what would happen in the realm of institution–performance interaction. Thus, the relative shares of the channels and exogenous variables in total impact can be viewed as a consensual estimation of both their actual and expected contributions. With this perspective, we can now identify some of the most important implications of our results for institutional priority setting, sequencing, and packaging as well as timing and scale aspects in reform programs.

Linkage Length and Impact Transmission

A negative but insignificant correlation was observed between linkage length evaluated in terms of the number of en-route variables and the magnitude of impact transmitted by various channels. This correlation suggests that, although channels with more en-route variables have a lower value, this need not necessarily be always true. However, in absolute terms, since reform regions have a larger correlation coefficient than other regions, impact transmission is lower for longer chains than for smaller chains. As the lower impact transmission by longer chains means weaker linkages and longer gestation among the en-route variables, this result suggests that the performance impact of the reform process, by and large, is notable more for its direct effect than for its indirect effect through institutional strengthening. If this is so, performance gains realized in the reform countries cannot be sustained unless the reform is taken to the next stage where the focus shifts toward institutional strengthening by concentrating on the longer chains essential for institutional thickening and interlinkages.

Longer chains, though good for institutional strengthening and institutional thickening, may not lead to any immediate impact on water sector performance in view of two factors. First, in the case of channels involving longer institutional chains, the initial effect of a change in institutional aspects may be moderated or distorted by weakness or inefficiency of the en-route variables. Second, time plays an implicit role, as some or all of the en-route variables may need differential time frames to capture and transmit the effects of an initial institutional change. This suggests the critical role of the time-related dynamics of institutional change and its performance impact. Since changing just one institutional aspect will not accomplish the reform goals without changes in other aspects with critical institutional and performance linkages, the institutional chains and their underlying institutional aspects have to be ranked in terms of the magnitude, significance, and gestation period of their impact. Since the channels involving lower and slower performance impact are also essential for sustaining the operational capacity of water institutions, there has to be a proper packaging of institutional variables covering those with a larger and more immediate performance impact as well as those with lower and slower performance impact. While the first group has the tactical role of sustaining economic and political pressure for reform by bringing immediate performance returns, the second group is critical for ensuring the long-term sustainability of institutional reform through a gradual but concerted effort to strengthen institutional linkages.

Institutional Priority Setting, Sequencing, and Packaging

The number, sequence, and configuration of variables in the linkage chains underlying the channels with large and significant impact provide invaluable information for designing the reform program, complete with institutional priority setting, sequencing, and packaging. While the inference on institutional priority is based on the relative size and significance of the institutional variables underlying various impact-transmission channels, the inference on sequencing is based on the order and configuration of the variables underlying these channels or linkage chains. Setting priorities for the institutional variables is straightforward, as it is based on the intensity of institutional linkages as reflected by the number of their impact-transmission channels as well as on the relative magnitude and share of their performance impact. Our results are unequivocal for giving top priority to administrative aspects, which account for 61 percent of the total impact calculated from all coefficients, and 52 percent of the impact calculated with significant coefficients. Their key role in overall institutional and sectoral performance is understandable in view of their importance both for water administration performance and for water law and policy performance. Since performance improvement is predicated more on implementation-related institutional aspects than on mere legal prescription or policy statements, there is a dichotomy of a poor law–policy regime with better implementation and a better law–policy regime with a poor implementation.

Priority should be given to the application of science and technology, building a strong information base, creating an independent body for water pricing, broadening functional specialization within water administration, and formulating an effective user participation policy. There is also an issue of sequencing not only among these aspects themselves but also between these and other institutional aspects. Science and technology application is especially a critical first step for building an information base, which can, in turn, enhance the effectiveness of water pricing. Similarly, an efficiently functioning network of WUAs at various levels is a precondition for an effective property-rights arrangement, both of which, together, set the necessary institutional framework for promoting institutional aspects such as cost recovery, accountability, conflict resolution, and water transfers. Institutional aspects related to balanced functional specialization, user participation policy, and property-rights format also deserve priority, as some of their channels, though not significant, have the potential for a large performance impact over the long run. Since the insignificant channels are an indication of weak or dormant linkages among the variables in the linkage chains, they can be strengthened by adopting either a package approach suitable for simultaneous reform in several related institutional and performance variables or spacing scheme to sequence their change within an appropriately defined time frame.

Strengthening Impact-Transmission Channels

Efforts to strengthen the impact-transmission channels are crucial for enhancing the performance contributions of significant channels and for turning some of the insignificant channels into the significant ones. Our empirical results enable us to establish priorities among channels only in terms of their relative share and significance of impact. But, there are other considerations, especially those related to the nature and relative significance of their long-term impact on institutional strengthening and performance improvement. Although these considerations are beyond our present model of institution–performance interaction, they can be addressed case by case, giving due weight to factors such as local conditions, reform stage, and reformers' expectations. For countries at the reform threshold, strategic considerations require priority for channels involving direct effects, as they can yield the quicker performance returns needed to counter political resistance and consolidate performance gains. In contrast, for countries in an advanced stage of reform, sustainability considerations require priority for channels conveying indirect effects through lengthy linkage chains, as they can deepen the process of institutional thickening so crucial to ensure the resilience and sustainability of the reform process. Similarly, the institutional and performance variables figuring in the linkage chains of a greater number of channels deserve priority over others, because any reform effort involving them is likely to strengthen all the channels in which they are involved.

In many cases, the significant channels also have the largest share, whereas most of those with a lower and marginal share are insignificant. Such a direct association between the size and significance of the impact transmitted by the channels has important implications. Since experts and policymakers attach a premium to the channels and their associated institutional variables with a large institutional and sectoral performance impact, these channels are likely to be significant and remain at the top of the priority hierarchy. Thus, when institutional reform improves the performance contribution of one or more institutional and performance variables, their larger performance impact itself ensures the significance of the channels in which they operate. By targeting the institutional and performance variables underlying both the significant channels with lower shares and their insignificant counterparts with higher shares, their relative importance and significance can be improved. This also suggests, implicitly, how institutional reform can alter both reality and perception.

Thrust and Scale in Institutional Reform

Although reform components and priorities are more or less the same across country groups, there are considerable differences in the thrust, scale, and effectiveness of initiated reforms. Since the reform countries have already undertaken significant reforms in various water institution components, further institutional reforms, involving both substantial and marginal changes, are likely to be more effective and less costly in view of the upstream and downstream linkages created by the reforms already undertaken. As a result, the impact of the reforms on institutional and sectoral performance is likely to be faster and more effective in the reform countries than in other countries. From the perspective of path dependency and institutional hierarchy, since information application mostly succeeds the application of science and technology, the dominant role of information adequacy in reform countries suggests that these countries should have already made substantial progress in technology application within their water administration. Despite a marginal variation in the number of significant channels among the country groups, the overall share of significant channels in total impact is far higher in reform countries (73 percent) than the same in other countries (56 percent). This result implies the following four important and interrelated aspects.

First, as noted already, the larger performance impact in reform countries owes more to the larger contributions of institutional variables through their direct impact-transmission channels than their indirect impact through institutional strengthening. Second, in reform countries, unlike others, most of the channels with a larger share of total impact are significant. Such a higher share of significant channels in total impact suggests that the institutional linkages are stronger in the reform countries. But, the strength is more visible in the case of intra-institutional linkages than in interinstitutional linkages. Third, although the insignificant channels are many, they have only a small share of the total impact, even in reform countries. Since this means that most of the total impact comes from only a few channels, the extent of institutional linkages contributed by recent reforms appears to be low, due either to slower development of these linkages or to limited institutional coverage of reforms. To enhance and sustain their institutional and sectoral performance, the future reform programs in reform countries have to concentrate on both the already significant and the currently insignificant channels. Finally, in some reform countries with a mature water sector, additional performance benefits can likely be obtained only with a substantial and higher dose of reform effort. This is not the case in countries lacking recent reforms or at the reform threshold. The intuition here is that performance return increases in the initial stages of reform, but decreases in the later stages. However, performance returns may not be observable without undertaking a critical minimum level of reform in the first place.

The larger impact conveyed by the significant channels also suggests the issue of scale and dose in reform effort. That is, since the variables associated with these channels produce a larger impact, both institutional and sectoral performance can be enhanced by a larger dose of reform effort in the context of these variables. The scale of effort also has a time dimension as the additional reform effort can be undertaken either simultaneously or sequentially with an appropriate time lag. But, the issue of when, how and where to make the additional reform effort depends on whether the performance impact associated with an exogenous variable is immediate or delayed, substantial or marginal, and direct or indirect. Since the speed of impact transmission depends on the nature and configurations of variables in the linkage chains, the final answer to the issue of scale and timing requires the evaluation of all channels, considering specifically their immediate and long-term implications for institutional strengthening and performance improvement.

Since our model assumes linear effect for all variables, information on the scale aspects has to be derived outside our model context. Usually, the nature of the effects associated with each key institutional aspect can be understood based on careful thinking and detailed observations in a given context. For instance, the performance impact of an additional unit of reform effort on user participation policy can be evaluated for a given region through a detailed review of its institutional linkages, the extent of reforms in related areas, and observations on current and past performance of this policy. The linear specification of our model does not give us any direct information on scale aspects, but it does provide some idea of the scale aspects involved in impact transmission. The scale in impact transmission can be addressed in terms of the size of the coefficients associated with the en-route variables. Thus, when all the coefficients of the en-route variables have a value of less (more) than one, it means that the effects of the exogenous variables will be transmitted less (more) than proportionately. However, the en-route variables in many contexts are likely to have mixed values for their coefficients, some with fractional values and others with values greater than one. The ultimate scale of impact transmission will, therefore, depend upon the size configuration of the coefficients of the en-route variables. Since the scale issue in the impact-transmission process is as, if not more, important than the scale in institutional change, the impact-transmission channels must be strengthened to make the underlying coefficients larger and more significant.

The Role of Time in Institutional Reform

The issue of timing cannot be explicitly addressed within the framework of our model, which does not explicitly incorporate the time dimension, but our results provide some basis for deriving useful inferences and hypotheses on this count. From a design perspective of institutional reform, the relative performance impact of institutional variables and their transmission channels suggests a clear choice between variables with fewer channels but larger impact and those with more channels and smaller impact. However, the choice is not as easy as it seems because of the intervening roles of institutional amenability, political feasibility, and the time lag between institutional strengthening and impact transmission. The choice will naturally tilt toward variables such as internal consistency and centralization tendency within water law in view of their stronger and significant performance impact and their amenability to reform with less political resistance. While the legal reforms needed to promote internal consistency and privatization may be politically easier and quicker, they take time to mature and yield perceptible performance impact.

In contrast, although political difficulties will delay property-rights reform, once such reforms are undertaken, their performance impact will be faster. In addition, once property-rights reforms are in place, institutional reforms in related spheres can become easier. Such a facilitative role for downstream reforms is critical to reduce the transaction costs of the overall reform program. More importantly, since property-rights reforms have intricate linkages with use efficiency, accountability, conflict resolution, cost recovery, and water transfers, they are also likely to contribute as much to the process of long-term institutional thickening as to immediate performance improvement. Such a process is indispensable in laying the foundation for institutional sustainability and long-term performance improvement. These considerations suggest the need for assigning higher priority to variables with stronger institutional and performance linkages, such as water rights, notwithstanding their lower immediate performance contributions. The choice is still difficult between institutional aspects with quicker reform prospects but delayed impact and those with difficult reforms but fast impact. There are tradeoffs between immediate performance benefits and long-term institutional and performance gains, but these can be resolved through appropriate institutional priority setting, sequencing, and packaging.

IMPLICATIONS FOR REFORM PROSPECTS

In addition to the implications noted for theory, policy, and reform design and implementation, some significant observations also emerge from our theoretical review, analytical framework, and empirical analysis of institution-performance interaction. These observations relate to some of the positive aspects, especially those related to the international environment, that enhance prospects for institutional reform both nationally and globally.

Global Consensus on Reform Thrust

The cross-country review of water sector and water institution goes far beyond simple documentation and comparative analysis. Although both the nature and direction of the institutional changes observed among countries vary by country-specific economic, political, and resource realities, some common trends and patterns are identifiable. These include the increasing importance assigned to market-based allocation, decentralization and privatization, integrated water resource management, and economic viability and physical sustainability. As physical, financial, and ecological constraints limit the relevance of supply-side solutions, countries are trying their best, within their political economy constraints, to set right the institutional foundation necessary to promote demand-side solutions. These commonalities vouch for the existence of considerable global consensus on the major thrust and focus of institutional reform within the water sector, despite differences in detail and format. Our empirical results concerning priorities, packaging, and sequencing provide some quantitative dimensions on this consensus. Although location-specific adjustments are also essential, nevertheless, a common agenda for institutional reform, applicable to most contexts, can be developed.

Role of Institutional Transaction Costs

Our cross-country review also suggests that the conditions are ripe for water institutional reform in many countries. Examples of institutional change in most countries can be taken as observational evidence that the opportunity costs of institutional change are surpassing the corresponding transaction costs. But, the fact that institutional changes are uniform neither across institutional components nor across water subsectors suggests that both opportunity and transaction costs vary considerably by context. The cross-country review of recent reforms suggests that institutional changes within the water sector are prompted by both endogenous factors (e.g., water scarcity, performance deterioration, and financial unviability) and exogenous factors (e.g., macroeconomic crisis, political reform, natural calamities, and technological progress). These factors act together to raise the opportunity costs of institutional change, reduce the corresponding transaction costs, and create a pro-reform climate. From a policy perspective, the synergy between these factors can be exploited well with appropriate timing and sequencing of reforms where water subsectors and institutional components are prioritized in terms of their performance impact, fiscal significance, facilitative roles for downstream reforms, and political acceptability.

Institutional Pluralism

Institutional change in the past was often marred by ideological attachment to some institutional forms. Today, there is a considerable consensus on the need for pluralistic institutional arrangements. In line with such consensus and the dominant view in institutional economics, we also favor institutional pluralism as the foundation of any institutional policy or reform program. Since society needs a variety of interlinked institutions to govern different spheres of human interaction, markets alone cannot be considered the ideal or universal institutional arrangement. Moreover, markets cannot perform without being embedded in a nexus of rules, obligations, and public interventions. Nor can the state be effective without reliance on markets and the delegation of some of their functions to private and other non-governmental groups. We agree that the pervasive and unrealistic dichotomy between the state and market has to be discarded, and a governance structure that can accommodate a broader array of institutional arrangements, mixing state and markets, should be considered.

Institutional change that strengthens the process of voluntary exchanges and interactions is desirable, but the market process itself does not have to shape the direction of institutional change, as institutional selection through market mechanisms can be myopic and inefficient and lead to deadlocks. Some institutions are amenable to market selection or transaction cost criteria, but many others can be explained mainly by social and political factors. Institutions evolve naturally through time and respond to economic, social, and political forces, but purposive changes are also necessary to expedite the process, shape the direction of institutional change, and create imaginative collective forms of coordination mechanisms. Institutional pluralism as a guiding principle of institutional reform is also consistent with our positive approach to institutions and institutional change.

Political Economy Opportunities

Political economy constraints are often overestimated, but equally powerful political economy opportunities are generally underestimated. For instance, the negative roles of interest groups are often overestimated, and the power of normalizing aspects such as the constitution and collective efforts to avert socially harmful economic decline are often underestimated. In addition to factors such as altruism and ideology, mechanisms such as the constitution, congress or parliament, multiparty system, and independence of bureaucracy broaden the time horizon of policymakers and dilute the negative effects of excessive power and self-interest in institutional change. Although the natural process of institutional evolution is often obstructed by rent seeking, path dependency, ideology, and political risk, many other factors enhance the reform prospects.

From the particular perspective of water sector, with increasing water scarcity and emerging financial and performance crises, the rents derived from subsidized water supply are threatened. The widespread and dominant trend toward political liberalization and democratization and the emergence of the middle classes as an outcome of economic development and education have also reduced the political predominance of a few groups and improved the political balance necessary for group-neutral reforms. Progress in water and information technologies, pressures from donor agencies, and requirements of international agreements tend to turn the political balance towards reform. With the emergence and political influence of pro-reform constituencies, political impetus is also building for institutional reform. Our cross-country review of recent institutional reforms has demonstrated the presence of significant political economy opportunities, and many countries have indeed utilized them to their advantage either by design or by chance. For instance, macroeconomic reforms (e.g., China, India, and Mexico) and water-related natural disasters such as droughts (e.g., California), floods (e.g., China), and soil salinity (e.g., Australia and Pakistan) have magnified the fiscal and social implications of the opportunity costs of institutional change. In contrast, sociopolitical reform attempts (e.g., in Chile during the 1970s, Spain during the 1980s, China since the 1980s, and South Africa since the 1990s) have reduced the transaction costs directly as the institutional changes in the water sector form only part of a nationwide reform.

Supply Side of Institutional Change

The supply side of institutional change used to be one of the most ignored dimensions of institutional economics. Now, it is receiving increasing attention in view of its role in minimizing the transaction costs of institutional reforms. From the demand–supply perspective of institutional change, the state has to play a central role both as the supplier of institutional change and as a promoter of other supply sources such as research and information systems. Equally crucial is also the role of international donor and technical agencies. Scale economic considerations give the state and these agencies an efficiency edge in lowering the overall transaction costs of institutional change. Although path dependence limits the institutional choice to only those that are consistent with the current state and configurations of institutions, the transaction costs can still be minimized by the way the institutional options are designed, structured, timed, sequenced, and packaged. Similarly, timing can also better exploit the pro-reform climate fostered by crisis. Thus, design issues such as priority setting, sequencing, and packaging are all part of the supply side of institutional change. Institutional design aspects minimize transaction costs directly and by virtue of their role in the formation of pro-reform political coalitions, they also lower those costs indirectly. Since the supply of institutional innovation also depends on advances in the knowledge of the institutional change process itself, policy research of the present type can reduce transaction costs and augment institutional supply. With an increasing integration of the world economic system under the ongoing process of globalization, documentation and dissemination of cross-country experience in the realm of water sector reforms can also minimize the costs and risks involved in experimenting with new institutions.

Sequential Reform Strategy

The positive aspects noted so far are mostly exogenous to the policy apparatus. However, the sequential reform strategy outlined here is essentially endogenous, as policymakers can use it to enhance reform prospects from within. Despite their urgency, institutional reforms within the water sector need not be undertaken in one go. They can be spaced within a well-planned time frame. The cost of transacting institutional reform in a given political economy context can be minimized, and the usual inertia associated with the stupendous nature of the reform task can be overcome through a gradual but sequential reform strategy. Since such a strategy continuously builds on the synergy generated by reforms already undertaken in key areas, subsequent reforms become easier to transact both politically and institutionally. This means that there are intricate and functional linkages between the transaction costs of subsequent reforms and the opportunity costs of earlier reforms. These linkages may seem abstract and theoretical, but their practical influence within the political economy of the reform process can be neither ignored nor underestimated.

Since institutional synergy reduces the transaction costs of subsequent reforms, and the immediate performance impacts of initial reforms ensure a steady flow of economic benefits, a sequential strategy can enhance the prospects for institutional change by weakening political resistance while precipitating endogenous pressures for further reforms. Apart from its virtues from a political economy perspective, a sequential strategy is also well suited for international lending agencies committed to promoting institutional change within the water sector. Sequential strategy provides a natural framework for developing temporally and operationally linked long-term lending programs in the institutional sphere of the water sector. Such programs are mutually advantageous for both the borrowing countries as well as the lending agencies. While the countries have an inherent incentive to adhere to the reform schedule in view of the performance-based and sequentially linked funding commitments, the lending agencies can ensure more effective monitoring of reform progress and better planning of their long-term investment portfolio.

LIMITATIONS AND CAVEATS

Despite its important theoretical and policy contributions, our study is not free from limitations and caveats. The macro and formal perspective of both water institutions and the water sector taken in this study involves a sacrifice of micro details, including informal institutions that play an important role in grass-roots decisions on water use and management. As micro and informal institutions lack international comparability and remain largely outside the ambit of purposive policy changes, our focus on macro and formal institutions is both an analytical necessity and a practical requirement. Although a finer decomposition of institutional and performance aspects is possible and desirable, we have focused only on some major institutional and performance aspects important for policy formulation. Likewise, the model of institution–performance inter-action does not exhaust all the intricate linkages among institutional aspects, but concentrates only on some of the key layers of institutional and perfor-mance linkages evident in the process of institution–performance interaction.

The model equations can be estimated with a variety of functional forms involving quadratic and logarithmic transformation, but, to make the analysis simple and transparent, we rely only on simple linear form for estimating all equations. Similarly, our inability to incorporate explicitly the effects of exogenous factors such as historical forces, political arrangements, demo-graphic condition, resource endowment, and economic development within the model of institution–performance interaction is also understandable in view of data limitations, including the analytical mismatch between subjective information obtained from individuals and objective data related to countries. Although our analysis provides some indirect inferences about the role of a few time-related aspects, analytical issues and data limitations have made it difficult to explicitly incorporate time in all its dimensions. From our empiri-cal analysis, a generic institutional reform program can be specified, complete with priority setting, packaging, sequencing, and other implementation aspects. However, we have deliberately refrained from such an attempt, as we consider this study more as a framework for a solution rather than the solution itself. This is partly to avoid a stereotypical approach and partly to recognize location-specific aspects in reform design and implementation.

Despite its limitations and constraints, the study has succeeded in address-ing its twofold objectives. The cross-country comparative review of water institutional changes attempted with an institutional transaction cost and polit-ical economy perspective indicates how factors – both endogenous and exoge-nous to the water sector – guide countries through the stages of the institutional change process. The empirical evaluation, on the other hand, demonstrates the inner dynamics of institution–performance and shows how insights into this process can be used to derive reform design and implemen-tation principles. More importantly, it has opened up an entirely new way of looking at institutional change that can facilitate a better understanding of the constraints and opportunities that are inherent in the institutional structure itself. The present study can also be extended in many directions, especially for testing alternative institutional combinations (packages) and their institu-tional and performance impacts. The large body of perception-based data on many country-specific institutional aspects also opens up another interesting avenue for developing an index to gauge the relative health of water institu-tions across countries or even across regions within the same country. In view of these and other possibilities for further extensions, we consider this study not as an end, but as a beginning of many future works in the realm of the insti-tutional economics of water.

Appendix A: Questionnaire

COMPARATIVE STUDY OF WATER INSTITUTIONS AND THEIR IMPACT ON WATER SECTOR PERFORMANCE IN SELECT COUNTRIES

REQUEST to RESPONDENTS

Knowing full well the value of your time and information, it is our intention to use them as efficiently as we can and, of course, with full acknowledgment of your specific views and contributions (unless stated specifically to the contrary). Thanks, in advance, for your cooperation and active support for this pioneering study.

(A) Definitions

1. *Water institution:*   An entity defined interactively by water law, water policy, and water administration at the formal and informal as well as macro and micro levels. The focus here is only on formal and macro dimensions.

2. *Water sector:*   Covers all consumptive uses of water such as irrigation, domestic consumption, and industrial processing from both surface and nonsurface sources as well as reclaimed or recycled sources. Nonconsumptive uses such as hydropower generation, navigation, and instream ecological needs are considered only to the extent that they affect consumptive uses directly or indirectly. However, in the context of this questionnaire, water sector is viewed from a more general and macro perspective.

3. *Water sector performance:*   Covers physical performance (demand vs. supply), operational performance (allocational ease and its efficiency), and financial performance (cost recovery and pricing efficiency).

(B) Notes

1. This questionnaire is intended essentially to highlight major issues as a starting point to initiate discussion and *elicit a gut-feeling response* of country experts, specialists, and policymakers. Since it does not exhaust all issues (especially the country-specific ones), *additional issues brought to our attention would be most welcome.* Your comments and suggestions on and modifications and refinements of specific issues are of utmost value as we plan to fine tune this questionnaire and send it to many experts worldwide subsequent to this initial and personalized survey.

2. Given the nature of the subject under study, questions with straightforward quantitative answers are interspersed with questions that allow only qualitative or *judgmental responses.* The latter set of questions can be quantified by carefully *choosing a value on a 1 to 10 scale (1 = the least and 10 = the best)* along with the reason(s) justifying the choice of the assigned value.

3. Interconnectivity among issues makes the questions not only interrelated but also repetitive. The repetition of the same questions in different contexts is deliberately intended to cross-check the response as well as to capture the multifarious effects of the same aspect in different institutional and performance contexts.

4. *Kindly try to answer all the questions in all four sections* of this questionnaire. Since we aim at evaluating the interlinkages among the three components of a water institution (water law, water policy, and water administration), *answers to all questions are critical.*

5. Besides the structural questionnaire and open-ended discussion, we seek your help and guidance in obtaining published and unpublished materials and data on water institution and water sector performance.

(C) Background Information

1. Respondent's name (optional) . . . .

2. Specialization   Economist/Engineer/Legal expert/

                                      Other (specify) . . . .

3. Affiliation . . . .

4. Address . . . .

    . . . .

    . . . .

    . . . .

    Email: . . . .

    Phone: . . . .

    Fax: . . . .

5. Any other relevant information: . . . .

    . . . .

---

1. WATER LAW

1.1. **Legal Treatment of Different Water Sources** (*Tick one or more*)

   (a) Surface and groundwater are treated alike   . . . . . .
   (b) They are treated differently   . . . . . .
   (c) Laws discriminate between water development and
        use by public and private parties   . . . . . .
   (d) Law distinguishes water development and use across
        sectors such as irrigation, domestic, and industrial uses . . . . . .
   (e) There is differential priority and treatment of
        consumptive and nonconsumptive uses.   . . . . . .

1.2. **Legal Linkages between Water and Water-Related Resources**

1.2.1. In your perception, how strong are the legal linkages
        (*on a 1 to 10 scale*)?
   (a) Between land and groundwater   . . . . . .
   (b) Between land and surface water   . . . . . .
   (c) Between forest and environment and water   . . . . . .

1.3. **Property-Rights Status** *(Local Level)*

1.3.1. Does water law allow private water rights?   Yes/No

1.3.2.   If yes is it in the form of (*tick one or more*):
(a)   Individual rights   . . . . . .
(b)   Group and collective rights   . . . . . .
(c)   Other forms (specify)   . . . . . .
. . . .
. . . .

1.3.3.   If no what are the constraints (*tick one or more*)?
(a)   Public control is needed for equity   . . . . . .
(b)   Administering private rights is socially difficult   . . . . . .
(c)   Gaps in water control institutions and technologies   . . . . . .
(d)   Others (specify)
. . . .
. . . .

1.4.   Property-Rights Status (*General*)

1.4.1.   Basis for general rights in surface water (*Tick one or more*)
(a)   None or not clear   . . . . . .
(b)   Common or state property   . . . . . .
(c)   Riparian system   . . . . . .
(d)   Appropriative system   . . . . . .
(e)   Correlative system (equal or proportional sharing)   . . . . . .
(f)   Any other, please specify   . . . . . .
. . . .

1.4.2.   Basis for general rights in groundwater (*Tick one or more*)
(a)   Open access   . . . . . .
(b)   Common or state property   . . . . . .
(c)   Appropriative system   . . . . . .
(d)   Correlative system (equal or proportional sharing)   . . . . . .
(e)   Any other, please specify   . . . . . .
. . . .

1.4.3.   Is there legalized intersectoral prioritization?   Yes/No

1.4.3.1.   If yes, specify the priority order (*by placing rank number*)
(a)   Domestic use   . . . . . .
(b)   Irrigation   . . . . . .
(c)   Industrial and commercial uses   . . . . . .
(d)   Power generation   . . . . . .
(e)   Navigation   . . . . . .
(f)   Environmental purpose (e.g., instream needs)   . . . . . .

1.4.3.2. What is the main basis of such prioritization?
(*Tick one or more. If more than one, indicate relative
importance on a 1 to 10 scale*)
(a) Equity concerns . . . . . .
(b) Resource conditions . . . . . .
(c) Economic considerations . . . . . .
(d) Any other, specify (e.g., historical reasons)

. . . .

. . . .

1.5. Conflict Resolution/Coordination

1.5.1. Are the conflict-resolution mechanisms explicitly
specified in law? Yes/No/Not Clear

1.5.2. If yes, indicate the kind of conflict-resolution mechanisms
(*Tick one or more*)
(a) Administratively/bureaucratically rooted system
(Water Resource Dept., Irrigation Dept., etc.) . . . . . .
(i) Local administration/govt. . . . . . .
(ii) National Water Council . . . . . .
(b) Relatively more decentralized system
(i) River boards . . . . . .
(ii) Basin organization . . . . . .
(iii) Any others, specify (e.g., WUAs)

. . . .

. . . .

. . . .
(c) Tribunals . . . . . .
(d) Judicial/legislative/constitutional . . . . . .
(e) Any others, specify . . . . . .

. . . .

1.5.3. What are the legally specified mechanisms for transboundary
conflicts (interstate and international)? (*Tick one or more*)
(a) River boards . . . . . .
(b) Basin organizations . . . . . .
(c) Tribunals . . . . . .
(d) Others, specify

. . . .

1.5.4. In your opinion, how effective are the legal provisions for
conflict-resolution and coordination mechanisms
(*on a 1 to 10 scale*)?
(a) Local level (among users) . . . . . .
(b) National level (among regions and sectors) . . . . . .
(c) International level (among nations) . . . . . .

1.6. Accountability of Water Sector Officials and Water Users

1.6.1. Are there explicit legal provisions for ensuring the accountability
of officials, water suppliers, and users? Yes/No/Not Clear

1.6.2. If yes, specify the legal instruments for the accountability
of the following (*tick one or more in each case*):
(a) Officials (i) Indemnity clause in water law . . . . . .
(ii) Penalty provisions in water law . . . . . .
(iii) Other administrative actions . . . . . .
(b) Users (i) Sanctions and tortious liabilities . . . . . .
(ii) User-oriented or decentralized
mechanisms (e.g., WUAs) . . . . . .
(iii) Actions by local government,
irrigation department,
water supply agency, etc. . . . . . .

1.6.3. In your opinion, how effective are the accountability provisions
(*on a 1 to 10 scale*)?
(a) For officials . . . . . .
(b) For users . . . . . .

1.6.4. Do the accountability provisions vary by (*Tick one or more*)
(a) Water sources . . . . . .
(b) Use categories . . . . . .
(c) User groups . . . . . .
(d) None . . . . . .

1.7. Intragovernmental Responsibility in Water Law

1.7.1. Please indicate (*by ticking*) current intragovernmental responsibility

Govt. level	Surface water	Ground- water	Recycled water	Water quality	Environment
National	. . . . . .	. . . .	. . . .	. . . . . .	. . . .
State	. . . . . .	. . . .	. . . .	. . . . . .	. . . .
Local	. . . . . .	. . . .	. . . .	. . . . . .	. . . .

1.7.2.   Does the existing division of legal responsibility favor
         an integrated treatment of water planning and
         development?   Yes/No

1.7.3.   If yes, how strong is the favorable effect
         (*on a 1 to 10 scale*)?   . . . . . .

1.7.4.   Are there legally conceivable property rights in water
         quality (i.e., pollution permits)?   Yes/No

1.7.5.   Specify (*by ticking*) the legal provisions for pollution control.
         (a)   Quality standards   . . . . . .
         (b)   Pollution control legislation   . . . . . .
         (c)   Any other, specify

               . . . .

1.7.6.   In your opinion, how effective are the overall legal provisions
         in protecting water quality (*on a 1 to 10 scale*)?   . . . . . .

1.8.   Overall Evaluation

1.8.1.   Does the present law contribute to centralization?   Yes/No

1.8.2.   In your opinion, how strong is the tendency
         toward centralization (*on a 1 to 10 scale*)?   . . . . . .

1.8.3.   How favorable are the legal provisions for private sector,
         nongovernmental organization (NGO)/community participation
         in water development/management (*on a 1 to 10 scale*)?
         (a)   Private sector   . . . . . .
         (b)   NGO   . . . . . .
         (c)   Community   . . . . . .

1.8.4.   In your opinion, how integrated are water laws with
         other laws related to land, forest, and environment
         (*on a 1 to 10 scale*)?   . . . . . .

1.8.5.   In your opinion, how relevant are the water and related
         laws for the current situation (*on a 1 to 10 scale*)?   . . . . . .

1.8.6. How strong is water law (*on a 1 to 10 scale*) in addressing new challenges in the sphere of
    (a) Water-sharing conflicts   ......
    (b) Environmental concerns   ......
    (c) New water technologies   ......

---

2. WATER POLICY

2.1. Water Policy Implications in Other Policies and Law
(*Tick one or more*)
    (a) Water law   ......
    (b) Agricultural policy   ......
    (c) Fiscal policies   ......
    (d) Credit and investment policies   ......
    (e) Environmental policies   ......

2.2. Priority of Uses

2.2.1. If intersectoral use priority is not explicit in water law, is it stated – explicitly or implicitly – in other policies?   Yes/No

2.2.2. If yes, specify the order (*by placing a rank*)
    (a) Domestic use   ......
    (b) Irrigation   ......
    (c) Industrial and commercial use   ......
    (d) Power generation   ......
    (e) Navigation   ......
    (f) Environmental purpose (instream use, etc.)   ......

2.2.3. Is such prioritization rooted (*tick one or more*) in
    (a) Equity concerns   ......
    (b) Resource conditions   ......
    (c) Economic considerations   ......
    (d) Any other, specify (e.g., historical reasons)   ......
    ....

2.3. Project Selection Criteria

2.3.1. Indicate (*by ticking*) the dominant criteria used in water
project selection

Criterion		*Irrigation project*	*Urban project*	*Multipurpose scheme*
(a)	Benefit–cost ratio	. . . .	. . . . . .	. . . .
(b)	Internal rate of return	. . . .	. . . . . .	. . . .
(c)	Equity factors	. . . .	. . . . . .	. . . .
(d)	Ecological factors	. . . .	. . . . . .	. . . .
(e)	Any other, specify			
	. . . .	. . . .	. . . . . .	. . . .

2.3.2. In case more than one criterion is used, please indicate your
judgment as to the *percentage (or proportion)* of projects using
each criterion

Criterion		*Irrigation project*	*Urban project*	*Multipurpose scheme*
(a)	Benefit–cost ratio	. . . .	. . . . . .	. . . .
(b)	Internal rate of return	. . . .	. . . . . .	. . . .
(c)	Equity factors	. . . .	. . . . . .	. . . .
(d)	Ecological factors	. . . .	. . . . . .	. . . .
(e)	Any other, specify			
	. . . .	. . . .	. . . . . .	. . . .

2.3.3. If the project selection criteria vary by the type of project, please
indicate (*by ticking*).

Criterion		*Local fund*	*Foreign fund/ aid*	*New const- ruction*	*Improv- ing old projects*	*Managerial improvement/ institutional improvement*
(a)	Benefit–cost ratio	. . .	. . . .	. . .	. . . .	. . . .
(b)	Internal rate of return	. . .	. . . .	. . .	. . . .	. . . .
(c)	Equity factors	. . .	. . . .	. . .	. . . .	. . . .
(d)	Ecological factors	. . .	. . . .	. . .	. . . .	. . . .
(e)	Any other, specify					
	. . . .	. . .	. . . .	. . .	. . . .	. . . .

2.3.4. Do you feel that the recent trend in project-selection
criteria is toward economic orientation?   Yes/No

2.4.   Pricing and Cost Recovery

2.4.1   How often are water prices or charges revised? (*Please tick*)

	Irrigation	*Domestic use Urban/Rural*	*Industrial*
(a) Often	......	......	......
(b) Infrequently	......	......	......
(c) Rarely	......	......	......
(d) Not revised	......	......	......

2.4.2.   Water pricing is based on (*Please tick*)

(a) Full cost recovery	......	......	......
(b) Partial recovery	......	......	......
(c) Full subsidy	......	......	......

2.5.   Interregional and Intersectoral Water Transfers

2.5.1.   Are there well-established policies or precedents for
   (a)   Interregional water transfers   Yes/No
   (b)   Intersectoral water transfers   Yes/No

2.5.2.   If yes, what is the dominant basis for such transfers?
   (*Tick one or more*)

	Interregional	*Intersectoral*
(a) Equity concerns	....	....
(b) Resource conditions	....	....
(c) Economic considerations	....	....
(d) Any other, specify	....	....

2.5.3.   What is the dominant means for such water transfers?
   (*Tick one or more*)

	Interregional	*Intersectoral*
(a) Purely a political decision	....	....
(b) Administrative dictates	....	....
(c) Negotiation	....	....
(d) Water market: (i) Macro	....	....
(ii) Micro	....	....
(e) Any other, specify	....	....

2.5.4. What is the organizational basis for water transfers?
(*Tick one or more*)

		Interregional	Intersectoral
(a)	River boards	. . . .	. . . .
(b)	Basin-level organizations	. . . .	. . . .
(c)	Tribunals	. . . .	. . . .
(d)	Other decentralized systems (Stakeholders, WUAs, etc.)	. . . .	. . . .

2.5.5. Efficiency and extensiveness of water transfers (*on a 1 to 10 scale*)

		Interregional transfers	Intersectoral transfers
(a)	How extensive are they?		
	(i) Macro level	. . . .	. . . .
	(ii) Micro level	. . . .	. . . .
(b)	How smooth are they?		
	(i) Macro level	. . . .	. . . .
	(ii) Micro level	. . . .	. . . .

2.6. Other Policies Affecting Water Development/Use

2.6.1 Other policies affecting water development/use

		Tick	(*1 to 10*)
(a)	Agricultural policies	. . . . .	. . . .
(b)	Energy and power policies	. . . . .	. . . .
(c)	Soil conservation policies	. . . . .	. . . .
(d)	Pollution control and environmental policies	. . . . .	. . . .
(e)	Fiscal policies (structural adjustment)	. . . . .	. . . .
(f)	Credit and investment policies	. . . . .	. . . .
(g)	Foreign investment and aid policies	. . . . .	. . . .
(h)	Others, specify (e.g., trade policies)		
	. . . .	. . . . .	. . . .

2.7. Privatization and Decentralization Tendencies

2.7.1. Do state policies favor water sector privatization?   Yes/No

2.7.2. If yes, how favorable are those policies (*on a 1 to 10 scale*)?

(a)	Irrigation	. . . . . .
(b)	Urban domestic use	. . . . . .
(c)	Rural domestic use	. . . . . .
(d)	Industrial and commercial use	. . . . . .

2.7.3. How extensive is private sector participation (*on a 1 to 10 scale*)?
    (a) Irrigation   . . . . . .
    (b) Urban domestic use   . . . . . .
    (c) Rural domestic use   . . . . . .
    (d) Industrial and commercial use   . . . . . .

2.7.4. In your opinion, how well are users disposed toward private sector involvement in the water sector? (*Tick one*)
    (a) Favorable overall   . . . . . .
    (b) Favorable in particular sector   . . . . . .
    (c) Not favorable   . . . . . .
    (d) Indifferent   . . . . . .
    (e) Opposed   . . . . . .

2.7.5. Do state policies favor user participation and decentralization?   Yes/No

2.7.6. If yes, how favorable are these policies (*on a 1 to 10 scale*)?

	Planning	*Development*	*Management*
(a) Irrigation	. . . . . .	. . . .	. . . .
(b) Urban domestic use	. . . . . .	. . . .	. . . .
(c) Rural domestic use	. . . . . .	. . . .	. . . .
(d) Industrial and commercial use	. . . . . .	. . . .	. . . .

2.7.7. How extensive is user participation (*on a 1 to 10 scale*)?

	Planning	*Development*	*Management*
(a) Irrigation	. . . . . .	. . . .	. . . .
(b) Urban domestic use	. . . . . .	. . . .	. . . .
(c) Rural domestic use	. . . . . .	. . . .	. . . .
(d) Industrial and commercial use	. . . . . .	. . . .	. . . .

2.7.8. How well are government officials disposed toward user participation and decentralization? (*Tick one*)

	User Participation	*Decentralization*
(a) Favorable overall	. . . .	. . . .
(b) Favorable in selective contexts	. . . .	. . . .
(c) Not favorable	. . . .	. . . .
(d) Indifferent	. . . .	. . . .
(e) Opposed	. . . .	. . . .

2.7.9.   How effective is participation of NGOs (users, private
         sector, and foreign funding and technical agencies) in the
         water sector (*on a 1 to 10 scale*)?

	Resource Development			Distribution	Management
	Planning	*Finance*	*Execution*		

I. Irrigation
    (a) User groups   ....
    (b) Private sector   ....
    (c) Foreign aid/
         Funding
         agencies   ....
    (d) Foreign private
         technical firms   ....

II. Domestic Use
    (a) User groups   ....
    (b) Private sector   ....
    (c) Foreign aid/
         Funding
         agencies   ....
    (d) Foreign private
         technical firms   ....

2.8.   Policies toward Water Technologies, Extension, and Recycling

2.8.1.   How effective are these policies (*on a 1 to 10 scale*)?
    (a)   Water technology policies
          (i)   Measuring devices   ......
          (ii)   Recycling technologies   ......
          (iii)   Drip systems   ......
          (iv)   Sprinkler systems   ......
          (v)   Any other, specify
                  ....
    (b)   Water technology policies
          (i)   Water-saving methods   ......
          (ii)   Climate and rain forecasts   ......
          (iii)   Drought-resistant crops and farming practices   ......
          (iv)   Water quality and sanitation   ......
          (v)   Any other, specify
                  ....

    (c)   Water technology policies
           (i)   Regulatory policies   . . . . . .
           (ii)   Incentive policies   . . . . . .
           (iii)   Research, extension, and education   . . . . . .
           (iv)   Any other, specify

                   . . . .
    (d)   Technological application policies
           (i)   Satellites and remote sensing   . . . . . .
           (ii)   Computers   . . . . . .
           (iii)   Geographical information system   . . . . . .
           (iv)   Management information system   . . . . . .
           (v)   Any other, specify

                   . . . .

2.9.   Linkage Between Water Law and Water Policy

2.9.1.   How well does water policy reflect water law
        (*on a 1 to 10 scale*)?   . . . . . .

2.10.   Overall Evaluation

2.10.1. How effective is the overall water policy in addressing
        sectoral challenges (*on a 1 to 10 scale*)?   . . . . . .

---

3.   WATER ADMINISTRATION

3.1.   Government Branches and Departments Influencing the Water Sector

3.1.1.   Indicate your judgment on the relative role and influence
        of government branches on the water sector (*on a 1 to 10 scale*)

	Irrigation use	Domestic use	Industrial
(a) Central or federal government	. . . .	. . . .	. . . .
(b) State or regional government	. . . .	. . . .	. . . .
(c) Local government	. . . .	. . . .	. . . .
(d) Statutory bodies and authorities	. . . .	. . . .	. . . .

3.1.2.   Is there an exclusive department for water?   Yes/No

3.1.3.   If not, indicate (*on a 1 to 10 scale*) the influence of departments
         on the water sector
         (a)   Water resources/irrigation department   . . . . . .
         (b)   Agricultural department   . . . . . .
         (c)   Environment and forest department   . . . . . .
         (d)   Urban and local administrative department   . . . . . .
         (e)   Legal department   . . . . . .
         (f)   Others, specify (e.g., economic affairs, finance)   . . . . . .

3.1.4.   To what extent is administrative coordination achieved
         (*on 1 to 10 scale*)?   . . . . . .

3.1.5.   Is there a specialized agency for different subsectors?   Yes/No

3.1.6.   If yes, name the agency for each subsector:
         Surface water   . . . .
         Groundwater   . . . .
         Water quality   . . . .
         Recycling   . . . .
         Irrigation   . . . .
         Urban use   . . . .
         Rural use   . . . .
         Hydropower   . . . .

3.1.7.   If there is no exclusive department for water sector or
         specialized agencies for different subsectors, indicate
         (*on a 1 to 10 scale*) the extent to which this lacuna
         deters better water administration . . . .

3.2.   Organizational Basis and Structure of Water Administration

3.2.1.   How is the water administration organized? (*Tick one*)
         (a)   On administrative division (geographical basis)   . . . . . .
         (b)   On hydrogeological regions   . . . . . .
         (c)   River basins   . . . . . .
         (d)   Mixture of all   . . . . . .

3.2.2. How strong is the functional capacity in the following
spheres (*on a 1 to 10 scale*)?
(a) Planning and design . . . . . .
(b) Implementation . . . . . .
(c) Financial management . . . . . .
(d) Operation and maintenance . . . . . .
(e) Rehabilitation and resettlement . . . . . .
(f) Environmental monitoring . . . . . .
(g) Research, training, and extension . . . . . .
(h) Interagency or departmental relationships . . . . . .
(i) Others, specify (e.g., public relations, accountability) . . . . . .

3.2.3. Is functional specialization within the water administration
balanced? Yes/No

3.2.4. If no, what are the gaps in the existing administrative set-up?
(*Please list them with their priority ranking*)

3.3. Financing and Staffing Pattern

3.3.1. Do you feel the water administration budget is adequate
to meet the modernization and strengthening objectives? Yes/No

3.3.2. If yes, how serious is the budget constraint
(*on a 1 to 10 scale*)? . . . . . .

3.3.3. Is the water administration overstaffed? Yes/No

3.3.4. If yes, how wide is the scope for staff reduction
(*on a 1 to 10 scale*)? . . . . . .

3.3.5. Can privatization and community participation
lead to redundancy in water administration? Yes/No

3.3.6. If yes, how strong is the staff-reduction effect
(*on a 1 to 10 scale*)?
(a) Privatization . . . . . .
(b) User participation . . . . . .

3.3.7. If no, do privatization and user participation complement
but not substitute in the staffing context? Yes/No

3.4. Water Pricing and Fee Collection Bodies

3.4.1. Is there an independent body for determining water price?   Yes/No

3.4.2. If yes, state the name of the body and its relationship
to water administration
(a) Name   . . . .
(b) Administrative relationship . . . .

3.4.3. If no, which agencies are involved in price determination?
(*Please list them for various water uses such as irrigation,
water supply, etc.*).

3.4.4. Are the price determination and fee collection
functions performed by the same agency?   Yes/No

3.4.5. If no, which agency performs fee collection?
(*Please list them*)

3.5. Regulatory and Accountability Mechanisms

3.5.1. What are the regulatory mechanisms and how effective
are they at the implementation stage?

		Mechanism (*Tick*)	*Effectiveness* (*on a 1 to 10 scale*)
(a)	Legal regulations	. . . .	. . . .
(b)	Administrative directions	. . . .	. . . .
(c)	Pollution control agencies	. . . .	. . . .
(d)	River boards	. . . .	. . . .
(e)	Basin organizations	. . . .	. . . .
(f)	Groundwater regulations		
	(i) Depth restrictions	. . . .	. . . .
	(ii) Spacing regulations	. . . .	. . . .
(g)	Withdrawal restrictions	. . . .	. . . .
	(Water rights, quota)		
(h)	Limits on moving water across	. . . .	. . . .
	regions (surface water)		
(i)	Any other, specify	. . . .	. . . .

3.5.2. In what way are the legal provisions of accountability administratively (or organizationally) translated and how effective are they in practice?

		(Tick)	*(on a 1 to 10 scale)*
(a)	**Within formal water administration**		
	(i) Administrative supervision	. . . .	. . . .
	(ii) Financial auditing (public accounts committees)	. . . .	. . . .
	(iii) Work auditing	. . . .	. . . .
	(iv) Grievance cells	. . . .	. . . .
	(v) Monitoring procedure for sectoral and regional water allocation	. . . .	. . . .
	(vi) Interministerial committees	. . . .	. . . .
	(vii) Any other, specify	. . . .	. . . .
(b)	**Outside formal water administration**		
	(i) Local user groups	. . . .	. . . .
	(ii) NGOs	. . . .	. . . .
	(iii) Local administration (government)	. . . .	. . . .
	(iv) Any other, specify (statutory bodies)	. . . .	. . . .

3.6.   Information Basis of Water Sector

3.6.1. Is there a separate wing within water administration for water data collection, updating, and maintenance?   Yes/No

3.6.2. If yes, please state the name of the agency

3.6.3. If no, which other agency or agencies maintain water data? (*Please list them*)

3.6.4. Are water data published regularly?   Yes/No

3.6.5. Are water data computerized?   Yes/No

3.6.6. How adequate and reliable (*on a 1 to 10 scale*) are water data for planning purposes?
        (a) Adequacy   . . . . . .
        (b) Reliability   . . . . . .

3.6.7. How strong (*on a 1 to 10 scale*) is the information flow
between irrigation and water departments and water and
land research institutes, experiment stations, and universities
and experts?
(a) Research institutes   . . . . . .
(b) Experiment stations   . . . . . .
(c) Universities and experts   . . . . . .

3.6.8. How strongly (*on a 1 to 10 scale*) does the water
administration influence the research agenda of the
research institutes, experiment stations, and universities
and experts?
(a) Research institutes   . . . . . .
(b) Experiment stations   . . . . . .
(c) Universities and experts   . . . . . .

3.6.9. Do you feel the ongoing research adequately addresses the
emerging issues in the water sector (*on a 1 to 10 scale*)?   . . . . . .

3.7.   Use of Science and Technology in Water Administration

3.7.1. Please indicate (*on a 1 to 10 scale*) the extent to which
the following science and technology components are
used within water administration
(a) Computers   . . . . . .
(b) Remote sensing and satellite   . . . . . .
(c) Research and experimental information   . . . . . .
(d) Modern accounting and auditing techniques   . . . . . .
(e) Management information system   . . . . . .
(f) Geographic information system   . . . . . .
(g) Wireless communication   . . . . . .
(h) Water-measuring technology   . . . . . .
(i) Computerized dynamic regulation
of canal and water delivery networks   . . . . . .
(j) Any other, specify   . . . . . .

3.8.   Overall Evaluation

3.8.1. How strong are the administrative and technical linkages
between water administration and the research system
(*on a 1 to 10 scale*)?   . . . . . .

3.8.2. How adequate is the administrative set-up to operationalize
water policy and water law (*on a 1 to 10 scale*)?   . . . . . .

---

4.   WATER SECTOR & WATER INSTITUTION: OVERALL PERFORMANCE

4.1. Physical Performance (*on a 1 to 10 scale*)
(a)   Ability to bridge overall demand–supply gap   . . . . . .
(b)   Physical health of water development projects   . . . . . .
(b)   Conflict-resolution efficiency (low cost and less time)   . . . . . .
(c)   Smoothness of water transfers across sectors and regions . . . . . .
(d)   Smoothness of water transfers between users   . . . . . .

4.2. Financial Performance (*on a 1 to 10 scale*)
(a)   Actual investment vs. investment requirements   . . . . . .
(b)   Cost recovery vs. expenditure   . . . . . .

4.3. Economic Efficiency (*on a 1–10 scale*)
(a)   Extent to which water prices cover supply cost   . . . . . .
(b)   Extent to which water prices cover scarcity value   . . . . . .

4.4. Equity Performance (*on a 1 to 10 scale*)
(a)   Equity between regions   . . . . . .
(b)   Equity between sectors   . . . . . .
(c)   Equity among social groups   . . . . . .

4.5. Progressivesness of Water Institution
(*on a 1 to 10 scale*)   . . . . . .
(Key considerations here include factors such as
effectiveness, flexibility, adaptability, technological
applications, innovation, openness to change, etc.).

Appendix B: List of experts who provided inputs and data

(The following titles and addresses reflect individuals' positions at the time of their contribution)

1. Sawfat Abdel-Dayem, Rural Development Department, World Bank, Washington, D.C., USA.
2. Hamden Abdelkader, Agence Génie Rural, Ministry of Agriculture, Tunis, Tunisia.
3. Reiichi Abe, CTI Engineering Co., Ltd., Tokyo, Japan.
4. Terence Abeysekara, Economist, World Bank Mission, Colombo, Sri Lanka.
5. Ahmed M. Adam, Ministry of Irrigation and Water Resources, Khartoum, Sudan.
6. Pedro Arrojo Agudo, Depatamento de Análisis Económico, Universidad de Zaragoza, Zaragoza, Spain.
7. José Newton Mamed Aguiar, Diretor de Operacoes, Endereco Av. Duque de Caxias, Fortaleza, Brazil.
8. Amilpa Enrique Aguilar, International Consultant, Mexico City, Mexico.
9. Muhamad Ait Kadi, Director General, Agence Génie Rural, Rabat, Morocco.
10. Guy J. Alaerts, EASEN, and International Institute for Hydraulic and Environmental Engineering, Delft, The Netherlands.
11. Luis Miguel Albisu, Unidad de Economía y Sociología Agrarias, Servicio de Investigación Agraria, Diputación General de Aragon, Zaragoza, Spain.
12. Angel A. Alejandrino, National Hydraulic Research Center, Quezon City, Philippines.
13. Omar Aloui, Economist, Agro Concept, Rabat, Morocco.
14. Denisard Oliveira Alves, Faculdade de Economia, Universidade de São Paulo, São Paulo, Brazil.
15. P.B. Anand, Development and Project Planning Centre, University of Bradford, Bradford, England.
16. Julio Barragan Arce, University of Minnesota, St. Paul, Minnesota, USA.

17. Saul Arlozoroff, International Consultant, Tel Aviv, Israel.
18. Luiz Gabriel de Azevedo, World Bank Mission, Brasilia, Brazil.
19. Gerhard R. Backeberg, Research Manager, Water Research Commission, Pretoria, South Africa.
20. Jonathan Baldry, Department of Economics, University of New England, Armidale, Australia.
21. Tissa Bandaragoda, International Water Management Institute (IWMI), Pakistan Office, Lahore, Pakistan.
22. Banduratne, Deputy Director, National Planning Department, Colombo, Sri Lanka.
23. Zanetta Eduardo Bartholin, Director, Commision Nacional de Riego (CNR), Ministerio Obras Publicas (MOP), Santiago, Chile.
24. George Bawtree, Manager, Competition and Pricing, Sydney Waters, Sydney, Australia.
25. Mhamed Belghiti, Agence Génie Rural, Rabat, Morocco.
26. Hassan Benabderrazik, Agro Concept, Rabat, Morocco.
27. Eyal Benvenisti, Faculty of Law, Hebrew University, Jerusalem, Israel.
28. Krzysztof Berbeka, Cracow University of Economics, Cracow, Poland.
29. Laudo Asesor Bernardes, Cabinete do Ministro, Ministerio do Medio Ambiente, dos Recursos Hidricos e da Amazonia Legal (MMARHAL), Brasilia, Brazil.
30. Armando Bertranou, CONICET, Consejo Nacional de Investigaciones Cientificas y Técnicas, Buenos Aires, Argentina.
31. Alfred Birch, Senior Technical Advisor (Asian Development Bank), Water Resources Secretariat, International Irrigation Management Institute, Colombo, Sri Lanka.
32. Alejandro Vergara Blanco, Professor of Law, Pontífica Universidad Católica de Chile, Santiago, Chile.
33. Benedito Braga, Department of Hydraulic and Sanitary Engineering, University of São Paulo, Brazil.
34. Marcos E.F. Brandao, Consultant, Secretariat of Water Resources, Brasilia, Brazil.
35. Eberhard Braune, Department of Water Affairs and Forestry, Pretoria, South Africa.
36. Emiunuo Rodríguez Briceno, Mexico City, Mexico.
37. João Castro Caldas, Instituto Superior de Agronomia, Lisbon, Portugal.
38. Bernardo Lopez Camacho, Jefe Departamento de Aguas Subterraneas, Canal de Isabel II, Madrid, Spain.
39. Elias Fereres Castiel, Instituto de Agricultura Sostenible, Cordoba, Spain.
40. Juan Carlos Jofre Chamy, Comisión Nacional de Medio Ambiente, Santiago, Chile.

41. Mohamed Chaouni, Divisia de la Legislatia d'Eaux, Administration de Hydraulique, Rabat, Morocco.
42. Henrique Marinho Leite Chaves, Especialista em Gerenciamente de Projectos, Convenio SRH/DNOCS/IICA, Instituto Interamicano de Cooperacao para a Agricultura, Brasilia, Brazil.
43. Dongcheng Beidajie Choyangmen, District Manager, Beijing, China.
44. Alan Conley, Director, Information Service, Department of Water Affairs and Forestry (DWAF), Pretoria, South Africa.
45. Manuel Contijoch Escontria, Director General, FIRCO, Ministry of Agriculture and Former Deputy Director General, CNA, Mexico City, Mexico.
46. Oscar de Moraes Cordeiro Netto, Professor Adjuncto, Departamento de Engenharia Civil, Universidade de Brasilia, Brasilia, Brazil.
47. Eduardo P. Corsiga, Quezon City, Philippines.
48. Marca A. Cruz, Metropolitan Waterworks and Sewerage System, Quezon City, Philippines.
49. Ralph J. Daley, United Nations University, Hamilton, Ontario, Canada.
50. Danasuriya, Additional Director (Institutional Development), Irrigation Management Division, Irrigation Secretariat, Colombo, Sri Lanka.
51. Baryohay Davidoff, Agricultural Water Conservation Unit, Sacramento, California, USA.
52. Rudolf de Munnik, GIS Specialist, ISCW, ARC, Pretoria, South Africa.
53. Cesare Dosi, University of Padova, Department of Economics, and Fondazione Eni Enrico Mattei, Padova, Italy.
54. Rachid Doukkali, Département des Sciences Humaines, Institut Agronomique et Vétérinaire Hassan II, Rabat, Morocco.
55. Joseph Draizin, Director, Planning Department, Water Commission, Tel Aviv, Israel.
56. Herbert Drummond, SGAN Quadra 601 Conj. 1 Sala 302, Brasilia, Brazil.
57. Rolfe Eberhard, University of London, New York, NY, USA.
58. Nihal Fernando, World Bank Mission, Colombo, Sri Lanka.
59. Mohamed Larbi Firdawcy, Department of Agriculture, Rabat, Morocco.
60. Antonio Coch Flotats, Jefe de la Oficina de Planificación Hidrología, CHE, MMA, Zarargoza, Spain.
61. Robert French, Centre for Water Policy Research (CWPR), Univerisity of New England, Armidale, Australia.
62. Alberto Garrido, Departamento de Económia, Universidad Politécnica de Madrid, Madrid, Spain.
63. R. Gary, Illinois Department of Natural Resources, Springfield, Illinois, USA.

64. Raj Goyal, Manager, Commercial and Economic Services, Sydney Waters, Sydney, Australia.
65. Siripong Hungspreug, Director Project Planning Division, Royal Irrigation Department, Bangkok, Thailand.
66. Ahmed Hajji, Office National de l'Eau Potable, Rabat, Morocco.
67. Tatsuo Hamaguchi, Water Resources Department, Tokyo, Japan.
68. Gu Hao, Director General, Department of Water Administration and Water Resources (DOWAWR), Ministry of Water Resources (MOWR), Beijing, China.
69. Guillermo Donoso Hariss, Director, Departmento de Económia Agraria, Pontifica Universidad Católica de Chile, Santiago, Chile.
70. Mehmood W. Hassan, International Irrigation Management Institute, Lahore, Pakistan.
71. Robert Hearne, CATIE, Turrialba, Costa Rica.
72. Liu Heng, Assistant Director, Nanjing Institute of Hydrology and Water Resources (NIHWR), MOWR, Nanjing, China.
73. José Alberto Herreras Espino, Presidente, SYNCONSULT, S.L., Madrid, Spain.
74. Paul Herrington, University of Leicester, Leicester, England.
75. Ivanildo Hespanhol, Department of Hydraulic and Sanitary Engineering, Universidade de São Paulo, São Paulo, Brazil.
76. Pieter Heyns, Department of Water Affairs, Namibia.
77. A.K.M. Shawsul Hoque, Bangladesh Water Development Board, Dhaka, Bangladesh.
78. Ted Horbulyk, University of Calgary, Calgary, AB, Canada.
79. Richard Howitt, University of California, Davis, California, USA.
80. Ching-Kai Hsiao, National Chung-Hsing University, Taichung, Taiwan.
81. Pieter Huisman, Integrated Water Management, The Netherlands.
82. H. Koensatwanto Inpasihardo, Irrigation Systems Research and Investigation, Jakarta, Indonesia.
83. Antonio Embid Irujo, Deparmento a Derecho Público, Universidad de Zaragoza, Zaragoza, Spain.
84. Maria Iskandarani, Center for Development Research, Bonn, Germany.
85. Shirazul Islam, Engineers' Institution, Bangladesh, Dhaka, Bangladesh.
86. Brobwen Jackman, School of Law, University of New England, Armidale, Australia.
87. Mohammed Jellali, Director General, Administration de Hydraulique, Rabat, Morocco.
88. Sam H. Johnson III, Council for International Development, Tucson, Arizona, USA.
89. Wayne R. Jordan, Texas Water Resources Institute, College Station, Texas, USA.

90. Xu Zi Kai, Engineer, NIHWR, MOWR, Nanjing, China.
91. Elisha Kally, Water Expert, Tel Aviv, Israel.
92. Menachem Kantor, Former Water Commissioner, Kibutz Maagan Michael, Israel.
93. Gian N. Kathpalia, Surya Foundation, New Delhi, India.
94. Ratneshwar Lal Kayastha, Ministry of Water Resources, His Majesty's Government of Nepal, Katmandu, Nepal.
95. Jerson Kelman, Federal University of Rio de Janeiro, Rio de Janeiro, RJ, Brazil.
96. Karin Kemper, World Bank, Washington, DC, USA.
97. Julio Thadeu S. Kettelhut, Departamento de Gestão de Aguas Federais, Secretario de Recursos Hidricos (SRH), MMARHAL, Brasilia, Brazil.
98. Janusz Kindler, Warsaw University of Technology, Institute of Environmental Engineering Systems, Warsaw, Poland.
99. Johann Kirsten, Head, Department of Agricultural Economics, University of Pretoria, Pretoria, South Africa.
100. Yoav Kislev, Department of Agricultural Economics, Hebrew University of Jerusalem, Rehovot, Israel.
101. Federico Aguilera Klink, Department of Economics, University of Laguna, Tenerife Island (WS), Spain.
102. Reinhard Kuschke, Agro-meteorology Specialist, ISCW, ARC, Pretoria, South Africa.
103. Ruth Lapidoth, Faculty of Law, Hebrew University, Jerusalem, Israel.
104. Mohamed Firdawcy Larbi, Director of Research, Department of Agriculture, Rabat, Morocco.
105. Henrique Marinho Chaves Leite, SRH/DNOCS/IICA, Instituto Interamericano de Cooperação para a Agricultura, Brasilia, Brazil.
106. James van der Linde, Director of Water Supply, Hermanus, Western Cape, South Africa.
107. Jiang Liping, Water Resources Engineer, World Bank Mission, Beijing, China.
108. Changming Liu, United Research Center for Water Problems, Chinese Academy of Sciences, Beijing, China.
109. Ramon Llamas, Departamento de Geodinamica, Universidad Complutense, Madrid, Spain.
110. Bernardo Lopez-Camacho, Jefe Departamento de Aguas Subterraneas, Canal de Isabel II, Madrid, Spain.
111. Janet Love, MP, Auckland Park 2006, Johannesburg, South Africa.
112. Zhang Hai Lun, Advisor, Nanjing Institute of Hydrology and Water Resources, MOWR, Nanjing, China.
113. Barkat Ali Luna, National Development Consultants, Lahore, Pakistan.
114. Zhang Hai Lung, NIHWR, MOWR, Nanjing, China.

115. Larry MacDonald, Boulder, Colorado, USA.
116. Gordon Maclear, Geohydrologist, DWAF, Cape Town, Western Cape, South Africa.
117. Josefina Maetsu, Director, Ecotech Research and Consulting Ltd., Madrid, Spain.
118. Rodrigo Maia, Laboratório de Hidráulica, Recursos Hídricos e Ambiente, Faculdade de Engenharia de Universidade do Porto, Porto Codex, Portugal.
119. Tomas A. Sancho Marco, Presidente, Confederación Hidrografica del Ebro, Ministerio de Medio Ambiente, Zaragoza, Spain.
120. Manuel Omedas Margeli, Secretario Tecnico de Presidencia, Confederacion Hidrografica del Ebro (CHE), MMA, Zaragoza, Spain.
121. Piet Maritz, Director, Agricultural Engineering, National Department of Agriculture, Pretoria, South Africa.
122. Warren Martin, Water Management Task Force, Ministry of Land and Water Conservation, GONSW, Sydney, Australia.
123. José Maria Santafe Martinez, Jefe de Area de Planes y Programas, Ministerio de Medio Ambiente, Madrid, Spain.
124. Warren Musgrave, Advisor, Premier's Department, Government of New South Wales (GONSW), Sydney, Australia.
125. Antonio Massarutto, Dipartimento di Scienze Economiche, Università di Udine, Udine, Italy.
126. Martin Mateo, San Juan, Spain.
127. Jennifer McKay, Policy and Law Group, University of South Australia, Adelaide, Australia.
128. Ruth Meinzen-Dick, International Food Policy, Research Institute, Washington, DC, USA.
129. Billy Mejia, Institutional Development Division, National Irrigation Administration, Quezon City, Philippines.
130. Kevin Melville, Senior Economist, Sydney Waters, Sydney, Australia.
131. Douglas Merrey, IWMI, Colombo, Sri Lanka.
132. Dries van der Merve, Institute for Soil, Climate and Water Agricultural Research Council, Pretoria, South Africa.
133. José Eduardo Mestre, Basin Council Expert, Queretero, Mexico.
134. Josu Mezo, Analistas Socio-Politicas, Gabinete de Estudios, Madrid, Spain.
135. Peter Millington, Peter Millington & Associates, NSW, Australia.
136. Marcus Moench, ISET (a nonprofit research group), Boulder, Colorado, USA.
137. Khalid Mohtadullah, Water and Power Development Authority (WAPDA), Lahore, Pakistan.

138. M.P. Mosley, NIWA, Christchurch, New Zealand.
139. Eugenia Gerente Muchnik, Departmento Agroindustrial, Fundación Chile, Santiago, Chile.
140. U. Myo Myint, Director, Irrigation Department, Yangon, Myanmar.
141. Mikiyasu Nakayama, Utsunomiya University, Tochigi, Japan.
142. Navaratne, Deputy Commissioner, Agrarian Services Department, Colombo, Sri Lanka.
143. Dolora Nepomuceno, Laguna Lake Development Authority (LLDA), Manila, Philippines.
144. Van Tuu Nguyen, World Bank, Washington, DC, USA.
145. José Olivares, International Consultant, Santiago, Chile.
146. Martin Gonzalo Pacheco, Director (Hydraulics), SYNCONSULT, S.L., Madrid, Spain.
147. Enrique Palacios, Collegio de Postgraduados, Programa de Hydrociencias, Mexico City, Mexico.
148. Douglas Parker, University of Maryland, College Park, Maryland, USA.
149. Humberto Pena, Director General de Aguas, Ministerio de Obras Públicas (MOP), Santiago, Chile.
150. Nelson Pereira Munoz, Jefe Dpto. Ejecutivo, Comisión Nacidad de Riego, Santiago, Chile.
151. John J. Pigram, Executive Director, CWPR, University of New England, Armidale, Australia.
152. G.T. Keith Pitman, operations, Evaluation Department, World Bank, Washington, DC, USA.
153. Rogelio Galvan Plaza, Oficina de Planificación Hidrológica, Zaragoza, Spain.
154. José Maria Pliego Gutierrez, Director General, Sociedad Espanola de Estudios para la Fija a Traves del Estrecho de Gibralter, Madrid, Spain.
155. Monica Porte, Presidente, Associação Brasiliera de Recursos Hidricos, Universidade de São Paulo, São Paulo, Brazil.
156. Ruben Porte, Department of Hydraulic and Sanitary Engineering, Universidade de São Paulo, São Paulo, Brazil.
157. Dirk J. Pretorius, Remote Sensing Specialist, Institute for Soil, Climate, and Water (ISCW), Agricultural Research Council (ARC), Pretoria, South Africa.
158. Halla M. Qaddumi, Yale University, New Haven, Connecticut, USA.
159. Yu Qiyang, Engineer, DOWAWR, MOWR, Beijing, China.
160. Osman Qumar, World Bank Office, Islamabad, Pakistan.
161. Michael Racznski, Coordinador, Programa de Construcción y Rehabilitación de Obras de Riego Medianas y Menores, Santiago, Chile.
162. George E. Radosevich, Resources Administration and Development International, Inc., Boulder, Colorado, USA.

163. Muhammad Idris Rajput, Sindh Irrigation Department, Pakistan.
164. K.V. Raju, Institute for Social and Economic Change, Bangalore, India.
165. Kikeri Ramu, Private Consultant, Denver, Colorado, USA.
166. Ranjith Ratnayake, Director, Water Resources Development, Ministry of Irrigation and Power (MOIP), Colombo, Sri Lanka.
167. Akanda Abdur Razzaque, Engineers' Institution of Bangladesh, Dhaka, Bangladesh.
168. Collin Reid, Chief Manager, Water and Transport, Independent Pricing and Regulatory Tribunal, New South Wales, Sydney, Australia.
169. Steven Renzetti, Department of Economics, Brook University, Ontario, Canada.
170. Fernardo A. Rodriguez, Director de Departamento, SRH, MMARHAL, Brasilia, Brazil.
171. Emiliano Rodriquez, Irrigation Engineer and Consultant, Queretero, Mexico.
172. Mieczyslaw Rutkowski, Regional Board of Water Management, Middle Vistula River Basin, Warsaw, Poland.
173. Abdin M.A. Salih, UNESCO Cairo Office, Cairo, Egypt.
174. Tomas A. Sancho Marco, Presidente, CHE, MMA, Zaragoza, Spain.
175. Ampara Núñez Sandoval, Empresa de Metropolitina de Obras Sanitarias, Santiago, Chile.
176. Ernesto Bohórquez Schulbach, Secretario Ejecutiva, CNR, MOP Santiago, Chile.
177. Michael Schur, Ernst and Young, South Africa.
178. Uri Shamir, Water Research Institute, Haifa, Israel.
179. Joshuwa Shvartz, TAHAL Water Company, Tel Aviv, Israel.
180. José Simas, World Bank Mission, Mexico City, Mexico.
181. Larry D. Simpson, Water Resource Management Consultant, World Bank Mission, Brasilia, Brazil.
182. Hong Sinara, No. 23, Mao Tse Toung Road, Phnom Penh, Cambodia.
183. Gaylord Skogerboe, IWMI, Pakistan Office, Lahore, Pakistan.
184. Soenarno, Senior Water Resources Engineer, Directorate General of Water Resources Development, Ministry of Public Works, Jakarta, Indonesia.
185. Miguel Solanes, Economic Commission for Latin America and the Caribbean, United Nations, Santiago, Chile.
186. Oudet Souvannavong, Sustainable Irrigated Agriculture Project, Lao PDR.
187. Geoff Spencer, World Bank, Washington, DC, USA.
188. Yuri N. Steklov, Economic Affairs Officer, Economic and Social Commission for Asia and Pacific, United Nations, Bangkok, Thailand.

189. Robyn Stein, Water Law Expert, Johannesburg, South Africa.
190. Ashok Subramanian, World Bank, Washington, DC, USA.
191. N. Suryanarayan, Deputy Director General (Water Resources Planning), Ministry of Water Resources, Government of India, New Delhi, India.
192. Kumiyoshi Takeuchi, Yamanashi University, Japan.
193. Jean-François Talec, Agence de L'Eau Loire-Bretange, Orleancs Cedex, France.
194. Donald M. Tate, Environment Canada, Ottawa, Ontario, Canada.
195. U. Myint Thwin, Deputy Director, Water Resources Utilization Department, Yangon, Myanmar.
196. Dirgha N. Tiwari, Katmandu, Nepal.
197. Cid Pompeu Tomanik, Pauru, Brazil.
198. Stefania Tonin, Fondazione Eni Enrico Mattei, Veneziz, Italy.
199. José Luis Trava, Commisión Nacional del Agua (CNA), Mexico City, Mexico.
200. Claus Triebel, Deputy Director General (Utilization), DWAF, Pretoria, South Africa.
201. Rodolfo C. Undan, Department of Agriculture, Elliptical Road, Dilliman, Quezon City, Philippines.
202. Consuelo Varela Ortega, Departamento de Económia, Universidad Politécnica de Madrid, Madrid, Spain.
203. B. George Verghese, Senior Fellow, Center for Policy Research, New Delhi, India.
204. Douglas Vermillion, IWMI, Colombo, Sri Lanka.
205. Eduardo J. Viesca de la Garza, Water Law Expert, Secretaría de Hacienda y Credito Público, Xochimilco, Mexico City, Mexico.
206. J.P. Villaret, World Bank, Washington DC, USA.
207. M.F. Vilyoen, University of the Free State, Blomfontein, South Africa.
208. Justus Wesseler, Oosterbeek, The Netherlands.
209. Wijayratna, International Irrigation Management Institute, Colombo, Sri Lanka.
210. L.T. WijeSooriya, Irrigation Department, Colombo, Sri Lanka.
211. Eric Wilkinson, Northern Colorado Water Conservancy District, Loveland, Colorado, USA.
212. Christina Wood, World Bank, Washington, DC, USA.
213. Mei Xie, World Bank, Washington, DC, USA.
214. Pham Xuan Su, Ministry of Agriculture and Rural Development, Hanoi, Vietnam.
215. Wei Yao-Rong, Legislative Affairs Commission, Beijing, China.
216. Dan Yaron, Department of Agricultural Economics, Hebrew University of Jerusalem, Rehovot, Israel.

217. Moon Yongkwan, Korea Water and Resources Corporation, Daejeon City, Korea.
218. Zou Youlan, Operations Officer, World Bank Mission, Beijing, China.
219. Slim Zekri, Department de Gestion de Développement, Tunis, Tunisia.
220. Jia Zemin, NIHWR, MOWR, Nanjing, China.
221. Mao Zhi, Irrigation Studies Section, Wuhan University of Hydraulic and Electrical Engineering (WUHEE), Wuhan, China.
222. Xu Zikai, NIHWR, MOWR, Nanjing, China.

Appendix C: mathematical analog for impact-transmission channels

The purpose of this Appendix is to show the derivation of the mathematical analog for the 63 impact-transmission channels associated with the exogenous variables listed in Table 10.1. The mathematical analog of the channels is represented in terms of the partial derivatives of the 10 equations in Model B with respect to the exogenous variables as well as to some of the endogenous variables entering as independent variables in a few equations. To compactly represent the partial derivatives, notations, rather than full names, are used to denote the variables. Thus, the 16 exogenous variables in the model are denoted by X_i ($i = 1, 2, \ldots, 16$) and the 10 endogenous variables by Y_j ($j = 1, 2, \ldots, 10$). For ready reference, the names and notations used for these variables are tabulated below.

Variable name	Notation used
LPRSRF	X_1
PGPIUP	X_2
POELWL	X_3
POPAWE	X_4
AIBDWP	X_5
PGPIPP	X_6
LOEPRV	X_7
AACCME	X_8
ABALFS	X_9
AARINF	X_{10}
LTRWSA	X_{11}
LINTRE	X_{12}
LOECEN	X_{13}
PPSCRI	X_{14}
AORGBA	X_{15}
AEXTST	X_{16}
LCRMEE	Y_1
PIRSWE	Y_2
PCOREC	Y_3

Variable name	Notation used
ASBUDC	Y_4
LACPRE	Y_5
LOEFWL	Y_6
POEFWP	Y_7
AOEFWA	Y_8
WIPOEV	Y_9
WSPOEV	Y_{10}

With the assigned notations for all the exogenous and endogenous variables, the 10 equations of Model B can be equally represented as:

$$Y_1 = F_1(X_1, X_2, X_4, X_9, X_{10}, X_{16})$$

$$Y_2 = F_2(X_1, Y_1, X_2, X_{16})$$

$$Y_3 = F_3(X_1, X_2, X_4, X_5)$$

$$Y_4 = F_4(X_2, X_5, Y_3, X_6)$$

$$Y_5 = F_5(X_1, X_3, Y_3, X_7, X_8)$$

$$Y_6 = F_6(X_1, X_5, Y_5, X_7, X_{11}, X_{12}, X_{13})$$

$$Y_7 = F_7(X_2, X_3, X_4, Y_3, X_6, X_{14}, Y_1)$$

$$Y_8 = F_8(X_5, X_8, X_9, X_{10}, X_{15}, Y_4, X_{16})$$

$$Y_9 = F_9(Y_6, Y_7, Y_8)$$

$$Y_{10} = F_{10}(Y_9, X_4, Y_3, X_{10}, Y_4, X_{16}).$$

Since the first nine equations are sequentially linked with the 10th equation, the 10 equations of Model B can also be written as a single equation:

$$Y_{10} = F_{10} \| F_9 \langle F_6 \{X_1, F_1(X_1, X_2, X_4, X_9, X_{10}, X_{16}), F_5 [X_1, X_3, F_3(X_1, X_2, X_4, X_5), X_7, X_8], X_7, X_{11}, X_{12}, X_{13}\},$$

$$F_7 \{X_2, X_3, X_4, F_3 (X_1, X_2, X_4, X_5), X_6, X_{14}, F_2 [X_1, F_1 (X_1, X_2, X_4, X_9, X_{10}, X_{16}), X_2, X_{16}]\},$$

$F_8 \{X_5, X_8, X_9, X_{10}, X_{15}, F_4 [X_2, X_5, F_3 (X_1, X_2, X_4, X_5), X_6],$
$X_{16}\}\rangle,$

$X_4, F_3 (X_1, X_2, X_4, X_5), X_{10}, F_4 [X_2, X_5, F_3 (X_1, X_2, X_4, X_5), X_6],$
$X_{16}\|.$

Notice that this equation is defined exclusively in terms of the 16 exogenous variables. By differentiating this equation with respect to each of the 16 exogenous variables, a mathematical description of all the impact-transmission channels can be provided and their impact transmission can be quantitatively evaluated in terms of the relevant value of the partial derivatives. As explained in Chapter 10, the partial derivative with respect to an exogenous variable is nothing but its coefficient in the relevant equation.

As we differentiate the single equation noted above with respect to X_1 (*LPRSRF*), we obtain the following differential chain:

$$\frac{\partial Y_{10}}{\partial X_1} = \frac{\partial F_{10}}{\partial X_9} \left\langle \frac{\partial F_9}{\partial F_6} \left\{ \frac{\partial F_6}{\partial X_1} + \frac{\partial F_6}{\partial F_1} \frac{\partial F_1}{\partial X_1} + \frac{\partial F_6}{\partial F_5} \left[\frac{\partial F_5}{\partial X_1} + \frac{\partial F_5}{\partial F_3} \frac{\partial F_3}{\partial X_1} \right] \right\} \right.$$

$$+ \frac{\partial F_9}{\partial F_7} \left\{ \frac{\partial F_7}{\partial F_3} \frac{\partial F_3}{\partial X_1} + \frac{\partial F_7}{\partial F_2} \left[\frac{\partial F_2}{\partial X_1} + \frac{\partial F_2}{\partial F_1} \frac{\partial F_1}{\partial X_1} \right] \right\}$$

$$\left. + \frac{\partial F_9}{\partial F_8} \left\{ \frac{\partial F_8}{\partial F_4} \frac{\partial F_4}{\partial F_3} \frac{\partial F_3}{\partial X_1} \right\} \right\rangle + \frac{\partial F_{10}}{\partial F_3} \left\{ \frac{\partial F_3}{\partial X_1} + \frac{\partial F_4}{\partial F_3} \frac{\partial F_3}{\partial X_1} \right\}.$$

As we expand this differential chain, we find 10 terms, each of which is defined by a product of two or more partial derivatives representing respectively the impact transmitted by the 10 channels associated with *LPRSRF*. Thus, the differential chain captures the total impact of a marginal change in *LPRSRF* transmitted in 10 different channels.

Similarly, when we differentiate the single equation with respect to X_2, the following differential chain captures the total impact of a marginal change in *PGPIUP* transmitted through 11 channels.

$$\frac{\partial Y_{10}}{\partial X_2} = \frac{\partial F_{10}}{\partial F_9} \left\langle \frac{\partial F_9}{\partial F_6} \left\{ \frac{\partial F_6}{\partial F_1} \frac{\partial F_1}{\partial X_2} + \frac{\partial F_6}{\partial F_5} \frac{\partial F_5}{\partial F_3} \frac{\partial F_3}{\partial X_2} \right\} \right.$$

$$+ \frac{\partial F_9}{\partial F_7} \left\{ \frac{\partial F_7}{\partial X_2} + \frac{\partial F_7}{\partial F_3} \frac{\partial F_3}{\partial X_2} + \frac{\partial F_7}{\partial F_2} \left[\frac{\partial F_2}{\partial F_1} \frac{\partial F_1}{\partial X_2} + \frac{\partial F_2}{\partial X_2} \right] \right\}$$

$$+ \frac{\partial F_9}{\partial F_8} \left\{ \frac{\partial F_8}{\partial F_4} \left[\frac{\partial F_4}{\partial X_2} + \frac{\partial F_4}{\partial F_3} \frac{\partial F_3}{\partial X_2} \right] \right\} \bigg/ + \frac{\partial F_{10}}{\partial F_3} \left\{ \frac{\partial F_3}{\partial X_2} \right\}$$

$$+ \frac{\partial F_{10}}{\partial F_4} \left\{ \frac{\partial F_4}{\partial X_2} + \frac{\partial F_4}{\partial F_3} \frac{\partial F_3}{\partial X_2} \right\}.$$

We can verify that the differential chain has 11 products of partial derivatives, the sum of which defines the total impact of a marginal change in *PGPIUP* on the ultimate dependent variable of the system, *WSPOEV*, representing the overall performance of water sector.

The differentiation of the single equation with respect to X_3 (*POELWL*) yields the following differential chain:

$$\frac{\partial Y_{10}}{\partial X_3} = \frac{\partial F_{10}}{\partial F_9} \left\langle \frac{\partial F_9}{\partial F_6} \left\{ \frac{\partial F_6}{\partial F_5} \frac{\partial F_5}{\partial X_3} \right\} + \frac{\partial F_9}{\partial F_7} \frac{\partial F_7}{\partial X_3} \right\rangle$$

As can be seen, this differential chain involves two product terms. These terms capture the impact of a marginal change in *POELWL* transmitted through its two impact-transmission channels.

The differentiation of the single equation with respect to X_4 (*POPAWE*) yields the following differential chain:

$$\frac{\partial Y_{10}}{\partial X_4} = \frac{\partial F_{10}}{\partial F_9} \left\langle \frac{\partial F_9}{\partial F_6} \left\{ \frac{\partial F_6}{\partial F_1} \frac{\partial F_1}{\partial X_4} + \frac{\partial F_6}{\partial F_5} \frac{\partial F_5}{\partial F_3} \frac{\partial F_3}{\partial X_4} \right\} \right.$$

$$+ \frac{\partial F_9}{\partial F_7} \left\{ \frac{\partial F_7}{\partial X_4} + \frac{\partial F_7}{\partial F_3} \frac{\partial F_3}{\partial X_4} + \frac{\partial F_7}{\partial F_2} \frac{\partial F_2}{\partial F_1} \frac{\partial F_1}{\partial X_4} \right\}$$

$$\left. + \frac{\partial F_9}{\partial F_8} \left\{ \frac{\partial F_8}{\partial F_4} \frac{\partial F_4}{\partial F_3} \frac{\partial F_3}{\partial X_4} \right\} \right\rangle \bigg/ \frac{\partial F_{10}}{\partial X_4} + \frac{\partial F_{10}}{\partial F_3} \frac{\partial F_3}{\partial X_4} + \frac{\partial F_{10}}{\partial F_4} \frac{\partial F_4}{\partial F_3} \frac{\partial F_3}{\partial X_4}.$$

This differential chain has nine terms. All terms except one involve the products of two or more partial derivatives. While these terms capture the indirect effects of *POPAWE*, the one with a single partial derivative captures its direct effect. In any case, these nine terms capture, respectively, the value of impact transmitted through the nine channels associated with *POPAWE*.

By differentiating the single equation with respect to X_5 (*AIBDWP*), we obtain the following differential chain consisting of eight terms, each representing the impact transmitted by the eight channels associated with *AIBDWP*:

$$\frac{\partial Y_{10}}{\partial X_5} = \frac{\partial F_{10}}{\partial F_9} \left\langle \frac{\partial F_9}{\partial F_6} \left\{ \frac{\partial F_6}{\partial F_5} \frac{\partial F_5}{\partial F_3} \frac{\partial F_3}{\partial X_5} \right\} + \frac{\partial F_9}{\partial F_7} \left\{ \frac{\partial F_7}{\partial F_3} \frac{\partial F_3}{\partial X_5} \right\} \right.$$

$$+ \frac{\partial F_9}{\partial F_8} \left\{ \frac{\partial F_8}{\partial X_5} + \frac{\partial F_8}{\partial F_4} \left[\frac{\partial F_4}{\partial X_5} + \frac{\partial F_4}{\partial F_3} \frac{\partial F_3}{\partial X_5} \right] \right\} \right\rangle$$

$$+ \frac{\partial F_{10}}{\partial F_3} \frac{\partial F_3}{\partial X_5} + \frac{\partial F_{10}}{\partial F_4} \left\{ \frac{\partial F_4}{\partial X_5} + \frac{\partial F_4}{\partial F_3} \frac{\partial F_3}{\partial X_5} \right\}.$$

The differentiation with respect to X_6 (*PGPIPP*) yields the following differential chain involving three terms corresponding to three impact-transmission channels associated with the exogenous variable in question:

$$\frac{\partial Y_{10}}{\partial X_6} = \frac{\partial F_{10}}{\partial F_9} \left\langle \frac{\partial F_9}{\partial F_7} \left\{ \frac{\partial F_7}{\partial F_6} \right\} + \frac{\partial F_9}{\partial F_8} \left\{ \frac{\partial F_8}{\partial F_4} \frac{\partial F_4}{\partial X_6} \right\} \right\rangle + \frac{\partial F_{10}}{\partial F_4} \frac{\partial F_4}{\partial X_6}.$$

Similarly, the differentiation with respect to X_7 (*LOEPRV*) and X_8 (*AACCME*) yields the following differential chains involving two terms each, representing the magnitude of the impact transmitted by the two channels associated with each of these exogenous variables:

$$\frac{\partial Y_{10}}{\partial X_7} = \frac{\partial F_{10}}{\partial F_9} \left\langle \frac{\partial F_9}{\partial F_6} \left\{ \frac{\partial F_6}{\partial F_5} \frac{\partial F_5}{\partial X_7} \right\} + \frac{\partial F_9}{\partial F_6} \frac{\partial F_6}{\partial X_7} \right\rangle \text{ and}$$

$$\frac{\partial Y_{10}}{\partial X_8} = \frac{\partial F_{10}}{\partial F_9} \left\langle \frac{\partial F_9}{\partial F_6} \left\{ \frac{\partial F_6}{\partial F_5} \frac{\partial F_5}{\partial X_8} \right\} + \frac{\partial F_9}{\partial F_8} \left\{ \frac{\partial F_8}{\partial X_8} \right\} \right\rangle.$$

As we differentiate the single equation with respect to X_9 (*ABALFS*), we obtain the following differential chain:

$$\frac{\partial Y_{10}}{\partial X_9} = \frac{\partial F_{10}}{\partial F_9}\left\langle \frac{\partial F_9}{\partial F_6}\left\{\frac{\partial F_6}{\partial F_1}\frac{\partial F_1}{\partial X_9}\right\} + \frac{\partial F_9}{\partial F_7}\left\{\frac{\partial F_7}{\partial F_2}\frac{\partial F_2}{\partial F_1}\frac{\partial F_1}{\partial X_9}\right\} + \frac{\partial F_9}{\partial F_8}\left\{\frac{\partial F_8}{\partial X_9}\right\}\right\rangle.$$

This differential chain involving three terms captures both the individual and the joint impact of a marginal change in *ABALFS* as transmitted through the three channels associated with this variable. Similarly, the differentiation with respect to X_{10} (*AARINF*) yields the differential chain involving four terms corresponding to the four channels associated with this exogenous variable:

$$\frac{\partial Y_{10}}{\partial X_{10}} = \frac{\partial F_{10}}{\partial F_9}\left\langle \frac{\partial F_9}{\partial F_6}\left\{\frac{\partial F_6}{\partial F_1}\frac{\partial F_1}{\partial X_{10}}\right\} + \frac{\partial F_9}{\partial F_7}\left\{\frac{\partial F_7}{\partial F_2}\frac{\partial F_2}{\partial F_1}\frac{\partial F_1}{\partial X_{10}}\right\} + \frac{\partial F_9}{\partial F_8}\left\{\frac{\partial F_8}{\partial X_{10}}\right\}\right\rangle$$

$$+ \frac{\partial F_{10}}{\partial X_{10}}.$$

As can be seen, the last term captures the direct effect whereas the others capture the indirect effect transmitted through one or more en route variables.

When we differentiate the single equation with respect to X_{11} (*LTRSWA*), X_{12} (*LINTRE*), X_{13} (*LOECEN*), X_{14} (*PPSCRI*) and X_{15} (*AORGBA*), we obtain the following differential chains involving just a single term representing the impact transmitted by the single channel associated with each of these exogenous variables:

$$\frac{\partial Y_{10}}{\partial X_{11}} = \frac{\partial F_{10}}{\partial F_9}\left\langle \frac{\partial F_9}{\partial F_6}\left\{\frac{\partial F_6}{\partial X_{11}}\right\}\right\rangle,$$

$$\frac{\partial Y_{10}}{\partial X_{12}} = \frac{\partial F_{10}}{\partial F_9}\left\langle \frac{\partial F_9}{\partial F_6}\left\{\frac{\partial F_6}{\partial X_{12}}\right\}\right\rangle,$$

$$\frac{\partial Y_{10}}{\partial X_{13}} = \frac{\partial F_{10}}{\partial F_9}\left\langle \frac{\partial F_9}{\partial F_6}\left\{\frac{\partial F_6}{\partial X_{13}}\right\}\right\rangle,$$

$$\frac{\partial Y_{10}}{\partial X_{14}} = \frac{\partial F_{10}}{\partial F_9}\left\langle \frac{\partial F_9}{\partial F_7}\left\{\frac{\partial F_7}{\partial X_{14}}\right\}\right\rangle \text{ and}$$

$$\frac{\partial Y_{10}}{\partial X_{15}} = \frac{\partial F_{10}}{\partial F_9} \left\langle \frac{\partial F_9}{\partial F_8} \left\{ \frac{\partial F_8}{\partial X_{15}} \right\} \right\rangle.$$

The differentiation with respect to X_{16} (*AEXTST*) yields the following differential chain involving five terms representing the value of the impact transmitted by the five channels associated with this variable:

$$\frac{\partial Y_{10}}{\partial X_{16}} = \frac{\partial F_{10}}{\partial F_9} \left\langle \frac{\partial F_9}{\partial F_6} \left\{ \frac{\partial F_6}{\partial F_1} \frac{\partial F_1}{\partial X_{16}} \right\} + \frac{\partial F_9}{\partial F_7} \left\{ \frac{\partial F_7}{\partial F_2} \frac{\partial F_2}{\partial F_1} \frac{\partial F_1}{\partial X_{16}} + \frac{\partial F_7}{\partial F_2} \frac{\partial F_2}{\partial X_{16}} \right\} \right.$$

$$\left. + \frac{\partial F_9}{\partial F_8} \left\{ \frac{\partial F_8}{\partial X_{16}} \right\} \right\rangle + \frac{\partial F_{10}}{\partial X_{16}}.$$

The last term with a single partial derivative captures the direct effect while others involving the product of two or more partial derivatives capture the indirect effect associated with a marginal change in *AEXTST*.

Bibliography

Abdulrazzak, M.J. (1995), 'Water supplies versus demand in countries of the Arabian Peninsula', *Journal of Water Resources Planning and Management*, **121** (3), 227–34.

Acheson, James M. (1994a), *Anthropology and Institutional Economics*, monographs in economic anthropology, no. 12, New York: University Press of America.

Acheson, James M. (1994b), 'Welcome to Nobel country: a review of institutional economics', in James M. Acheson (1994a), pp. 3–42.

Adam, Ahmed M. (1997), 'Sudan' in Ariel Dinar and Ashok Subramanian eds.

Adelman, Irma and T.F. Head (1983), 'Promising developments for conceptualizing and modeling institutional change', working paper no. 259, Gianni Foundation, University of California at Berkeley, Berkeley, CA.

Adelman, Irma and Jan-Berndt Lohmoller (1994), 'Institutions and development in the nineteenth century: a latent variable regression model', *Structural Change and Economic Dynamics*, **5** (2), 329–59.

Adelman, Irma, and Cynthia Taft Morris (1967), *Society, Politics, and Economic Development: A Quantitative Approach*, Baltimore, MD: Johns Hopkins Press.

Adelman, Irma and Cynthia Taft Morris (1974), 'Growth, income distribution, and equity-oriented development strategies', *World Development*, **4** (1), 67–76.

Adelman, Irma, Cynthia Taft Morris, Habib Fetini, and Elise Golan-Hardy (1992), 'Institutional change, economic development, and the environment', *Ambio*, **21** (1), 106–10.

Aekaraj, Sukontha and Saravuth Chevapraset (1999), 'Protection and rehabilitation of the Chao Phraya River in Thailand: national policy and strategies', in United Nations (1999b), pp. 99–105.

Agence Loire-Bretange (1998), 'Financial assistance and charges: 30 years of experience of the Loire-Brittany River Basin bodies', fax sent by Agence Loire-Bretange.

Alam, A.F.M. Nural (1997), 'Sustainable development of water resources in Bangladesh', in United Nations (1997).

Alchian, Armen A. (1950), 'Uncertainty, evolution, and economic theory', *Journal of Political Economy*, **58** (2), 211–21.

Alesina, Alberto (1994), 'Political models of macroeconomic policy and fiscal reforms', in Stephan Haggard and Steven B. Webb, (eds) (1994a), pp. 37–57.

Alston, Lee J. (1996), 'Empirical work in institutional economics: an overview', in Lee J. Alston, Thrainn Eggertsson, and Douglass C. North (eds) (1996a), pp. 25–30.

Alston, Lee J. and Joseph P. Ferrie (1996), 'The economics and politics of institutional change: paternalism in agricultural labor contracts in the U.S. south: implications for the growth of the welfare state', in Lee J. Alston, Thrainn Eggertsson, and Douglass C. North (eds) (1996a), pp. 307–41.

Alston, Lee J., Thrainn Eggertsson, and Douglass C. North (eds) (1996a), *Empirical Studies in Institutional Change*, Cambridge, MA: Cambridge University Press.

Alston, Lee J., Thrainn Eggertsson, and Douglass C. North (1996b), 'Introduction', in Lee J. Alston, Thrainn Eggertsson, and Douglass C. North (eds), pp. 1–5.

Amer, Mohamed Hassan (2000), 'Country position paper: Egypt', in ICID (2000a), pp. 96–111.

Archibald, Sandra O. and Mary E. Renwick (1998), 'Expected transaction costs and incentives for water market development', in K. William Easter, Ariel Dinar, and Mark Rosegrant.

Arlosoroff, Saul (1997), 'The Public Commission on the Water Sector Reform (the general ideas underlying its recommendations)', *International Water and Irrigation Review*, 1–9.

Arriens, Wouter Linklaen, Jeremey Bird, Jeremey Berfoff, and Paul Moseley (eds) (1996), 'Towards effective water policy in the Asian and Pacific region', vol. 2, country papers, Manila: Asian Development Bank.

Artana, Daniel, Fernando Navajas, and Santiago Orbiztondo (1999), 'Governance and regulation: a tale of two concessions in Argentina', in William Savedoff and Pablo Spiller (eds), pp. 197–248.

Axelrod, R. (1984), *'The Evolution of Cooperation*, New York: Basic Books.

Baltazar, Menlchor O. (1999), 'Protection and rehabilitation of the Pasig River in the Philippines', in United Nations (1999b), pp. 73–92.

Bangladesh Water Development Board (2000), 'Gorai River Restoration Project', draft feasibility report, The Government of the People of Bangladesh, Ministry of Water Resources, Bangladesh Water Development Board, vol. 1, main report, October.

Barraque, Bernard, Jean-Marc Berland, and Edith Floret-Miguet, 1998, 'Selected emerging issues in water quality control policies', in Francisco Nunes Correia (ed.), 1998b, pp. 73–102.

Barraque, Bernard, Jean-Marc Berland, and Sophi Cambon (1998), 'France', in Francisco Nunes Correia, (ed.) (1998a), pp. 85–182.

Barrett, Scott and Kathryn Graddy (2000), 'Freedom, growth, and the environment', *Environment and Development Economics*, **5**, 433–56.

Barzel, Y. (1989), *Economic Analysis of Property Rights*, Oxford: Cambridge University Press.

Bates, Robert H. (1989), *Beyond the Miracle of the Market: The Political Economy of Agrarian Development in Kenya*, Oxford: Cambridge University Press.

Bates, Robert H. (1994), 'Social dilemmas and rational individuals: an essay on the new individualism', unpublished manuscript.

Bates, Robert H. (1996), 'Institutions as investments', development discussion paper no. 527, Cambridge, MA: Harvard University.

Bates, Robert H. and Anne O. Krueger (eds) (1993), *Political and Economic Interactions in Economic Policy Reform*, Oxford: Blackwell.

Beaumont, Peter (1994), 'The myth of water wars and the future of irrigated agriculture in the Middle East', *International Journal of Water Resources Development*, **10** (1), 9–21.

Berbeka, Krzysztof (2000), 'Water pricing in selected accession countries to the European Union: current policies and trends', Part II, country descriptions, contract number: B4-3040/99/130877/MAR/B2, Cracow, December.

Betlem, Ilja (1998a), 'Relationship between water policy and environmental policy', in Francisco Nunes Correia (ed.) (1998b), pp. 143–80.

Betlem, Ilja (1998b), 'River basin planning and management', in Francisco Nunes Correia (ed.) (1998b), pp. 73–102.

Bhaskar, Roy (1979), *The Possibility of Naturalism: A Philosophical Critique of the Contemporary Human Sciences*, Brighton: Harvester.

Binswanger, Hans P. and Vernon W. Ruttan (eds) (1978), *Induced Innovations: Technology, Institutions, and Development*, Baltimore, MD: Johns Hopkins University Press.

Bos, M.G. (1997), 'Performance indicators for irrigation and drainage', *Irrigation and Drainage Systems*, **11** (2), 119–37.

Boyer, Robert (1987), 'Regulation', Robert Boyer (ed.), in *The New Palgrave*, London: Macmillan.

Boyer, Robert and J. Rogers Hollingsworth (1997a), 'From national embeddedness to spatial and institutional nestedness', in J. Rogers Hollingsworth and Robert Boyer (eds), pp. 433–77.

Boyer, Robert and J. Rogers Hollingsworth (1997b), 'The variety and unequal performance of really existing markets: farewell to Doctor Pangloss?', in J. Rogers Hollingsworth and Robert Boyer (eds), pp. 49–54.

Brinkerhoff, D.W. (1994), 'Institutional development in World Bank projects: analytical approaches and intervention designs', *Public Administration and Development*, **14** (1), 135–51.

Bromley, D.W. (1985), 'Resources and economic development', *Journal of Economic Issues*, **19** (September), 779–96.

Bromley, D.W. (1989a), *Economic Interests and Institutions: The Conceptual Foundations of Public Policy*, New York: Basil Blackwell.

Bromley, D.W. (1989b), 'Institutional change and economic efficiency,' *Journal of Economic Issues*, **23** (3), 735–59.

Buchanan, J.M. and G. Tullock (1962), *The Calculus of Consent*, Ann Arbor: The University of Michigan Press.

Burness, H.S. and J.P. Quirk (1980), 'Economic aspects of appropriative water rights system', *Journal of Environmental Economics and Management*, **7** (4), 372–8.

Burt, C.M. and S. Styles (1997), *Irrigation Modernization Study*, appendix 'Irrigation indicators', Washington, DC: World Bank–IPTRID–IIMI.

Bush, P.D. (1987), 'The theory of institutional change', *Journal of Economic Issues*, **21** (3), 1075–116.

Caldwell, B.J. (1982), *Beyond Positivism: Economic Methodology in the Twentieth Century*, London: Allen and Unwin.

Canadian National Committee on Irrigation and Drainage (CNCID) (2000), 'Country position paper: Canada', in ICID (2000a), pp. 41–8.

Challen, Ray (2000), *Institutions, Transaction Costs, and Environmental Policy: Institutional Reform for Water Resources*, Cheltenham, UK: Edward Elgar.

Chang, Ha-Joon (1994), 'State, institutions, and structural change', *Structural Change and Economic Dynamics*, **5** (2), 293–313.

Cheung, S.N.S. (1968), Private property rights and sharecropping', *Journal of Political Economy*, **76**, 1107–122.

Chong, Alberto and Cesar Calderon (2000), 'Institutional quality and income distribution', *Economic Development and Cultural Change*, **49**, 761–86.

Ciriacy-Wantrup, S.V. (1956), 'Concepts used as economic criteria for a system of water rights', *Land Economics*, **32** (4), 295–312.

Clague, Christopher (1994), 'Bureaucracy and economic development', *Structural Change and Economic Dynamics*, **5** (2), 273–91.

Clague, Christopher (ed.) (1997a), *Institutions and Economic Development: Growth and Governance in Less-Developed and Post-Socialist Countrie'*, Baltimore, MD and London: Johns Hopkins University Press.

Clague, Christopher (1997b), 'Introduction', in Christopher Clague (ed.) (1997a), pp.1–12.

Clague, Christopher (1997c), 'The new institutional economics and economic development', in Christopher Clague (ed.) (1997a), pp. 13–36.

Coase, Ronald H. (1937), 'The nature of the firm', *Economica*, **4** (2), 386–405.

Coase, Ronald H. (1960), 'The problem of social cost', *Journal of Law and Economics*, **3** (1), 1–44.

Colby, Bonnie (1990), 'Transaction costs and efficiency in Western waters', *American Journal of Agricultural Economics*, **72** (5), 1184–92.

Coleman, James S. (1987), 'Norms as social capital', in G. Radnitzky and P. Bernholz (eds), *Economic Imperialism: The Economic Approach Applied Outside the Field of Economics*, New York: Paragon House, pp. 133–55.

Coleman, James S. (1990), *Foundations of Social Theory*, Cambridge, MA: The Belknap Press of Harvard University Press.

Commons, J.R. (1934), *Institutional Economics*, New York: Macmillan.

Commons, J.R. (1968), *Legal Foundations of Capitalism*, Madison, WI: University of Wisconsin Press.

Cook, Karen Schweers and Margaret Levi (eds) (1990), *The Limits of Rationality*, Chicago: The University of Chicago Press.

Cooter, R.D. and T. Ullen (1988), *Law and Economics*, New York: Harper Collins.

Coriat, Benjamin and Giovanni Dosi (1998), 'The institutional embeddedness of economic change: an appraisal of the "evolutionary" and "regulationist" research programmes', in Klaus Nielsen and Bjorn Johnson (eds), *Institutions and Economic Change,* Cheltenham, UK: Edward Elgar, pp. 3–32.

Correia, Francisco Nunes (ed.) (1998a), *Institutions for Water Resources Management in Europe*, Rotterdam, The Netherlands: A.A. Balkema Publishers.

Correia, Francisco Nunes (ed.) (1998b), *Selected Issues in Water Resources Management in Europe*, Rotterdam, The Netherlands: A.A. Balkema Publishers.

Correia, Francisco Nunes, Eduardo Beja Neves, Maria Alzira Santos, and Joaquim Evaristo Da Silva (1998), 'Portugal', in Francisco Nunes Correia (ed.) (1998a), pp. 449–536.

Cukierman, Alex, Steven B. Webb, and Bilin Neyapti (1998), 'Measuring the independence of central banks and its effects on policy outcomes', *World Bank Economic Review*, **6** (3), 353–98.

Dahlman, Carl J. (1979), 'The problem of externality', *Journal of Legal Studies*, **22** (1), 141–62.

Dales, J.H. (1968), 'Land, water, and ownership', *Canadian Journal of Economics*, **1** (4), 791–804.

David, Paul (1985), 'Clio and the economics of QWERTY', *American Economic Review*, **75**, 332–7.

David, Paul (1994), 'Why are institutions the "carriers of history"? Path dependence and the evolution of conventions, organizations and institutions', *Structural Change and Economic Dynamics*, **5**, 205–20.

Davis, L.E. and D.C. North (1970), 'Institutional change and American economic growth: a first step towards a theory of institutional innovation', *Journal of Economic History*, **30** (March), 131–49.

Demsetz, Harold (1964), 'The exchange and enforcement of property rights', *Journal of Law and Economics*, **3** (October), 1–44.

Demsetz, Harold (1967), 'Toward a theory of property rights', *American Economic Review*, **57** (2), 347–59.

Department of Environment, Transport and the Regions (DETR), 1998a, *Water Charges in England and Wales: A New Approach*, London: DETR.

Department of Environment, Transport and the Regions (DETR) (1998b), *Water Charges in England and Wales*, London: DETR.

Department of Land and Water Conservation (DLWC) (1997), *Report to the Minister on NSW Water Reforms*, Water Management Task Force, Government of New South Wales, Sydney.

Department of Water Affairs and Forestry (DWAF) (1997), *White Paper on a National Water Policy for South Africa*, Pretoria: DWAF.

Department of Water Affairs and Forestry (DWAF) (1999), 'National Water Act (Act No. 36 of 1998) for South Africa', Pretoria: *National Gazette* 20615, 12 November.

DiMaggio, P. and W. Powell (1983), 'The iron cage revisited', *American Sociological Review*, **48**, 147–70.

Dinar, Ariel (ed.) (2000), *The Political Economy of Water Pricing Reforms*, New York: Oxford University Press.

Dinar, Ariel and J. Latey (1991), 'Agricultural water marketing: allocative efficiency and drainage reduction', *Journal of Environmental Economics and Management*, **20**, 210–23.

Dinar, Ariel and Edna Lohman (eds) (1995), *Water Quantity/Quality Disputes and Their Resolutions*, New York: Praeger.

Dinar, Ariel and Ashok Subramanian (eds) (1997), 'Water pricing experience: an international perspective', technical paper no. 386, Washington, DC: World Bank.

Dollery, Brian (1995), 'Institutional change, property rights and economic performance in post-apartheid in South Africa', *Development Southern Africa*, **12** (6): 851–62.

Donahue, John M. and Barbara Rose Johnston (1998), *Water, Culture, and Power: Local Struggles in a Global Context*, Washington, DC: Island Press.

Douglas, Mary (1986), *How Institutions Think?*, New York: Syracuse University Press.

Easter, K. William, Ariel Dinar, and Mark Rosegrant (eds) (1998a), *Markets for Water: Potential and Performance*, Boston: Kluwer Academic Publishers.

Easter, K. William, Ariel Dinar and Mark Rosengrant (1998b), 'The performance of water markets; transaction cost, interjurisdictional barriers and institutional options', in Richard Just and Sinya Natanyahn (eds), *Conflict and Cooperation on Trans-boundary Water Resources*, Boston: Kluwer Academic Publishers, pp. 299–313.

Easter, K. William, Mark Rosegant and Ariel Dinar (1999), 'Formal and informal markets for water: institutions, performance and constraints', *World Bank Reseach Observer*, **14** (1), 99–116.

Economic and Social Commission for Asia and the Pacific (ESCAP) (1997), 'Current status and future trends of water and sustainable development in Nepal, in United Nations (1997), pp. 94–104.

Economic Intelligence Unit (2000a), 'Myanmar (Burma)', country profile, *The Economist*, London.

Economic Intelligence Unit (2000b), 'Namibia, Swaziland', country profile, *The Economist*, London.

Economic Intelligence Unit (2000c), 'Sudan', country profile, *The Economist*, London.

Eggertsson, Thrainn (1990), *Economic Behavior and Institutions*, Cambridge: Cambridge University Press.

Eggertsson, Thrainn (1996a), 'A note on the economics of institutions', in Lee J. Alston, Thrainn Eggertsson, and Douglass C. North (eds) (1996a), pp. 6–21.

Eggertsson, Thrainn (1996b), 'The economics of control and the cost of property rights', in Susan Hanna, Carl Folke, and Karl-Goran Maler (eds), *Rights to Nature: Ecological, Economic, Cultural, and Political Principles of Institutions for the Environment*, Washington, DC: Island Press, pp. 157–78.

Esty, C. Daniel and Michael E. Porter (2000), 'Measuring national environmental performance and its determinants', in *The Global Competitiveness Report 2000*, Geneva, Switzerland: The World Economic Forum.

Falkenmark, Malin (1999), 'Forward to the future: a conceptual framework for water dependence', *Ambio*, **28** (4): 356–61.

Falkenmark, Malin and Gunnar Lindh (1993), 'Water and economic development', in Peter H. Gleick (ed.) (1993).

Farley, Peter J. and Benjamin M. Simon (1996), 'Privatizing Government Irrigation Projects in New Zealand', *Water Resources Bulletin*, **32** (3), 585–94.

Feeny, David (1993), 'The demand for and supply of institutional arrangements', in Vincent Ostrom, David Feeny, and Hartmut Picht (eds), *Rethinking Institutional Analysis and Development: Issues, Alternatives, and Choices*, San Francisco: Institute for Contemporary Studies Press, pp. 159–209.

Field, Alexander James (1981), 'The problem with neoclassical institutional economics: a critique with special reference to the North/Thomas model of pre-1500 Europe', *Explorations in Economic History*, **18** (April), 174–98.

Food and Agriculture Organization (FAO) (1996), 'Food production: the critical role of water', technical background document for the World Food Summit: 7, Rome: FAO.

Fox, Irving K. (1976), 'Institutions for water management in a changing world', *Natural Resources Journal*, **16** (4), 743–58.

Frederiksen, Harald D. (1992), 'Water resources institutions: some principles and practices', World Bank technical paper no. 191, Washington, DC: World Bank.

Frederiksen, Harald D. (1998), 'International community response to critical world water problems: a perspective for policy makers', *Water Policy*, **1**, 139–58.

Fusfeld, D.R. (1980), 'The conceptual framework of modern economics', *Journal of Economic Issues*, **14**, 1–52.

Garrido, Alberto (1997), 'A mathematical programming model applied to the study of water markets within the agricultural sector', paper presented at the 8th European Agricultural Economists Association Congress, Edinburgh, UK, September.

Gazmuri, Renado and Mark Rosegrant (1994), 'Chilean water policy: the role of water rights, institutions, and markets', paper prepared for the Irrigation Support Project for Asia and the Near East (ISPAN), International Food Policy Research Institute, Washington, DC.

Gleick, Peter H. (1993), 'Water in the 21st century' in Peter H. Gleick (ed.), *Water in Crisis: A Guide to the World's Fresh Water Resources*, New York: Oxford University Press.

Gleick, Peter H. (1998), *The World's Water: The Biennial Report on Fresh Water Resources*, Washington, DC: Island Press.

Government of India (GOI) (1992), *Report of the Committee on Pricing Irrigation Water*, New Delhi: Planning Commission.

Government of India (GOI) (1995), *Report of the High Level Committee on Private Sector Participation in Irrigation and Multi-purpose Projects*, New Delhi: Ministry of Water Resources.

Government of Sudan (2001), *National Water Policy of Sudan*, Khartoum: Ministry of Water and Irrigation.

Granovetter, Mark (1985), 'Economic action and social structure: the problem of embeddedness', *American Journal of Sociology*, **91**, 481–510.

Gray, Cheryl W. and Daniel Kaufmann (1998), 'Corruption and development', *Finance and Development*, **35** (1), 7–10.

Greif, Avner (1989), 'Reputations and coalitions in medieval trade: evidence on the Maghribi traders', *Journal of Economic History*, **49**, 857–82.

Greif, Avner, Paul Milgrom, and Barry R. Weingast (1994), 'Coordination, commitment, and enforcement: the case of the merchant guild', *Journal of Political Economy*, **102**, 745–77.

Griffin, Ronald C. (1991), 'The welfare analytics of transaction costs, externalities, and institutional choice', *American Journal of Agricultural Economics*, **73** (August), 601–14.

Groenewegen, John (1996), *Transaction Cost Economics and Beyond*, Dordrecht: Kluwer Academic Publishers.

Groenewegen, John, Frans Kerstholt, and Ad Nagelkerke (1995), 'On integrating new and old institutionalism: Douglass North building bridges', *Journal of Economic Issues*, **29** (2), 467–74.

Guggenheim, Scott (1992), 'Institutional arrangements for water resources development' in Le Moigne, et al, (1992).

Hage, Jerald and Catherine Alter (1997), 'A typology of inter-organizational relationships and networks', in J. Rogers Hollingsworth and Robert Boyer (eds), pp. 94–127.

Haggard, Stephan (1997), 'Democratic institutions, economic policy, and development', in Christopher Clague (ed.) (1997a), pp. 121–52.

Haggard, Stephan and Steven B. Webb (eds) (1994a), *Voting for Reform: Democracy, Political Liberalization, and Economic Adjustment*, Washington, DC: World Bank.

Haggard, Stephan and Steven B. Webb (1994b), 'Introduction', in Stephan Haggard and Steven B. Webb (eds), pp. 1–36.

Hall, Peter Christopher (1986), *Governing the Economy: The Politics of State Intervention in Britain and France*, Cambridge: Polity Press.

Ham, Gee Bong (1997), 'Water and sustainable development in the Republic of Korea', in United Nations (1997), pp. 128–30.

Hanna, Susan, Carl Folke, and Karl-Goran Maler, (eds) (1996), 'Property rights and natural environment', in Susan Hanna, Carl Folke, and Karl-Goran Maler (eds), *Rights to Nature: Ecological, Economic, Cultural and Political Principles of Institutions for the Environment*, Washington, DC: Island Press, pp. 1–10.

Harsanyi, John C. (1977), *Rational Behavior and Bargaining Equilibrium in Games and Social Situations*, Cambridge, MA: Cambridge University Press.

Hartman, L.M. and D. Seastone (1970), *Water Transfers: Economic Efficiency and Alternative Institutions*, Baltimore, MD: Johns Hopkins Press.

Hayek, F.A. (1976), *The Mirage of Social Justice*, Chicago: University of Chicago Press.

Hayes-Roth, F., D.A. Waterman, and D.B. Lenat (1983), *Building Expert System*, Reading, MA: Addison-Wisely.

Hazin, L.S. (1998), 'New strategy in urban water management in Mexico: the case of Mexico's Federal District', *Natural Resource Forum*, **22** (3), 185–92.

Hearne, Robert (1998), 'Opportunities and constraints for improved water markets in Mexico', in K. William Easter, Ariel Dinar and Mark Rosegrant (eds).

Hearne, Robert and K. William Easter (1995), 'Water allocation and water markets: an analysis of gains-from-trade in Chile', technical paper no. 315, Washington, DC: World Bank.

Hearne, Robert and K. William Easter (1997), 'The economic and financial gains from water markets in Chile', *Agricultural Economics*, **15**, 187–99.

Hee, Lee Chan (1998), 'Water quality management in the Republic of Korea', in United Nations (1998), pp. 133–40.

Heyns, Piet (1997), 'Namibia', in Ariel Dinar and Ashok Subramanian (eds).

Heyns, Piet (1999), 'Water management in Namibia: achievement and future prospects', paper prepared for the visit of the Parliament Standing Committee on Agriculture and Environment of the Swedish Parliament, Department of Water Affairs, Windhoek.

Hodgson, Geoffrey M. (1993), *Economics and Evolution: Bringing Life Back into Economics*, Cambridge, MA: Polity Press and Ann Arbor, MI: University of Michigan Press.

Hodgson, Geoffrey M. (1998), 'The approach of institutional economics', *Journal of Economic Literature*, **36** (1): 166–92.

Hoffman, R.R. (1987), 'The problem of extracting knowledge of experts from the perspective of experimental psychology', in *Artificial Intelligence Application in Natural Resources Management*, **1** (2), 35–48, Artificial Intelligence Application, University of Idaho, Moscow, ID.

Hollingsworth, J. Rogers and Robert Boyer (eds) (1997), *Contemporary Capitalism: The Embeddedness of Institutions*, Cambridge: Cambridge University Press.

Howe, C.W., D.R. Schurmeier, and W.D. Shaw (1986), 'Innovative approaches to water allocation: the potential for water markets', *Water Resources Research*, **22** (4), 439–45.

Howitt, Richard E. (1994), 'Effects of water marketing on the farm economy', in Harold O. Carter, et al. (eds), *Sharing Scarcity: Gainers and Losers in Water Marketing*, Berkeley, CA: University of California, Agricultural Issues Center.

Howitt, Richard (1998), 'Spot prices, option prices, and water markets in California', in K. William Easter, Ariel Dinar, and Mark Rosegrant (eds).

Huntington, Samuel (1991), *The Third Wave: Democratization in the Late Twentieth Century*, Norman, OK: University of Oklahoma Press.

Hurwicz, L. (1972), 'Organised structures for joint decision making: a designer's point of view', in M. Tiute, R. Chisholm, and M. Radnor (eds), *Interorganisational Decision Making*, Chicago: Aldine, pp. 37–44.

Hurwicz, L. (1998), 'Issues in the design of mechanisms and institutions', in F.T. Loehman and D.M. Kilgur (eds), *Designing Institutions for Environmental and Resource Management*, Cheltenham, UK: Edward Elgar, pp. 29–56.

Indonesian Delegation (1996), 'Country paper for Indonesia', in Arriens, et al. (eds).

International Commission on Irrigation and Drainage (ICID) (2000a), *Draft ICID Strategy for Implementing Sector Vision*, water for food and rural development and country position papers, New Delhi.

International Commission on Irrigation and Drainage (ICID) (2000b), 'Country profile: Canada', *ICID Newsletter*, **3**, 12–13.

Isham, Jonathan and Satu Kahkonen (1999), 'Institutional determinants of the impact of community-based water services: evidence from Sri Lanka and India', IRIS Working paper, University of Maryland, College Park, MD.

Ismaji, Tri Harjun (1998), 'A study of water pollution problems in the Brantas River Basin, Indonesia', in United Nations (1998).

Israel, Arturo (1987), *Institutional Development: Incentives to Performance*, Baltimore, MD and London: The Johns Hopkins University Press.

Italian National Committee on Irrigation and Drainage (INCID) (2000), 'Country position paper: Italy', in ICID (2000a), pp. 213–24.

Jarayabhand, Srisuda, Supa Sokultanjaroenchai, and Chanin Tongdhamachart (1998), 'Sources and nature of pollution in the rivers of Thailand', in United Nations (1998), pp. 141–3.

Johnson, Bjorn and Klaus Nielsen (1998), 'Introduction', in Klaus Nielsen and Bjorn Johnson (eds), *Institutions and Economic Change*, Cheltenham, UK: Edward Elgar pp. xiii–xxviii.

Johnson, Sam H. (1997), 'Irrigation management transfer: decentralizing public irrigation in Mexico', *Water International*, **22** (3), 159–67.

Johnston, John (1984), *Econometric Methods*, 3rd edn, New York: McGraw-Hill Book Company.

Kahneman, Daniel and Amos Tversky (1984), 'Choices, values, and frames', *American Psychologist*, **39** (4), 341–50.

Kaufmann, Daniel, Aart Kraay, and Massimo Mastruzzi (2003), 'Governance matters III: governance indicators for 1996–2002', draft, Washington DC: The World Bank, 8 May.

Ke Lidan (1997), 'Water law and water management', in Qian Zhengying (ed.), *Water Resources Development in China*, Beijing/New Delhi: China Water and Power Press/Central Board of Irrigation and Power.

Kennedy, Peter (1987), *A Guide to Econometrics*, 2nd edn, Cambridge, MA: The MIT Press.

Keohane, Robert O. (1988), 'International institutions: two approaches', *International Studies Quarterly*, **32** (4), 379–96.

Kiser, Larry and Elinor Ostrom (1982), 'The three worlds of action: a metatheoretical synthesis of institutional approaches', in Elinor Ostrom (ed.), *Strategies of Political Inquiry*, Beverly Hills, CA: Sage Publications, pp. 179–222.

Kliot, Nurit, Deborah Shmueli, and Uri Shamir (1997), *Institutional Frameworks for Management of Transboundary Water Resources*, Haifa, Israel: Water Research Institute, Technion (Israel Institute of Technology).

Knack, Stephen and Philip Keefer (1986), 'Institutions and economic performance: cross-country tests using alternative institutional measures', *Economics and Politics*, **7** (3), 207–27.

Knight, Jack (1995), 'Models, interpretations, and theories: constructing explanations of institutional emergence and change', in Jack Knight and Itai Sened (eds) (1995a), pp. 95–120.

Knight, Jack and Itai Sened (eds) (1995a), *Explaining Social Institutions*, Ann Arbor, MI: The University of Michigan Press.

Knight, Jack and Itai Sened (1995b), 'Introduction', in Jack Knight and Itai Sened (eds), (1995a), pp. 1–14.

Kraemer, R. Andreas and Frank Jager (1998), 'Germany', in Francisco Nunes Correia, (ed.) (1998a), pp. 183–325.

Kunte, Arundhati, Kirk Hamilton, John Dixon, and Michael Clemens (1998), 'Estimating national wealth: methodology and results', Environment Department papers, no. 57, Washington, DC: World Bank.

Kwun, Soon-kuk (2000), 'Country position Paper: Korea' in ICID (2000a), pp. 241–55.

Landa, J.T. (1994), *Trust, Ethnicity, and Identity: Beyond the New Institutional Economics of Ethnic Trading Networks, Contract Law, and Gift Exchange*, Ann Arbor, MI: The University of Michigan Press.

Landry, Rejean (1996), 'A framework for the study of incomplete institutions', colloquium presentation at the Workshop in Political Theory and Policy Analysis, Indiana University, Bloomington, IN, 21 October.

Lazonick, William (1991), *Business Organization and the Myth of the Market Economy*, Cambridge and New York: Cambridge University Press.

Le Moigne, Guy, Shawki Barghouti, Gershon Feder, Lisa Garbus, and Mei Xie (eds) (1992), 'Country experiences with water resources management: economic, institutional, technological, and environmental issues', World Bank technical paper no. 175, Washington, DC: World Bank.

Le Moigne, Guy, Ashok Subramanian, Mei Zie, and Sandra Giltner (1994), 'A guide to the formulation of water resources strategy', technical paper no: 263, Washington, DC: World Bank.

Levi, Margaret (1990), 'A logic of institutional change', in Karen Schweers Cook and Margaret Levi (eds).

Li Quan (1999), 'Institutional design and the performance of trade blocs', paper prepared for International Studies Association annual meeting, Washington, DC, February.

Libecap, Gary D. (1978), 'Economic variables and the development of the law: the case of western mineral rights', *Journal of Economic History*, **38** (June), 338–62.

Libecap, Gary D. (1989), *Contracting for Property Rights*, Cambridge, MA: Cambridge University Press.

Livingston, Marie Leigh (1987), 'Evaluating the performance of environmental policy: contribution of neoclassical, public choice, and institutional models', *Journal of Economic Issues*, **21** (1), 281–93.

Livingston, Marie Leigh (1993), 'Normative and positive aspects of institutional economics: the implications for water policy', *Water Resources Research*, **29** (4), 815–21.

Lo, Carlos Wing-Hung, and Shui-Yan Tang (1994), 'Institutional contexts of environmental management: water pollution control in Guangzhou, China,' *Public Administration and Development*, **14** (1), 53–64.

Lorek, Maciej (2000), 'Poland – country description', in Krzysztof Berbeka.

Mahaweli Economic Authority (MEA) (1997), *Progress Report – 1997*, Colombo: Ministry of Mahaweli Development.

Maia, Rodrigo (2000), 'Sharing the waters of the Iberian Peninsula', paper presented at the 10th World Water Congress, Melbourne, Australia, March.

March, J.G. and J.P. Olsen (1989), *Rediscovering Institutions: The Organizational Basis of Policies*, New York: Free Press.

Marglin, Stephen A. (1991), 'Understanding capitalism: control versus efficiency', in Bo Gustafasson (ed.), 'Power and Economic Institutions', Cheltenham, UK: Edward Elgar, pp. 225–52.

Marshall, Alfred (1948), *Principles of Economics*, 8th edn, New York: Macmillan.

Massarutto, Antonio (1999), 'Water institutions and management in Italy', draft working paper, Department of Economic Science, University of Udine, Italy, 25 May.

McCann, Laura, and K. William Easter (1999), 'Transaction costs of policies to reduce agricultural phosphorous pollution in Minnesota River', *Land Economics*, **75** (3), 402–14.

McDonald, A. and D. Kay (1988), *Water Resources: Issues and Strategies*, London: Longman Scientific and Technical Publishers Ltd.

Milgrom, Paul and J. Roberts (1992), *Economic Organizations and Management*, Englewood Cliffs, NJ: Prentice Hall.

Milliman, J.W. (1959), 'Water law and private decision-making: a critique', *Journal of Law and Economics*, **2** (1), 41–63.

Ministerio de Obras Publicas Y Transportes (MOPT) (1993), *Plan Hidrologico Nacional Memoria*, Madrid: Ministerio de Obras Publicas.

Ministry for the Environment (1999), 'Making every drop count: water 2010', The National Agenda for Sustainable Water Management draft report, Wellington, New Zealand, July.

Molle, Francois (2001), 'Water pricing in Thailand: theory and practice', DORAS–DELTA research report no. 7, Kasetsart University, Institut de Recherche pour le Développement, DORAS Center, Bangkok, Thailand.

Morris, Cynthia Taft and I. Adelman (1988), *Comparative Patterns of Economic Development*, Baltimore, MD: Johns Hopkins University Press, pp. 1850–914.

Musgrave, Warren F. (1997), 'Australia', in Ariel Dinar and Ashok Subramanian (eds).

Myint, Ohn (1997), 'Sustainable development of water resources in Myanmar', in United Nations (1997), pp. 86–93.

Myint, U Myo, U Aung Kyaw, and U Myint Thwin, (1996), 'Country paper of Myanmar', in Arriens, et al. (eds), pp. 103–12.

Nam, Le Duc (1997), 'Current status and future trends of water and sustainable development in Vietnam', in United Nations (1997), pp. 141–3.

Nanni, Marcella (1996), *Preliminary Report on National Water Resource Laws and Institutions in Sri Lanka*, Water Policy and Law Advisory Programme, CGP/INT/620/NET, Colombo: Food and Agriculture Organization.

Nash, Linda (1993), 'Water quality and health', in Peter H. Gleick (ed.) (1993).

Nelson, Douglas and Eugene Silberberg (1987), 'Ideology and legislator shirking', *Economic Enquiry*, **25**, 15–25.

Nelson, Joan (ed.) (1990), *Economic Crisis and Policy Choice: The Politics of Adjustment in the Third World*, Princeton: Princeton University Press.

Nepalese Delegation (1996), 'Country paper on Nepal', in Arriens *et al.* (eds), pp. 113–17.

Nguyen, Thai Lai (1999), 'Protection and rehabilitation of the Red River in Vietnam', in United Nations (1999b), pp. 106–13.

Nishat, A. and I.M. Faisal (2000), 'An assessment of the institutional mechanisms for water negotiations in the Ganges–Brahmaputra–Meghna Basin', *International Negotiation*, **5** (2), 289–310.

North, Douglass C. (1981), *Structure and Change in Economic History*, New York: Norton.

North, Douglass C. (1983), 'A theory of economic change', *Science*, **219**: 163–64.

North, Douglass C. (1986), 'The new institutional economics', *Journal of Institutional and Theoretical Economics*, **142**, 230–7.

North, Douglass C. (1988), 'Institutions and a transaction cost theory of exchange', Political economy working paper no. 144, Washington University, St. Louis, MO.

North, Douglass C. (1990a), *Institutions, Institutional Change, and Economic Performance*, Cambridge, MA: Cambridge University Press.

North, Douglass C. (1990b), 'Institutions and their consequences for economic performance', in Karen Schweers Cook and Margaret Levi (eds).

North, Douglass C. (1990c), 'A transaction cost theory of politics', *Journal of Theoretical Politics*, **2** (4): 355–67.

North, Douglass C. (1993), 'The new institutional economics and development', paper prepared for the Conference on Public Choice and Development: The New Institutional Economics and Third World Development, London, 16–18 September.

North, Douglass C. (1994), 'Economic performance through time', *American Economic Review*, **8** (2), 359–68.

North, Douglass C. (1995), 'Five propositions about institutional change', in Jack Knight and Itai Sned (eds) (1995a), pp. 15–26.

North, Douglass C. (1997), 'The contribution of the new institutional economics to an understanding of the transition problem', WIDER annual lectures 1, World Institute for Development Economics Research, Helsinki, Finland.

North, Douglass C. and Robert P. Thomas (1970), 'An economic theory of the growth of the Western world', *Economic History Review*, **23** (March), 1–17a.

North, Douglass C. and Robert P. Thomas (1971), 'The rise and fall of the manorial system: a theoretical model', *Journal of Economic History*, **31** (4), 777–803.

North, Douglass C. and Robert P. Thomas (1973), *'The Rise of the Western World: A New Economic History*, Cambridge, MA: Cambridge University Press.

North, Douglass C. and Barry R. Weingast (1989), 'Constitutions and commitment: the evolution of institutions governing public choice in seventeenth century England', in Torsten Persson and Guido Tabellini (eds), *Monetary and Fiscal Policy: Vol. 1. Credibility*, Cambridge, MA: Cambridge University Press.

North, Douglass C. and Barry R. Weingast (1996), 'The evolution of modern institutions of growth: constitutions and commitment: the evolution of institutions governing public choice in seventeenth-century England', in Lee J. Alston, Thrainn Eggertsson, and Douglasss C. North (eds) (1996a), pp. 129–33.

Office of Water Services (OFWAT) (1999a), *Report on Tariff Structure and Charges: 1999–2000*, Birmingham, UK: OFWAT.

Office of Water Services (OFWAT) (1999b), *Future Water and Sewerage Charges 2000–05*, Birmingham, UK: OFWAT.

Olson, Mancur (1965), *The Logic of Collective Action*, Cambridge, MA: Harvard University Press.

Olson, Mancur (1982), *The Rise and Decline of Nations: Economic Growth, Stagflation, and Social Rigidities*, New Haven, CT: Yale University Press.

Orloci, J., K. Szesztay, and L. Varkonyi (1985), *National Infrastructure in the Field of Water Resources*, Paris: UNESCO.

Ostrom, Elinor (1986), 'An agenda for the study of institutions', *Public Choice*, **48**, 3–25.

Ostrom, Elinor (1990), *Governing the Commons: The Evolution of Institutions for Collective Action*, Cambridge, UK: Cambridge University Press.

Ostrom, Elinor (1999), 'Institutional rational choice: an assessment of the institutional analysis and development framework', working paper, Workshop in Political Theory and Policy Analysis, Indiana University, Bloomington, IN.

Ostrom, Elinor, Roger B. Parks, and Gordon P. Whitaker (1978), *Patterns of Metropolitan Policing*, Cambridge, MA: Ballinger.

Ostrom, Elinor, Roy Gardner, and James Walker (1994), *Rules, Games and Common Pool Resources*, Ann Arbor, MI: University of Michigan Press.

Ostrom, Vincent (1980), 'Artisanship and artifact', *Public Administration Review*, **40** (July–August), 309–17.

Ostrom, Vincent and Elinor Ostrom (1972), 'Legal and political conditions of water resource development', *Land Economics*, **48** (1), 1–14.

Ostrom, Vincent, Charles M. Tiebout, and Robert Warren (1961), 'The organization of government in metropolitan areas: a theoretical enquiry', *American Political Science Review*, **60** (4), 831–42.

Oswald, Odile (1992), 'An expert system for the diagnosis of tank irrigated systems: a feasibility study', working paper no. 22, International Irrigation Management Institute, Colombo, Sri Lanka.

Pattanee, Surapol (2000), 'Country position paper: Thailand', in ICID (2000a), pp. 427–35.

People's Republic of China (1988), *Water Law of the People's Republic of China*, Beijing: Ministry of Water Resources.

People's Republic of China (1997), *China Water Resources News*, (4 December), Beijing: Ministry of Water Resources.

Perdock, Peter J. (1998), 'Netherlands', in Correia, Francisco Nunes (ed.) (1998a), pp. 327–447.

Philippines Delegation (1996), 'Country paper of the Philippines', in Arriens, et al, (eds), pp. 127–36.

Picciotto, Robert (1995), 'Putting institutional economics to work: from participation to governance', discussion paper no. 304, Washington, DC: World Bank.

Poland National Committee on Irrigation and Drainage (PNCID) (2000), 'Country position paper: Poland', in ICID (2000a), pp. 363–9.

Polanyi, Karl (1957) [1944], *The Great Transformation: The Political and Economic Origins of Our Time*, Boston: Beacon Press.

Polanyi, Michael (1962), *Personal Knowledge: Towards a Post-Critical Philosophy*, New York: Harper & Row.

Porat, M. and M. Rubin (1977), *The Information Economy* (nine volumes), Office of Communications Special Publication 77-12, US Department of Commerce, Washington, DC: Government Printing Office.

Posner, Richard A. (1980), 'A theory of primitive society, with special reference to law', *Journal of Law and Economics*, **23** (1) (April), 1–53.

Posner, Richard A. (1986), *Economic Analysis of Law*, Boston: Little Brown.

Postel, S.L. (1993), *The Last Oasis: Facing Water Scarcity*, Worldwatch Institute Environmental Alert Studies, New York: Worldwatch Institute.

Postel, S.L. (1999), *Pillar of Sand: Can the Irrigation Miracle Last?*, New York: W.W. Norton.

Postel, S L., G.C. Daily, and P.R. Ehrlich (1996), 'Human appropriation of renewable fresh water', *Science*, **271**, 785–8.

Qishun, Zhang and Zhang Xiao (1995), 'Water issues and sustainable social development in China', *Water International*, **20** (3), 122–8.

Rahman, Shafi-ur (1998), 'Status of water quality and water quality management in the rivers of Bangladesh', in United Nations (1998).

Randall, Alan (1974), 'Coasian externality theory in a policy context', *Natural Resources Journal*, **14** (January), 34–54.

Rasphone, Sitahng (1996), 'Country paper of the Lao People's Democratic Republic', in Arriens, et al (eds), *The Economics and Management of Water and Drainage in Agriculture*, Boston, Kluwer Academic Publishers.

Rausser, Gordon C. and Leo Simon (1992), 'The political economy of transition in Eastern Europe', in Christopher Clauge and Gordon C. Rausser (eds), *The Emergence of Market Economies in Eastern Europe*, Cambridge, MA: Basil Blackwell, pp. 245–70.

Rausser, Gordon C. and Pinhas Zusman (1991), 'Organizational failure and the political economy of water resources management', in Ariel Dinar and David Zilberman, (eds).

Rawls, John (1971), *Theory of Social Justice*, Cambridge, MA: Harvard University Press.

Rees, Yvonne and Thomas Zabel (1998a), 'United Kingdom', in Francisco Nunes Correia (ed.) (1998a), pp. 537–670.

Rees, Yvonne, and Thomas Zabel (1998b), 'Regulations and enforcement of discharges to water', in Francisco Nunes Correia (ed.) (1998b), pp. 181–222.

Rees, Yvonne, Thomas Zabel, and Jonathan Buckland (1998), 'Overview of water resources management issues', in Francisco Nunes Correia (ed.) (1998b), pp. 7–38.

Regmi, Dev Raj, Laxman Sharma, and Y.L. Vaidya (1998), 'Sources and nature of pollution in the rivers of Nepal', in United Nations (1998), pp. 115–17.

Remmer, Karen L. (1998), 'Does democracy promote interstate cooperation? Lessons from the Mercosur region', *International Study Quarterly*, **42** (1), 25–52.

Renault, Daniel (1998), *On Reliability in Irrigation Service: Conceptual Approach and Definitions*, Colombo, Sri Lanka: International Irrigation Management Institute.

Riker, William H. (1962), *The Theory of Political Coalitions*, New Haven, CT: Yale University Press.

Riker, William H. (1995), 'The experience of creating institutions: the framing of the United States Constitution', in Jack Knight and Itai Sened (eds) (1995a), pp. 121–44.

Rivera, Marcelino M. and Luis M. Sosa (1998), 'Sources and nature of pollution in the rivers of the Philippines', in United Nations (1998), pp. 131–3.

Rosegrant, M.W. and C. Ringler (1999), 'Impact on food security and rural development of reallocating water from agriculture', EPTD discussion paper no. 47, Washington, DC: International Food Policy Research Institute.

Royal Government of Cambodia (1996), 'Country paper of Cambodia', in Arriens, et al. (eds), pp. 7–22.

Rutherford, Malcolm (1995), 'The old and the new institutionalism: can bridges be built?', *Journal of Economic Issues*, **29** (2), 443–50.

Ruttan, Vernon W. (1978), 'Induced institutional change', in Hans P. Binswanger and Vernon W. Ruttan (eds).

Ruttan, Vernon W. (1988), 'Cultural endowments and economic development: what can economists learn from anthropology?', *Economic Development and Cultural Change*, **36**, 247–71.

Ruttan, Vernon W. (1999), 'Induced institutional innovation', paper presented at the Conference on Induced Technology Change and the Environment, International Institute for Applied Systems Analysis, Laxenberg, Austria.

Ruttan, Vernon W. and Y. Hayami (1984), 'Toward a theory of induced institutional innovation', *Journal of Development Studies*, **20** (July), 203–23.

Saghir, Jamal, Manuel Schiffler, and Mathewos Woldu (2000), *Urban Water and Sanitation in the Middle East and North Africa: The Way Forward*, Washington, DC: World Bank.

Saleth, R.M., (1996), *Water Institutions in India: Economics, Law, and Policy*, New Delhi: Commonwealth Publishers.

Saleth, R.M. (1998), 'Water markets in India: economic and institutional aspects', in K. William Easter, Mark W. Rosegrant, and Ariel Dinar, (eds).

Saleth, R.M. (1999), 'Irrigation privatization in India: options, framework, and experience', *Economic and Political Weekly*, **34** (26), A86–A92.

Saleth, R.M. (2002), 'Introduction', in R.M. Saleth (ed.), *Water Resources and Economic Development*, Cheltenham: Edward Elgar.

Saleth, R.M. and John B. Braden (1995), 'Minimizing the potential distortions in a spot water market: a multilateral bargaining approach', in Ariel Dinar and Edna Lohman, (eds).

Saleth, R.M. and Ariel Dinar (1999a), 'Water challenge and institutional response: a cross-country perspective', World Bank policy research working paper no. 2045, Washington, DC: World Bank.

Saleth, R.M. and Ariel Dinar (1999b), 'Evaluating water institutions and water sector performance', World Bank technical paper no. 447, Washington, DC: World Bank.

Saleth, R.M. and Ariel Dinar (2000), 'Institutional changes in global water sector: trends, patterns, and implications', *Water Policy*, **2** (3), 175–99.

Saleth, R.M. and G.S. Sastry, (2004), 'Water and sanitation sector in Karnataka, India: status, performance, and change', *Water Policy* (forthcoming).

Saleth, R.M., John B. Braden, and J. Wayland Eheart (1991), 'Bargaining rules for a thin spot water market', *Land Economics*, **67** (3), 326–39.

Sampath, R.K. (1990), 'Measures of inequity for distribution of large public surface irrigation systems: a welfare-theoretic approach', in R.K. Sampath and R.A. Young (eds), *Social, Economic and Institutional Issues in Third World Irrigation Management*, Boulder, CO: Westview Press.

Santos Alzira, Maria and Rui Rodrigues (1998), 'Water resources information policy', in Francisco Nunes Correia, (ed.) (1998b), pp. 39–72.

Savedoff, William, and Pablo Spiller (1999), *Spilled Water: Institutional Commitment in the Provision of Water Services*, Washington, DC: Inter-American Development Bank.

Schmid, A.A. (1972), 'Analytical institutional economics: changing problems in the economics of resources for a new environment', *American Journal of Agricultural Economics*, **54** (5), 893–901.

Schmitter, C. Philippe (1997), 'Levels of spatial coordination and the embeddedness of institutions', in J. Rogers Hollingsworth and Robert Boyer (eds), pp. 311–19.

Schotter, A. (1981), *The economic theory of social institutions*, Cambridge: Cambridge University Press.

Scrimgeour, Frank (1997), 'New Zealand', in Ariel Dinar and Ashok Subramanian, (eds).

Seckler, David, Upali Amarasinghe, David Molden, Radhika de Silva, and Randolph Barker (1998), 'World water demand and supply, 1990 to 2025: scenarios and issues', research report, International Water Management Institute, Colombo, Sri Lanka.

Sharma, Kem Raj (2000), 'Country position paper: Nepal', in ICID (2000a), pp. 299–316.

Shepsle, K.A. (1979), 'Institutional arrangements and equilibrium in multidimensional voting models', *American Journal of Political Science*, **23**, 27–60.

Shepsle, K.A., and Barry R. Weingast (1981), 'Structure induced equilibrium and legislative choice', *Public Choice*, **37**, 503–20.

Shepsle, K.A. and Barry R. Weingast (1984), 'When do rules of procedures matter?': structure induced equilibrium and legislative choice', *Journal of Politics*, **46** (1), 206–21.

Shiklomanov, Igor A. (1993), 'World fresh water resources', in Peter H. Gleick (ed.) (1993).

Shim, Soon-Bo (1996), 'Korean experience and challenges in water resources planning and management', in Arriens, et al. (eds), pp. 236–49.

Shubik, Martin (1982), *Game Theory in the Social Sciences*, Cambridge, MA: The MIT Press.

Shubik, Martin (1984), *A Game-Theoretic Approach to Political Economy*, Cambridge, MA: The MIT Press.

Simon, Herbert A. (1957), *Models of Man*, New York: John Wiley & Sons.

Simon, Herbert A. (1961) [1949], *Administrative Behavior*, 2nd edn, New York: Macmillan.

Sina, Chea (1998), 'Sources and nature of pollution in rivers of Cambodia', in United Nations (1998), pp. 98–100.

Sina, Chea (1999), 'Protection and rehabilitation of the Tonle Sap River in Cambodia', in United Nations (1999b), pp. 4–7.

Sisovann, Ouk (1997), 'Water and sustainable development in Cambodia', in United Nations (1997), pp. 23–9.

Sjostrand, Sven-Erik (1995), 'Toward a theory of institutional change', in John Groenewegen, Christos Pietelis, and Sven-Erik Sjostrand (eds), *On Economic Institutions: Theory and Applications*, Brookfield, VT: Edward Elgar, pp. 19–44.

Sosa, Luis M. (1997), 'Current status and future trends on water sustainable development in the Philippines', in United Nations (1997), pp. 118–27.

Sosongko, Djoko (1999), 'Protection and rehabilitation of the Cisadane River in Indonesia', in United Nations (1999b).

Souk, Boun (1998), 'Status of water quality management and pollution control in the Lao People's Democratic Republic', in United Nations (1998), pp. 110–12.

Souk, Boun (1999), 'Nan Ngum River water quality protection and rehabilitation in the Lao People's Democratic Republic', in United Nations (1999b), p. 36.

Souvannabouth, Phouang Phanh (1997), 'Water resources development in Lao People's Democratic Republic', in United Nations (1997), pp. 74–9.

Stein, Johan (1997), 'How institutions learn: a socio-cognitive perspective', *Journal of Economic Issues*, **31** (3), 729–39.

Su, Pham Xuan (1996), 'Country paper of Vietnam', in Arriens, et al. (eds), pp. 165–71.

Su, Pham Xuan (1998), 'Water resources potential and water quality in the rivers of Vietnam', in United Nations (1998), pp. 145–54.

Sutardi (1997), 'Water and sustainable development: current status and future trends in Indonesia', in United Nations (1997).

Thai Delegation (1996), 'Country paper of Thailand', in Arriens et al. (eds), pp. 155–60.

Tool, M.R. (1977), 'A social value theory in neo-institutional economics', *Journal of Economic Issues*, **11** (December), 823–49.

Tu, Dao Trong (2000), 'Country position paper: Vietnam', in ICID (2000a), pp. 445–50.

Twight, Charlotte (1992), 'Political transaction-cost manipulation: an integrating theory', *Journal of Theoretical Politics*, **6** (2), 189–216.

United Nations (1997), *Sustainable Development of Water Resources in Asia and the Pacific: An Overview*, Economic and Social Commission for Asia and the Pacific, New York: United Nations.

United Nations (1998), *Sources and Nature of Water Quality Problems in Asia and the Pacific*, Economic and Social Commission for Asia and the Pacific, New York: United Nations.

United Nations (1999a), *Assessment of Water Resources and Water Demand by User Sectors in the Philippines*, Economic and Social Commission for Asia and the Pacific, New York: United Nations.

United Nations (1999b), *Water Quality of Selected Rivers in Asia: Protection and Rehabilitation*, Economic and Social Commission for Asia and the Pacific, New York: United Nations.

United Nations (2000), *Economic Survey of Europe*, No. 2/3, Economic Commission for Europe, Geneva: United Nations.

Upadhyay, Lakshman Prasad and Dev Raj Regmi (1999), 'River water quality management in Nepal: problems and solutions', in United Nations (1999b), pp. 37–40.

Varis, Olli (1999), 'Water resources development: vicious and virtuous circles', *Ambio*, **28** (7), 599–603.

Vaux, Henry and Richard Howitt (1984), 'Managing water scarcity: an evaluation of inter-regional transfers', *Water Resources Research*, **20**, 785–92.

Veblen, Thorstein B. (1899), *The Theory of the Leisure Class: An Economic Study in the Evolution of Institutions*, New York: Macmillan.

Veblen, Thorstein B. (1914), *The Instinct of Workmanship and the State of the Industrial Arts*, New York: Augustus Kelley.

Veblen, Thorstein B. (1919), *The Place of Science in Modern Civilization and Other Essays*, New York: Huebsch.

Vermillion, Douglas L. (1997), 'Impact of irrigation management Transfer: A Review of Evidence', Colombo, Sri Lanka: IIMI.

Vira, Bhaskar (1997), 'The political Coase theorem: identifying differences between neoclassical and critical institutionalism', *Journal of Economic Issues*, **31** (3), 761–79.

von der Fehr, Nils-Henrik M. and Lise Sandsbraten (1997), 'Water on fire: gains from electricity trade', *Scandinavian Journal of Economics*, **99** (2), 281–97.

Wade, Robert (1982), 'Employment, water control, and water supply institutions: South India and South Korea', Discussion Paper: 182, Institute of Development Studies, University of Sussex, Brighton, UK.

Wai, Oo Tun and U Win Thein (1998), 'Sources and nature of pollution in the rivers of Myanmar', in United Nations (1998), pp. 113–15.

Wallis, John and Douglass C. North (1986), 'Measuring the transaction sector in the American economy, 1870–1970' in S. Engerman and R. Gallman (eds), *Long-Term Factors in American Economic Growth*, NBER Studies in Income and Wealth, vol. 51, Chicago: The University of Chicago Press, pp. 95–148.

Wallis, John and Douglass C. North, (1988), 'Should transaction costs be subtracted from gross national product?', *Journal of Economic History*, **48** (3), 763–70.

Water Resources Secretariat (WRS) (1997), *Approach for Comprehensive Water Resources Management in Sri Lanka*, Colombo, Sri Lanka: WRS.

Weingast, Barry R. (1993), 'Constitutions as governance structures', *Journal of Institutional and Theoretical Economics*, **149** (March), 286–311.

White, Louise G. (1990), *Implementing Policy Reforms in LDCs: A Strategy for Designing and Effecting Change*, Boulder and London: Lynne Rienner Publishers.

Wijkman, J. and L. Timberlake (1984), *Natural Disasters: Acts of God or Acts of Man?*, London: Earthscan Publishers Ltd.

Wilber, C.K. and R.S. Harrison (1978), 'The methodological basis of institutional economics: pattern model, story-telling, and holism', *Journal of Economic Issues*, **12** (1), 61–89.

Wilks, S. and M. Wright (eds) (1987), *Comparative Government–Industry Relations: Western Europe, the United States and Japan*, Oxford: Clarendon Press.

Williamson, Oliver E. (1975), *Markets and Hierarchies, Analysis and Antitrust Implications: A Study in the Economics of Internal Organization*, New York: Free Press.

Williamson, Oliver E. (1985), *The Economic Institutions of Capitalism: Firms, Markets, Relational Contracting*, New York: Free Press.

Williamson, Oliver E. (1993), 'Transaction cost economics and organizations theory', *Industrial and Corporate Change*, **2** (2), 107–56.

Williamson, Oliver E. (1994), 'Institutions and economic organization: the governance perspective', annual bank conference on development economics, Washington, DC: World Bank.

Williamson, Oliver E. (1999), 'Public and private bureaucracies: a transaction cost economics perspective', *Journal of Law, Economics, and Organization*, **5**, 306–47.

World Bank (1992), 'Asia water resources study: stage 1', vol. 2, annexes, Agricultural Division, Asia Technical Department, Washington, DC: World Bank.

World Bank (1993), 'Republic of Tunisia: agricultural sector investment loan', Staff appraisal report no. 12229-TUN, Washington, DC: World Bank.

World Bank (1994), 'Kingdom of Morocco: water resources management project', project appraisal report no. 15760-MOR, Washington, DC: World Bank.

World Bank (1995), 'Socialist Republic of Vietnam: irrigation rehabilitation project', staff appraisal report no. 13702-VN, Washington, DC: World Bank.

World Bank (1996), 'Philippines: water resources development project', staff appraisal report no. 15297-PH, Washington, DC: World Bank.

World Bank (1997), *World Development Report: 1997*, Washington, DC: World Bank.

World Bank (1998), 'India water resources management sector review: initiating and sustaining water sector reforms', report no. 18356-IN, Washington, DC: World Bank.

World Bank (1999a), 'Republic of Indonesia: water resources sector adjustment loan', report no. P 7304-IND, Washington, DC: World Bank.

World Bank (1999b), 'Socialist Republic of Vietnam: Mekong Delta water resources project', project appraisal document, Washington, DC: World Bank.

World Bank (2000a), *World Development Report: 2000*, Washington, DC: World Bank.

World Bank (2000b), 'Argentina: water resources management, policy elements for sustainable development in the 21st century', report no. 20729-AR, Washington, DC: World Bank.

World Bank (2000c), 'Sudan: options for the sustainable development of the Gezira Scheme', report no. 20398-SU, Washington, DC: World Bank.

World Bank, Asian Development Bank, FAO, UNDP, and Water Resources Group, in Cooperation with the Institute of Water Resources Planning, Vietnam (1996), *Vietnam Water Resources Sector Review*, main report, Washington, DC: World Bank.

World Economic Forum (1997), *The World Competitiveness Report*, Geneva, Switzerland: WEF.

World Resources Institute (1990), *World Resources: 1990*, Washington, DC: WRI.

World Resources Institute (1999), *World Resources*, Washington, DC: WRI.

Yaffey, Michael (1998), 'Moral standards and transaction costs: long term effects', in Klaus Nielsen and Bjorn Johnson (eds), *Institutions and Economic Change*, Cheltenham, UK and Northampton, MA: Edward Elgar, pp. 258–90.

Yang, Youngseok (1997), 'Crafting institutions and the determination of their hierarchy in environmental policy-making: the Platte River as a case study', *Journal of Economic Issues*, **31** (3), 834–40.

Yaron, Dan (1997), 'Israel', in Ariel Dinar and Ashok Subramanian (eds).

Young, M.D., and J.C. McColl (2002), *Robust Separation: A Search for a Generic Framework to Simplify Registration and Trading Interests in Natural Resources*, Policy and Economics Research Unit, CSIRO Land and Water, Adelaide, Australia, 48pp.

Zekri, Slim (1997), 'Tunisia', in Ariel Dinar and Ashok Subramanian, (eds).

Zilberman, David, Ariel Dinar, Neal MacDougall, Madu Khanna, Cheryl Brown, and Fredrico Castillo (1998), 'Private and institutional adaptation to water scarcity during the California drought, 1987–1991', staff paper 9802, Economic Research Service, Washington, DC: US Department of Agriculture.

Index

University of Plymouth Library

Subject to status this item may be renewed
via your Voyager account

http://voyager.plymouth.ac.uk

Exeter tel: (01392) 475049
Exmouth tel: (01395) 255331
Plymouth tel: (01752) 232323

To our children
Joel and Shira,

representing the next generation that will benefit by knowing
what it takes to manage the planet's scarce water